Fifth Edition

MANAGING CLASSROOM BEHAVIOR

A REFLECTIVE CASE-BASED APPROACH

James M. Kauffman
University of Virginia

Patricia L. Pullen
Charlottesville, Virginia

Mark P. Mostert
Regent University

Stanley C. Trent
University of Virginia

TOURO COLLEGE LIBRARY
Kings Hwy

WITHDRAWN

PEARSON

Boston   Columbus   Indianapolis   New York   San Francisco   Upper Saddle River
Amsterdam   Cape Town   Dubai   London   Madrid   Milan   Munich   Paris   Montreal   Toronto
Delhi   Mexico City   Sao Paulo   Sydney   Hong Kong   Seoul   Singapore   Taipei   Tokyo

Vice President and Editor in Chief: Jeffery W. Johnston
Executive Editor: Ann Castel Davis
Editorial Assistant: Penny Burleson
Vice President, Director of Marketing: Quinn Perkson
Marketing Manager: Erica DeLuca
Senior Managing Editor: Pamela D. Bennett
Production Editor: Sheryl Glicker Langner
Operations Supervisor: Central Publishing
Project Manager, Central Publishing: Laura Messerly
Senior Art Director: Jayne Conte
Cover Designer: Central Design
Cover Art: Superstock
Full-Service Project Management: GGS Book Services
Composition: GGS Book Services
Printer/Binder: R.R. Donnelley/Harrisonburg
Cover Printer: R.R. Donnelley/Harrisonburg
Text Font: AGaramond 10/12

Credits and acknowledgments borrowed from other sources and reproduced, with permission, in this textbook appear on appropriate page within text.

Every effort has been made to provide accurate and current Internet information in this book. However, the Internet and information posted on it are constantly changing, so it is inevitable that some of the Internet addresses listed in this textbook will change.

Library of Congress Cataloging-in-Publication Data

Managing classroom behavior : a reflective case-based approach / James M. Kauffman ... [et al.]. — 5th ed.
    p. cm.
  Includes bibliographical references and index.
  ISBN-13: 978-0-13-705679-8
  ISBN-10: 0-13-705679-6
  1. Classroom management. 2. Classroom management—Case studies. 3. Case method. I. Kauffman, James M.

LB3013.M326 2011
371.102'4—dc22   2009042106

www.pearsonhighered.com

10 9 8 7 6 5 4 3
ISBN-10:   0-13-705679-6
ISBN-13: 978-0-13-705679-8

PREFACE

When teachers are not successful in helping students learn and enjoy school, the reason is likely to be, in large measure, the difficulty they experience in managing classroom behavior. Many teachers who become discouraged, feel "burned out," or leave the profession attribute their unhappiness in teaching to their difficulty in managing students' behavior. Managing students' behavior has always been a demanding task, but it becomes more exacting with each passing year. What experienced teachers tell us, what we read, and what we see in schools—all reliable indicators—tell us that disruption, aggression, disinterest in school, social withdrawal, and other forms of undesirable behavior are increasingly common in nearly all schools. Federal and state laws applying to *all* students have made teaching even harder, and demands for higher academic performance have not made students more tractable. Without effective strategies for dealing with unacceptable and troublesome behavior, teachers are unlikely to seek a career in teaching and even less likely to enjoy and be successful in their chosen profession. Furthermore, students are very unlikely to learn what they should when their teachers are unhappy and feel defeated.

We understand both the immensity of the challenge of dealing with students' behavior in today's schools and the importance of preparing teachers for that challenge. This book represents our efforts to help prospective and in-service teachers meet that challenge as reflective practitioners of the profession of teaching. Our experience in working with students of teaching, whether before they begin teaching or after, has led us to the conclusion that the typical expository style of textbooks and the typical lecture-discussion format of courses are inadequate.

In the late 1980s, we began experimenting with a different approach—the case method of teaching, which has been used for decades in schools of business and law. We found much in the case method to recommend it, and we became convinced that it could become the model for some, but not all, of the courses we teach in education. The case-based approach, it seemed to us, was a "natural" for an applied course in classroom behavior management because successful management requires the kind of reflection and analytical skills case analysis demands. Nevertheless, we discovered that teaching cases without readings that provide a foundation of basic concepts about reflection on behavior management issues was also unsatisfactory. For a course in classroom behavior management, we found no texts that presented the information we found most pertinent in a manner designed to encourage reflective analysis of teaching practices. This book was born, in our minds, of necessity. Over the years, we have collected and written cases of our own and used them in our teaching. The cases included in this book are stories we have found useful in helping teachers think through the complexities of dealing effectively with troublesome classroom behavior.

In Part I, we provide an overview of basic concepts that our experience leads us to believe are essential to classroom behavior management. Each chapter begins with an advance organizer—an outline of the major headings, giving the reader a preview of the questions we will be addressing. The body of each chapter is organized around a common framework: (1) an opening statement about the topic of the chapter, (2) one or more vignettes (except in the opening chapter) illustrating problems of the type we will be discussing, (3) the major questions on which we are asking the reader to reflect, (4) consideration of the questions for reflection, (5) a brief chapter summary, and (6) suggestions for connecting particular cases to the chapter.

Our intention is not only to present basic concepts succinctly but also to induce in readers a process of self-questioning that carries forward from the first chapter to the last and that is intimately connected to how one analyzes cases. We have not prepared a "cookbook" or behavior management manual. Rather, our approach is based on the assumptions that asking good questions is a prerequisite for finding good answers. Thus, although we make some specific suggestions regarding behavior management, we raise more questions than we answer. Our writing style is, we hope, both readable and conducive to reflection about questions and answers.

In Part II, we offer cases for analysis. Some are cases we wrote following interviews with teachers, others were written by teachers or intern teachers themselves or by parents and edited by us. All the cases are factual—they are not hypothetical—and the only changes in the facts of the cases are those necessary to protect the identities of the individuals about whom they are written or to detach them from a particular place or date. Each case suggests problems and analyses to which several of the chapters in Part I are relevant. One aspect of the case-based approach that is frustrating, yet that makes case-based teaching and learning particularly challenging and exciting, is the multitude of perspectives from which one can view any given case and the multiple problems each case presents. That is also one of the strengths of a case-based approach—it reflects the real-life complexities we do not ordinarily encounter in brief vignettes, hypothetical examples, and the straightforward exposition of principles.

Case-based teaching is relatively new in teacher education, compared to training in business or medicine. Consequently, you may not have any prior experience in case analysis. The process of case analysis is one you can learn only by doing it. Your instructor will lead you and your fellow students through the analysis of cases by asking you to prepare study questions and by guiding your discussion of various aspects of the cases. If your experience is anything like that of the students with whom we have used these materials, you will find case-based learning highly intriguing and rewarding. We hope you enjoy both parts of this book and find them useful in thinking about how you manage students' behavior.

NEW TO THE FIFTH EDITION

Although the fifth edition follows the same overall structure as the first four editions, we have added some new features. Specifically, new to the fifth edition are:

- A new chapter (Chapter 2) on planning for the school year and managing the physical environment
- A new feature, **Case Connection**, making explicit links between chapters in Part I and specific cases in Part II (at the end of each chapter, we suggest a case or cases with particularly high relevance to the chapter's content)
- A completely rewritten Chapter 8
- Four new cases and deletion of five cases from the previous edition
- Use of APA reference style, with all references listed at the end of the book rather than at the end of each chapter
- Revisions of all chapters for improved readability and updating
- Inclusion of all case descriptions in the text (rather than including parts of cases in the instructor's manual only)

ACKNOWLEDGMENTS

We wrote or edited all of the cases included in this book. However, we are indebted to many other teachers, parents, and university colleagues for drafting cases or telling us their stories. We also acknowledge with thanks the assistance of Gary D. Jacobs, Walsh University; David Majsterek, Central Washington University; and Cheryl Zaccagnini, Shippensburg University in reviewing this edition and giving us their recommendations.

J.M.K.
P.L.P.
M.P.M.
S.C.T.

CONTENTS

Part 1   Developing a Reflective Approach to Problems   1

Chapter 1   Analyzing Cases   2

Questions for Reflection   2

How will analyzing cases help me in the classroom?   3

How should I analyze a case?   3

What are the issues that I should attend to first?   4

What actions should I take to resolve the issues?   5

What knowledge will I need to formulate an action to resolve the issues?   6

What are the perspectives of the people involved in the plan, and what can I predict about their behavior?   7

What might be the consequences of my actions?   8

Summary   10   •   Case Connection   10

Chapter 2   Planning for the Year and Managing the Physical Environment   11

Sue   11

Lisa   12

Questions for Reflection   13

What do I need to know about my class before school starts?   13

GETTING INFORMATION FROM OTHERS   13

CUMULATIVE FOLDERS   14

What do I do with the information I find?   15

How can I plan ahead for behavior management?   16

RULES   17

SPACE   18

Summary   20   •   Case Connection   20

Chapter 3   Identifying Behavior Problems   21

Sally   21

Sam   22

Questions for Reflection   23

Could this problem be a result of inappropriate curriculum or teaching?   23

What do I demand and prohibit, and what should I?   24
  DEMANDS   26
  PROHIBITIONS   26

Why do certain behaviors bother me, and what should
  I do about them?   27

Is this behavior developmentally significant?   29
  ACADEMIC FAILURE   29
  AGGRESSION   30
  DEPRESSION   31
  PROBLEMS WITH PEERS   32

A Note About Multiple Problems   32

Should I focus on a behavioral excess or a deficiency?   33

Will resolution of the problem solve anything else?   33
  Summary   34   •   Case Connection   34

Chapter 4   Analyzing Behavior Problems   35

Tammy   36

Trisha   36

Questions for Reflection   37

What are my assumptions about why students behave
  the way they do?   37

What are the most important alternative explanations
  of the misbehavior?   38

Are there causes of the misbehavior that I can control to a
  significant degree?   39

How should I define the behavior I am concerned about and
  identify its antecedents and consequences?   40
  DEFINING BEHAVIOR   40
  IDENTIFYING ANTECEDENTS   41
  IDENTIFYING CONSEQUENCES   42
  IDENTIFYING CHAINS OF EVENTS   42
  IDENTIFYING COERCIVE INTERACTIONS   44
  IDENTIFYING THE PATTERNS AND STAGES OF MISBEHAVIOR   45

How might I identify the probable cognitive and affective
  aspects of the misbehavior?   47

How should I measure the behavior problem and
  behavior change?   48

What's a reasonable goal?   50

How do I accomplish a functional assessment of behavior
  and write a positive behavior intervention plan?   50

What is required for prevention and early intervention?   51
  Summary   52   •   Case Connection   52

Chapter 5   Changing Behavior   53

Mary   54

Tom   54

Questions for Reflection   55

Have I tried the simplest and most obvious strategies?   55

What approaches to helping students change their behavior are most likely to be successful?   59

How might I use the five operations of a behavioral approach?   60

POSITIVE REINFORCEMENT   60

NEGATIVE REINFORCEMENT   63

EXTINCTION   63

RESPONSE COST PUNISHMENT   64

PUNISHMENT BY PRESENTING AVERSIVES   65

A NOTE ON CORPORAL PUNISHMENT   66

How can I capitalize on the cognitive and affective aspects of behavior change?   66

TALKING WITH STUDENTS   67

CHOOSING CONSEQUENCES FOR STUDENTS' BEHAVIOR   67

TEACHING SELF-CONTROL PROCEDURES   67

TEACHING SOCIAL SKILLS   67

Is my approach positive and supportive of appropriate behavior?   68

Can I use an instructional approach to prevent this behavior problem?   69

PRECORRECTING PROBLEMS   69

INTERRUPTING THE ACTING-OUT CYCLE   71

Special Note on Digital Resources   73

Summary   74   •   Case Connection   74

Chapter 6   Talking with Students   75

Sarah   76

Natalie   76

Questions for Reflection   77

How does classroom talk differ from talking in other places?   77

How is talking with students about their behavior related to my teaching goals?   78

How can I avoid unproductive talking with students about their behavior?   79

What verbal and nonverbal communication skills must I model and teach?   82

LISTENING   82

USING PROXIMITY   83

SPEAKING BODY LANGUAGE   83

ESTABLISHING EYE CONTACT AND VARYING FACIAL EXPRESSIONS   83

PAUSING, REFLECTING, AND PROBING   83

DESCRIBING, NOT JUDGING   84

CHOOSING THE BEST WORDS   84

USING THE BEST VOICE   84

SETTING THE RIGHT PACE   85

SUMMARIZING   85

QUESTIONING   85

WAITING   86

How can talking with students teach them about personal responsibility?   86

How should I talk with students about appropriate behavior?   88

How should I talk with students about unacceptable behavior?   89

How should I talk with angry or aggressive students?   90

How should I talk with students who are withdrawn?   92

Summary   93   •   Case Connection   93

Chapter 7   Using Peer Influence   94

Sally   95

Marcus   95

Questions for Reflection   96

How might I use observational learning and vicarious consequences to affect the behavior of my students' peers?   96

MODELS WHO ARE LIKELY TO BE IMITATED   97

REWARDING THE MODEL AND TARGET STUDENT   97

LIMITS OF VICARIOUS EFFECTS   98

What type of group contingency might I use to create desirable peer pressure?   99

INDEPENDENT GROUP CONTINGENCIES   99

DEPENDENT GROUP CONTINGENCIES   100

INTERDEPENDENT GROUP CONTINGENCIES   100

COOPERATIVE LEARNING   100

SCHOOL-WIDE PLANS   101

CAUTIONS ABOUT GROUP CONTINGENCIES   101

How might I engage peers as confederates?   102

How might I use peer tutors as a classroom resource?   103

CHOOSING AND TRAINING TUTORS   103

LIMITATIONS OF PEER TUTORING   104

What options should I consider in teaching social skills?   104

Summary   105   •   Case Connection   106

Chapter 8 **Working with Other Teachers and Other Professionals   107**

Jennifer   108

Penny   110

Questions for Reflection   111

What do I need to know about working with someone whose views are much like mine?   111

How do I work with someone who doesn't share my views about how to solve an educational problem?   112
Finding Out About Other People's Views   112
Making Your Views Clear   112
Finding Mutual Objectives   113

How and what can I learn from other teachers?   113
Listening and Reading   113
Watching   113
Learning   114

How do I share my ideas with others most effectively?   114
Sensitivity and Tactfulness   114
Clarity and Terseness   114
Acceptance   114

What does it take to make collaboration benefit me and my students?   115

What are the limits of collaboration?   116

When am I better off "doing my own thing"?   116
Summary   117   •   Case Connection   117

Chapter 9 **Working with Parents and Families   118**

Miss Adams   118

Marie   119

Questions for Reflection   120

Why should I involve parents and families?   121

Who are the parents of my students?   122
Understanding Economic Stresses on Families   122
Understanding Parents from Different Cultural or Ethnic Backgrounds   123

What are my prejudices?   127

What is the reciprocity of parent-child interaction?   128

What are the school guidelines for communicating with parents?   129

When and how should I involve parents, especially parents of tough kids?   130
The Sooner, the Better   130

LETTERS   131
PARENT CONFERENCES   131
ABUSIVE PARENTS   133

In what ways can I involve parents and families?   134
HOME-NOTE PROGRAMS   134

Why is it so hard to involve parents?   134
Summary   136   •   Case Connection   136

Part 2   Cases for Analysis and Discussion Reflection   137

Alone in the Dark,   Alan Stean   138

Avoiding the Issue,   Johnny's Teachers   141

Caught in the Middle,   Leann Grossley   144

Charley,   Ms. Russell   149

Grandma's Boy,   Helen Jamison   154

James's Uncertain Future,   Dan Parker   160

Lenny,   Sara Olson   163

One Bad Apple,   Elaine Brown   167

Richard's Mother,   Polly Dudley   171

Stealing Time,   Robert Carter   175

The Contract with Parrish and Son,   Rebecca Phillips   180

The First Parent Conference,   Christine Walker   184

The One That Got Away,   Charles Allen   189

The Truth About Alice,   Janet Lane   193

They Failed Derrick,   Melinda Smith   196

What You Don't Know Can Hurt You!   John McCullum   203

What's Inclusion Got to Do with It?   Anita Atkinson   206

When Secrets Disable,   Cathy Schrock   211

Where to Now?   Connie Ballard   215

Winnie,   Patty Gray   219

References   226
Index   229

PART ONE

Developing a Reflective Approach to Problems

Chapter 1 Analyzing Cases
Chapter 2 Planning for the Year and Managing the Physical Environment
Chapter 3 Identifying Behavior Problems
Chapter 4 Analyzing Behavior Problems
Chapter 5 Changing Behavior
Chapter 6 Talking with Students
Chapter 7 Using Peer Influence
Chapter 8 Working with Other Teachers and Other Professionals
Chapter 9 Working with Parents and Families

CHAPTER ONE

Analyzing Cases

Questions for Reflection
How will analyzing cases help me in the classroom?
How should I analyze a case?
What are the issues that I should attend to first?
What actions should I take to resolve the issues?
What knowledge will I need to formulate an action to resolve the issues?

What are the perspectives of the people involved in the plan, and what can I predict about their behavior?
What might be the consequences of my actions?
Summary
Case Connection

Case-based teaching has certain advantages, but only if you have an orientation to analyzing cases. Consequently, we start with some questions and suggestions about case analysis. After all, this is a *case-based book,* and we want you to get in the habit of reflecting on what you read. We want you to be able to apply the principles you read about in subsequent chapters to the cases in this book and to your own practices as a teacher. You'll likely be able to do that only if you have a systematic way of trying to make sense of the circumstances teachers face. We provide illustrations of some of these circumstances throughout the chapters. However, we describe such circumstances more extensively in the cases in Part II.

QUESTIONS FOR REFLECTION

As you encounter cases in your reading and study, we suggest that you ask yourself some important questions about cases. You might start with these:

- How will analyzing cases help me in the classroom?
- How should I analyze a case?
- What are the issues that I should attend to first?
- What actions should I take to resolve the issues?
- What knowledge will I need to formulate an action to resolve the issues?

- What are the perspectives of the people involved in the plan, and what can I predict about their behavior?
- What might be the consequences of my actions?

How will analyzing cases help me in the classroom?

Studying cases has been part of university programs in business, law, and medical schools for decades. These professions have long understood the benefits of analyzing real-life problems on paper before heading into the real world. All of the cases in this book are real—none is fictitious—and some are daunting in their scope and depth of problems. They are all real-life problems of teachers and parents, like those included in Kauffman and Landrum (2009b).

Many, if not most, of the problems encountered in the cases that students study are common problems that appear daily in given professions, which means that the resolutions students find in cases often generalize into the world. This generalization helps them to make better decisions quicker when they obtain a job.

How should I analyze a case?

So, case analysis might help you make better decisions. But how do you analyze a case? Where do you begin? Are some *issues* more important than others? What *knowledge* is most important? Will some *actions* have better *consequences* than others? And why should you be concerned about the consequences? Why is understanding of the *perspectives* of those in the case important, and why would you worry about an administrator's or a parent's perspectives on your plan?

A case can be analyzed in many different ways (see Goor & Santos, 2002; Kolodner, 2003; Mostert, 1998; Silverman, Welty, & Lyon, 1992; Sudzina, 1998, 1999). We suggest a five-part method developed by our colleagues Joanne and Robert McNergney of the University of Virginia. We are grateful to them for sharing their method with us. Even though we delineate the five parts of a case here, it is important to understand that these parts are interdependent and sometimes difficult to see separately. When you analyze the cases, it's helpful to ask the following questions:

1. What are the *issues* in this case, and which issue is the most important?
2. What are the *actions* I could take to resolve this issue?
3. What *knowledge* do I need to implement my action?
4. What are the *perspectives* of the people involved in the implementation of my plan?
5. What might be the *consequences* of my actions?

Always read a case and obtain the facts first. Without all the facts, you can't accomplish the rest of the case analysis. Ask yourself questions like these.

- Who is in the case?
- What happens in the case?
- Where does the problem occur? During reading? At recess?
- Is there an important *sequence* of events in the case? If so, can you determine the antecedents and the consequences of the behavior?
- If several teachers are involved in the case, how much teaching experience do the main characters have?
- Is the student's culture different from your culture?

Carefully determining the facts should lead you to the *issues. Roget's Thesaurus* gives synonyms for the word *issue: a situation that presents difficulty, uncertainty, or perplexity.* There are many difficult situations in the cases and in our classrooms that perplex us, ranging from suspicion of child abuse, threats of suicide, poor academic achievement, and noncompliance to lack of parental involvement or a distrustful parent who watches every move in the classroom.

What are the issues that I should attend to first?

Safety and legal issues are always the first concerns. Is there a safety issue presented in the case? Is either the student's or the teacher's safety in jeopardy? Is child abuse suspected? Has the student threatened suicide? Suspected child abuse could be both a safety and a legal issue because in most states, teachers are considered "reporters" of child abuse and are legally bound to report *suspected* child abuse to child protective services. Consider the following vignette:

> Adrian's mother, Mrs. Beckett, never answered the notes I sent home and was barely polite the few times I phoned her. It was clear that she was not going to be part of any home/school behavior management plan, so I persuaded the principal to mentor Adrian, give him stickers for good work and compliment him for good behavior. But because I believed so strongly in collaboration with parents and because I wanted to develop rapport with this parent, I scheduled a home visit to explain the results of the educational assessment for Adrian's approaching triennial evaluation.
>
> The speech-language pathologist, Susan, accompanied me to explain her testing results also. Our first impression when Mrs. Beckett let us in was how spotless and ordered the apartment was. As Susan said, "It was uncomfortably clean. You would never have guessed that children lived there." Mrs. Beckett asked us to sit at the dining room table and then pointed to Adrian and his younger brother and yelled, "Sit on the sofa! Now!" They sat.
>
> During the explanations of the assessments, I said, "I'm so proud of Adrian. He has worked very hard lately and is completing all of his work neatly and accurately." When I mentioned his name, Adrian approached his mother with one of his assignments. Before Adrian could show his mother his paper, Mrs. Beckett slapped the table close to Adrian with a cutoff razor strap attached to her wrist with a leather thong and yelled, "Sit down!"
>
> Susan, Adrian, and I jumped, and Adrian backed away, apologizing, "I'm sorry, Mamma. I'm sorry." Susan and I were amazed that we had not seen the razor strap attached to Mrs. Beckett before she banged it on the table. But as Susan later observed, "I guess you don't expect a mother to have a razor strap around her arm when you go for a home visit."

If Mrs. Beckett would wear her razor strap when school faculty visited, Susan and I suspected that she wore it all the time and that she probably thumped her children and not the table when no one else was around. Susan and I were also amazed that Mrs. Beckett was so volatile. We thought this was definitely a safety issue: a mother with a short fuse and a ready razor strap. We involved Child Protective Services (CPS).

One of the cases we know involves a mother who wants her son tested for what she considered "learning problems." After many pleading letters from the mother, the school finally tested the son but only when an advocate became involved 18 months after the initial request. The school was not in compliance with the special education law, which was clearly a legal issue.

Usually there are multiple issues in a case. Most children do not present one problem but a cluster of problems, and we are compelled to determine which issue to work on first. Always remember, safety first, for the kids as well as for yourself.

What actions should I take to resolve the issues?

Actions are the plans you implement to resolve the *issue*. What *actions* could you take in a case to *prevent* problems in similar situations? For example, the action the speech-language pathologist and I took about Mrs. Beckett's suspected abuse of her children was to call CPS. Consider the following vignette:

> I'm a single mother, and I have to work, but I think I'd rather dig ditches than continue teaching. Even though I'm a speech-language pathologist and have no training in teaching, I am desperate to move my children away from the crime in the big city. So I've accepted the only available job in the small school system in which I was educated.
>
> I foolishly thought that a classroom of 12 students with mild mental retardation in a middle school wouldn't be so hard. What a doofus I am! There are *no* materials appropriate for my class. Even though all the texts are too hard for them, there's no money to purchase any new texts. When I asked the principal what reading program the previous teacher used with the class, he said, "Don't worry much about actually teaching these kids anything. They're retarded and probably won't amount to much. And anyway, we don't have money to buy any new reading material." (He actually said this!) And if there were money, would I know which text to purchase? Nope. And these kids are bad! They fight and hit each other on a daily basis, curse each other and me, and won't pay attention in class or complete the few assignments that I give them. And I have no idea how to get them to behave.
>
> Last week, two of the girls got into a knock-down-hair-pulling-scratching cat fight, and when I tried to separate them, I got hit. One of the boys in the class grabbed me and shoved me under the desk, and said, "Now you stay there, you crazy little white woman, 'till I get help." Seemed like a good plan to me! But I can't spend every day hiding under my desk. All I can do is hold on until spring while I search the want ads for another job—*any* job, as long as it's not in the classroom. So far, I can't seem to find anything that offers the same benefits as my miserable teaching job, and I definitely need insurance for my children and me. It's going to be a long winter.

There are lots of issues in the preceding, including the following:

1. An unsafe, out-of-control classroom where children are physically and verbally aggressive
2. No behavior management plan
3. Teaching out-of-field—teacher is a speech-language pathologist, not a classroom teacher
4. Inappropriate curriculum—texts seem too hard
5. No funds to provide another curriculum

The action the teacher would implement for the preceding case would depend on which of the issues she chose to remediate. For example, if the teacher decided that teaching out-of-field is the most pressing issue, she could ask for reassignment as a speech-language pathologist, and if there were no such jobs available, she could resign. But she has already said that leaving the classroom without another job that provided benefits is not an option. She has to teach, even though she is miserable. The physical and verbal aggression presents a safety issue and should be addressed immediately. Because many educators say that the best behavior management tool teachers have is good instruction, she should address this issue first, along with the violence. But if you consider the last issue, no funding, how would she do this? The following might be actions to consider:

1. Obtain appropriate texts by pleading for funds from an advocacy organization (e.g., the ARC, formerly known as the Association for Retarded Citizens).
2. Contact parents for collaboration in obtaining appropriate texts.
3. Develop and implement a behavior management plan that reinforces nonaggressive behaviors, attention to teacher presentations, and correctly completed assignments.
4. Enroll in education courses that will help the teacher manage academic and social behavior competently.

If she is already stressed, taking a night class might be the last straw, so enrolling in a course may not be an option—particularly if the school system won't pay for the course. If she decides to plead with the ARC and parents to help her acquire appropriate texts, she needs to know two important facts: (1) the academic achievement of the students and (2) what texts or commercial programs would best serve the needs of her students. The teacher knows how to test and interpret the language and articulation deficits of her students and could develop a speech and language program, but she does not know where her students are in their academic or social skills or how to determine these skill deficits. She needs more knowledge if she is to implement an appropriate action.

What knowledge will I need to formulate an action to resolve the issues?

Let's assume that this benighted soul decides to press for better texts and to develop a behavior management plan. She needs to know where her students are in their academic skills because, as she already knows, if the texts are too hard, the students won't complete tasks or pay attention during instruction—a clear path for chaos in the classroom. However, if the texts are too easy, the students will be bored and will find inappropriate ways to ease the boredom. The child study committee is a logical place to ask for help, but before she pleads for help from the child study committee, she needs to consult the following for information:

1. *Students' cumulative folders*, including the individualized education programs (IEPs), where she can possibly determine her students' academic levels, previous behavior problems and how they were handled, and names of faculty who have worked with the students before.
2. *Personnel* who have worked with the students in the past, who might be able to elaborate on successful academic and social skills programs.
3. *Parents* who could possibly provide more information about academic and social skills problems and how they handle these issues at home. Even if the parents have little information to share, she should develop rapport with them. The parents could also petition the school board for more funding.
4. *The school psychologist* may have tested the students and may have time to help her develop a behavior management plan.

In this case, the teacher determined that 10 of her 12 middle school students had been retained two years, were reading on first-grade or primer level, and had been notorious trouble-makers their entire academic careers. Eight students were from single-parent families, and grandparents were raising two. Most of the parents or guardians blamed the school for their children's behavior problems, and, as one grandmother said, "The schools don't teach my grandson, and so he finds something to do. Ain't always what's best for him, though." Indeed. This teacher also discovered that the texts she was asked to use were on fifth-grade level—clearly too hard for her students.

Armed with the knowledge that reading texts were too difficult for her class, this teacher may now take the following actions:

1. Contact the special education supervisor and other administrators to ask for appropriate texts and to investigate programs that the students had used successfully in the past.
2. Contact the parents and ask for help to obtain appropriate texts.
3. Contact ARC and ask for funding.
4. Present this information to the child study committee that might have more appropriate texts available.
5. Ask the child study committee to help her make a behavior management plan.

What are the perspectives of the people involved in the plan, and what can I predict about their behavior?

Perspectives are the values of the people involved in the case. Teachers, students, parents, and administrators might view situations depicted in the case differently. How do the values of the characters in the case determine how they will react? Are some of their actions predictable? There are some cases when you'll probably say out loud to a character in the case, "No, don't do that!" because you can see what the predictable reaction of the child or parent will be. If you know the perspectives of the characters, you may be able to *predict* how these folks will behave in a given situation. The predictive quality of knowing how a person will react in a situation helps you formulate a better plan of action. In the preceding case about the speech-language pathologist teaching out-of-field, the principal stated his perspective about children with mental retardation. He said, "Don't worry much about actually teaching these kids anything. They're retarded and probably won't amount to much. And anyway, we don't have any money to buy any new reading material."

From his stated perspective on students with mild mental retardation—that they won't amount to much anyway and that there is not money for new material—the speech-language pathologist could predict that it would be a waste of her time to ask the principal for money to purchase new materials. She could also predict that he won't invest much time or effort in searching for funds from parents, community leaders, or the school board. The teacher will have to hunt for money to purchase appropriate texts. We might hope that the principal will support her efforts, but he is not going to start any campaigns to purchase appropriate curriculum materials for this class.

The grandmother who was a guardian of one of the boys in the class said, "The schools don't teach my grandson, and so he finds something to do. Ain't always what's best for him, though." Her stated perspective is that her grandson has a behavior problem in school because the school doesn't teach him and that if he were involved in academics in school, he might not find inappropriate ways to amuse himself. What can the teacher predict from the grandmother's statements that would influence her actions? Would the grandmother be supportive of petitioning the school board for appropriate texts? She might. She also might be more supportive of the teacher and more willing to collaborate with school personnel if she knows that the teacher is working hard to obtain material so that she really can teach her students.

People often do not consider the perspectives of the characters involved in problems they encounter, and they lose valuable time formulating actions that won't work because of the values of the folks in the case. Consider the following true story about Raymond, married two weeks to a divorcee with a 4-year-old girl, Katy:

Raymond's new wife, Betty, met him at the door when he came home from work and said, "You have to spank Katy right now."

Raymond was startled. Katy had always been a model child around him, and there had never been any reason to do more than ask her to sit down and be quiet. He and Betty had never discussed behavior or discipline problems because there didn't seem to be any.

He said, "Betty, I don't believe in spanking children. There is never a good enough reason to hit a child."

"Well, there is this time, and you have to spank her."

"What in the world did she do, Betty?"

"She called me a bitch."

"Well, you spank her. You were the one she called a bitch."

"I would, except she crawled under the porch, and I can't reach her. You have to go get her, bring her out here, and spank her."

Betty insisted that Raymond fetch Katy, so he changed clothes, and armed with a flashlight, he crawled through spiders, mice feces, and dirt to reach Katy, who was in the farthermost corner under the house. When he was about six inches from Katy's face, he opened his mouth to say he-knew-not-what—how was he to persuade her to leave her safe haven of spiders and rat feces so her mother could spank her?—when she said, "Did that bitch run you up under beneath the porch too?" Raymond collapsed laughing, and he and Katy held onto each other, howling with laughter. Katy escaped a spanking. Betty was just glad "for those howling idiots to come from under the porch."

Betty predicted from Raymond's stated perception—"There is never a good enough reason to hit a child"—that Raymond would probably never spank his children. If Katy warranted a spanking, then Betty would have to do it. Katy is now an adult, and Raymond never spanked her or her two younger siblings. Understanding the perspective of the people involved in your cases can save you time when you plan your actions.

What might be the consequences of my actions?

All actions have *consequences*—some good, some bad. You must determine what the consequences of your action *might* be. Suppose that the speech-language pathologist/teacher in the earlier case decides to ask her supervisor for help. The teacher hopes that after explaining the academic skill level of her class and the inappropriateness of the texts the class is expected to use, the supervisor will try to find the funds for new materials. However, a bad consequence might be that the supervisor not only doesn't have the funds and doesn't know how to obtain them, but she would also be angry with the teacher for asking for something that she can't have.

The consequences of asking the child study committee for help in developing a behavior management plan might be that the committee would make a plan and help the teacher implement the plan and that this would significantly reduce the aggressive behaviors in class. Or the committee might dismiss the teacher's pleas as whining. Or the committee might be too busy to help her. It might be better to take the chance on the more positive consequence.

Sometimes, the bad consequence that might occur far outweighs the positive one, and the school personnel might revise their actions. Consider the following:

I had been on the child study committee for 10 years, and I felt that we had had a positive effect at the school—until Mrs. Randolph. Gerry Randolph was a first-grader who was absent three to four days a week, and his teacher was a bit frantic trying to keep up Gerry's skills. The teacher said, "He's not God's brightest light, but he certainly is average, and he wants to come to school. But I can't teach him if he's not here!" On the days that Mrs. Randolph allowed Gerry to attend school, she sat in her car in the school parking lot all day and waited for Gerry. The first-grade teacher, the visiting teacher (called a school social worker in some states), and the principal made separate visits to Mrs. Randolph's home and explained to her why Gerry should attend school regularly and that she could be held legally responsible if she did not see that Gerry came to school every day unless he was ill. Gerry often expressed how much he liked school and how much he wanted to come to school. He even volunteered that he could get himself ready every day if someone would pick him up. But Mrs. Randolph just wouldn't allow him to come to school. On several mornings, the visiting teacher, Anne Gregory, had tried to persuade Mrs. Randolph to allow her to drive Gerry to school, but Mrs. Randolph would hold Gerry tightly in her arms and refuse to allow him to leave, even when Gerry reached his arms toward Anne and begged his mother to allow him to go with the visiting teacher.

During a child study meeting, the committee decided to send the visiting teacher and the school system's lawyers to Gerry's house and physically remove him from home and drive him to school. The committee felt that after a couple of visits, Mrs. Randolph might be more amenable to having her son come to school. "She can sit in the parking lot, or we can bring her to school with Gerry and allow her to sit in the classroom. But Gerry must come to school."

Thank goodness Mrs. Randolph's Department of Social Services (DSS) case-worker was present at the meeting when we discussed forcibly taking Gerry from his mother. She said, "Mrs. Randolph is receiving treatment for a serious mental illness, and if you drag her child from her, she is likely to commit suicide before Gerry gets to school."

The principal was visibly shaken by this news and promised the DSS worker that we would not follow this action. The committee thought that Gerry's safety was another issue that we had not considered carefully enough. We asked the DSS workers to look into foster placement for Gerry.

Later, when committee members discussed this plan with the school lawyer, he asked, "Are you nuts? School personnel can't pull children from their mother's arms!"

Sometimes, there may be drastic and terrible consequences for implementing certain actions—consequences that would render your action useless or even dangerous. No evaluation of a case, no plan of action is complete until both *good* and *bad* consequences are considered.

Summary

Studying cases will help you make better decisions more quickly. Case analysis should follow a systematic pattern. Every case can be analyzed for the following elements:

- *Issues:* Problems encountered in a case; safety and legal issues should be the first considerations
- *Actions:* Plans formulated to resolve the *issues*
- *Knowledge:* Information teachers need from theory, other professionals, practice, texts, or experience to formulate a plan of *action*

- *Perspectives:* Understanding of the values of the people involved in the case gives predictability to how they will react to your *actions*
- *Consequences:* Understanding the *good* and *bad* effects of your plans of *action*

Case analysis requires addressing each of these elements of a case.

Case Connection

Every case requires analysis, but you might find the following cases particularly useful for your first case analysis:

Avoiding the Issue   Johnny's Teachers
Charley   Ms. Russell

CHAPTER TWO

Planning for the Year and Managing the Physical Environment

Questions for Reflection
What do I need to know about my class before
  school starts?
  Getting Information from others
  Cummulative folders
What do I do with the information I find?

How can I plan ahead for behavior management?
  Rules
  Space
Summary
Case Connection

Managing classroom behavior begins with advance planning. You need to be prepared for your students from the first day of the school year. Arranging the physical environment—your desk, students' desks, work areas, and the materials that you and your students need—is also important. Get these things wrong, and you'll complicate your work for the rest of the year. Get them right, and things will be easier and more efficient from the beginning.

The better you are at planning for the year, thinking ahead about behavior management, and learning what you need to know about your students, the easier your job of behavior management will be. And the easier and more efficient you are in managing classroom space and things in it, the easier your job will be as a manager of behavior. So, planning and thinking ahead about students and your classroom are things you'll definitely want to do. Just think about the following vignettes and how Sue could have saved herself and everyone else lots of grief and how Lisa was justifiably upset about what happened to Fred at school:

Sue

My husband and I were walking on the downtown mall late one evening when a small boy with long blonde hair and big blue eyes approached. He was smoking, and for a moment I thought he was a midget, until I realized that he was a classmate of Paul, one of my students with special needs. Christopher smiled and said, "Hey Miz Gordon, got any money you can give me?"

We talked with Christopher for a moment, but when he understood that we weren't sharing any money with him, he scurried to another couple. I was startled. A smaller than average, eight-year-old boy was roaming around the mall by himself at 11:00 PM, smoking and begging for money!

My aide always picked up Paul for me, but on Monday, I decided to fetch him. I wanted to schedule a time with his teacher, Sue Landers, when we could discuss Christopher. I was hoping she would tell me that she had contacted social services for Christopher, but I also wanted to see if he really was what Paul referred to as "that scary bully." As I walked into the classroom, I saw Christopher sitting close to the door, isolated from the other students. He smiled, waved, winked at me, and simultaneously kicked a classmate on her way to the pencil sharpener. Mrs. Landers yelled at Christopher, who grinned and winked at her.

Later, during our meeting, I asked Sue if this was typical of Christopher, and she said, "When Christopher realizes that someone is entering or leaving the class, he scoots his desk close enough to hit, kick, pinch, or spit on them. I'm surprised that he didn't hit or kick you!" I was relieved.

But what upset Sue the most was that sometimes when she was helping another student with her back to him, Christopher sometimes left the classroom. And it took a long time and a lot of adults to find him. She told me that one time he'd left school and walked home.

"He's so smart," Sue said. "But he's a mess. And he's totally messed up my class. I'm not sure what to do with him. But I know I missed the picture about where he should sit in my classroom!"

Lisa

I was thrilled when the elementary school evaluation committee determined that my son, Fred, had severe auditory discrimination problems at the end of his first-grade year. I'd begged and pleaded with the school to evaluate Fred, but his homeroom teacher, the principal, and the counselor didn't believe that he had any learning problems—just behavior problems. A friend of mine who was a special education teacher in another district composed a letter for me demanding that the school comply with the law and evaluate my son. They did. Finally!

Overwhelmed with work, a pending divorce, and two children, I didn't have time for a parent-teacher conference at the beginning of Fred's second grade. After a couple of weeks, Fred told me that his language arts teacher, Mrs. Anderson, made him sit in the hall every day, and he said, "I like sitting out there. Don't have to do any work."

I was confused. There hadn't been any phone calls, notes, or emails from Mrs. Anderson informing me that Fred was having problems in class. I also suddenly realized that Fred hadn't brought home any language arts seatwork—something I needed to see.

I scheduled a conference with Mrs. Anderson, and the meeting didn't make me angry—just sad and nervous for my son's progress. When I asked what problems Fred exhibited, Mrs. Anderson responded that he never followed directions, never completed seatwork, and was very disruptive. I was puzzled, and asked, "Well, what does his special education teacher, Miss Hamilton, say about this?"

Mrs. Anderson looked confused. "I don't understand."

"Mrs. Anderson, no one told you that even though Fred has an IQ around 130, he has serious auditory discrimination problems and receives help every day?"

"Well, I only have Fred for language arts, and I never knew that he's one of Miss Hamilton's students. I thought that his misconduct was just a *behavior* problem. No one ever mentioned to me that Fred had a learning disability."

A few days later, Mrs. Anderson, Miss Hamilton, the special education teacher, and I met. We devised a plan to assist Fred in the classroom. Even though I was annoyed that these teachers had not provided the help for which my son qualified—nor had they contacted me when he continually misbehaved—I was grateful that Fred was finally going to receive academic and behavioral assistance.

It was hard for me to grasp why Fred's language arts teacher never understood that he qualified as a student with a learning disability. I pledged to myself that I would hereafter schedule a parent-teacher conference at the beginning of *every* school year—before Fred stepped into the school—and take every teacher a copy of my son's IEP.

QUESTIONS FOR REFLECTION

As you plan for the year and the arrangement of your classroom, you'll need to consider two primary questions:

1. What do I need to know about my students before school starts?
2. How do I plan ahead for behavior management?

What do I need to know about my class before school starts?

The first thing you should do in getting ready for a new school year is to know as much about your students as you can *before* school starts. According to Wong and Wong (2009), "Finding out about your students is important in an effectively run classroom" (p. 8). It is. So, you might ask yourself questions like these:

- Where do I find the information I need?
- What do I do with the information I find?

Sources of information about your students are school faculty and staff, the cumulative folders, psychological folders, and the parents. Use them all. You can't know too much, but you need to realize that sometimes information may be wrong. However, if you don't have *any* information, you can't even make that judgment!

GETTING INFORMATION FROM OTHERS   Some school systems have team leaders who attend the induction workshops for new teachers, and these leaders share pertinent information about class rolls to the inductees. Other systems have departmental meetings during the before-the-students-arrive workweek when teachers share information about students. For example, fourth-grade teachers might meet with fifth-grade teachers to share information about the rising fifth graders. This is usually when teachers will suggest that Johnny and Harry not sit next to each other or that Susie's mother is a very concerned parent who will observe the classroom three mornings a week.

One way to begin information gathering is to copy your class roster and submit it to the special education teachers and the school counselors. Ask them if they will highlight the students who qualify for special education, those who have been evaluated but didn't qualify, and those who have behavior problems. Ask them to hand the form back to you or return it to your mailbox. Then read the highlighted students' cumulative and psychological folders if you can get them. You don't want to be in the dark about students if you don't have to be.

CUMULATIVE FOLDERS   If you're a high school teacher who will be teaching more than a hundred students, you can't read the cumulative folders of *all* of your students, but you can determine pertinent information about *some* of them. And even if you're an elementary or special education teacher, you may not find the time to read about *all* of your students, but you should learn about as many of them as possible. Here are some examples of the kinds of questions you might find answers to by reading cumulative folders:

Is there important medical information in the folder?
1. Is the student diabetic?
2. Does the student have seizures?
3. Does the student take prescription drugs for ADHD, such as Ritalin?
4. Does the student take any other medication for a serious illness?
5. Does the student have a visual or auditory impairment?
6. Is the student morbidly obese or does he or she have other eating or weight problems?

If the answer to any of the preceding questions is yes, then you should talk with the school nurse about the medical condition and how to handle this in the classroom. For example, one fifth-grade teacher and a diabetic student developed a signal when the student was to go to the resource room to eat his snack, which he was embarrassed to do in front of the class. Often, medical conditions should be discussed with the parents. What you need to know is how this medical condition will affect the student's functioning in the classroom and how you will need to adapt the classroom environment for the student.

What other questions might I be able to answer by looking at the cumulative folder?
- If the student is in foster care, is it because of neglect or abuse, incarceration of parents, or because of illness or the death of a parent?
- Does the student qualify for special education services? Is there a separate psychological folder for this student?
- Has the student ever been evaluated for services as a child with disabilities but did not qualify for services?
- Does the student attend school regularly? If the student's attendance is sporadic, why?
  1. Are absences due to illness?
  2. Are absences due to family pressures, such as babysitting or protecting an abused parent?
  3. Are absences due to neglectful parents who are not committed to their child going to school regularly?

Regular attendance is important, and if the student doesn't attend regularly and doesn't have a medical condition, then why is he or she consistently absent? The answers to the preceding will probably not be in the cumulative folder, but they should prompt you to chase down the school social worker for the facts.

- Has the student attended many different schools?
  1. If so, why? Are the parents in military service?
  2. Does the parent have a job that requires the family to move often?
  3. Are parents on the move to keep a step ahead of protective services?

Whatever the reason for many transfers, changing schools is often hard for children and sometimes predicts low academic achievement and/or behavior problems. If the student's parents are not moving because of job requirements, they may be trying to outrun protective services, which may suspect abuse, or they may be escaping an abusive spouse who is stalking them. Be particularly watchful of those students.

- Does the student have siblings?
   1. How many siblings are there?
   2. Do any of the student's siblings attend the same school?
   3. If the student is a "tough kid," are any of his siblings also considered "tough kids"?
- What names of professionals who have worked with the student are in the folder, and why are these names important?

You look for names of professionals because they may have pertinent information about the student—information they won't place in the folder. For example, a colleague of ours became very frustrated in trying to meet with the mother of a new student. Even though this mother routinely made appointments for both home visits and school conferences, she never appeared. When the colleague spoke with the visiting teacher from the child's previous school, she learned that the mother prostituted herself for drugs and that the grandmother was the responsible adult to contact because the children lived with her, even though she wasn't considered the legal guardian.

- Is there a separate discipline folder? And, if so, where is the discipline folder kept?

Sometimes discipline folders are locked in the principal's office, and teachers aren't aware of its existence. If there is a discipline folder, it records the serious misbehavior(s) that might have precipitated a suspension or expulsion—discipline referrals. You need to know just how tough your tough kids are.

It may be difficult to find the time to follow all of the suggestions in this chapter, particularly reading the cumulative folders. If you don't have time to read all the folders that were highlighted before the students arrive, *don't stop reading them*. Try to read one a week until you understand your difficult students.

What do I do with the information I find?

You might ask specifically: What do I do with the information I get from cumulative folders? Remember, you're looking for patterns of behavior that will affect school achievement. So, you might keep questions like these in mind:

- What academic comparisons can I make?
   1. Has the student *usually* achieved well academically?
   2. Has the student *rarely* achieved as expected academically?
   3. Is the student failing now, but there was a time when he or she was successful? And, if so, why is the student failing now?
   4. Is the student significantly better in one subject than another? Knowing students' areas of relative strength and weakness can help you understand things like enthusiasm for or avoidance of particular activities.
   5. If the student qualifies as a special needs student, has his or her academic performance improved, or has the student's achievement declined?
   6. If the student is in foster care, after a period of adjustment, has his or her academic achievement improved since he or she was removed from home?

- What behavioral and social comparisons can I make?
    1. Does the student consistently misbehave at specific times or for specific teachers?
    2. Has the student routinely been a behavior problem, or was there a time when she or he was compliant?
    3. If the student qualifies as a student with disabilities, has his or her behavior improved since evaluation and identification?
    4. If the student is in foster care, has her or his behavior improved since removal from the home?

Comparing the information in the folder may indicate that the academic or social programs implemented for the student need revision, or this information may show that a student needs a full evaluation for possible identification as a student with special needs, or the data may indicate that the department of social services should step in and provide protection.

For example, carefully read the grade reports that are usually in the cumulative folder. Low grades accompanied by big changes in behavior for students who have previously achieved at a high level may mean that the student has experienced a family trauma—death, divorce, moving, new baby, or remarriage of a parent—and the low achievement or behavior is temporary. Or it could be an indication that he or she developed a major illness that you could document by checking the medical information in the folder. It could also mean that the student's friends are not into academics and peer pressure is responsible for the decline. Low grades could also mean that the material has gotten too hard and the student may need help, particularly if the low grades continue over a year and are accompanied by an increase in misbehavior. Whatever the reason for the decline in grades, previous grades indicate that at one time the student was capable of achieving and might succeed again if the proper adaptations were made.

If the student has always earned below-average grades, he or she may have low cognitive functioning and may need help, or the student may be from a family that doesn't value education, so neither does he or she. Both possibilities require some preplanning in order to motivate the student and may even require that you refer the student to the child study committee (the educators who study students and make recommendations about what to do next).

If the student is significantly better in one subject than another, he or she may have a mild learning disability and may misbehave during instruction in order to escape feeling inadequate.

If a student is in foster care, read the folder with great care. You want to determine whether the student's behavior and academic achievement has improved during foster care, or is the student angry, noncompliant, and disinterested in academics. It's an unfortunate fact that many foster homes are as abusive as the ones from which the students have been removed. Also, the attachment children have for their parents is so strong that even if the parents have been abusive, many children want to return home and are often very angry when they can't. Whatever the case, even if the student seems happy and well adjusted with the foster parents, contact the social worker. The social worker is your link to the foster parents, the natural parents, and the safety net for your student, should he or she show up bruised or otherwise traumatized. *Know who your foster care students are, and be extra vigilant with them.*

How can I plan ahead for behavior management?

Tough kids may fit the category of folks who are so contrary that they would argue with a fence post. These are the students who make teachers and other students edgy, frustrated, and angry. They use noncompliance to suck teachers into arguments they can't win. Their mantra regarding reasonable expectations seems to be, "I'm not going to do it, and you can't make me!"

Unfortunately, many of us persist in arguing with our tough kids, placing more sanctions on their noncompliance until somebody wins—almost always the tough kid. They are very good at their "kingpin" job and do not easily relinquish this power. Why should they? The short-term payoffs for them are huge. They get out of doing academic work. They control their classmates and teachers. They derive great joy from pushing our buttons and watching us blast off. Other tough kids learn from them and become tougher. A few easily implemented strategies will help keep the lid on the tough kids' eruptions from day one. You might give special thought to two items: rules and space.

RULES   Rules are a vital part of classroom structure in all grades. Here are some general guidelines to follow:

- *Don't pile on the rules.*   Try to keep the list short. Don't have more than five rules, and because compliance is a hurdle for tough kids, always have a compliance rule first. Here are three good rules to start with:
  1. Do what teachers ask immediately.
  2. Keep your hands and feet and everything else to yourself.
  3. Raise your hand and wait to be called on before talking, unless we have free time.
- *Be careful how you word your rules.*   Try to follow these guidelines:
  1. Keep the wording positive when possible (i.e., say what to do, not what not to do; positive rules are also a guide for you in what to recognize as good rule-following behavior).
  2. Make your rules specific. No ambiguity. Students need to know exactly what is expected.
  3. Make your rules describe behavior that is observable and measurable. Rules that describe feelings or other internal states or that require subjective judgments are full of ambiguity and will cause you trouble.
  4. Link following the rules to good consequences. What good thing will happen if students follow the rules, and what mild punishments will result from not following the rules?
  5. Post rules and consequences so that you can refer to them. (see Rhode, Jenson, & Reavis, 1993, p. 22)
- *Rules that aren't specific, observable, or measurable aren't good classroom rules.*   In the following rules, the words "respect," "good citizen," or "best" can have wide interpretation among students and teachers:
  1. Be responsible.
  2. Be a good citizen.
  3. Demonstrate respect for others.
  4. Respect others' rights.
  5. Do your best. (Rhode, Jenson, & Reavis, 1993, p. 22)

The preceding are concepts that you want to teach or discuss with your class; however, they don't make good classroom rules. They're much more the kind of school-wide rules that all of the teachers in a school might agree on.

- Have a hierarchy of positive and negative consequences posted beside the rules. The following is an example:

If You Follow the Rules, You Can Earn the Following:
  1. Extra free time.
  2. A turn at the class "grab bag."
  3. Lottery tickets for mystery prize.
  4. Lunch with the teacher [or, for older children, homework pass].

If you don't Follow the Rules:
1. Loss of extra free time.
2. Get a phone call to your parents.
3. Go to in-school suspension.
4. Lose school privileges (for example, lunch with your friends).

When you establish the rules, display them in a prominent place where your students can see them. One of the first principles of rules is to discuss the requirements and the consequences—both positive and negative. As we'll discuss in later chapters, remember, too, that rules need to be reviewed, and you need to be particularly positive in recognizing rule-following. Rules alone do little to improve behavior. Rules plus positive recognition for following them are much more effective.

SPACE   After you know who's going to be in your class and what rules you'll have, you have to organize the physical aspects of your classroom. "People who are not organized send a loud message that they are not ready to teach" (Wong & Wong, 2009, p. 92). The way you organize and manage the physical aspects of your classroom tells students a lot about you. "Proactive planning of the physical space includes the layout of furniture and the design of accesses and pathways" (Evertson & Poole, 2008, p. 132). A dirty or disorganized classroom space doesn't encourage the kind of behavior you want.

We've been in some classrooms when the teachers had to rake through piles of debris to find their student rosters, their lesson plans, students' corrected assignments, or their personal belongings. Not good! And one classroom we saw was so filthy that the students had to move to another room because mice had nested in the classroom's filth. *Definitely,* not good! Although these are truly outrageous examples, teachers must still organize and prepare their classrooms. First of all, the room *must* be clean from the beginning. And keeping it reasonably clean and well organized is important. Yes, a custodian will likely be responsible for cleaning your room, but a custodian can and will do only so much. YOU are responsible for how your room looks and for the efficient organization of space and materials.

Here are four basic rules of organization that will help you arrange your room:

1. *Separate school from personal work.*   The students are your priority. Don't get sidetracked by a personal matter.
2. *Clear your desktop.*   Have labeled vertical files where you can see categories of papers rather than a catchall pile of papers and materials on your desk.
3. *Create a place for incoming and outgoing papers.*   Know where to put papers incoming for you and where to put papers to be returned to the students.
4. *Consolidate, consolidate, consolidate.*   Get small boxes, clear plastic containers, magazine files, and desk organizers. The few minutes you spend to consolidate will save you hours of searching for items. (Wong & Wong, 2009, p. 94)

Although it's important to provide a clean and comfortable room for your students, it's also vital to organize your work so you can be prompt and accurate when teaching. Know the exact location of your daily lesson plans, where your students' completed assignments are kept, where the new assignments are housed, and where daily or weekly assessments of students' academic and behavioral achievements are kept. Also, have a list of parents with their contact information easily available. This kind of organization is much more important than decorating your bulletin boards before your students arrive. "Research proves that a school's and classroom's cleanliness, orderliness, and character influences the students' behavior and the ability of a teacher to teach" (Wong & Wong, 2009, p. 92).

Placement of desks and furniture is another important issue. First of all, be sure that you have enough desks for all your students. If you're missing a desk or have one that's damaged, request what you need before school starts. Not having enough desks or chairs or having those that are broken is asking for trouble; avoid it if you can.

We also recommend that you think about these things: (1) learning your students' names, (2) keeping troublesome students apart, and (3) avoiding known problems. First, it's a good idea to assign students to specific seats so they know where to go. Letting students pick their places is asking for confusion and conflict, and problem students are likely to sit together. If you assign seats and have a seating chart, you avoid potential problems. You can also make a seating chart to help you learn your students' names. Not learning their names quickly leaves you at a disadvantage. Second, if you know that particular students are troublesome or tend to make trouble together, assign them to seats where you can see them easily and they're not likely to set each other off. Finally, you might have found out (by talking to others or by reading the cumulative folders) that a particular student needs to be close to or far from you or tends to exhibit a particular problematic behavior that you can manage more easily if you put him or her at a particular location (e.g., if a particular student tends to leave the classroom unexpectedly, don't seat that student near the door; don't put a student who's highly distractible in a high traffic area).

Because of the different grade levels, it's difficult to suggest specific instructions for organizing your desks. For example, if you teach first grade and use direct instruction, you must have an area where small groups may receive instruction while allowing you to monitor the other students while you teach. If you teach a foreign language in high school, you need to place the desks so that you can hear and see all the students, and they can see you. However, here are some specific suggestions that will assist you in organizing your room regardless of grade:

1. Have an area for students who need isolation.
2. Keep traffic areas clear. Don't put desks, chairs, or tables in front of doors, water fountains, sinks, pencil sharpeners, or your desk. Also, make sure that the teacher's desk and other equipment don't interfere with the flow of traffic.
3. Make sure that your desk is away from the door so that no one can take things from your desk and quickly walk out. And keep your personal items—keys, handbag, and so on—in a safe and secure location.
4. Arrange work areas and desks so that you can easily see the students, and they can see you.
5. Keep clear access to storage areas, bookcases, cabinets, and doors.
6. Plan areas for students' belongings. For example, provide space for their books, lunch bags, umbrellas, and jackets.
7. Display your classroom rules in a prominent place.
8. Have a place for listing the day or week's assignments.
9. Have a method ready for matching students to a desk. You could place name cards on the desk or use an overhead transparency or PowerPoint to correlate desk arrangements with student names. (suggestions in Wong & Wong, 2009)

If you have difficulty moving your desks and furniture around, ask for help. If you don't have time to decorate your bulletin boards, do it later. Decorating your room should be the last item on your list.

Summary

The more you accomplish in planning before the school year begins, the better you can manage your classroom. First, learn as much about your students as possible from teachers, cumulative folders, school counselors, or parents. Then neaten up and organize your classroom. Assign your students to seats, make a seating chart, and pay careful attention to where you assign your students to sit. Exhibit your carefully worded rules in a prominent place where every student can see them. Finally, organize your desks and classroom furniture so that the students can see you, you can see them, and students you know are easily distracted are not placed in a high traffic area.

Case Connection

Many cases involve the kind of planning we suggest, but you might find the following cases to present particular problems for analysis related to the content of this chapter:

The Truth About Alice   Janet Lane
What You Don't Know Can Hurt You!   John McCullum

CHAPTER THREE

Identifying Behavior Problems

Questions for Reflection

Could this problem be a result of inappropriate curriculum or teaching?

What do I demand and prohibit, and what should I?
Demands
Prohibitions

Why do certain behaviors bother me, and what should I do about them?

Is this behavior developmentally significant?
Academic Failure

Aggression
Depression
Problems with Peers

A Note about Multiple Problems

Should I focus on a behavioral excess or a deficiency?

Will resolution of the problem solve anything else?

Summary

Case Connection

Managing classroom behavior is a complex task requiring self-questioning and careful reflection that even the best teachers must work to acquire and maintain. This self-questioning and reflection should begin as soon as you become concerned about the behavior of a student or group. First impressions about a problem can be misleading. Our experiences in classrooms with children and youth lead us to believe that even outstanding teachers sometimes jump to conclusions about what the problem is rather than taking a more reflective, analytical approach to identifying it. As a consequence of not being sufficiently reflective and analytical, a teacher can waste a lot of time and energy dealing with an issue that isn't the most important while neglecting a more significant problem. In the following vignette, consider two teachers' reflections on their initial mistakes in identifying problems.

Sally

Kevin was a first-grader who drove me nuts by doing all kinds of things that were not just irritating but kept me from being able to teach effectively. It seemed to me that he was always out of his seat when he was supposed to be working. He grabbed things from other kids and pestered them when they were working. He yelled out things to me when I was across the room. He whined. At first, I thought if I could only keep him in his seat I'd be making a lot of progress. So I devised a plan for rewarding him for working at his desk—at first, you know, for just a couple of minutes at a time, then for gradually longer periods. And he began staying in his seat more. But I realized after a while that the other problems weren't getting any better and that there was a bigger problem. The bigger problem was noncompliance. Kevin just about never did what I told or asked him to do, and staying in his seat to do his work was just one of those things. When I finally figured out that getting him to be reasonably obedient was the real problem, I started teaching compliance as a skill in short lessons (each lesson lasting just a few minutes). Then I really saw a change in all these things that at first I saw as separate problems. I wish I'd gotten the bigger picture right away, before I spent a couple of weeks on just keeping Kevin in his seat.

Sam

A couple of years ago, the kids in the high school where I taught often wore hats. A lot of the boys wore baseball hats or painters' hats just about everywhere they went. The school administration didn't have any rules about wearing hats, so I had to make my own. I have this "thing" about wearing hats in homes, restaurants, schools, and so on. It seems impertinent to me. The way I was raised, you just don't do it. I think it's disrespectful, and I just want to grab these guys' hats and tell them to keep them off until they get outside. So I spent a lot of my time and psychic energy on hats. I made a strict no-hats rule in my classroom, and I enforced it successfully most of the time. But I ended up having some serious conflicts with kids, too, especially because I was the only teacher in the school who strictly prohibited hats. I wish I'd been able to see at the time that the real problem was my intolerance for a cultural custom that differs from mine. Sure, I have a right to my feelings, but the real issue was how I could exercise control of myself, not a custom of these kids that many see as harmless.

Effective teaching requires much more than keeping students' behavior under control. Yet, without reasonable control over students' classroom behavior, you will have no chance whatever of being effective. Behavior management skills are necessary but not sufficient for good teaching. Because behavior management skills are necessary, some people make the mistake of judging a teacher's competence solely on the basis of how well the class is controlled. But because controlling behavior isn't sufficient by itself, people may make the mistake of judging a well-managed class as indication that the teacher is more concerned about control than teaching. We hope that as you study issues in behavior management you will carefully examine your own concerns and values about controlling the students you teach. You might ask yourself questions like these:

- How much control is enough?
- How do I judge the amount of control necessary in a given circumstance?
- What means of control are legitimate?
- How do I learn to relinquish and regain control?
- How do I want students in my class to perceive my control and their own self-control?

To a large extent, these and similar questions can't be answered for you. They are matters that you must address for yourself—as a teacher exercising informed, professional judgment (see Skinner & Greene, 2008).

QUESTIONS FOR REFLECTION

We suggest that when you believe a behavior problem in your classroom needs attention and correction, you begin at the beginning—by asking yourself questions that will help you focus on what the problem really is. Only after you've identified it accurately can you feel secure in analyzing the problem and planning ways to manage it. The questions you need to ask yourself include the following:

Could this problem be a result of inappropriate curriculum or teaching?

What do I demand and prohibit, and what should I?

Why do certain behaviors bother me, and what should I do about them?

Is this behavior developmentally significant?

Should I focus on a behavioral excess or a deficiency?

Will resolution of the problem solve anything else?

Could this problem be a result of inappropriate curriculum or teaching?

As teachers, we have a tendency to overlook the fact that what and how we teach can contribute directly to our students behaving in ways that we find irritating, perplexing, or unacceptable. This tendency comes, in part, from the difficulty of keeping the students' perspective in mind while concentrating on teaching. It's easy to forget how frightening new tasks can be, how overwhelming assignments and expectations can look, how boring and mindless requirements can seem, how devastating criticism can be, or how irritating it is to be unengaged in activity (have nothing worthwhile to do) and spend long periods simply waiting (See Kauffman & Landrum, 2009a).

It's easy to fall into the trap of assuming that because most students learn what we're trying to teach, *all students can* or that *all students will* respond similarly to our teaching methods. In fact, expecting *all students* to respond in the same way to instruction is part of the folly of the No Child Left Behind Act (NCLB) of the early years of the twenty-first century and part of the reason that public education has been seen as tragicomic (Kauffman, 2010).

Consider life in the classroom as a student might experience it. For example, imagine yourself as a student who sees no point in what she or he is being asked to learn, one who finds the materials or instructions utterly confusing, one who sincerely believes that she or he can't do what's expected, one who's expected to repeat again and again a lesson already mastered, one who's expected to listen attentively once more to instructions he or she has heard and comprehended and followed many times already, one who often hears criticism but seldom receives recognition for work well done. If you're one of those students, you're prone to misbehave—to talk to and distract your neighbors, daydream, become irritable, make hostile remarks, and so on. Adults, including teachers themselves, respond in like manner to similar conditions. Think of your own behavior, or the behavior of some of your colleagues, in poorly taught classes, at boring faculty meetings, or useless in-service sessions. You know what it's like to act crazy because you're in a situation that you find stultifying! Adults, too, are vulnerable to inappropriate behavior, given certain conditions. Before assuming that there's more to the problem you're having with a student or a class, reflect on questions like these:

- How relevant to or functional in the student's life is the curriculum?
- Do I have the option of teaching something more relevant and functional?
- To what extent could I individualize instruction?
- How successful is this student or group in the curriculum?
- Am I using an approach to teaching that provides too little structure, too much direction, too little positive feedback, or too much criticism?

- How frequently do my students have an opportunity to respond to academic tasks?
- What percentage of time are my students actually actively engaged in learning?
- How and how much could I change the teaching strategies I use?

Behavior problems aren't always a result of a teacher's poor choices of curriculum or teaching strategies, but these must be the first factors you examine. No other questions are appropriate until you can conclude that the *what* and *how* of instruction aren't the likely source of the problem. That is, you shouldn't proceed until you're satisfied that what you're asking students to learn is important to their lives, that they're being challenged by assignments but not overwhelmed by failure, that they have frequent opportunities to respond as well as listen, and that they're having a high degree of success and are receiving frequent positive feedback about their performance. These are essential elements of effective, systematic instruction (see Engelmann, 1997; Rosenshine, 1997, 2008). If they don't characterize what happens in your classroom, then the first order of business is putting these elements of effective instruction into practice.

We're aware of the difficulties teachers can encounter in using effective teaching practices. The best efforts of excellent teachers sometimes fail to convince students of the importance or relevance of the subject matter. Sometimes teachers are given little or no control over what they teach, the materials they use, or the instructional methods they employ. In such cases, it may be difficult to resist pressures from administrators or supervisors who impose curricula and methods on a schoolwide basis. Sometimes teachers are faced with overwhelming problems in being able to meet the instructional needs of individual students. They may have too many or too diverse a group of students to be able to serve them all adequately, or they may be told no one is going to help them. Advocacy for additional resources to meet students' needs may be ignored or receive hostile responses. Teaching isn't an easy profession. It sometimes demands taking risks, sometimes dictates compromise, and always requires struggling with dilemmas. You might ask yourself other questions:

- If I'm uncertain about whether my teaching strategies or curriculum are contributing to behavior management problems, what steps could I take to resolve my uncertainty?
- How might I evaluate whether my teaching approximates best practice?

What we consider best instructional practices are summarized by the descriptions in Table 3.1. Note that we have arranged the characteristics in order so that the first letters can be used as a mnemonic—CLOCS-RAM. Table 3.1 is our attempt to summarize principles in a way that will help you remember them. We've obtained these principles from reading these sources: Bateman (2004), Carnine, Silbert, Kame'enui, & Tarver (2005, 2010); Coyne, Kame'enui, & Carnine (2006); Engelmann (1997); Forness, Kavale, Blum, & Lloyd (1997); Lloyd, Forness, & Kavale (1998); Rosenshine (1997, 2008), Walker (1995), and Walker, Ramsey, & Gresham (2004).

You may want to compare your own practice to the characteristics we list in Table 3.1. We don't assume that there are no other characteristics of best instructional practices that could be listed. However, we do consider these to be the most basic features of best instructional practices. Without any of them, a teacher is likely to be less than optimally successful and to create a classroom environment in which misbehavior is likely.

What do I demand and prohibit, and what should I?

Assuming that you're satisfied with the what and how of your academic instruction and that they don't set up circumstances under which students' misbehavior is predictable, you should next consider your expectations for students' behavior. You'll need to consider what you demand of your

TABLE 3.1 Characteristics of Best Instructional Practices

Keys to offering effective instruction:

1. *Clarity:*   The student must know exactly what to do (i.e., have no doubt about what is expected).
2. *Level:*   The student must be able to do the task with a high degree of accuracy (i.e., be able to get at least 80 percent correct), but the task must be challenging (i.e., the student should not easily get 100 percent correct repeatedly).
3. *Opportunities:*   The student must have frequent opportunities to respond (i.e., be actively engaged in the task a high percentage of the time).
4. *Consequences:*   The student must receive a meaningful reward for correct performance (i.e., the consequences of correct performance must be frequent and perceived as desirable by the student).
5. *Sequence:*   The tasks must be presented in a logical sequence so that the student gets the big idea (i.e., steps must be presented and learned in order that the knowledge or skill is built on a logical progression or framework of ideas, which is a systematic curriculum).
6. *Relevance:*   The task is relevant to the student's life and, if possible, the student understands how and why it is useful (i.e., the teacher attempts to help the student see why in his or her culture the task is important).
7. *Application:*   The teacher helps the student learn how to learn and remember by teaching memory and learning strategies and applying knowledge and skills to everyday problems (i.e., teaches generalizations, not just isolated skills, and honors the student's culture).
8. *Monitoring:*   The teacher continuously monitors student progress (i.e., records and charts progress, always knows and can show what the student has mastered and the student's place or level in a curriculum or sequence of tasks).

students and what you'll not tolerate in two areas: academic performance and social behavior. You'll also need to question your expectations for both the class as a group and for individual students. The specific behavior demanded and prohibited varies considerably from teacher to teacher. Some teachers have very different expectations for individual children, compared to those they hold for the class as a whole. In some cases, management problems aren't so much a result of students' behavior as they are a result of teachers' inappropriate expectations.

There's much greater agreement among teachers about what behavior is prohibited than about what's demanded. That is, teachers find it easier to specify what they won't tolerate than to specify the appropriate behavior they demand. Perhaps this is a result of our culture's focus on punishment as the primary means of behavior control. Yet, knowing what to demand of students—and therefore what to reward with recognition and praise—is a key to good behavior management. Adults' expectations for children are matters of constant debate in U.S. culture, and teachers' expectations for their students are a central point of controversy. Ask yourself questions like these:

- How do I arrive at my expectations for students?
- To what extent are my expectations biased by labels or stereotypes?
- Are my expectations based on cultural standards that discriminate unfairly against some students?
- Are my expectations based on cultural traditions that aren't necessary for, or are even inconsistent with, effective teaching?

With these questions in mind, we consider the kinds of academic and social behavior most teachers demand and prohibit.

DEMANDS   Most teachers demand a set of academic and social behaviors that describe a good or "teachable" student, and for good reason—they make good teaching easier (see Kauffman & Landrum, 2009a; Walker, 1995). For example, most teachers indicate that the following types of behavior are critical for success in their classrooms: following their established classroom rules, listening to their instructions, following written instructions and directions, complying with commands, doing in-class assignments as directed, avoiding breaking classroom rules even when encouraged to do so by peers, producing work of acceptable quality for the student's skill level, and having good work habits (e.g., making efficient use of class time, being organized, staying on task). Far less agreement is found regarding demands for behaviors such as these: using social conventions appropriately (e.g., saying "thank you," "please"), volunteering for classroom activities, working on projects with other students, sharing materials with others in a work situation, and initiating conversations with peers in informal situations.

PROHIBITIONS   Teachers generally agree that they won't tolerate certain types of behavior in their classrooms, again, for good reason—they make good teaching harder (see Kauffman & Landrum, 2009a; Walker, Ramsey, & Gresham, 2004). Among those behaviors considered intolerable by the vast majority of teachers are the following: inappropriate sexual behavior, stealing, physical aggression, destruction of property, behaving inappropriately to correction, refusing to obey classroom rules, disturbing or disrupting the activities of others, self-injury, lewd or obscene gestures, ignoring teacher's warnings or reprimands, creating disturbance during class activities, cheating, and being verbally aggressive toward others. Considerably less consistency among teachers is found in teachers' intolerance of behaviors such as the following: pouting and sulking, asking irrelevant questions or making irrelevant remarks, refusing to play games with others, ignoring the social initiations of others, and refusing to share.

Opinions about teachers' expectations—what they demand and prohibit—vary widely among educators and the public. One commonly heard criticism of teachers' expectations are that they're too low, that teachers get about what they expect from students and they expect too little. Another criticism is that teachers' expectations are too traditional and self-serving. According to this criticism, teachers set expectations for their students based primarily on the way they themselves were taught. Furthermore, their expectations are designed primarily to make their jobs more comfortable rather than to create effective environments for learning and to avoid criticism in a system that places a high value on conformity. This stifles innovation and maintains the status quo in schools. Another criticism is that teachers' expectations are not sensitive to cultural and ethnic differences in behavioral styles or norms; thus, they are unnecessarily restrictive and oppressive. In any given situation, every teacher must consider the extent to which these criticisms are justified. Often, in our opinion, they aren't (see Kauffman, 2010).

A major concern of educators is that teachers' expectations shouldn't be too high or too low. Expectations that are too high are problematic because students and teachers are too frequently confronted with failure. Students become demoralized because they almost never are able to measure up to the teachers' standards. Teachers, too, become demoralized and drop all expectations because they lose confidence that their students can succeed. Expectations that are too low don't challenge students, convey to students the idea that they aren't capable of meeting higher standards, and result in low achievement and frequent misbehavior. Low expectations become self-fulfilling prophecies.

High expectations for some students will be too low for others, depending on what the students have experienced and learned. Getting the expectations just right requires a high degree of knowledge of, and sensitivity to, students' abilities and histories of success and failure. "The same high expectations for all students" may sound egalitarian and be consistent with some educators' philosophies. The problem with this philosophy, however, is that individual differences are ignored (See Kauffman & Landrum, 2009a).

Nearly every teacher insists on some basic classroom rules that apply to all students. It's as if the teacher has said, "If you want to be a part of this classroom, then there are certain things you have to do and certain things you must not do." Yet, most teachers have more specific expectations for one or more individuals in the class. For certain students, the teacher may interpret the standard expectations differently or articulate a different set of demands and prohibitions. Having different expectations for different students presents a dilemma, however; on the one hand, having the same expectations for everyone ignores individual differences, and on the other hand, individual expectations could be based on favoritism or negative bias. This isn't an easy dilemma to resolve. It's part of the extremely difficult task of creating classrooms and schools that are both sensitive to individual differences and consistently enculturating.

Another major concern is that expectations must be communicated clearly and consistently. Sometimes behavior problems arise because the teacher hasn't articulated clearly and frequently what's demanded and prohibited in the classroom. The teacher may feel that her or his expectations have been communicated, but if the students are asked, they can't state what their teacher expects. Perhaps the teacher has never discussed, posted, or reviewed any classroom rules. Some teachers and administrators have so many rules that students can't reasonably be expected to remember them all. We have been in schools in which the rules were several single-spaced typewritten pages in length and in classrooms where twenty or more rules were posted. This kind of rule "overkill" doesn't result in effective communication of expectations.

Sometimes teachers state one set of expectations verbally but in subtle ways convey a different set of expectations through their nonverbal behavior. For example, a teacher might state that students need to raise their hands and wait to be called on before speaking, yet respond to students who call out answers. A teacher might also say that showing respect for others in the class is expected but respond to some students with sarcasm. Teachers may also fall into a pattern of changing expectations from day to day so that students are never quite certain which rules are in effect or how they'll be enforced.

Very likely, you'll be able to state what you demand and prohibit in your classroom. Once you've done so, however, you'll need to reflect on several questions about those expectations:

- Are my expectations justifiable, and if so, on what grounds?
- Have I clearly, repeatedly, and consistently communicated those expectations?
- Are my expectations biased against certain groups of students?
- Do I hold the same expectations for everyone, or do I make exceptions for certain individuals?
- If I make exceptions, how do I justify and communicate them?

Why do certain behaviors bother me, and what should I do about them?

We've been discussing expectations as if they're somehow objectively determined with little reference to teachers as individuals with highly personal, emotional responses to children's behavior. This is because, to a great extent, teachers must be able to take a detached, objective view of their behavior and that of students. Nevertheless, teachers must maintain a high level of self-awareness and understanding of how their personal responses to behavior affect their interactions with students.

One's expectations for behavior—what one considers polite, proper, crass, threatening, profane, annoying, unacceptable, and so on—are to some extent a result of one's upbringing in a particular culture and family. Expectations may be modified by exposure to other cultures, groups, and individuals, and they can be partly based on personal values, biases, preferences, and sensitivities. Some teachers' expectations are based on what they believe children need to learn if they're going to have friends, be employable, and avoid incarceration or institutionalization. These expectations might be considered universal in our culture. And some kinds of behavior, like throwing things at or hitting a teacher, cursing the teacher, or refusing to comply with reasonable requests, are seen by nearly everyone in nearly every culture as unacceptable.

Some expectations, however, are based primarily on more limited social conventions or personal preferences. Sometimes it's difficult to judge whether an expectation is based primarily on broad social or cultural norms or on personal preferences. Consequently, all teachers need to be aware of multicultural issues in education.

Student teachers and those new to the profession are sometimes unprepared for the "tacky" or "trashy" behavior many children may exhibit in the classroom. Many children engage in behavior that may seem intended to challenge, threaten, badger, humiliate, irritate, agitate, or disgust others, including their teachers. Behavior of this type could indicate that a child has serious emotional problems, but often it doesn't. Furthermore, some individuals may find certain behaviors annoying, offensive, or threatening, whereas others don't. The language children use at school, particularly certain forms of address and various words that some consider vulgar, is a type of behavior about which teachers often have very different opinions. One teacher may bristle at a student's use of the word *nerd* or *dork* (or any other word describing someone unfavorably), whereas another may feel these words are a legitimate part of all youngsters' vocabulary. The mannerisms of certain children may elicit excruciating tension in one teacher but be easily tolerated by another. The way you respond to a given type of behavior may say a lot about how you were reared and enculturated in school yourself. It may also say a lot about how secure and competent you feel as a teacher. Sometimes it merely indicates a hypersensitivity to certain characteristic behaviors of an individual child.

Given that certain behavioral characteristics may "set us off," how should we deal with them as professional educators? All of us find certain idiosyncrasies or characteristics of other people particularly grating and have our pet peeves, and it's legitimate to have especially intense reactions to some types of behavior that others may be able to tolerate far more easily. But teachers must be very careful not to foist their personal standards on their students and not to become peevish or tyrannical in response to personal irritations. They must also be aware of how certain types of behavior may make them defensive and distract attention from important issues. Behavioral standards and personal preferences raise issues of the rights of students and teachers, teachers' responsibility to exercise self-control, and the recognition of developmental risk.

- When do I have a right to impose my personal standards on my students?
- When do my students have a right to behave as they wish?
- How do I determine whether my expectations are consistent with broad social or cultural demands or are primarily idiosyncratic?
- How do I recognize that I react intensely to a particular student's behavioral characteristics, yet avoid treating this student unfairly?

These aren't easy questions to answer, and they frequently demand careful reflection. You may need to solicit the opinions and suggestions of other teachers, an administrator, a parent, or others more detached from the situation to help you weigh these issues.

Imagine that you've become aware that a behavior irritates you primarily because it offends your personal values or sensitivities. You consider it inappropriate or bothersome, but you realize that in the broader social context it's trivial. You consider it "tacky" and grating, but you know that it's essentially harmless. It might be wearing a hat indoors, as Sam described in an earlier vignette, or it might be a child's tone of voice that you consider grating or disrespectful. What should you do about it? You might try to change it. On the other hand, you might try to learn to live with it. Perhaps it isn't worth trying to change; maybe it isn't something you feel you can learn to tolerate. In either case, considerable self-control might be required on your part to deal effectively with the situation. Sometimes teachers find that managing their own behavior—learning techniques of self-control—is the better solution to dealing with irritating student behavior. Unfortunately, some teachers find it difficult to ignore irritating but unimportant misbehavior, and they become embroiled in conflicts about trivia.

Also unfortunately, some teachers learn to ignore or tolerate behaviors that they shouldn't. They allow students to behave in ways that have serious consequences. Some types of behavior shouldn't be ignored or tolerated because they entail developmental risk for students. That is, these behaviors are signs that students have serious problems that are likely to become worse without effective intervention.

Is this behavior developmentally significant?

Developmentally significant behavior problems are those that have serious long-term consequences for children. That is, if the problems aren't resolved, it's highly likely that the children who exhibit them will have increasing difficulties in becoming self-sufficient, reasonably well-adjusted adults. Many of these behaviors are seen by teachers at school. It's extremely important that teachers recognize the seriousness of these behaviors and intervene as early and effectively as possible to change them (see Kauffman & Brigham, 2009). Although there may be other types of developmentally significant behavior, most of them fall into one of four primary categories: academic failure, aggression, depression, and problems with peers. We base our description of these problems on the following: Cullinan (2007); Forness, Kavale, & Walker (1999); Gresham, Lane, McIntyre, MacMillan, Lambros, & Bocain (2001); Kauffman & Brigham (2009); Kauffman & Landrum (2009a); Kerr & Nelson (2010); Liapusin & Scott (2008); Walker, Forness, Kauffman, Epstein Gresham, Nelson, and Strain (1998); and Walker, Ramsey, & Gresham (2004).

ACADEMIC FAILURE   Children who fail to acquire basic academic skills in the early grades, those who fail grades or earn failing grades in courses, and those who drop out of school are at high risk for social and economic difficulties. In fact, failure to learn basic skills in reading and math in the early grades is likely to lead to later failure and dropping out of school. At least a moderate level of success in academics is necessary for most children to develop a healthy self-image. Students who aren't academically competent are often shunned or rejected by their peers. Thus, identifying that a student's skills lag seriously behind grade level and taking steps to bring them up to grade expectations is critically important.

At first thought, identifying and remediating deficient academic skills as early as possible seems like a straightforward task. A little reflection, however, will bring out some of the persistent problems in defining and dealing with academic failure.

- How do I establish performance expectations for a particular grade level or age of student?
- How far behind grade expectation is far enough to merit special attention? That is, how much failure does a child have to experience or how far behind the rest of the class must a child fall before I become seriously concerned?
- If I perceive that a student is failing significantly behind, how should I intervene?
- How can I tell whether my efforts to help are merely making matters worse?
- When I've exhausted my own knowledge in trying to improve the student's performance, whom should I consult?
- Under what conditions should I conclude that I don't have, and can't acquire quickly enough, the skills or resources necessary to address the problem effectively?

These are only a few of the questions you must consider in dealing with academic failure. Questions such as these have sparked much controversy among educators for many decades, and the answers aren't obvious. Nearly all educators agree that a teacher has an obligation to see that every child in her or his class experiences frequent success and achieves at the highest level possible. Nevertheless, nearly everyone who has been a teacher has experienced failure in dealing with a student's failure—despite his or her best efforts, the teacher hasn't been able to help a student experience an acceptable level of success in the classroom and approximate the achievement of the peer group. The way teachers assess their limitations and deal with their failures as teachers is extremely important for the education profession and even more important for the futures of the students they have been assigned to teach.

Academic failure usually brings with it a variety of behavior problems. Children who don't keep up with their peers in academics seldom have a strong sense of personal worth and dignity. They have little to lose, and sometimes, much to gain in the way of attention from peers and adults by getting into trouble. If they don't become persistently annoying to others, they may withdraw from social interaction and become morose. In either case, such students are laying the groundwork for further academic failure, which leads to an increasing tendency toward aggression, depression, or both. Breaking the vicious cycle of academic failure and maladaptive behavior may require attention to multiple aspects of the problem. Besides academic remediation, the teacher needs to be ready to intervene in other developmentally significant behavior problems.

AGGRESSION   Numerous writers have noted that aggression is endemic in the United States—"as American as apple pie," as some have put it. Violence is the primary active ingredient in popular media. Hostile aggression and other antisocial behavior, both physical and verbal, are pervasive in many neighborhoods and schools. Homicide is one of the leading causes of death among adolescents and young adults. Because of its pervasiveness in U.S. culture, and because of the long-held misconception that it isn't a highly significant indicator of mental illness, hostile aggression is often ignored. We are not referring here to the adaptive assertiveness that is necessary for survival in a humane society. We are referring to hyperaggressive behavior that harms others or destroys property, drives others away by threats or intimidation, prompts counteraggression, and is incompatible with learning prosocial behavior or academic skills. It's behavior that's inappropriate for one's age and the social circumstances in which it occurs (see Kauffman & Brigham, 2009).

Extremely aggressive behavior carries an extremely high risk of other developmental problems. The earlier in life a child's behavior is highly aggressive (compared to other children of the same age), the longer a child's history of aggressive acts, the greater the variety of settings in which a child is aggressive (e.g., playground, classroom, bus, home, neighborhood), and the more varied a child's aggressive acts (e.g., hitting, kicking, biting, pinching, scratching, throwing things, threatening, extorting), the worse the prognosis is for later adjustment and achievement (Kauffman & Landrum, 2009a). Thus, early intervention to stop aggression and teach more prosocial behavioral alternatives is critically important.

If a child stands out from his or her peers as being highly aggressive, teachers are doing the child and society no favor by ignoring it, assuming the child will outgrow it or justifying it on grounds that the expression of aggression may help to reduce it (Kauffman & Brigham, 2009). Engaging in aggressive antisocial acts isn't good for children; it doesn't help them develop appropriate behavior but increases the likelihood of further aggression, maladjustment, and social and academic failure. Effective means must be sought to stop it and replace it with more adaptive, self-enhancing behavior.

As is the case with the other topics we've discussed, easy answers to most of the questions raised by students' aggression are not to be found. Following are questions every teacher must consider.

- What aggressive acts fall within the developmentally appropriate range for youngsters of a particular age, social background, and gender?
- When is aggressive behavior acceptable because it falls within cultural norms, although it violates the teacher's expectations?
- How much aggression should be tolerated in the classroom, given the teacher's best efforts to reduce it, before the student is excluded?

Questions such as these will likely stir controversy among educators for many decades to come.

Nevertheless, we feel confident in stating that hyperaggression is a developmentally significant type of behavior that teachers must take seriously (Kauffman & Brigham, 2009). The more clearly a child is verbally and physically more aggressive than the norm for his or her age, the more teachers should be concerned for the child's future. We also feel confident in stating that educators' responses to students' aggression mustn't be counteraggressive. That is, truly effective interventions in aggression don't involve adults' aggression against students. The response to aggression must be, to the greatest extent possible, nonviolent and instructive (Kauffman & Brigham, 2009). We discuss this matter further in subsequent chapters (see especially Chapter 5).

DEPRESSION Only within the past few decades have developmental psychologists, mental health professionals, and educators begun to understand the nature and extent of the problem of depression among children (Reinemann & Schnoebelen, 2008). Suicide and suicide attempts by children and adolescents have increased dramatically during the past twenty-five years, and suicide is now one of the leading causes of death among adolescents and young adults. Furthermore, studies of the thoughts and feelings of children and adolescents have revealed that they become depressed in much the same way adults do and that depression is a far more frequent problem among minors than previously thought. Depression is often a problem related to aggressive behavior, social withdrawal, hyperactive and inattentive behavior, and academic failure.

The signs of depression in children and adolescents may be similar to those in adults. Any radical change in behavior should be taken as a signal that the student may be experiencing depression. If a student exhibits one or more of the following characteristics over a period of weeks, he or she should be evaluated for depression by a mental health professional:

- Inability to experience pleasure, or depressed mood
- Sudden change in appetite or weight
- Disturbance of sleep (insomnia or constant drowsiness)
- Exaggerated, excessive, or retarded physical movement
- Loss of energy, feelings of fatigue
- Feelings of worthlessness, self-reproach, excessive guilt
- Inability to think, concentrate, or make decisions
- Talk about suicide

Signs of depression are often ignored by teachers. Frequently, depressed students don't disrupt the class (although this isn't always the case), so it's easier for the teacher not to become involved with their behavior. Ignoring depressed students may compound their problems, however, because depressed students often feel isolated, neglected, or "invisible." They often have given up on themselves and see themselves as unworthy of other people's concern.

How should you respond to students whom you suspect are depressed? Perhaps the most important thing you can do is persist in attempts to establish communication with these students, to reach out to them and let them know you have noticed them and aren't going to give up on them. You should also ask others to help; a school psychologist or counselor, for example, can evaluate students and, if necessary, make referrals to mental health professionals. In some cases, you may encounter problems that call for difficult personal or professional judgments. Some depressed individuals are extremely manipulative and are masters at getting others entangled in their problems in ways that aren't helpful. If possible, seek the advice of a mental health professional who's familiar with the student.

PROBLEMS WITH PEERS   Children and adolescents who don't have friends their own age or who are in frequent conflict with members of their peer group are at high risk for other developmental problems. Those who have serious academic problems aren't typically popular among their peers. Those who are aggressive are, understandably, typically rejected by their classmates. Those who are depressed often cut themselves off from social interaction with others. Whatever the reason, the student who ends up a loner isn't headed down a developmental path likely to lead to personal fulfillment and satisfactory adult adjustment.

Healthy psychological and social development depends on friendships—close, mutually gratifying relationships that involve giving and receiving support in dealing with life's vicissitudes. Teachers frequently overlook or downplay the importance of peer relationships in school. The focus in schools tends to be on individual achievement and deportment, with social relationships relegated to a secondary or even minor role. When thinking about a student who's exhibiting problem behavior, you should inquire about his or her friendship patterns and social interactions (see Kauffman & Landrum, 2009a):

- To what extent is this student accepted or rejected by peers?
- Does this student have friends, including a best friend?
- When this student interacts with others, who initiates the interaction?
- How sensitive is this student to influence, positive and negative, from the peer group?
- If this student has friends, who are they and what are they like?

The last question is one that research has shown is particularly important to ask in the case of antisocial students. Some students whose behavior is developmentally dangerous do have friends, but they are the wrong kinds of friends—other antisocial students. The fact that a student is enmeshed in a social group doesn't mean that he or she doesn't have peer-related problems. Running with the wrong crowd, admiring and imitating the behavior of deviant peers, and choosing to associate primarily with those who exhibit significant problematic behavior are risk factors for a variety of negative outcomes.

These and more specific questions should help you assess the extent to which peer problems are an issue, a topic to which we return in Chapter 7.

A NOTE ABOUT MULTIPLE PROBLEMS

Finally, we note that academic failure, aggression, depression, and problems with peers aren't mutually exclusive categories of behavior. Academic failure often is accompanied by aggressive behavior, depression, poor peer relations, or all of these. Not all depressed students are socially withdrawn; a substantial percentage manifest aggressive behavior as part of their depression. The prognosis usually is worse for an individual with multiple, interrelated problems. Students who fail academically and are aggressive and depressed are at particularly high risk for severe and protracted personal problems. The co-occurrence of problems is sometimes referred to in the literature as *comorbidity*. Regardless of the term used to refer to multiple problems, the meaning and implications are essentially the same: students with multiple problems are typically at higher risk than those who have a single problem (see Forness, Kavale, & Walker, 1999; Kauffman & Landrum, 2009a; Tankersley & Landrum, 1997).

Should I focus on a behavioral excess or a deficiency?

When we think of behavior management, we typically think first of things we want students to stop doing—behavioral excesses. Just as important, however, are the things students don't do but should—behavioral deficiencies. The aggressive student needs to learn alternative nonaggressive ways of interacting with others. Trying to reduce excessive behavior without at the same time increasing deficient behavior is a common tactical blunder that contributes to many teachers' behavior management difficulties.

Because it's so easy to focus on getting rid of maladaptive behavior and forget the importance of teaching alternative adaptive behavior, some have suggested always thinking of "behavior pairs." A behavior pair includes both a behavior that should be increased and one that should be decreased. For example, completing schoolwork might be paired with not paying attention to work. This pairing would help the teacher focus on what's desired and what should be rewarded (completing work), not just on what's undesirable (inattention). The pairs chosen must be opposites—things that are very difficult or impossible to do simultaneously—so that increasing the desirable behavior is virtually certain to decrease the undesirable behavior.

The pairing of behaviors to be increased and decreased helps the teacher avoid thinking only of the negative side of the student's behavior. This is critically important because effective and humane behavior management relies very little on punishment and is primarily a matter of supporting desirable behavior.

Before assuming that you've identified a behavior management problem with sufficient clarity, ask yourself these questions:

- How do I want this student to behave?
- Can I describe in positive terms what I want the student to do?
- For each behavior I want the student to stop or decrease, have I identified an alternative behavior that I want the student to learn or exhibit more often?

Will resolution of the problem solve anything else?

Some behavior management problems seem overwhelming because so many things need changing. It's hard to know where to begin. Some problems seem insurmountable because the behavior is so extreme. It's hard to know how much change is reasonable to expect. When faced with such problems, teachers can easily become hopeless or adopt strategies that are self-defeating. They may begin attacking problems at random or choose to work on trivial behaviors, or they may reach the unfortunate conclusion that unless they can resolve a problem completely, their efforts will be wasted. An important skill in behavior management is identifying problems in ways that help one know where to begin and how to judge progress. We offer two caveats about managing difficult behavior problems. First, you shouldn't expect to solve all problems at once. Second, you shouldn't expect to resolve all problems entirely.

The more difficult the management problem, the more important it is to address first things first—to look for key behaviors that, if changed, will make the greatest difference overall. People who are very experienced in managing difficult children are able to identify the behavior in a constellation of problems that holds the key to generalized improvement. For example, Patterson and his colleagues, (e.g., Patterson, Reid, & Dishion, 1992; see also Kauffman & Landrum, 2009a; Kazdin, 2008) who have helped hundreds of families achieve better control of aggressive children, have found that not minding (disobedience to parents and teachers) is a key behavior. Rather than starting with other aggressive acts, Patterson, Kazdin, and others have found that it's often better to start dealing with an aggressive child by working on compliance or obedience. Furthermore, experience shows that it's wise to begin a behavior management program by concentrating on one important behavior and dealing with it very consistently. The temptation to deal with multiple problems at one must be resisted. Thus, if you're confronted by a child or class with multiple problems, you should ask yourself the following:

- Can I identify one behavior that seems likely to be the key to general improvement?
- If I resolve this one problem, what else is likely to change?
- How can I develop a consistent, effective plan for attacking this key behavior?

Teachers often are judged harshly by others, and they sometimes fall prey to harsh self-judgment. And teachers, like most other people, are impatient with behavioral change that's slow or incomplete. Sometimes it's difficult to know whether the amount of change achieved in a behavior is worth the teacher's effort or whether change is occurring rapidly enough to meet a reasonable goal. Teachers may benefit from asking themselves the following questions:

- Has the change in behavior made a significant difference in the classroom, even if the change isn't total and complete?
- Is the change worth my investment of time and energy?
- How much more change should I try to accomplish?
- What is a reasonable goal?

Teachers vary considerably in what they see as worthwhile progress. Too often, in our judgment, teachers devalue progress or behavioral change because they expect themselves to accomplish a radical and permanent transformation of a pupil or their class.

Summary

Skillful classroom behavior management requires that teachers first engage in careful reflection about the nature of the problem. Before attempting to analyze a management problem in detail or develop a management strategy, teachers must consider their own behavior, values, sensitivities, and knowledge about pupil behavior. The behavior management problem may be a consequence of inappropriate curriculum or teaching strategies. Teachers' demands and prohibitions may be poorly communicated or overly lax, too strict, or inappropriate for the class or for certain students. They must examine the reasons that certain behaviors of their pupils are bothersome and decide whether self-control (personal tolerance) or intervention to change the pupil's behavior is more appropriate. Teachers must be particularly concerned about academic failure, aggression, depression, and problems with peers, as these behaviors carry particularly high risk for continuing developmental problems. They also must take care to give at least as much concern to what they want students to do as they give to what they want students not to do. In dealing with multiple behavior problems, teachers must begin with a single key behavior, which, if changed, will likely produce more generalized improvements. Teachers must also weigh carefully their goals and standards for judging success.

Case Connection

Identifying the problem is always an issue, but you might give special attention to how the problem might have been analyzed in the following cases:

The Contract with Parrish and Son   Rebecca Phillips
Winnie   Patty Gray

CHAPTER FOUR

Analyzing Behavior Problems

Questions for Reflection

What are my assumptions about why students behave the way they do?

What are the most important alternative explanations of the misbehavior?

Are there causes of the misbehavior that I can control to a significant degree?

How should I define the behavior I am concerned about and identify its antecedents and consequences?

Defining Behavior
Identifying Antecedents
Identifying Consequences
Identifying Chains of Events

Identifying Coercive Interactions
Identifying the Patterns and Stages of Misbehavior

How might I identify the probable cognitive and affective aspects of the misbehavior?

How should I measure the behavior problem and behavior change?

What's a reasonable goal?

How do I accomplish a functional assessment of behavior and write a positive behavior intervention plan?

What is required for prevention and early intervention?

Summary
Case Connection

Skilled professionals in all fields analyze problems carefully before attempting to solve them. Physicians, engineers, lawyers, and merchants, as well as teachers and school administrators, are typically more successful when they are able to figure out why a problem exists and how bad it is before they start doing something to change it. People with little knowledge of a field of study or professional practice sometimes become impatient with a competent practitioner's approach to a problem because they believe the analysis should be simple and quick. The competent practitioner knows that apparently simple problems can be unexpectedly complex and understands that time spent in analysis can save time in the long run and prevent embarrassing, costly, or tragic errors. Two examples of teachers' reflections on their analysis of behavior problems can be found in the vignettes, Tammy and Trisha.

Tammy

When I first started working on the problems I had with Kevin, I wasn't aware of how often he failed to do what I told him. Actually, I had quite a few kids in my class who were non-compliant pretty frequently, but Kevin was really by far the worst. The thing that helped me most when it came to getting a handle on the problem was keeping track of my directions and Kevin's compliance for a while. I kept a daily record of how often I told Kevin to do something and the percentage of times he did what I told or asked him to do.

It was a little extra work to remember to keep track of my directions and his compliance, but it wasn't too bad. I was surprised by the numbers—by how often I was giving him a command of some sort and by the low percentage of the time he obeyed me. He seemed to give me the most trouble during reading, which he doesn't do very well, especially when I was working with another group. He also had lots of trouble during less-structured activities like lunch break and art. So I focused my record keeping on reading and lunch period, which included noon recess. I carried a little card in my pocket, and every time I told or asked him to do something, I just made a tally mark. Then, if he complied within about a minute, I circled the tally. I divided the card into two sections, the top for reading and the bottom for lunch period.

By keeping track, I had a daily record of how often I was telling Kevin to do things and how often he complied in those two situations. I did this for about five days before I started the compliance training, so I had a pretty objective basis for judging whether the training was making a difference on compliance in reading and math. Of course, subjectively I felt things were getting a lot better too, but the data on the cards helped me confirm that he really was improving.

Trisha

It took me a while, but I finally figured out something that was a really effective reward for Sammy, this kid who was such a whiner and a crier. He was so spoiled by his mother and grandmother that there just seemed to be nothing I could offer him that he was interested in working for. Then one day I was talking to him about other things and he said something about not liking the name Sammy. He said his name was Sam, like his daddy's name, and that's what he wanted to be called. He thought Sammy was a "baby name," as he put it, and he didn't want to be called that anymore. So then I thought, aha! There's something he maybe cares enough about that I can use it as leverage to get him to stop crying. This is a kid who would have 10 or 15 crying fits just about every day, most of them lasting for just a couple of minutes but some going on for an hour. I think we really turned the corner with him when I had a little talk with him about his crying and his name, and I told him I'd have to call him Sam and so would all the other kids, as long as he wasn't crying. If he cried, we could call him Sammy, but otherwise we'd use his grown-up name.

If you approach a behavior management problem with the questions we posed in Chapter 3, you have already started the process of problem analysis. You will have begun eliminating wrong explanations for the behavior and are ready to analyze in more detail the extent of the problem, its possible causes, and where you might find a point of leverage in changing it. Understanding the possible and probable cause(s) of behavior is often critical to choosing means for trying to change it. Measuring the level of the problem and having a way of judging progress are essential for making good decisions about whether to try a different strategy and when to consider a problem resolved.

Setting clear and reasonable goals helps teachers avoid getting discouraged or becoming overly optimistic. In brief, as you analyze problems, you need to ask yourself important questions about your assumptions and intentions.

- What are my assumptions about why students behave the way they do?
- Can I identify causal factors that I can change?
- What is sufficient evidence that I'm making progress in changing behavior?
- Exactly what am I trying to accomplish?
- What is the student trying to get?
- Could I help this student get what he or she is after in a better way?

These and other questions are part of a careful analysis of behavior management problems leading to well-planned strategies for change. They're also part of the functional behavioral assessment (FBA) that is required by federal special education law (IDEA, the Individuals with Disabilities Education Act).

QUESTIONS FOR REFLECTION

We suggest that after you've made an initial identification of a behavior management problem, you analyze the problem further before planning an intervention strategy to change it. Your analyses should include possible causal explanations for the misbehavior, measurement of its level and trend, and the goals you hope to accomplish. A careful analysis will greatly increase your chances of devising a management plan that is effective and efficient. The questions you need to ask yourself include the following:

- What are my assumptions about why students behave the way they do?
- What are the most important alternative explanations of the misbehavior?
- Are there causes of the misbehavior that I can control to a significant degree?
- How should I define the behavior I'm concerned about and identify its antecedents and consequences?
- How might I identify the probable cognitive and affective aspects of the misbehavior?
- How should I measure the behavior problem and behavior change?
- What's a reasonable goal?
- How do I accomplish a functional assessment of behavior and write a positive behavior intervention plan?

What are my assumptions about why students behave the way they do?

Everyone makes certain assumptions about why people behave as they do. These assumptions are important because they're often the basis for attempts to change behavior. Examining your assumptions about the causes of behavior is important because beliefs are related to actions; what you do may change as a result of a change in your beliefs. But what you do also affects what you believe. Beliefs and actions influence each other, along with other factors, in a person's environment.

Historically, philosophers, religious leaders, and scientists have offered a variety of explanations for human behavior. Their explanations might be grouped into four basic categories:

1. *Biological:*   Physiological or biochemical factors such as brain damage, disease, drugs, or malnutrition
2. *Environmental:*   Events in the objective external world, such as the consequences of behavior, the settings in which it occurs (e.g., signs or signals that certain behavior is expected or prohibited), and the examples provided by others

3. *Psychological:* Internal mental characteristics or phenomena such as thoughts, feelings, or emotional states
4. *Spiritual:* Supernatural or mystical forces such as god(s), devil(s), or other spirits.

Present-day explanations also include all four of these categories. None of these categories is completely rejected by most people, although most people believe more in some than in others, particularly in cases of highly unusual behavior. In analyzing a behavior problem, it's important first to clarify the basic assumptions with which you approach human behavior.

- How do I typically explain people's behavior?
- What's the basis for my beliefs about behavior?
- To what extent are my beliefs based on scientific evidence about the causes of behavior?

The general notions you have about the causes of human behavior will likely influence significantly how you attempt to explain the misbehavior about which you're concerned.

What are the most important alternative explanations of the misbehavior?

Most people believe that human behavior has multiple causes, some of which are more important than others for explaining particular acts or patterns of conduct. For example, a person might believe that biological, psychological, and environmental factors are all involved to some degree in causing human behavior (see Pinker, 2002). However, in explaining why a given student behaves in a particular way in the classroom, this person might also believe that the most important causes are psychological (e.g., feelings of self-efficacy, predictions of the consequences of behavior) and environmental (e.g., the consequences of behavior and signals that certain behavior is expected). One job of a teacher is identifying the most likely and most relevant explanations of classroom behavior for individual students and specific circumstances.

We suggest that teachers pay particular attention to explanations of behavior that are supported by ample empirical research and that offer teachers the possibility of a reasonable measure of control. Concentrating on relevant and reliable explanations means, in our opinion, that you pay particular attention to environmental and psychological causes. These are the causes most directly related to teaching and the ones supported by the most scientific evidence. We aren't suggesting that other explanations have no relevance or validity, but simply that in most cases the strongest research support and the greatest opportunity for you to control what happens are likely to be found in explanations having to do with environmental and psychological variables (Cullinan, 2007; Kauffman & Landrum, 2009a; Kerr & Nelson, 2010; Landrum & Kauffman, 2006; Walker, Ramsey, & Gresham, 2004).

Some of the potential causes of behavior problems are things that teachers can't control, at least not directly. In nearly all cases of misbehavior caused by biological factors, the teacher can only make a referral or ask for assistance from a health care professional or social worker. Sometimes misbehavior is a result of brain dysfunction, disease, or problems of diet or health. You must be aware of these possibilities and refer the student for evaluation by qualified health care providers when appropriate. Sometimes misbehavior is a result of abuse or neglect at home or is related to other home or family conditions over which you don't have any direct control. Again, it's extremely important to be aware of these potential sources of problems and request evaluation or assistance when needed (see Kauffman & Brigham, 2009).

Being unaware of or ignoring potential causes of problem behavior can result in unfortunate outcomes. For example, missing or ignoring signs of malnutrition, seizures, abuse, and so on will result in failure to address critical aspects of the problem and could frustrate your attempts to ameliorate it. You must be keenly aware of possible causes of behavior problems other than those that are most obvious. This requires extensive knowledge of child development and a high level of sensitivity to children's life circumstances.

When analyzing a behavior problem, you should consider the range of possible causes and try to make sure that no plausible explanation for the behavior is ignored.

- What possible reasons for the behavior can I identify?
- Have I asked for an evaluation by other professionals to eliminate certain explanations for the behavior that might be important?

We offer two cautions: first, possible or plausible causal factors often remain matters for speculation, not proof. In many cases, the precise cause(s) of misbehavior can't be identified with certainty. Furthermore, there are typically several plausible causes, not just one. Second, finding the cause(s) doesn't necessarily lead directly to an effective intervention. That is, the cause doesn't necessarily tell us the "cure." Some causes can't be reversed (e.g., brain damage, a history of abuse), but some interventions are effective even though the cause isn't known. For example, stimulant medication may benefit a hyperactive child even though the cause of the hyperactivity can't be found. Consistent consequences may result in improvement of an aggressive student's behavior even though we can only speculate about the causes of aggression (Kauffman & Landrum, 2009a).

Where does this leave you, as a teacher, who is trying to analyze a behavior problem? We reiterate two points made earlier. First, it's important to recognize the possible range of causes of behavior and request the services of other professionals who may be able to rule out certain causal factors or to obtain help that you may not be able to provide. Second, you should give your greatest attention to the causal factors that you can alter.

Are there causes of the misbehavior that I can control to a significant degree?

Teachers often can make a difference in the lives of their pupils by getting involved in matters that extend beyond the classroom or school. For example, some teachers make repeated home visits for the purposes of understanding and improving the home lives of their students by working with parents. Others are able to make a significant contribution to improving students' lives by counseling students or obtaining health and social services for them outside the school environment. We caution that you can become over-involved in students' lives and neglect your own needs (and those of your partner or family). We also recognize that there are limits to parental involvement in behavior management (see Chapter 9). Furthermore, circumstances, such as living in a community far from the school in which you teach, may preclude your extensive involvement with your pupils outside the classroom or school. Yet, you might ask yourself whether there are circumstances or conditions outside your classroom or school that may be contributing to a pupil's misbehavior and that you might be able to change.

Clearly, conditions and events in the classroom and school can contribute to behavior management problems. As we mentioned in Chapter 3, the curricula and teaching strategies teachers use, the demands and prohibitions of teachers and administrators, and the influence of peers are critical factors that can set the stage for appropriate or inappropriate student behavior. Of all the possible factors that can contribute to behavior problems, events and conditions in the classroom are the factors over which the teacher has the greatest control. Furthermore, a substantial body of empirical research suggests that teachers often can improve their students' behavior substantially if they change certain classroom conditions. In fact, teachers can most productively view behavior management problems as instructional problems. Your most important consideration is arranging the classroom environment to teach appropriate behavior. We elaborate on this concept in Chapter 5.

Of all the questions you could ask yourself about the causes of behavior, we believe the single most important one is this: What's happening in my classroom that might contribute to misbehavior? That is, how could I be teaching my student(s) to misbehave, albeit inadvertently? Or, how am I failing to teach my student(s) to behave the way I'd like them to? You can examine events and conditions in the classroom and their possible effects on behavior in a variety of ways. In our opinion, the most useful way of analyzing what happens in your classroom—what students are being taught—is to define the behavior of concern as an observable event and then examine what happens immediately before it occurs (antecedent events) and after (consequences) (see Alberto & Troutman, 2009; Darch & Kame'enui, 2004; Kauffman & Brigham, 2009; Kerr & Nelson, 2010; Walker, Ramsey, & Gresham, 2004).

How should I define the behavior I am concerned about and identify its antecedents and consequences?

Defining a behavior problem isn't always as simple as it first appears. Many times, students exhibit a wide array of "trashy" behaviors that are irritating and divert attention from the central issue (recall, for example, Sally's description in Chapter 3). Sometimes it's difficult to focus on the problem and describe it as a particular behavior the student does or doesn't do. Nevertheless, a precise description of what the student does or doesn't do is extremely important for identifying antecedents and consequences and devising an intervention plan. Moreover, a precise description is important for measurement of the problem—assessing its severity and evaluating progress or success (Alberto & Troutman, 2009; Kauffman, 2010; Kerr & Nelson, 2010).

DEFINING BEHAVIOR   Defining a problem as something a student does or doesn't do requires that you observe carefully just how the student behaves and describe it clearly as an action. You must describe the behavior objectively and precisely enough that nearly anyone else observing the student independently could state whether or not the behavior occurred. You must take care not to describe the problem as your reaction or interpretation (e.g., "He irritates me") or the student's internal state (e.g., "She goes off into her dream world"), as these are too subjective and measurement of them will be too unreliable. "She cries," "She looks off into space with a blank expression," "He rummages in his desk," "She talks without permission," or "He doesn't complete his homework" are behavioral definitions that are probably objective enough that, with some clarifications, two or more independent observers could agree about whether or not they occurred in most instances.

If you have defined a behavior precisely and objectively, you'll be able to observe when it begins and when it stops. That is, the behavior won't be described as a state of being ("unmotivated," "hostile," or "reticent," for example) but as a measurable event or episode (e.g., "slept," "cursed or hit someone," "didn't respond to a direct question"). A good test of whether you've defined a problem appropriately for our discussion here is to ask yourself these questions:

- Could I count occurrences of this behavior so that I could state how many times it occurred today?
- Could I measure the duration of these episodes so that I could state how many minutes of the period the student was engaging in this behavior?
- Could I glance at the student and tell whether or not the student was engaged in the behavior at that instant?

Once you've defined the behavior so that you can observe its occurrence accurately, you'll be able to observe what happens just before and just after it occurs. As we discuss further in Chapter 5, the events that occur just before and just after a behavior can have a powerful influence. In fact, one explanation of behavior is that it's almost entirely a function of its antecedents and consequences. We urge you to take careful note of the events surrounding the behavior you're concerned about, because you may be able to alter these surrounding events and thereby modify it.

IDENTIFYING ANTECEDENTS   You might begin by noting the antecedents. What are the events or conditions that immediately precede instances of the problem behavior? You may need to keep anecdotal records or other written notes in order to describe a pattern of when, where, and under what conditions the behavior most often occurs. Your objective in examining the antecedents of the behavior should be to anticipate it—to predict it accurately. If you find that the behavior occurs only under certain conditions or immediately after certain events, then you might be able to resolve the problem completely or in part by changing the antecedents. For example, if you find that the student nearly always exhibits the problem behavior when you give an instruction or make a request, you might try varying the way you present the task to avoid the problem. Sometimes giving a student a choice rather than a direct instruction (e.g., "Which of these pages would you like to do first?" rather than "I want you to complete these two pages.") will make a significant difference in his or her compliance.

A particularly useful way of conceptualizing behavior problems is called precorrection, a type of lesson plan that we discuss further in Chapter 5 (Colvin, 2004; Colvin, Sugai, & Patching, 1993; Kauffman & Brigham, 2009). Teachers who use precorrection see misbehavior as an error or mistake that they can teach the student to avoid. Precorrection requires taking proactive measures to keep misbehavior from occurring in the first place, not reactive measures taken after it has occurred (see also Darch & Kame'enui, 2004). The teacher tries to anticipate the misbehavior and replace it with a desired behavior.

The critical step in using precorrection, after defining the problem objectively and defining the behavior the teacher would like to see instead, is describing the context in which the problem usually happens. Skilled teachers often can identify the antecedent—that is, the situation, circumstance, condition, or context in which a troublesome behavior is utterly predictable. If they can, then they may be able to modify the context to avert the trouble, saving them and everyone else the hassle of dealing with the problem. Good teachers find ways of helping students avoid making mistakes over and over, whether the skill being taught is academic or social. Helping students avoid a repetition of errors requires identifying a predictable pattern of behavior, beginning with the context in which the error is likely (e.g., in basketball, a particular play—perhaps a fast break; in music, a particular passage—perhaps a rest; in school conduct, a particular social demand—perhaps responding to a transition from one activity to another).

We aren't suggesting that the antecedents of troublesome behavior can always be identified or that you can always alter them. Some behavior patterns are extremely hard to figure out. Sometimes the antecedents may be internal events or states. For example, a student experiencing high levels of anxiety or having a psychotic condition may be responding to perceptions or thoughts that you can't observe directly. Sometimes the antecedents are things you can't change. For example, you may find that the student exhibits the problem behavior whenever there's an announcement on the school intercom, a condition that you aren't able to alter. At the least, however, identifying the antecedents should help you anticipate problems and know where and when to focus your intervention.

IDENTIFYING CONSEQUENCES   Equally as important as noting the antecedents is identifying the consequences—events that occur soon after the behavior you're concerned about (Alberto & Troutman, 2009; Kauffman & Brigham, 2009; Kerr & Nelson, 2010). What does the student "get" out of the behavior? You must remember that appearances can be deceiving; the student may appear to get nothing or to receive only negative consequences for the behavior, yet he or she persists in doing it. A rewarding consequence, or a punishing one, for one person is not necessarily the same for another. You must also look for multiple consequences.

Sometimes the "payoff" for behavior has several components, and the nature and sequence of these components can be highly significant. In the classroom, for example, a student may frequently misbehave in ways that result in criticism or punishment from adults (perhaps including restrictions or extra work) and scorn of peers. A consequence of this kind of behavior is the attention—often the undivided attention—of one or more adults, several peers, or perhaps the entire class. Although the misbehaving student seems to earn only punishment, the attention that goes with the punishing consequences may be a sufficient reward that outweighs the intended effect of the punishment. For some students, seeing adults get upset is a very powerful rewarding consequence. Enticing the teacher into an emotional outburst may, for these students, be well worth enduring any punishment adults are likely to devise (Kauffman & Landrum, 2009a; Walker, Ramsey, & Gresham, 2004).

IDENTIFYING CHAINS OF EVENTS   Antecedents, behaviors, and consequences occur in continuous strings or chains of events. To analyze relationships among them, you may need to keep a running record of the sequence of events. Here's an example, drawn from a case written by John Shearer, "Foul Language: Classroom Trouble" included in *The Intern Teacher Casebook* (edited by Judith H. Shulman and Joel A. Colbert and published by the ERIC Clearing House on Teacher Education). It recounts a sequence of events in a junior high school classroom. The incident involves a student's (Richard's) use of language that the teacher (John) considers foul:

1. John asks for volunteers to name sources of pollution
2. Richard raises his hand and says, "I know, teacher! Farts!"
3. Boisterous laughter and noises from the class
4. John calls the class to order and cautions Richard to stop
5. Richard flails his arms in the air and says, "Teacher, teacher! Malcolm just told me to [sexually graphic phrase]!"
6. Howling, whistling from the class

We could label the first three events in this sequence in what is called an ABC analysis. For example, we might label these events as follows:

Antecedent ⟶	*Behavior* ⟶	*Consequence*
J asks for volunteers	R raises hand, says, ". . . Farts!"	Laughter, noises from class

We might go on to label the next three in a similar fashion:

Antecedent ⟶	*Behavior* ⟶	*Consequence*
J calls for order, cautions R	R flails arms, makes sexual comment	Class howls, whistles

Notice that in such analyses, a given behavior can be both a consequence for the behavior it follows and an antecedent for the next behavior in sequence. Thus the teacher's behavior can be a consequence for the student; likewise, the student's behavior can be a consequence for the teacher. We might have chosen to diagram the sequence of ABCs as follows:

Antecedent ⟶ *Behavior* ⟶ *Consequence*
R raises hand, says, ". . . Farts"   Laughter, noises from class   J calls for order

    In interactions, individuals provide consequences and antecedents for each other in an ongoing chain of events. Where you start the analysis—which event you choose to label antecedent and whose behavior you choose as the focus—depends on your purpose. The purpose of an ABC analysis is to clarify the sequence of classroom events from a particular perspective, either the student's or the teacher's. It helps one understand what each party is responding to and what each is getting out of the interaction. ABC analyses are usually done for the events surrounding a specific behavior problem episode.

    Doing an ABC analysis requires that the sequence of events be recorded accurately. Few teachers will have the help of someone who can observe classroom interactions and record them accurately, although sometimes a classroom aide or support staff (e.g., school psychologist, consulting teacher) can do so. If you must do the analysis yourself, you should attempt to jot notes to yourself whenever possible and reconstruct the sequence of events as soon after the episode as possible. Recalling the exact behaviors and their sequence is critically important. We suggest that if you plan to do an ABC analysis, you use a form similar to the one shown in Table 4.1. We have added some possible written items to Table 4.1 to illustrate how it might be used. Note that in our example, Chris is successful in avoiding his teacher's (Ms. P.'s) expectations and his involvement in academic work with the class. You may want to recall the example shown in Table 4.1 when we discuss turn-taking interactions. The example shows how "turns" operate, with teacher and student each setting up the other for the next "turn" in an interaction.

    Whenever you are perplexed by classroom behavior, you may need to answer these questions:

- What is the precise sequence of events surrounding this problem?
- Can I clearly identify the ABCs of the interactions that are troublesome?
- Most important, can I identify a predictable pattern of behavior, including the situation, circumstance, or context in which it usually occurs?

    Answering these questions is particularly important for resolving the negative interactions that are called coercion. Answering them is also important to functional behavioral assessment (FBA), which means finding out what consequences a student obtains by specific misbehavior in a given setting.

TABLE 4.1 **Forms for Recording ABC Analysis**

Antecedents	Behaviors	Consequences
Ms. P. asks class to open books to p. 43	Chris does not open his book and pounds his book with his fist	Ms. P. says "Chris, open your book."
Chris opens his book but closes it again	Ms. P. walks to Chris's desk	Chris puts book inside desk
Ms. P. puts her open hand on Chris's shoulder	Chris brushes away Ms. P.'s hand and says, "Leave me alone."	Ms. P. moves away from Chris and talks to rest of class

IDENTIFYING COERCIVE INTERACTIONS   Antecedents, behaviors, and consequences sometimes are characterized by an escalating pattern of aversiveness. That is, starting with an antecedent that is aversive (unpleasant or painful, something the person would like to escape from or avoid), two parties attempt to control each other by increasingly powerful negative consequences. Positive consequences are not an outcome of these interactions. For example, abused and aggressive children often behave in ways that are extremely irritating to adults; they seem to "ask for" punishment, and adults typically oblige by providing it. Their irritating behavior typically is followed by harsh reprimands, if not physical abuse, from parents, which sets the stage for even more highly irritating acts. They and their parents become embroiled in a battle that someone "wins" (usually the parent when the child is younger) by being more obnoxious, threatening, or brutal, forcing the other party to stop. This type of interaction is known as coercion (see Kauffman & Landrum, 2009a).

Coercion is sometimes a feature of classroom interactions between teachers and pupils and of interactions among classroom peers. The pupil may find the teacher's expectations and demands aversive and may attempt to avoid them by misbehaving. The teacher finds this aversive and restates the demands or increases them, perhaps threatening or punishing the student. The student feels challenged to become more obnoxious, tempting the teacher to respond with more severe punishment or threats. This kind of coercive interaction continues until either the teacher or the student "wins" or an uneasy and temporary truce is made. Following is an example of a coercive classroom interaction.

Teacher asks student to complete a page of math problems

Student says, "I don't know how to do this crap!"

Teacher says, "Yes, you do, we just did some problems like these yesterday. Get started now."

Student slams the book closed, saying, "Ain't doin' it!"

Teacher goes to student's desk, opens the book, hands student a pencil, says in an angry tone, "Get started now!"

Student shoves book off the desk.

Teacher squeezes student's shoulder, growls, "Pick that book up, young man!"

Student jumps to his feet, says, "Get your hands off me, bitch! You pick it up! You can't make me do nothin'!"

Teacher yells, "That's it! I've had enough of this! Pick that book up and get to work now or you're outta here to the office!"

Many students are masters at drawing teachers into power struggles; they know how to start wars of will, and they often know how to win them. Students sometimes lay coercive "traps" for teachers by engaging in irritating conduct, knowing that many teachers will respond to them by engaging in a power struggle, often over minor misbehavior. The more skillful the teacher is at behavior management, the more tactics she or he has for ending the struggle early, typically by finding a way to disengage and avoid stepping into the trap. Clearly, coercive interactions aren't desirable, but they're common in many classrooms. Understanding the process of coercion is important in finding ways to deal effectively with it. We discuss the underlying process—negative reinforcement—in Chapter 5.

Becoming keenly aware of coercive interactions is critically important to the successful use of more positive behavior management strategies. In analyzing the ABCs of your classroom interactions, you should be especially concerned about those that involve a coercive process. Ask yourself questions about the early stages of the interactions.

- How do these interactions start?
- At what point could I avoid the process by disengaging from it?
- How could I start a different interaction that doesn't end in a power struggle?
- How could I try to replace coercive interactions with those ending in positive consequences?

Sometimes you might discover that in trying to find answers to these questions you need to consider both your own thoughts and feelings and those of your students. Equally important, however, is being able to find the typical pattern of misbehavior and then observing how it begins and the stages through which it may go so that you can find effective ways of short-circuiting it.

IDENTIFYING THE PATTERNS AND STAGES OF MISBEHAVIOR   Geoffrey Colvin and his colleagues at the University of Oregon have studied the classroom conduct of acting-out, aggressive students in great detail. Colvin has identified a typical cycle or sequence of phases that can help teachers see the early signs of misbehavior and take action to avoid an escalation of the problem (Colvin, 2004). In fact, most teachers, in reflecting on their experiences as children or youths or even their lives as adults, can probably recognize examples of these phases in their own conduct. Recalling or imagining how it feels to be in one of these phases or how these phases look to others, teachers are likely to be able to spot them in their students (see Kauffman & Brigham, 2009).

It's essential to recognize that all students are at least occasionally in the first and desirable phase: calm. When students are calm, they are on task and goal-oriented, follow classroom rules and expectations, respond well to praise and other forms of recognition, comply with suggestions, and take the initiative in classroom routines and academic work. The reason it's essential to recognize this phase in the behavior of students, as we discuss further in Chapter 5, is that taking action to sustain this phase is the single most important behavior management strategy. This is the phase you want to draw out as much as possible, as it's the phase in which students are most teachable.

The calm behavior that teachers rightfully desire is often disturbed by incidents that they can identify. Teachers should be as aware as possible of events in or out of school that may launch students into the second, problematic stage: trigger. In the trigger phase, something happens that's anxiety provoking or discomforting to the student. Triggers may include, for example, conflicts with other students or adults, such as provocations or teasing, denial of a need, or the infliction of anything unpleasant on the student; changes in routine; pressure to perform or lack of the skills needed to respond appropriately to demands; making errors or being corrected; problems at home or in the community, including threats, abuse, or gang-related events; substance abuse; or health, nutritional, or sleep problems. Teachers sensitive to these triggers may be able to respond to students who have experienced them in such a way as to avoid the explosions that they may set off. The main purpose of looking for the phases is to keep the student's behavior from moving up the scale of seriousness.

If a student has experienced a trigger in school or out of school, he or she may show signs of the third phase: agitation. A noticeable increase or decrease in behavior may indicate agitation. The agitated student might show an increase in behavior that demonstrates a lapse in ability to stay on task and concentrate. This could include such things as a lot of off-task behavior, moving in and out of groups, constant motion (especially of hands), darting eyes, vocal noises, or using a lot of nonconversational language (such as repetition of words or phrases). Alternatively, an agitated student might show a decrease in certain types of behavior. For example, the student might stare into space rather than comply with a request, mumble or say something indicating he is not certain what to do, shove his hands into his pockets or fold his arms rather than do an assigned task, or withdraw from social interaction with others. The perceptive teacher spots these increases or decreases in behavior quickly and recognizes that something needs to be done to keep the student from becoming more agitated.

Agitation is often a prelude to the fourth phase: acceleration. In the acceleration phase, the student is looking for ways to draw other people—either peers or adults—into a struggle. The student finds ways of inviting others to engage him or her in coercive interactions. Difficult students offer invitations that most peers and adults find difficult to turn down, and teachers often find that they've been drawn into the struggle before they know what has happened. Some students seem to have earned a Master of Engagement (M.E.) degree; they are exceedingly skilled at making themselves the center of attention by displaying behavior that others think they can't ignore. Sometimes their engaging behavior really can't be ignored because it's clearly intolerable in the classroom or is dangerous. The most difficult students have a special talent for engaging others in counteraggression or emotional upsets. These put the student in full control. The engaging behavior—the invitations to coercive interactions—include a lot of crafty moves. Difficult-to-manage students might use questioning and arguing, an especially useful ploy for adults who feel they must have the last word. They might use noncompliance and defiance, directly challenging the teacher's authority. They might comply with a request but do so with such inappropriate behavior that the teacher is unlikely to be happy with the compliance. They might engage in sustained off-task behavior that a teacher tends not to ignore. They might provoke others by teasing, nasty comments, gestures, and so forth. They might whine or cry or run away from the teacher, leave the room, or in some other way avoid or escape the task or situation. They might threaten or intimidate others through verbal abuse or physical acts. They might threaten to destroy property. A teacher's response to a student's engaging behavior in this acceleration phase must be quick but insightful. Without skillful management of this phase, a blowup is highly likely. However, in most cases, there is still a chance to divert the student from a full-blown tantrum or assault.

If the student isn't diverted, he or she goes "out of control" or enters phase five: peak. In this phase, one may see serious property destruction, physical assault, self-injury, hyperventilation, or a tantrum of considerable severity.

The peak phase can't last forever, simply because it's exhausting. The sixth phase, de-escalation, is sure to follow. After going out of control, students typically show signs of confusion. They may withdraw, deny that anything happened, or blame others. They may seek reconciliation or be responsive to clear directions. They don't want to discuss what happened at this point, but they may be willing to engage in some simple task.

Eventually, after a period of de-escalation, comes the final phase: recovery. The student may still be defensive and try to avoid discussing what happened, but he or she is likely to be relatively subdued in interactions with others and may show an eagerness for some sort of independent work. Recovery is a period of regaining equilibrium or getting back on track.

Figure 4.1 depicts the seven phases of acting-out behavior. It's important to understand that a given individual may move very quickly from one phase to the next, seem to skip a phase, or remain in one phase for a long time. The key concept here is that there are various levels of intensity of behavior ranging from calm, task-oriented, compliant behavior to peak, out-of-control behavior. The most problematic types of behavior are repeated; they don't occur just once but recur in a predictable pattern that skillful observers can recognize. The phases we've described and that are depicted in Figure 4.1 are a way of organizing observations and communication about these predictable patterns.

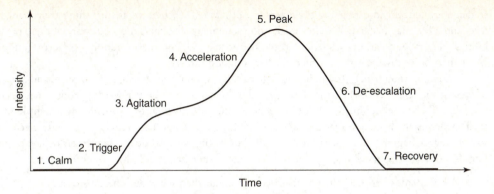

Phases of escalated behavior

FIGURE 4.1 Phases of the Acting-Out Cycle   *Source:* From *Managing Acting-Out Behavior* by Geoffrey Colvin. Copyright © 1992 by Behavior Associates. Reprinted by permission.

How might I identify the probable cognitive and affective aspects of the misbehavior?

Teachers who are experts in behavior management pay attention to more than what students do. They recognize that thoughts and feelings are intimately connected to the way people behave. They would like students to think rationally and feel good about themselves, and they know that helping students develop cognitive skills and appropriate affective responses is part of their responsibility. Furthermore, finding out what students think and how they feel, and reflecting on one's own cognitive and affective reactions, can provide useful insights into resolutions of behavior problems. We aren't referring here to analyzing unconscious motivations or hidden meanings. Rather, we're referring to paying attention to what students say and their reactions to situations, which reveal their thought processes, preferences, and emotional responses.

Teachers often suspect that students' thoughts and feelings cause them to misbehave, and often they would like to change the way students think or feel about things. Someone else's thoughts and feelings can't be manipulated directly, however. Furthermore, changing the way students think or feel won't necessarily change the way they behave. Teachers can directly control many of the antecedents and consequences of students' classroom behavior, however, and in this way they may be able to alter students' thoughts and feelings. But how does someone identify the thoughts and feelings that might be involved in behavior? The simplicity of the answer belies the complexity of the task: by watching and listening.

Observing and interpreting the affective components of students' behavior requires sensitivity to subtle individual differences and changes in posture, facial expression, behavior, and voice—the types of things we described in our discussion of the phases of acting-out behavior. Students who are the easiest to manage are likely also to be the easiest to "read." Those who are difficult to manage and interpret often express themselves in atypical ways or send mixed signals—verbal and nonverbal messages that contradict each other. In fact, they often put teachers in a quandary by saying one thing and doing another.

Teachers often learn much about students' thoughts and feelings indirectly through casual conversation. Perhaps most teachers could learn more by asking students directly what they think or how they feel about their own behavior and important aspects of the classroom and school. Some students are reticent in expressing their feelings, others tell teachers what they think they want to hear, and a few may make deliberately misleading statements. Teachers must be aware of these possibilities. Nevertheless, asking students is often better than relying solely on indirect interpretations. In Chapter 5, we discuss ways in which teachers might do this.

One important benefit of finding out what students think and feel about themselves and aspects of their school experience is that it often gives the teacher a clue about rewarding consequences for behavior. Trisha's reflection on Sam (at the beginning of this chapter) provides an example of a teacher identifying a student's feelings about something that could be used as a highly effective consequence. In Chapter 5, we discuss other benefits of talking with students about their behavior. For purposes of analyzing a behavior problem, however, we suggest you ask these questions:

- Are students giving me clues to their feelings about themselves and the classroom?
- Have I listened and observed carefully to detect the emotions that accompany their behavior?
- Have I asked the students directly what they think and feel about specific events or conditions?
- Can I connect what I observe and hear to a pattern or cycle of acting-out behavior?

How should I measure the behavior problem and behavior change?

Measurement is a fundamental requirement of many professional activities. Physicians, engineers, and economists, for example, typically rely heavily on measurements related to their analyses of problems and base their professional recommendations and judgments of success on measured outcomes (Kauffman, 2010). In education, measurement of students' academic skills is an accepted part of professional practice. Measurement of problem behavior is expected as an integral part of an intervention plan. A teacher can't assess the effects of teaching without a reliable, accurate means of monitoring behavior.

We recognize that there are many different types of measurement ranging from subjective impressions to extremely precise quantitative assessments. Choosing the most helpful and efficient type of measurement and choosing to measure the right things are keys to competent professional practice. Your choice of measurement may depend on how you answer several questions related to the problem behavior.

- How serious do I believe the problem is?
- How am I going to judge the success or failure of my interventions?
- With whom do I need to communicate about the problem and my success or failure in dealing with it?

Ordinarily, the more serious you believe the problem is, the more concerned you should be about devising a precise way of measuring it (see Alberto & Troutman, 2009; Kerr & Nelson, 2010). For minor problems, subjective impressions may suffice; for major problems, objective data are critical. More precise and objective measurement is needed for more serious problems for three reasons: (1) the consequences of the problem and its resolution are greater for both the student and the teacher; (2) the more serious the problem, the more imperative it will be for the teacher to communicate objective, reliable information about it to others; and (3) with more serious problems, subjective impressions can be very misleading.

Subjective impressions about behavior and behavior change are often included in summary reports of student progress. Some teachers keep diaries in which they record their impressions or reactions to students' behavior. These subjective, nonquantitative statements may be useful, but they have severe limitations in cases of serious behavior problems. Teachers seldom define problem behavior as precisely as they should when they record only their subjective impressions.

A systematic anecdotal record is a more precise level of measurement. Such a record requires that the teacher jot down observations about the student's behavior whenever it occurs or at regular times (e.g., daily). Anecdotal records can be quite helpful, but they do not allow one to make a careful assessment of the problem unless they include sufficient detail to allow an ABC analysis. An ABC analysis is actually a very careful anecdotal record in which specific events are recorded in time sequence to describe a behavior and its antecedents and consequences. A still more precise and quantitative level of measurement is often needed, however.

Direct daily measurement is extremely helpful in assessing serious problems and evaluating the effects of interventions. Measurement of this type requires that the teacher define the behavior as an objectively observable act, as we've suggested, and record occurrences of the behavior to establish its quantitative level. We can't detail the methods of direct daily measurement here (see Alberto & Troutman, 2009; and Kerr & Nelson, 2010 for more of the details). However, an example may show some of the advantages of such methods. We use the case of Trisha's work with Sammy, described in the vignette earlier in this chapter. We don't provide all of the details of Sammy's case but focus on those aspects related to direct daily measurement.

Sammy was a third-grader who, Trisha realized, had a serious problem because he frequently disrupted the class with loud crying and whining. His peers teased him when he cried, contributing further to the problem. Trisha knew Sammy cried a lot, but she didn't know how to describe how much he cried or how to measure changes in this problem behavior. She knew that his crying episodes sometimes lasted only a couple of minutes and that others lasted for as long as an hour.

We considered how Trisha could measure Sammy's crying in such a way that she would have a more objective basis than her subjective impressions or general descriptions ("He cries a lot!") for describing the seriousness of the problem and changes in his behavior. Trisha could have measured the duration of each crying episode by jotting down the time each crying episode started and when it stopped (using a stopwatch). This would have had certain advantages, as she could then have described total crying time in minutes per day, percentage of the day spent crying, and number of episodes per day. Because she was responsible for the entire class and had no aide or other person who could keep such a record, we needed to find a measurement system that she could manage, but one that would still give her an objective description. Trisha agreed that she could keep an index card handy and make a tally mark for each crying episode. This gave her the number of episodes per day, but not their duration. She kept a daily log sheet on which she wrote down the number of tallies for the day. (The first author, Kauffman, helped Trisha devise her measurement plan.)

By the time we began working with Trisha to resolve Sammy's crying, she had already tried several approaches: comforting, ignoring, and reprimanding him. None of these seemed to bring about improvement, although Trisha had no objective basis for judging the effects of her attempts to get Sammy to stop crying. She had given up on the problem until she could think of something new to try. We suggested, therefore, that she first record Sammy's crying episodes under "baseline" conditions before she tried anything else. After recording his crying episodes for 10 days, she reported that Sammy cried an average of about 17 or 18 times per day (see Figure 4.2). She felt that reducing the number to 6 or 8 times per day would be a reasonable goal. Next, Trisha tried totally and consistently ignoring Sammy when he cried. After five days of ignoring, the average was still about 15 (14, 15, 17, 15, 16 times per day), a little lower but not very close to her goal. Then she discovered that Sammy wanted to be called Sam. She designed an intervention in which she and his peers called him Sam—except when he was crying, when they tried to ignore him but could call him Sammy. Trisha also asked Sam to record his own behavior on her graph each day. The number of crying episodes then dropped to nearly zero (0, 0, 1, 4, 1, 0, 0, 0 for the next 8 days). Trisha continued counting for a while longer (during follow-up) but eventually was satisfied that the problem had been resolved.

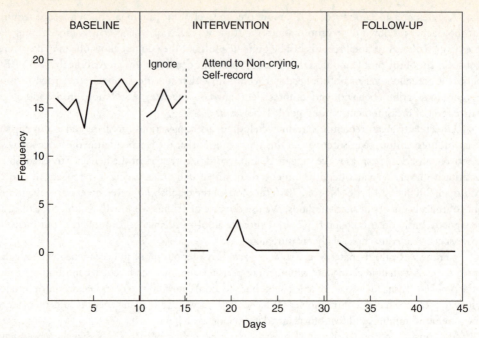

FIGURE 4.2   Sammy's Crying

Trisha's direct daily measurement helped her plot Sammy's progress more objectively and quantitatively than she could have using her subjective impressions. Her subjective impressions were useful, but her objective measurement gave her subjective perceptions a firmer base. Another method Trisha used was plotting her data daily on a graph, which is commonly done as a part of direct daily measurement. Her graph, shown in Figure 4.2, gave her a quick, easily interpretable picture of what was happening with Sammy's behavior.

What's a reasonable goal?

The ideal behavior management strategy resolves the problem immediately, completely, and permanently without creating any new ones. However, we nearly always have to settle for something less than the ideal. Teachers try to help their students learn patience and persistence and how to obtain gratification from partial successes. Teachers should be models of these characteristics by setting goals for themselves and their students that challenge but do not overwhelm. What does this mean for how you should approach setting a goal for the outcome of your intervention in a behavior management problem? We can't answer this question directly because it's a matter for careful reflection of each individual case.

We can, however, suggest that goals are more likely to be reasonable when teachers define the problem behavior precisely and devise a way of measuring it objectively and accurately. Precise definition and quantitative measurement often help teachers notice progress that they might not have perceived if they'd relied on more global, subjective impressions.

How do I accomplish a functional assessment of behavior and write a positive behavior intervention plan?

When a student is having extraordinary difficulty in school due to behavior problems, special education law may require a functional behavioral assessment, or FBA (Fox & Gable, 2004). Actually, neither the federal special education law (the Individuals with Disabilities Education Act, reauthorized in 2004) nor professionals in special education agree on just what a FBA is or how to do it.

The basic idea of FBA is to ascertain by looking at the pattern of the student's behavior in its school context—using strategies like the ABC analysis we have already discussed—just why a student is exhibiting a particular behavior. Presumably, if you can learn why the student is behaving in a particular way, then you can help him or her learn to achieve the same goal in a more socially acceptable manner. This is more easily said than done, but FBA is at least intended to promote the analysis of why students misbehave and connect that information to a reasonable plan to do something about it.

There's a lot of speculation about just what lawmakers and rulemakers intended or envisioned FBA to be. However, we think it's safe to assume that they intended to make the assessment of behavior functional—practical, useful, helpful in designing intervention plans, not simply an exercise in classification. This goal is entirely consistent with the purpose of this book. For details of current legal requirements related to FBA, you should contact your local special education administrator, who will know your state's requirements as well as the federal law.

Besides FBA, federal law may require a positive behavior intervention plan (BIP) for certain students. Again, consult your local special education administrator for details of the legal requirements, which are likely to change with each new reauthorization of the federal law and may vary from state to state. The procedures we suggest in this book are consistent with constructing a positive behavior intervention plan. There's nothing mysterious or peculiar about the essential features of a BIP that's outside the scope of our suggestions. If you implement our suggestions for analyzing behavior problems and changing behavior, then you'll have a good basis for completing a functional behavior assessment and writing a positive behavior intervention plan.

What is required for prevention and early intervention?

Why not do whatever we can to prevent the serious behavior management problems we call emotional or behavioral disorders from occurring in the first place or, at least, intervene effectively as early as we can when we see them? This is a reasonable question that any thoughtful person might ask. The answer isn't simple, though. Although just about everybody thinks prevention and early intervention are good ideas in the abstract, when it comes down to actually doing them they balk for a variety of reasons (Kauffman, 1999, 2003; Kauffman & Brigham, 2009; Kauffman, Mock, & Simpson, 2007; Kauffman, Simpson, & Mock, 2009). This is especially true when recognition of the problem involves the need for any kind of treatment, like mental health counseling or special education.

Someone is almost always going to bring up the fear that labeling and categorizing will cause harm. Then there's the fear of being wrong, the fear of acting too quickly because everything's going to work out okay—it's just a temporary problem, a phase, a rough patch in otherwise ordinary development. Sometimes, people argue that special education for the student will be just going from bad to worse, that the special education he or she gets will be second rate or worse. Or someone might say the problem is just the result of the teacher's poor instruction or poor behavior management skills or the child's home or culture or the teacher's perceptions or bias—something outside of the child and therefore the child doesn't actually have a behavior problem. These are legitimate concerns that must be taken seriously. There is the possibility that any of them (or any combination of them) could be true. But they can also be used as excuses to do nothing. Usually, the concerns we mentioned win out over concern for early identification and intervention, as Kauffman and Brigham (2009) point out.

A common belief is that the student's problem is merely a conduct disorder (CD), not an emotional disorder under special education law; the student is simply a "pain in the neck," not one who needs mental health services or special education. Usually, the person who says this will argue that the youngster is socially maladjusted, not emotionally disturbed, and that CD is not actually a disability. This is one of the worst, most damaging misconceptions about behavior problems. The mental health literature is overwhelming on this point: the hyperaggressive, disruptive behavior known as conduct disorder or CD is a serious mental health disability with a very poor prognosis, and the longer it is left untreated the worse the prognosis becomes (Kauffman & Landrum, 2009a).

What is required for prevention and early intervention? The short answer is that good teaching, good behavior management of the kind we will discuss further, and recognition of problems in their earliest stages (and talking about them) are all necessary. Remember that you can't prevent what you can't or don't anticipate. You can't talk about problems without labels and categories for them. You can't intervene effectively in problems you don't see. And hyperaggressive and disruptive behavior are among the most serious behavior problems. The most important things you can do as a teacher to prevent problems and intervene early in them are (a) providing excellent instruction, (b) emphasizing positive behavior management strategies (which we discuss further in the next chapter), and (c) recognizing the seriousness of acting-out, hyperaggressive, and disruptive behavior. We don't want to give the impression that depression and social withdrawal aren't serious, too. It's just that people often offer unconvincing or completely phony "explanations" of serious acting-out behavior or ignore it when they shouldn't.

Summary

Careful analysis of a problem prior to designing a plan for attacking it is an accepted part of professional practice. Analyses of behavior management problems should include an examination of your assumptions about the causes of behavior because your beliefs may significantly affect your choice of intervention strategies. Some explanations of behavior are more important than others for teachers. We suggest that you focus on the causal factors that have the greatest support in empirical research and offer you the greatest opportunity for control. For teachers, classroom events are usually the most important causal factors. Analysis of classroom events should begin with a precise definition of the problem behavior. Particularly important in analyzing the problem is identifying antecedents (events immediately preceding the behavior) and consequences (events immediately following). Sequences or chains of antecedents, behaviors, and consequences (ABCs) may be described to clarify interactions from a particular individual's perspective. Coercive interactions, in which each party struggles for control by presenting increasingly aversive consequences for the other, are especially important to analyze carefully. Acting-out behavior typically occurs in a pattern of phases: calm, trigger, agitation, acceleration, peak, de-escalation, and recovery. The cognitive and affective aspects of behavior should be identified through careful listening and observation as they may provide clues for resolving behavior problems. Analyzing behavior problems requires that the teacher select an appropriate approach to measurement. Direct daily measurement allows the most precise level of assessment and is particularly useful in evaluating the effects of interventions. A precise definition of behavior and an accurate measurement of it helps teachers set appropriate goals for behavioral change. Identifying and intervening in problems as early as possible is critically important.

Case Connection

Every case requires analysis of behavior, but you might study the following cases in particular and think about how the teacher or others might have analyzed the problem more explicitly and productively:

James's Uncertain Future   Dan Parker
Stealing Time   Robert Carter

CHAPTER FIVE

Changing Behavior

Questions for Reflection

Have I tried the simplest and most obvious strategies?

What approaches for helping students change their behavior are most likely to be successful?

How might I use the five operations of a behavioral approach?
Positive Reinforcement
Negative Reinforcement
Extinction
Response Cost Punishment
Punishment by Presenting Aversives
A Note on Corporal Punishment

How can I capitalize on the cognitive and affective aspects of behavior change?
Talking with Students

Choosing Consequences for Students' Behavior
Teaching Self-Control Procedures
Teaching Social Skills

Is my approach positive and supportive of appropriate behavior?

Can I use an instructional approach to prevent this behavior problem?
Precorrecting Problems
Interrupting the Acting-Out Cycle

Special Note on Digital Resources
Summary
Case Connection

A ttempts to change behavior, whether by parents, teachers, politicians, or employers, have traditionally been impromptu. As reliable scientific evidence regarding behavioral change is accumulated and professional practices are more widely shared and evaluated, behavior management is becoming less improvised and more planned. Today, it's possible for teachers to select from a wide variety of strategies for managing classroom behavior (see Evertson & Weinstein, 2006). Some are "packaged" as programs, books, or workshops under special titles or trademarks. Others are presented in textbooks or resource manuals that focus more on underlying principles and their application to unique circumstances. Our approach is to present principles and suggest some initial questions you might ask yourself in selecting a management strategy. We also offer some specific suggestions and cautions for using specific strategies. This implies that you won't thoughtlessly follow a standard plan or passively accept whatever we offer. Of course, we hope you'll follow our suggestions. But we hope you'll use your knowledge of behavior principles and best professional practices to select the strategies that have the highest probability of success. Our intention is to foster reflective professional practice rather than provide a "formula" or "recipe" for you to follow. The vignettes of Mary and Tom provide examples of the kind of thinking we hope to encourage.

Mary

Two years ago, I went through a truly horrible time. I had one of the most difficult groups of kids I've ever taught. I was in terrible shape physically, psychologically, and financially. My whole world seemed to be a mess. I had back problems. My two grown kids both lost their jobs and came back to live with me. My husband had run away. I was deeply in debt. Maybe it was understandable, but I wasn't positive with the kids in my class. I was cranky. I yelled at them a lot. They got on my nerves. I was unhappy, and so were they. One day my supervisor was in my class and gave me one of those looks—you know, like, "What's the matter with *you*?" That was enough to make me stop and think about what was happening in my class and how I'd gotten into a lot of negativism, criticism, nagging, and other depressing kinds of interactions. My life outside school was bad enough, but my experiences in my classroom were just adding to my exhaustion. I knew I had to pull myself together and not let my personal life outside the classroom determine the way I behaved in school. It was really, really hard to do that! For a while, I kept an informal tally (on an index card) of my positive and negative statements to kids. Then I worked hard on being more positive when kids were doing what I wanted them to. I talked about this with my aide, too, and she helped me by watching for kids who were doing what they were supposed to. Her signals helped me let kids know I noticed their good behavior and approved of what they were doing. Fortunately, I got things turned around to the way I usually teach, with lots more positive than negative interactions with my students.

Tom

My sixth-grade group ate lunch in my room. They brought their lunch trays into the room from the cafeteria. After they ate, they were supposed to go out into the hall to scrape their trays into a waste can and stack their trays on a trolley. Even though I thought I had stated the rule clearly—no more than four students at a time in the hall—I had a lot of difficulty with too many kids going out together. Once five or six of them got out into the hall together, they started horsing around, shoving, pushing, doing gross things with the leftovers, and so on. Naturally, this made a lot of noise and led to problems with teasing, threatening behavior, spilled food, and soiled clothing. Finally, it occurred to me that what might work was some sort of "pass" or object to make the rule easier to monitor, something tangible that would regulate traffic for me. So I got four pieces of bamboo to use as "batons" or passes. The rule was that you could go out to scrape your tray only when you had a baton. The kids actually thought it was kind of fun because they made a game of passing the baton to the next person of their choosing. It worked for this group, but I was aware that it could have created problems, too. Kids could have started doing bad things with the batons. We could have had fights and teasing and hard feelings over who got the baton next. But we didn't. Other things could have gone wrong. But they didn't. If it had backfired—and I was ready for it to do just that—I wouldn't have lost much, if anything, by trying. What I learned was that sometimes little gimmicks work, especially in regulating kids' turns or movement. After all, why do you suppose some stores have customers take a number so they know when it's their turn to be waited on?

The wide range of methods and materials for behavior management available today requires every teacher to use self-questioning. What have I tried, and how well have I implemented what I've done? Have I overlooked the simplest potential solution? What reasons do I have to believe that this approach might be successful? Given what I know about child development and this particular problem, what would be an appropriate strategy? Have I fallen into a pattern of negative or coercive interactions in trying to manage this problem? Am I employing best professional practices in dealing with this situation? Could I figure out how to precorrect the problem—to change the context somehow so that the problem doesn't occur in the first place, saving myself and my students a lot of needless hassle? These are only a few of the questions teachers must pose for themselves in tackling a behavior management problem after they have made an initial identification and analysis.

QUESTIONS FOR REFLECTION

When you've reached the point of planning a strategy for changing behavior, it's important to make a wise choice from the options you might try first. Sometimes people overlook the simplest and most obvious yet effective strategies. We recommend that you consider how you might approach the problem from both behavioral and cognitive perspectives. Whatever the theoretical basis for the strategies you choose, it's critically important that you focus on what you want the student to do and that you provide a positive, supportive environment for appropriate behavior. You should ask yourself at least the following questions:

- Have I tried the simplest and most obvious strategies?
- What approaches for helping students change their behavior are most likely to be successful?
- How might I use the five operations of a behavioral approach?
- How can I capitalize on the cognitive and affective aspects of behavior change?
- Is my approach positive and supportive of appropriate behavior?
- Can I use an instructional approach to prevent this behavior problem?

Have I tried the simplest and most obvious strategies?

Amid the demands of teaching and the availability of relatively sophisticated or technical information regarding behavioral change, it's easy to forget that simple, direct approaches can be effective. When simple strategies work, they have the advantage of saving time and energy. They also tend to be more "natural" and may avoid the problems associated with highly technical or "artificial" approaches, including difficulties in implementation and failure to obtain long-term improvement in behavior. They're also easier to explain and defend to parents, administrators, and other teachers.

We're *not* suggesting that you take a simplistic approach to behavior management—an oversimplified view that justifies the use of discredited or unethical strategies (e.g., lecturing, sarcasm, corporal punishment). Many classroom behavior problems are complex and have no simple solution. Experience and research show, however, that such simple things as clear and consistent instructions and other uncomplicated strategies sometimes quickly and effectively resolve seemingly intransigent problems.

Simple things may seem obvious to someone else who's taking a fresh look at a situation, but they're easy to overlook when you're the teacher responsible for managing a difficult child or class. We suggest that before attempting a more complicated or elaborate approach you try to get a fresh look at the problem yourself, through self-questioning and reflection, to see whether a simple strategy might work: What's the simplest, most direct approach I could take to this problem? Have I overlooked an obvious tactic that might work? If I *have* tried a simple, direct strategy, have I implemented it well and consistently?

If a simple approach resolves the problem, you'll have saved a lot of time and energy; if it doesn't, you'll have lost little or nothing. We can't catalog all the simple, direct, and effective strategies teachers might use. Teachers constantly amaze us with their creative but simple, direct solutions to common problems. We can, however, suggest several categories of interventions that are often overlooked. These include instructions, examples, and choices.

When faced with the problem of a student who either does things he or she shouldn't or fails to do what's desired, we believe the simplest, most direct approach a teacher can take is using *instructions*—telling the student what's expected. You may at first think that this approach is unrealistic because the student obviously has been told how to behave. After all, most students who present behavior problems have been talked to quite a lot. Nevertheless, you might reflect on your communication with this student and consider whether you've used instructions in the most effective way:

- ***Have I made the instruction as simple and clear as possible?*** Adults often clutter and complicate their instructions with too much verbiage. Consider the differences between the following: (1) "It's time to get ready to go out to recess, so pick up everything and put it away and get ready to go, because, like I've told you, we're not going to go out to recess until everything's cleaned up and put away where it belongs and you're in your seats." (2) "It's time for recess. Put your things away so we can go."
- ***Have I given the instruction in a clear, firm, non-tentative but polite and non-angry way?*** Adults are more likely to get compliance when they speak as if they expect compliance and treat the student with respect. Questions aren't instructions. For example, "Could you do this problem now?" indicates that you would like the student to do the problem but leaves you vulnerable to the response "No!" An alternative way of expressing your expectation might be "Please try this problem now."
- ***Have I made certain I have the student's full attention before giving the instruction?*** Students sometimes don't follow instructions because they never really "hear" them. Don't make the mistake of assuming that instructions are being received and processed when the student is doing something else or not looking at you when you give them. Sometimes it's helpful to have the student repeat the instruction to make sure it was heard.
- ***Have I given one instruction at a time?*** Sometimes adults are unaware that they're piling instruction upon instruction without waiting for compliance with the first before giving a second. When repeated instructions are given in a short period of time, the student will likely perceive the adult as nagging.
- ***Have I been careful not to give too many different instructions?*** Students often feel they're ordered about constantly. Instructions will be more effective when they're carefully considered and only essential ones are given.
- ***Have I waited a reasonable time for compliance before assuming that the instruction will not be followed?*** It's easy to make the mistake of demanding instantaneous obedience. Giving the student the "room" of a few minutes often avoids noncompliance.
- ***Have I monitored compliance?*** Students with behavior problems often "tune out" adults because they're convinced no one will notice whether they obey. They're accustomed to adults assuming that instructions will be ignored.
- ***Have I provided appropriate consequences for compliance?*** Positive consequences for compliance, perhaps in the form of attention, recognition, or praise, will probably increase the likelihood that your instructions will be followed in the future. Adults often forget that reasonable compliance with instructions is learned—it needs to be rewarded consistently when it's a new behavior for the student, one we hope the student will acquire.

Depending on your responses to these questions, you might want to consider modifying your use of instructions. We haven't exhausted the questions you might ask yourself. You might consider using models (drawing attention to other students who *are* following instructions), self-instruction (giving yourself audible instructions, then following them; asking the student to give himself or herself instructions and follow them), and making compliance with your instructions a kind of "game" (e.g., by interspersing "silly" or humorous instructions with serious ones).

We *don't* suggest that you train students to obey instructions without thinking. Unless students comply with most of the teacher's instructions, however, little learning will take place. Pupils who are highly noncompliant are at a severe disadvantage in school. They frustrate their teachers, but more important, they cut themselves off from many opportunities to learn. Helping students become reasonably compliant with classroom instructions is therefore a critical task of teachers.

Instructions depend on understanding the language used to describe an action or series of actions. People often take for granted that an individual will understand their instructions because they seem simple enough to them. "Oh, just write a little batch file and put it in the root directory" or "Now make sure you reduce the sauce before adding the mushrooms" may seem perfectly clear to some people, but to others these instructions are as dense as Mississippi mud. The person being instructed has a much better chance of doing what's expected if the action is modeled for him or her—that is, if the person is shown how to do it with step-by-step instructions and feedback. The individual might need to be shown repeatedly or might do better if given a chance to practice under supervision before being expected to know what to do the next time he or she hears the instructions.

Examples are simple but indispensable tools in teaching. For some reason, teachers often forget this even when teaching children social and interpersonal behavior. It's easy to forget that the social skills that teachers assume to be second nature are unfamiliar, even mysterious, to some youngsters. "You need to pay attention" may mean little or nothing to many students with serious attention problems. Many of these children must be shown examples of what they typically do when they aren't paying attention and how they might behave if they were paying attention. We and others have found that in teaching students to pay attention to their work it's typically necessary to (1) demonstrate for them the way they behave when they're *not* paying attention (e.g., looking around the room, playing with an object), (2) model for them the kind of behavior involved in paying attention (e.g., reading, writing answers, looking at the teacher when the teacher is talking), and (3) have them practice the behavior involved in paying attention and give them feedback on their performance. Being polite, sharing, waiting your turn, and so on are examples of other types of behavior that some students may not understand without being shown examples.

When instructions aren't working, we suggest that you ask yourself this question: Could I provide an example, model, or demonstration that would make my expectation clearer to this student? Can I show this student step-by-step just how I want him or her to behave? You might reflect further as follows:

• ***Have I provided both correct and incorrect examples and labeled them?*** Examples of desirable or correct behavior are essential. Typically, students will understand better what they're to do if you show them what is *not* correct as well as what *is* correct performance. Correct and incorrect examples must be labeled; that is, you must tell the observing student what is correct and what is incorrect (or appropriate and inappropriate).

• ***Have I demonstrated each step clearly and in sequence?*** Remember that unfamiliar tasks are difficult for most people to learn. The student will likely not acquire the skill you're trying to teach if you fail to give examples that are both clear and complete.

• ***Have I made sure the student is "with" me all the way?*** Watch for lapses in attention or points of confusion. Examples, like instructions, are useless if the student isn't paying close attention or doesn't comprehend what is happening.

• *Have I given corrective feedback when the student makes an error?* Students will learn slowly, or not at all, when they don't receive feedback about how they're doing.

• *Have I maintained a positive instructional atmosphere?* No one likes to be taught by someone who's impatient, uses sarcasm or ridicule, or otherwise causes embarrassment. Be careful to choose a time and place for giving examples that will avoid making the student feel inadequate or humiliated in the peer group. Maintain a supportive, positive attitude and recognize progress, even if it's slight.

Examples or models provided by the teacher can be extremely effective teaching. In addition, the models of behavior provided by peers can be extremely influential. We discuss peer models further in Chapter 6. Suffice it to say here that showing students how you want them to behave is a simple but often effective means of teaching. It's a strategy that's been used by master teachers in all fields for thousands of years.

One of the simplest but frequently overlooked techniques for managing problem behavior is giving people *choices.* Not only children in classrooms but also individuals in all kinds of social situations are likely to behave more constructively when they perceive that they have the power to make choices that are important to them. Conversely, people often behave badly when they feel "boxed in," perceiving that they have no choices. Students are likely to be less resistant to their teachers' instructions and control when they can choose certain features of their instruction or classroom environment. The savvy teacher is careful about the choices students are allowed to make for themselves.

Many teachers have found that students show less resistance to classroom demands and exhibit more appropriate classroom behavior when students are allowed to choose among several academic tasks, all of which are acceptable. For example, a student might be allowed to choose one of the following spelling tasks rather than being told which one he or she must complete:

1. Write each of 20 spelling words three times.
2. Write all 20 words one time in alphabetical order.
3. Look up and write the definitions for 15 words, and give the dictionary page number for 5 words.
4. Create 20 sentences, each using one of the spelling words.

Inventive teachers can find numerous alternatives to nearly any assignment, all of which have instructional value; allow a difficult student to choose the one he or she prefers (Kauffman & Landrum, 2009a).

Too few choices breed resentment and resistance to authority. Too many choices induce a kind of paralysis, leaving a person frustrated and unable to make a decision. For obvious reasons, some individuals shouldn't be allowed to make certain choices. We know that if some individuals are given certain choices, they're highly likely to make very bad ones. The teacher, then, is faced with this question: For a given individual, how many choices—and which ones—are appropriate?

Master teachers understand that choices must be structured for students to prevent catastrophic consequences and to foster interest and personal responsibility. That is, teachers can't allow students to make choices that will close off future options (e.g., deciding not to attend school or not to complete assigned work). On the other hand, teachers must try to encourage students to make wise choices and to present options that will heighten students' interest, satisfaction, and judgment. This requires helping students understand and be able to predict the consequences of their choices and constructing appropriate options in situations in which students haven't ordinarily had them.

Students sometimes make choices in situations that you can't control or structure. Under such circumstances, you can only try to help students make good choices. Our point is that *constructing* options is a simple strategy that can be used very creatively and often successfully to manage behavior.

The kinds of options we're referring to may appear to some teachers to be trivial, but to students they may be significant. They may involve such simple choices as which assignment or problem to do first, what color paper or pen to use, or where to sit for a particular activity. Students might be allowed to choose one of two or more tangible rewards or special activities when they've earned it or choose a friend with whom to work. When teaching, and especially when teaching a "difficult" student, you would be wise to ask yourself the following questions.

  • *What appropriate new options can I give this student?*   There are nearly always new choices that a student might be allowed, thereby increasing the student's stake in the classroom activity.
  • *Do I know that I can live with the choice the student makes?*   Be careful not to construct an option that's intolerable or unacceptable.
  • *Have I constructed an array of options that's consistent with the student's developmental level?*   The student's age, preferences, and decision-making abilities are important to take into consideration. The number and nature of options must be matched to the student's interests and ability to make choices.

What approaches for helping students change their behavior are most likely to be successful?

Teachers have many choices for approaching behavior management problems. More skillful behavior managers are aware of more options and able to make better choices among them. Regardless of the number of alternative approaches you may know about, it's important to be able to articulate your reasons for choosing one approach rather than another. Following are the primary questions we suggest you ask yourself when considering a particular approach.

  • *Is this approach consistent with professional practices?*   Teachers' practices must always reflect sound professional judgment. The fact that a particular approach has been used or suggested by other teachers doesn't necessarily mean that it's appropriate. Teachers must studiously avoid practices that are prohibited by law or school policy and those that are questionable on ethical grounds.
  • *Does my own experience or that of colleagues suggest that this approach might be effective?*   Teachers themselves are often good judges of what is and what isn't likely to work with a given class or student. We caution that some teachers find it easy to reject useful suggestions out-of-hand based on their personal biases; some cling to approaches that are familiar to them but are not very successful. Nevertheless, the judgment of highly skilled teachers must be viewed as an important test of the value of any suggested approach.
  • *What technical assistance can I find for helping me implement this approach?*   Guidance from colleagues, consultants, technical manuals, or professional publications is often a critical factor in determining whether an approach is successful. Trying to implement procedures on a seat-of-the-pants basis often leads to disappointment and sometimes to mistaken judgment about the value or workability of the approach. Some approaches are failures, even when skillfully implemented; some are failures because their implementation was flawed. When you select an approach to a problem, make sure you use it skillfully.
  • *What empirical research supports this approach?* In our view, support from empirical research should be a critical factor in selecting an approach to behavior management. Testimonial evidence alone ("I tried this, and it works!" or "I don't believe it's ever effective, because I've never been able to make it work!") doesn't seem to us as reliable as teachers' opinions that are supported by evidence obtained in carefully controlled research studies. Because we take the position that accumulated evidence from empirical research is the single best criterion for selecting strategies,

we describe approaches based on the research literatures of behavioral psychology and social learning, particularly as they apply to the classroom.

How might I use the five operations of a behavioral approach?

Research in behavioral psychology has produced a wide range of techniques for changing human behavior. Here, we briefly describe only five basic operations that provide the core strategies for building all others (Alberto & Troutman, 2009; Cullinan, 2007; Kerr & Nelson, 2010; Landrum & Kauffman, 2006; Walker, Colvin, & Gresham, 2004). With an understanding of these basic operations, teachers are able to create sound techniques for intervening to increase or decrease specific behaviors. We refer to "operations" because we are discussing "operant" behavior—actions that "operate" in the environment to produce certain outcomes. The operations we describe are ways of modifying the social environment so that specific behaviors will produce predictable consequences.

The five operations we describe here are all based on the principle that the events immediately following a behavior—its consequences—determine to a large extent how likely it is to occur again. Positive and negative reinforcement involve using consequences to *increase* the probability or rate of a behavior; extinction and punishment, whether by response cost or by presenting aversives, involve using consequences to *decrease* the probability or rate of a behavior. Each of these operations has advantages and disadvantages, and some should be used more frequently than others. In most classroom situations, teachers' interventions will involve combinations of operations.

POSITIVE REINFORCEMENT   Positive reinforcement is the staple of good behavior management, and it is a concept with which most teachers are familiar. It means that when the student behaves in a specific, desirable way, the consequence(s) will be positive—something the individual student is willing to work to obtain. Positive reinforcement has the effect of increasing the behavior that produces such consequences. Providing rewards for appropriate behavior is extremely simple in principle, but putting positive reinforcement into practice in ways that are effective and self-enhancing for the student sometimes requires great creativity and finesse on the part of the teacher. Teachers are sometimes unsuccessful in using positive reinforcement because they neglect the fine points that are critical in using the operation effectively. Following are questions you need to ask yourself if you wish to use positive reinforcement to increase the behavior you would like to see a student exhibit more frequently.

• *Am I sure the consequences I'm using are positive reinforcers (rewards) for this student?* Not everyone finds the same consequences reinforcing; what is rewarding for one person may not be for another. To use positive reinforcement successfully, you have to provide a consequence that's attractive to the particular student whose behavior you are trying to improve. Finding the right consequence is sometimes difficult. It must not only be something attractive to the student, but you must be able to control access to it. You might consider several categories of potential reinforcers:

1. Social reinforcers such as attention, praise, touching (these are among the most natural reinforcers, but they don't work for every student)
2. Activity reinforcers such as talking with friends, reading, playing a game or sport, caring for pets, tutoring a peer, playing a musical instrument, working at the computer, watching a video (this category is nearly inexhaustible for the creative teacher and might be seen as only slightly more artificial than social reinforcers)
3. Tangible reinforcers such as edibles, toys, clothing, money, or any type of token that has no inherent value but can be exchanged for other desired reinforcers (tangibles are often considered highly artificial reinforcers)

You might identify reinforcers by asking a student what he or she is willing to work for, by observing the student's preferences, or simply by trying out things you think might work. The ultimate test of whether a consequence is a positive reinforcer for a given individual is whether he or she will work to get it. Bear in mind, however, that you can offer a potential reinforcer in ways that will make it useless (i.e., that destroy its appeal). If you require too much work for earning a reward, if you offer the reward in too small or too large an amount, or if you are inconsistent in providing the reinforcer, for example, you may be unsuccessful. Finally, sometimes students receive consequences that appear to be punishing, not reinforcing, yet they continue to behave inappropriately. In many cases, some aspect of the apparent punishment, perhaps the attention or the emotional behavior of adults who are upset, is actually a rewarding consequence for misbehavior that outweighs the intended punishment.

• *Does getting the reinforcer depend on the student's exhibiting the appropriate behavior?* Reinforcers are typically useless unless they're made contingent on the behavior you want to increase. "Contingent" means that the reward is available when, and only when, the expected behavior is exhibited. If the reinforcer is given without the student behaving as expected, then the he or she is unlikely to be motivated to earn it; "earning it" means that it's not available until after the appropriate behavior is exhibited. Teachers often experience failure in attempts to reward students' appropriate behavior with attention because they fail to respond differently to desirable conduct and misbehavior. When students get attention—either positive or negative—regardless of how they behave, they're unlikely to learn to behave as you would like them to. If you can't control when the student has access to the reinforcer, then you probably can't use it to improve behavior. You must attempt to use reinforcers that are under your control—things you can regulate.

• *Is the reinforcer available soon after the student performs the appropriate behavior?* Much of behavior is controlled by immediate consequences. Smoking and overeating are common examples in which, even for many successful and well-adjusted adults, immediate positive consequences take precedence over long-term negative consequences. As people develop psychologically, they're able to tolerate greater delays in gratification and are controlled to a greater extent by long-term consequences in most areas of their lives. Young children and those whose psychological development is lagging, however, typically won't respond to rewards that are delayed for more than a few seconds. Many teachers underestimate the importance of immediacy in using positive reinforcement effectively. Often, finding a way to decrease the interval between appropriate behavior and reward will be key to making positive reinforcement effective. Remember, too, that for many students the behavior that is rewarded is the one that occurs immediately prior to their receiving a reward. Regardless of what you intend to reward, the reinforcer will likely strengthen whatever behavior the student has just exhibited. We offer this caution: be very mindful of the timing of your reinforcement.

• *Am I providing an appropriate unit of reward for the expected unit of behavior?* Reinforcers are, in effect, like wages; they must be fair and effective compensation for performance. Fairness isn't necessarily judged by what's typical. It's far more complicated than that. Perhaps the best way of determining what's fair is negotiating it with the student. Especially with young and developmentally delayed students and especially when the student is learning a new skill, we recommend that you require only a little performance for reinforcement. Frequent small rewards are typically more effective than infrequent large rewards.

• *Is the reinforcer a "natural" consequence or at least paired with one?* "Natural" reinforcers are those that exist, or should exist, in a humane environment and that effectively influence the behavior of most individuals. Most people agree that praise, recognition, and healthy recreational activities are natural reinforcers. "Artificial" reinforcers are those contrived for special purposes when natural consequences have failed (e.g., token systems in classrooms designed to remediate serious behavior problems). Natural reinforcers are preferred because they're likely to maintain behavior after artificial incentives are withdrawn. Artificial reinforcers are sometimes critical to initial success in changing behavior, and they shouldn't be shunned when they're necessary. For example, food or toys or tokens or some other tangible rewards might be necessary at first. When they're used, however, they should be paired with (i.e., delivered concurrently with) more natural rewards. For example, social attention, such as praise, should nearly always be given along with tangible reinforcement. In this way, with time, natural consequences are likely to take on some of the power of artificial incentives.

   • *Am I careful to respect entitlements?* One of the more difficult ethical and legal issues involving positive reinforcement is the question of the conditions and privileges to which students are entitled regardless of how they behave. People may disagree about whether every student has a fundamental right or entitlement to certain activities (e.g., recess, all classroom privileges) or whether they may be made contingent on a standard of classroom conduct. Activities and privileges that are considered entitlements can't be made contingent on desired behavior and thus can't be used as rewards. We can't draw the boundaries of classroom entitlements for you; we can only urge you to be aware of the issues and take precautions against ethical and legal questions being raised. One precaution is making sure that your principal approves of any program that involves making any "standard" activity contingent on a student's behavior. Another precaution is using *additional* activities or privileges beyond those granted routinely to all students as reinforcers whenever feasible. A final precaution is reviewing the conditions of your students' lives from the perspective that every student has the right to be treated fairly and equitably and to receive recognition and rewards for appropriate behavior.

   A problem that most teachers anticipate, and many experience, is the claim of entitlement to reinforcement by a student who hasn't behaved appropriately. That is, a student may deny that he or she hasn't met the criterion for reward or may argue that he or she should receive the same reward as another student. In some cases, teachers become so weary of the carping of students who haven't earned rewards that they eliminate special contingencies for students or groups with special needs. Some teachers become so frustrated by claims of entitlement that they conclude that positive reinforcement simply isn't worth the hassle. When teachers abandon positive reinforcement contingencies because of this problem, then students are winning a contest of wills, but both they and their teacher are losing opportunities for more constructive interactions.

   We have three suggestions for responding to inappropriate student claims of entitlement. First, you should be certain that every student in your class has a reasonable opportunity to earn frequent, meaningful rewards. Students' complaints sometimes mean that the opportunities for reward are simply too few, and you may need to alter your reward system accordingly. If rewards are scarce and given disproportionately, students may have a legitimate complaint. If the same contingencies don't apply to everyone, you may need to explain briefly and in simple language that different students need and earn different rewards.

   Second, you shouldn't become embroiled in arguments or long discussions about rewards. If you're confident that the reward system is fair to everyone in the class, then you have no need to offer repeated justifications or respond to nagging. Let one simple explanation of why the reward is given suffice; ignore further complaints.

   Finally, teachers should commit to memory the suggestions of Ginger Rhode, Bill Jenson, and Ken Reavis about how to make positive reinforcement work, using the mnemonic IFEED-AV as a reminder (Rhode, Jenson, & Reavis, 1998; see also Kauffman & Brigham, 2009). If you want to be successful in using positive reinforcement, make sure that you give it as *Immediately* after desirable behavior as possible, give it *Frequently,* show *Enthusiasm* for the student's behavior and the reinforcement, make *Eye contact* with the student when you deliver the reinforcement, *Describe* simply and clearly what the student has done to earn the reinforcement, build the student's *Anticipation* of earning the reinforcement, and provide *Variety* in the reinforcements the student can earn.

NEGATIVE REINFORCEMENT   The term *negative reinforcement* is frequently misunderstood to mean punishment. The term actually means reinforcing (strengthening) behavior by removing or preventing something unpleasant. That is, negative reinforcement strengthens whatever behavior allows the individual to escape or avoid a negative consequence. An everyday example may help to clarify how negative reinforcement works. Normally, people take analgesics to remove (escape from) pain; taking such pills when you're in pain is a behavior maintained by negative reinforcement.

But negative and positive reinforcement can also occur together and provide a "double whammy." Consider seat belts. People buckle their seat belts to avoid a negative consequence—injury or death; buckling up is a behavior that is negatively reinforced because it removes fear but also by positive reinforcement, because it brings a feeling of safety and perhaps praise by others. Students may study for a test at least in part to avoid negative consequences such as embarrassment or a low grade. But studying may be maintained in part by both negative reinforcement (avoidance of failure) and positive reinforcement (getting a good grade or learning privileges as well as—we always hope—the intrinsic satisfaction of learning).

Ordinarily, negative reinforcement shouldn't be a *prominent* part of classroom behavior management for two reasons. First, negative reinforcement relies on the presence or threat of negative (aversive) consequences. Although some negative consequences or their threat are an unavoidable part of everyday existence, including a reasonably demanding learning environment, good teaching and management don't rely primarily on threats. Second, deliberate negative reinforcement sets the stage for coercion—the use of force or intimidation to achieve one's objectives. A coercive relationship is one in which both parties vie for control by increasing the level of pain or discomfort of the other, as we discussed in Chapter 3. Whoever wins the contest is negatively reinforced; the losing party withdraws his or her pressure, providing negative reinforcement for the winner. Coercion is, unfortunately, a part of the family life of many students with behavior problems. To make coercion a part of their school experience adds insult to injury.

When devising a behavior management program, ask yourself the following questions about negative reinforcement: What part does negative reinforcement play in my students' motivation to learn and behave appropriately? Can I rely more on positive reinforcement and less on negative reinforcement to motivate my students? Am I becoming engaged in coercive interactions—power struggles—with my students? Power struggles are sometimes difficult, if not impossible to avoid. Nevertheless, they're a sign that your behavior management strategies need close scrutiny and possibly revision.

EXTINCTION   One way of eliminating behavior, whether desirable or undesirable, is to eliminate its reinforcement—an operation called *extinction.* When a behavior no longer produces the desired effect (positive or negative reinforcement), it will eventually fade away (be extinguished). Using an extinction procedure assumes that you can identify the reinforcer for the behavior you're trying to eliminate and that you can terminate the reinforcer. The concept of extinction is indispensable in a behavioral approach to classroom management, but the procedure is never appropriate as a *sole* strategy.

Extinction has two major disadvantages as the primary focus of an approach for reducing problem behavior. First, it's a slow process, especially for a behavior pattern that's become well established. Second, when an extinction procedure is first implemented, the behavior is likely to become worse before it starts to improve. When people don't get what they have come to expect as a consequence of their behavior, they first try harder to produce the usual result. For example, if a child is used to getting what he or she wants by throwing temper tantrums, his or her tantrums will at first become more severe when adults place them on extinction (i.e., resolutely refuse to give in to them). Furthermore, extinction by itself is of little value. It does little or nothing, without reinforcement for desirable conduct, to improve behavior.

The central feature of a skillful behavioral approach is a combination of shifting reinforcement away from undesirable behavior (i.e., extinction) and toward desirable behavior (i.e., positive reinforcement). The critical concept in the approach is making sure that students receive ample positive reinforcement—but only, or at least overwhelmingly, for behavior that's appropriate (see Kauffman & Brigham, 2009; Kerr & Nelson, 2010). When using extinction, the following are important questions to ask yourself.

• *Have I identified and effectively terminated reinforcement of the undesirable behavior?* Occasional reinforcement during extinction is likely to make the behavior even worse. Try to make sure that you keep the behavior from resulting *any* time in its former consequence.

• *Am I offering strong positive reinforcement for alternative appropriate behavior?* Remember, positive reinforcement for the behavior you want to encourage is a key to making extinction work.

RESPONSE COST PUNISHMENT   Like negative reinforcement, punishment is often misunderstood. Punishment does *not* necessarily mean causing pain, either physical pain or serious psychological distress. Punishment means providing a consequence that decreases the likelihood that a behavior will be repeated. True, punishment may involve causing physical or psychological distress, but the punishment procedures that are most effective for most individuals don't cause such trauma. The most effective punishment typically involves withholding or withdrawing a positive reinforcer contingent on a specific misbehavior. Punishment of this kind means that misbehavior "costs" something, hence the term **response cost**. It may mean the loss of money (i.e., a fine) or other possession or the withdrawal of a privilege (e.g., loss of a specific amount of time for television viewing, recess, or another valued activity).

Punishment of any kind, including response cost, can be abusive if it's excessive or capricious. Nevertheless, it appears that rearing children who are reasonably socialized and maintaining a humane social structure require the judicious use of punishing as well as positively reinforcing consequences. In fact, punishment is inevitable; it should just be done wisely (see Kauffman & Brigham, 2009; Kazdin, 2008; Newsom & Kroeger, 2005). When you're contemplating or evaluating the use of punishment, ask yourself the following questions.

• *Have I made every effort to use positive procedures to manage this student's behavior?* Punishment should never be your first resort. Consider it only after you've devised a behavior management scheme that emphasizes positive consequences for desirable conduct.

• *Am I generally positive toward my students, giving frequent praise and other forms of positive attention to them when their behavior is appropriate?* Punishment is most effective when it comes from people who are typically warm and loving toward the individual when his or her behavior is acceptable. If you're generally irritable or negative toward a student, your attempts to punish are likely to backfire. Punishment is most effective when it represents a stark contrast to the typical interactions between teacher and student.

• *Am I able to administer punishment matter-of-factly, without a display of anger and without nagging, threats, or moralizing (trying to induce guilt through sermonizing or shaming)?* Displays of anger and lectures that accompany punishment will almost certainly have exactly the opposite effect you intend. Repeated warnings are actually nagging or threats, which are counterproductive. If you're going to give a warning before punishing, give only one. After the student has been punished, don't lecture him or her; pick up classroom activities as if nothing had happened and emphasize positive consequences for appropriate behavior. Punishment should ultimately be designed simply to help students make better choices; it needs to be *educative* (Walker & Fecser, 2007).

• *Is the punishment immediate, fair, and consistent?* Delaying punishment, like delaying reinforcement, reduces its effectiveness. Effective punishment is reasonable—not trivial, but not out of proportion to the seriousness of the offense. And predictability is a critical feature of effective punishment. The student must know what behavior will result in punishment, and the punishment should be consistently applied for that behavior.

• *Does the punishment quickly produce behavioral change?* Effective punishment doesn't take a long time to work. If a change in behavior for the better isn't quickly apparent (after it is administered a few times), you should revise or discontinue it. It's better not to punish at all than to persist in ineffective punishment (which is abuse). Punishing more severely is seldom the answer. Changing the nature of the consequence or making punishment more immediate or consistent is more likely to produce good results.

• *Have I communicated my punishment procedures to all concerned parties?* The student(s), parents, and your school administrators should know what punishment procedures you intend to use. Your best insurance against legal entanglements and unprofessional conduct is to keep concerned parties fully informed and your procedures open to inspection by others.

PUNISHMENT BY PRESENTING AVERSIVES   Punishment may be accomplished in one of two ways, by either withdrawing valued commodities (as described in response cost) or by presenting aversive consequences such as reprimands, isolation, or noxious stimuli. Using noxious or painful consequences places the teacher in extremely dangerous territory, both legally and ethically, and our advice is to steer well clear of using them. Don't use corporal punishment. However, reprimands and *brief* social isolation may be appropriate when used carefully and skillfully along with the positive procedures we have discussed. All the questions and caveats we offered in our discussion of response cost apply as well to presenting aversive consequences. In addition, consider the following regarding reprimands.

• *Do I keep my reprimands brief and to-the-point?* Lectures and general criticisms tend to be wasted words, if not inducements to further misbehavior. "Randy, stop talking to Rachel" is preferable to "Randy, I've told you I simply won't tolerate this kind of behavior, and I want you to stop it right now and pay attention to your work. Now shape up!"

• *Do I keep my reprimands as private as possible?* Private reprimands are those given so that few, if any, of the student's peers can hear what is being said. Public reprimands are those that nearly everyone in the class can hear. Private reprimands, for which the teacher goes to the student and speaks quietly but firmly, are usually most effective. Public reprimands may sometimes be necessary, but more is lost than gained when the teacher uses primarily loud, public criticism or rebuke.

• *Do I make sure I have the student's attention and attempt to get eye contact before reprimanding?* Like instructions, reprimands will be ineffective if they're delivered to a student who is otherwise occupied. Use the student's name. Look directly at the student when speaking and use a direct, firm, but not angry tone of voice. There should be no misunderstanding about the fact that you're displeased with the student's behavior, but you shouldn't be visibly upset.

Brief social isolation is sometimes referred to as a **time-out**. Nearly every teacher is familiar with the term, yet many teachers misuse the procedure in attempts to punish misbehavior. The technical meaning of a time-out is *time out from positive reinforcement.* That is, it means an interval during which positive reinforcement can't be obtained. The implication is that positive reinforcement is readily available, except when the individual is in a time-out. As such, a time-out does not *necessarily* require physical isolation; it may not involve removal of the student from the group, only a period during which the student will be ignored or not allowed to earn the typical rewards for appropriate behavior. It may, however, involve placing the student for a brief period in a place where he or she is unable to interact freely with others and obtain attention and other positive reinforcers. When a time-out involves placing a student in a separate room, it becomes a highly controversial procedure and one that's easily abused. We recommend that you do *not* use any such isolation procedure without the explicit approval of your school administrator and the student's parents and with consultation from a professional with extensive experience in appropriate use of the procedure. Brief social isolation of a less radical nature, such as having the student "sit out" of a game or move to another seat in the classroom, is less risky. Even with this kind of time-out procedure, however, you should be sure to keep our previous questions and cautions regarding punishment in mind.

In addition, remember that longer time-outs aren't typically more effective than shorter ones. The *maximum* effective time-out period usually isn't more than five minutes. To use a time-out appropriately, you'll need a timer to signal when the time-out period has ended; you must *not* allow yourself to forget the student in a time-out. Finally, recall that a time-out means *time-out from positive reinforcement*, not merely a time out of the classroom or time out of your sight. Attempts to use a time-out often fail for one of two reasons: (1) the "time in" environment offers little positive reinforcement, so being excluded from it isn't punishing, or (2) the "time-out" environment is one in which the student obtains unintended reinforcement. The latter is often the case when the student is placed in a hallway or office, where interesting observations of and interactions with others are typically available.

A NOTE ON CORPORAL PUNISHMENT   Spanking, hitting, or otherwise punishing students physically still has its proponents. Depending on where you live, your school system's policies, and your own upbringing or thoughts on punishment, you may find justification for some form(s) of corporal punishment. The idea of corporal punishment is alive and well, as reported by the American Civil Liberties Union (2009) and the controversy on the topic carried by newspapers in their Dear Abby feature in March, 2009. Something's being alive and well does not attest to its virtue. *We can't overemphasize our view that we believe corporal punishment is not only unjustified but counterproductive.* We know that people offer many justifications for corporal punishment, but we think none of them is convincing. We realize that we are all human beings who become frustrated and may have relied on some form of corporal punishment when we shouldn't have, but that is reason for neither guilt nor for using corporal punishment again. We agree with Kazdin (2008) that punishment is unavoidable in child rearing, but that nonviolent (noncorporal) punishment is always a better choice, the wiser way to discipline children in the long run.

How can I capitalize on the cognitive and affective aspects of behavior change?

A behavioral approach provides anchor points for devising specific management techniques. The five operations and combinations and variations of them are a core that enables teachers to plan explicit strategies. Nevertheless, the nuances of behavior management require that you also approach students as thinking, feeling individuals. In fact, if you ignore the way students think and feel about their behavior and about your management techniques, you're going to be ineffective.

Sensitivity to meanings and emotions is required for effective behavior management. Next, we briefly highlight the importance of cognitive and affective aspects in talking with students, choosing consequences for students, teaching self-control, and teaching social skills.

TALKING WITH STUDENTS   In Chapter 6, we elaborate on the importance of teachers' verbalizations to students. Here, we merely wish to point out that your success with the strategies we've discussed may well depend on how you use them (see Kerr & Nelson, 2010). Students' understanding of contingencies and their emotional responses to them will be determined in part simply by what the teacher says and how she or he says it. Words and tones that convey a positive attitude, respect for the student, self-confidence, and firm expectations that the student will behave appropriately will make a significant difference in the probability of success. What really matters to students? How do they feel about important aspects of school and the classroom? It should seldom be the case that a student can say, "No one ever asked me."

CHOOSING CONSEQUENCES FOR STUDENTS' BEHAVIOR   "Different strokes for different folks" is a cliché that applies to selecting effective reinforcing and punishing consequences. Sensitivity to the student's preferences, which can be obtained only through careful observation and listening, is essential in choosing consequences of behavior that will have the desired effect. Talking with students about their behavior and its consequences is necessary. Nevertheless, talking is not enough. Watching and listening with understanding sometimes reveal that students' words don't reflect their true feelings. Many a student has fooled a teacher by saying, "I don't care." Sometimes verbal bravado masks real feelings; sometimes it doesn't. How can you tell what a student *really* feels about something? Perhaps another cliché will help: "Actions speak louder than words."

TEACHING SELF-CONTROL PROCEDURES   The ultimate goal of good behavior management is to help students learn to control their own behavior in self-enhancing ways. As we discuss in Chapter 6, teaching self-control is intimately connected to talking with students about their behavior. It's a way of getting them actively involved, cognitively and effectively, in their own self-growth.

TEACHING SOCIAL SKILLS   Some students acquire social skills easily. They don't seem to require explicit instruction in order to learn the patterns of social interaction that teachers consider acceptable. As is the case with academic skills, however, some students don't learn the critical social skills as easily as other students. Students who need a more explicit instructional program for learning social skills must be helped to think through the demands of social situations and their own options for dealing with everyday interpersonal problems (Darch & Kame'enui, 2004; Lane, 2004). The teacher must help these students become cognitively aware of others' expectations, their choices in responding to those expectations, and the probable outcomes of making given choices.

Finally, it's important that you try to understand how your students feel about the conditions of their lives, both in school and out of school. Your knowing how a misbehaving student feels won't, in itself, change the student's behavior, nor will it necessarily enable you to resolve the behavior problem by other means. Understanding the student's feelings will, however, improve your chances of developing a helpful relationship with the student. A helpful relationship is one in which the student is open to positive influence through your listening, talking, and providing consequences. A student is more likely to be open to positive influence by a teacher whose behavior indicates awareness of the student's feelings.

Our belief is that students' cognitive and affective changes generally follow their behavioral changes, although thoughts and feelings sometimes determine how a student behaves. Attempts to change students' feelings and patterns of thinking in the hope that these changes alone will be followed by behavioral improvement are, in our judgment, not very likely to be successful. Thus our prediction is that your best bet for helping students understand and feel better about themselves will be to put your primary effort into helping them change their behavior for the better, with secondary emphasis on affective and cognitive changes related to their behavior. Of course, the goal of teaching is to accomplish improvements in both behavioral and cognitive-affective domains. The following are questions to ask yourself: Where do I begin? Where do I put my greatest emphasis? How do I view the relationship between what students do and how they think and feel about what they do?

Building helpful relationships with students requires both technical skills in using the operations of a behavioral approach and the ability to see events through the eyes and minds of pupils. Understanding the rage, loneliness, self-congratulations, suspicion, sadness, joy, or other emotions of the individual student is desirable in itself because it enables you to relate to that student as another human being (See Cantrell & Cantrell, 2007). More important for you as a teacher, perhaps, such understanding might help you plan and thus make better choices about the way you talk to the student and the way you construct expectations and consequences in the classroom.

Is my approach positive and supportive of appropriate behavior?

In any attempt to modify behavior, you should reflect on the extent to which your approach emphasizes positive consequences for appropriate behavior. Negative reinforcement, extinction, and perhaps even punishment (within the guidelines we have suggested) may be justified as part of a management scheme. However, unless your approach is *overwhelmingly* positive and supportive of appropriate behavior, we feel it is professionally and ethically questionable. Remember that the positive support of behavior characterizes a successful school, and it should characterize your classroom (see Kauffman, 2010). Teachers need to ask themselves questions about their own behavior in the classroom and take action accordingly.

• *How frequently do I offer praise or other positive evaluations (e.g., smiles, pats, approval) of my students' appropriate behavior?* Most teachers overestimate their positive interactions with students. You may want to keep a tally of your positive and negative responses to students during specified periods for several days to see just what your ratio of positive to negative is. Yes, it's possible to overdo praise statements, but few teachers are in any danger of doing so. No, it's not enough just to make many positive statements and show approval to students; your positive attention must be contingent on the type of behavior you want your students to exhibit. Make sure that inappropriate behavior receives no rewarding consequences from you.

• *Do I ignore most minor misbehavior?* One of the most difficult behavior management strategies for most teachers is putting minor misbehavior on extinction—simply ignoring it and focusing attention on desirable behavior. It's very easy to fall into the trap of giving negative attention to minor misbehavior that results in inadvertent reinforcement of it. Attention—even negative attention in the form of reprimands—can be a positive reinforcer, particularly when a student seldom receives positive attention. Some misbehavior can't be ignored because it's dangerous or too disruptive. But most of the minor disruptions and irritating behavior we see in classrooms are best treated as if they didn't happen. No one can give you an exact formula for when and what to ignore and when and what *not* to ignore. Becoming a good judge of exactly what and when to ignore is an important aspect of becoming a master teacher.

• *Do I emphasize positive outcomes of desirable behavior rather than avoidance of negative consequences for inadequate performance?* The distinction between positive and negative reinforcement is subtle but important. Positive reinforcement induces a student to approach the teacher; negative reinforcement is based on avoidance. To the greatest extent possible, your behavior management strategies should be based on motivation to obtain rewarding consequences, not avoid unpleasantness. Unfortunately, the March 30, 2009, *Non Sequitur* cartoon drawn by Wiley Miller illustrated what too often happens in classrooms. The little girl, Danae, is asked by her father what she learned in school. She says she learned that good behavior makes you invisible. Make sure that's not what students are learning in your class.

• *Am I able to avoid getting drawn into power struggles and other forms of negative interactions with students?* Some students with behavior problems are masters at drawing adults into arguments and verbal power struggles—struggles that they typically win. Whatever you say, they will question. Before you know it, you're engaged in an argument and feeling emotionally upset, usually about something that in retrospect seems silly. Becoming aware immediately that you're being drawn in and terminating the interaction before it turns into a power struggle is an important skill for dealing with difficult students. In part, avoiding power struggles involves the recognition that you're responsible for your choices as a teacher and students are responsible for theirs.

• *Do students like being in my classroom?* One important test of whether your behavior management strategies are appropriate is whether students have generally positive feelings about your classroom. Successful schools, as Kauffman (2010) points out, are places kids like to be; so are successful classrooms. Certainly, you shouldn't expect that students will never express unhappiness with you or the demands you make of them. Good teachers care about much more than their popularity with students. Nevertheless, if over a reasonable period of time students obviously don't like being in your classroom, you're probably not meeting their needs in a professionally defensible way.

• *Are my students learning academic and social skills at a level commensurate with their abilities?* For the competent teacher, students' good feelings aren't enough. Students must make progress in acquiring the academic and social skills that are self-enhancing and that give them increased options in important areas of their lives.

Can I use an instructional approach to prevent this behavior problem?

Too often teachers fail to see that social behavior can be taught and that an effective *instructional* program is crucial for classroom deportment, just as it is for the development of academic skills. Behavior management is often simply reactive (responding to misbehavior after it occurs) rather than proactive (preparing a program to teach desired behavior so that the misbehavior does not occur). During the past decade, researchers at the University of Oregon have been particularly adept at explaining how to *teach* appropriate behavior. Here, we provide a brief explanation of the *precorrection* teaching strategy that we introduced in Chapter 4. Then we suggest strategies for managing the phases of the acting-out cycle depicted in Figure 4.2.

PRECORRECTING PROBLEMS   Precorrection requires the teacher to specify the problem—to define precisely what the student does that is predictable but unacceptable. It also requires the teacher to describe the context in which this behavior is highly likely. The **context** is the set of circumstances under which the behavior is predictable. The rationale is that if you can predict the circumstances under which a student will make a mistake (be it academic or social), then you can teach the student how to avoid the mistake and do what's expected. This means that it isn't enough merely to say what is unacceptable behavior; it's essential to say, in addition, what *is* expected instead (a matter that's easy to forget in the heat of working with a difficult student). Then, the problem is this: How can the context be modified to help the student avert the mistake and do what's expected?

The precorrection strategy is both anticipatory and instructional. The teacher may think it through in this way: In this context (perhaps a transition from one activity to another, during which Fred must move from one place in the classroom to another), this behavior is highly predictable (perhaps Fred's teasing another student). Here's the behavior I expect (perhaps that Fred will mind his own business while going through the transition). And here's the way I can modify the context to make the behavior I expect more likely to occur (perhaps by specifying a particular route for Fred to take, clarifying my expectations for behavior during transitions, and giving Fred special recognition for doing what I expect).

Teaching generally involves not only instructions about what's expected but also rehearsals, prompts, and rewards for correct performance. Clearly stated expectations are essential, as we have discussed in previous chapters. But many students have to have more than that if they're going to learn. They may have to practice the correct response under close supervision. This may involve the students actually doing the expected behavior or mentally rehearsing what they're supposed to do, step by step. Most teachers easily get the hang of helping students go through academic problems in a step-by-step fashion; athletic coaches have long understood that this is critically important. Yet, when it comes to social behavior, teachers often seem to forget the principles of rehearsing, prompting, and rewarding.

For Fred, the precorrection plan might involve a mini-lesson in which the teacher explains the route from point A to point B that he's to take and the expected behavior: "Mind your own business on the way, which means don't get involved with anybody else along the way, hands to yourself, mouth closed." Rehearsal could involve either talking through the expected routine or actually showing Fred what you expect him to do and then having him practice it a time or two while you watch and give him feedback. Prompts could involve giving Fred a hand signal or perhaps handing him a brief written reminder just before the transition. Strong reinforcement could be given by allowing Fred to earn a special privilege after he has a string of several successive days of appropriate transition behavior. Monitoring could mean just keeping a simple log indicating whether Fred behaved as expected (perhaps just a plus or minus noted on the teacher's calendar).

The precorrection strategy may be used with an individual student or with a group of students. Figure 5.1 shows a completed precorrection checklist and plan for a student, Jimmy. Remember that each part of the plan is an essential element in teaching desired behavior. Key questions in using the strategy are the following:

• ***Can I identify the context in which a predictable problem occurs?*** The context is the where and when. It's the situation or circumstance in which predictable behavior occurs.

• ***Have I specified the expected behavior?*** Can you describe what you want the student to do instead of the predictable behavior? Both you and the student(s) must be very clear about just what you want.

• ***How can I modify the context to make the expected behavior more likely to occur?*** Look for ways to change the situation, circumstance, or condition to make the predictable behavior less likely and the expected behavior more likely to occur.

• ***What is the best way I can help the student(s) rehearse the expected behavior?*** Think through and offer opportunities for the student(s) to practice. They will need a dry run, a tryout, a little drill to get the hang of it.

Teacher: <u>Pat Puller</u>   **Student:** <u>Jimmy Ott (6th grade)</u>   **Date:** <u>Oct. 11</u>

1. **Context** (where and when; situations, circumstances, or conditions in which predictable behavior occurs)

   Upon entering the classroom in the morning, where at least one other student is in the room

   Predictable Behavior (the error or misbehavior that you can anticipate in the context)

   Jimmy describes his deviant behavior or deviant intentions (e.g., how he drank or did drugs or got into a fight or stole something or is going to "take someone out")

2. **Expected Behavior** (what you want the student to do instead of the predictable behavior)

   Jimmy will talk about appropriate topics (anything not deviant) when he enters the class

3. **Context Modification** (how you can change the situations, circumstances, or conditions to make the predictable behavior less likely and the expected behavior more likely to occur)

   Meet Jimmy at the door and immediately ask a question demanding appropriate talk as an answer

4. **Behavior Rehearsal** (practice; dry run; try out; drill)

   Practice with Jimmy coming into class and responding to my question, then talking about appropriate topics

5. **Strong Reinforcement** (special reward for doing the expected behavior)

   Praise for appropriate talk on coming into the classroom, plus 5 minutes to talk with his choice of me, principal, cook, or custodian if no inappropriate talk before first period assignment is given (principal, cook, and custodian agreed and trained in how to handle conversation)

6. **Prompts** (gestures or other signals indicating "remember; do it now")

   Hand signal to Jimmy, when I first see him in the morning, worked out in advance to indicate "appropriate talk"

7. **Monitoring Plan** (record of performance; indicator of success that you can show someone)

   Jimmy and I to record daily successful school entry talk

FIGURE 5.1   A Completed Precorrection Plan

    • ***What reinforcement will be strong enough to serve as an effective reward for the expected behavior?*** You must find a consequence that is meaningful and arrange its occurrence when the expected behavior occurs.

    • ***How can I prompt the behavior I want?*** Prompts are gestures or other signals indicating, "Remember; do it now."

    • ***How can I monitor the behavior so that I have a reliable record of progress?*** A simple recording system will help you and others judge whether the student is behaving as you expect.

INTERRUPTING THE ACTING-OUT CYCLE   As we suggested in Chapter 4 and in our earlier discussion of positive reinforcement in this chapter, the key to successful behavior management is focusing on what you want the student to do. The natural inclination is not to do this. In fact, most teachers are inclined to wait until a student is misbehaving in an obvious and intrusive manner before getting into the act and attempting to do something helpful. By that time, a teacher's efforts to correct are often unsuccessful and the problem gets worse—the student moves up to more intense acting-out behavior and may even reach the peak phase. (You may want to review Figure 4.2 and our accompanying discussion of the acting-out cycle.)

    The most efficient and effective behavior management is achieved by concentrating on the earliest stages in the acting-out cycle. The principle is simple: If possible, keep the student in the calm phase; if not, then step in as early as possible to break the cycle and return the student to the calm phase. Following are a few questions and suggestions for responding to each phase.

• *What can I do to keep a student in the calm phase?* A well-structured classroom in which expectations are clear and in which a high-quality instructional program exists will help. The most important thing you can do in addition is to initiate positive interactions with the student. Hill Walker and his colleagues emphasize *noncontingent attention* as a key concept and strategy here (see Walker, Ramsey, & Gresham, 2004). The idea is to catch the student when he or she comes through the classroom door and, before there is any chance for the student to become agitated or begin accelerating misbehavior, engage him or her in productive behavior. Engage the student in pleasant conversation; ask the student to help you do a job that's nonthreatening; give the student an assignment to do a favorite task or in some other way recognize, approve, and engage the student.

As the class or day progresses, take the opportunity *frequently* to show attention and approval for calm behavior. Do *not* assume that calm behavior is its own reward for the student or that it is a phase you can ignore. It is, in fact, the phase to which you need to direct as much attention as possible from the beginning of the student's time with you. Keeping the student engaged from the get-go in focused, productive activity is the best way to perpetuate the calm phase and avoid classroom triggers and the subsequent escalation of misbehavior.

• *What should I do when I find that a trigger has occurred?* A **trigger** is an unresolved problem that upsets a person's calm. As we mentioned in Chapter 4, some triggers occur in the student's life before he or she enters your classroom. But regardless of where the trigger occurs, once you know it has happened, your best strategy is to move quickly to resolve the problem. Begin by letting the student know that you're aware of what has happened and offering to help, resolve the problem if you can. Just the reassurance that you know the student is experiencing discomfort, anxiety, frustration, or anger about the trigger may help. If you can resolve the problem right away, by all means do so. If you can't, then let the student know you will do what you can to help as soon as possible; meanwhile, help the student get focused on productive activity. If the trigger is something that is a recurrent problem, work out with the student how you will manage it together—identify the problem, possible solutions, the student's choices, and the outcomes of those choices. Time and energy spent helping students solve problems at this stage will save a world of effort and frustration.

• *What should I do when I see signs of agitation?* Again, let the student know that you recognize the signs (see also our suggestions for talking to students in Chapter 6). Give the student time and space; at this point, don't crowd the student or demand instant performance. It may be helpful to move toward or to move away from the student, depending on his or her individual characteristic response to proximity. It may also be beneficial to let the student do independent work or to engage in some type of movement activity. Again, if possible, involve the student in a plan to manage agitation if you see a recurring pattern of behavior. Work out with the student what you will do and what you will expect of him or her when you see signs of agitation. Look for a solution to this problem: What can you and the student do to get him or her to return to a non-agitated state? What you should *not* do is ignore the agitation and provide a reason for the student to move into the acceleration phase.

• *When a student is in the acceleration phase, what should I do?* Remember that in this phase the student is inviting someone to engage in a "my turn, your turn" interaction, looking to draw someone into an argument or battle of wills. Your best bet by far is to decline the invitation. This means that you must avoid doing things that are likely to escalate conflict; avoid showing your own agitation, making challenging or demeaning remarks, touching or grabbing the student, or lecturing. Maintain calm behavior and an attitude of respectful detachment; refuse to be drawn in. Wise teachers plan ahead for a student's acceleration and establish a negative consequence beforehand (e.g., office referral, calling the parents, calling the police). Then, to avert a crisis, the teacher is able to do the following calmly: state the behavioral expectation (e.g., "Robert, you need to sit down now . . ."); state the consequence of not meeting the expectation (e.g., ". . . or I will call your parents"); allow the student some time to make a decision (e.g., "You have a few seconds to decide"); and follow through with the consequence (e.g., if Robert doesn't take his seat, then call his parents; if he does sit down, then proceed with the class). If you answer the student's invitation to argue, become upset, become belligerent, or otherwise "mix it up" with the student, you will almost certainly regret it. Be cool, be calm, be respectful, be certain that you have a choice to offer the student, and be sure to follow through with what you say will happen if the student doesn't choose to do what you expect. Later—after the student has returned to calm behavior and is accessible to productive conversation—talk to the student about the incident and how such conflicts can be avoided.

• *What do I do with a peak phase?* The main consideration is safety—yours and your students'. Get help. Restrain or isolate the student if that can be done safely. Besides safety, you should think about long-term interventions that might avoid future peaks: making the school program more appropriate, getting additional evaluation of the student, obtaining counseling or other therapies to help the student manage problems more effectively, or changing your behavior management strategies. Once you hit the peak, it's too late to take preventive action except to keep anyone from getting hurt and to try to avoid a later peak.

• *What are the best tactics for the de-escalation phase?* Allow time for the student to cool down. Try to get him or her back on track with some routine, independent work. If possible, get the student to restore or clean up the physical environment if it was seriously affected.

• *What should I consider during the recovery phase?* Get back to normal routines, emphasizing attention on productive work and calm behavior. Talk to the student about the incident with emphasis on establishing plans to avoid future blowups. Express confidence that the student can learn to meet your expectations with help. Acknowledge any problem-solving behavior the student exhibits and focus on concrete plans for managing future issues.

SPECIAL NOTE ON DIGITAL RESOURCES

Resources for behavior management are increasingly available on the World Wide Web. However, we caution that some sites offer misleading information or, frankly, misinformation. Our recommendation is that you avoid any site recommending against the application of the principles we discuss in this book (regardless of the rationale) and that you view the information provided at that site with extreme caution. Many good sites are being developed on the Internet, and most provide links to other sites. Following are three that we recommend and that you might want to explore:

• The National Center on Education, Disability, and Juvenile Justice is found at www.edjj.org.
• The Oregon Social Learning Center is at www.OSLC.org.
• Sopris West has many helpful links at www.soledwest.com.

Summary

Today's teachers have available to them a wide variety of behavior management suggestions, including "packaged" techniques. We urge you to use a reflective, self-questioning approach that makes creative use of basic principles. Before implementing elaborate or sophisticated management strategies, we suggest that you try the simplest, most obvious professionally defensible procedures. These include using instructions, showing and describing examples, and providing choices to students. When implemented very skillfully, these and other simple approaches are often sufficient to resolve behavior problems. In selecting other options for behavior management, you must weigh them in the light of best professional practices, personal experience and that of colleagues, available technical assistance, and reliable empirical research. Research in behavioral psychology and social learning applied to classroom problems provides, in our opinion, a sound basis for devising behavior management strategies.

The five operations of a behavioral approach—positive reinforcement, negative reinforcement, extinction, response cost punishment, and punishment by presenting aversives—are based on the principle that consequences (events immediately following a behavior) can be altered to change behavior. Positive and negative reinforcement are ways of increasing the strength or probability of behavior; extinction and punishment are ways of decreasing or weakening it. The key to good behavior management is emphasizing positive reinforcement of appropriate behavior; the other four operations should play a secondary role. Teachers who use behavioral operations successfully must capitalize on the cognitive and affective aspects of behavior change.

Students' thoughts and feelings must be considered when you talk with students, choose consequences for students' behavior, and teach self-management techniques and social skills. Understanding students' thoughts and feelings is important in building helpful relationships. Behavior management should be positive and supportive of appropriate behavior so that students receive frequent teacher approval, the focus is on motivation to obtain rewarding consequences, and students like being in the classroom and learn important academic and social skills. Instructional approaches to behavior management include the precorrection strategy and focusing interventions on the earliest stages in the acting-out cycle.

Case Connection

All cases offer opportunities to think about changing behavior, but you might consider the particulars of behavior change strategies that teachers might have used in the following, especially what teachers did well and what they did not do well or didn't do at all:

Alone in the Dark   Alan Stean

One Bad Apple   Elaine Brown

The Contract with Parrish and Son   Rebecca Phillips

They Failed Derrick   Melinda Smith

CHAPTER SIX

Talking with Students

Questions for Reflection

How does classroom talk differ from talking
in other places?

How is talking with students about their behavior
related to my teaching goals?

How can I avoid unproductive talking with
students about their behavior?

What verbal and nonverbal communication
skills must I model and teach?

Listening

Using Proximity

Speaking Body Language

*Establishing Eye Contact and Varying Facial
Expressions*

Pausing, Reflecting, and Probing

Describing, Not Judging

Choosing the Best Words

Using the Best Voice

Setting the Right Pace

Summarizing

Questioning

Waiting

How can talking with students teach them
about personal responsibility?

How should I talk with students about
appropriate behavior?

How should I talk with students about
unacceptable behavior?

How should I talk with angry or aggressive
students?

How should I talk with students who are
withdrawn?

Summary

Case Connection

T alk is cheap—sometimes. It can also be very costly. Knowing when to hold your tongue can save you a world of trouble, especially when you're dealing with students who are masters in drawing adults into arguments or enticing others into a battle of insults. It's difficult to remember, when confronted by a direct verbal jab, that "a soft answer turneth away wrath" and that sometimes saying nothing is better than saying anything.

Knowing just what to say and how to say it aren't only a very large part of knowing how to give effective academic instruction, but also of knowing how to manage behavior skillfully. Skill in talking with students isn't just a matter of finding the right words but of being able to combine them with the right timing, intonation, eye contact, and nonverbal behavior to have a maximum effect. The skilled teacher knows not only what to say and how to say it but also how to listen—what to listen for, how to interpret what is said, and how to judge whether a productive conversation is possible at the moment or whether it would be better to wait for a more opportune moment.

Sarah

I was prepared for a lot of things in my first year. I'd even paid attention to some professors who had reminded me to think through how I was going to set up my class routine, the rules I wanted to impose, and what to do if certain unacceptable student behaviors popped up.

Looking back, though, having my own class has taught me far more than I ever imagined about talking with my students. I assumed that I was prepared for communicating with them. After all, I'd been able to talk to people all my life! Wow, was I wrong! David taught me the most. He was so unpredictable and very good at getting me hooked into verbal sparring matches. I remember one time when he really pushed all of my buttons. We were doing math, and I had instructed David to begin the written work I'd assigned. He turned his face to the wall, and that was that. I talked to him, but without eye contact I knew I wasn't getting anywhere. I tried everything from pleading and cajoling to shouting and yelling. Nothing. Not even a murmur. Then, as I walked away, he turned and said, quite deliberately: "You can't make me do anything I don't want to do!"

Well, that was all I needed. As I returned to his desk, I told him in no uncertain terms (I guess my voice was a little shaky, though) that I was the boss, and that he would toe the line or else. I still haven't figured out exactly why we ended up in the principal's office with David getting suspended, but in looking back I probably gave David exactly what he wanted.

Natalie

The cumulative folder from Anthony's former school described a child with mild mental retardation and hyperaggressive behavior, but my aide and I didn't need to read the folder. After four days in my classroom, several tantrums, and an aching jaw from a right to my chin, we knew he could accelerate from calm to explosion in a matter of seconds. Too often, we helped him along the way to a peak experience by what we said to him. Sometimes we were smarter and didn't get sucked into his verbal battles.

One morning, my aide was conducting an art lesson with Anthony's group when he began to brag about how frightened his mother was of him. My aide ignored him at first, but then tried to defuse him with mollifying statements. "That's a terrible way to talk about your mother! I know how much you love your mother. You don't want to talk about her like that!"

It didn't work. Anthony continued to engage my aide, to draw her in, to rant about how intimidated his mother was and how, if she ever crossed him again, the rescue squad would have to pick up what was left of her. Then he got up and began to strut around the art table while expounding on his acts of prior and future terror. When he began to threaten the other children in the group with comments like, "And you're next! The ambulance can pick you up, too," I intervened.

I had instituted a response cost system with Anthony—a laminated card with happy faces that I could mark off for misbehavior. When all the happy faces were crossed out, he lost his recess.

I picked up the card, approached Anthony, and said quietly, "Anthony, you only have one happy face left. You need to sit down and be quiet now, or you'll lose your last happy face." Then I chatted with one of the other students in his group. He sat down. I placed the card and a crayon in front of the aide and returned to my instructional group. Anthony earned his recess that day.

Some of the things teachers and students say to each other are not terribly important. Many, however, are critically important. They will make the difference between understanding and bewilderment or between conflict and harmony. A few words carefully chosen—or a few words spoken thoughtlessly—can have very dramatic results, as seen in the vignettes describing Sarah and Natalie.

QUESTIONS FOR REFLECTION

Talking with students is a complicated issue that permeates every level of behavioral assessment, the formulation of behavioral interventions, and the execution of behavior management plans. If you're constantly aware of effective communication skills and are able to put them into practice, you're more likely to accomplish your goals than if you forge ahead without careful reflection. As you approach the management of difficult students in your classroom, consider at least the following questions:

- How does classroom talk differ from talking in other places?
- How is talking with students about their behavior related to my teaching goals?
- How can I avoid unproductive talking with students about their behavior?
- What verbal and nonverbal communication skills must I model and teach?
- How can talking with students teach them about personal responsibility?
- How should I talk with students about appropriate behavior?
- How should I talk with students about unacceptable behavior?
- How should I talk with angry or aggressive students?
- How should I talk with students who are withdrawn?

How does classroom talk differ from talking in other places?

The language of the classroom is, for the most part and for most students, substantially different from the language of the home, the peer group, and the streets. It's typically more formal, more precise, and more directive than the conversational speech used by most students outside the classroom. Although this is true for most students, regardless of their cultural identity, the cultural bases of classroom talk are both very important and also highly controversial (see Hallahan, Kauffman, & Pullen, 2009; Powell & Caseau, 2004). Two critical issues become apparent to any teacher who reflects on talking with students: the acceptability of language (both the students' and the teacher's) and the adequacy of communication (both the ability to decode others' messages and the ability to encode messages that are understandable to others—to understand and to communicate).

- *What kind of language is acceptable in my classroom?* In Chapter 3, we discussed teachers' expectations for their students' conduct. Deciding where and how to draw the line on acceptable language is one of teaching's great challenges. Language may be discouraged or proscribed in school because it's thought to be foul, disrespectful, intimidating, impolite, or disruptive. The difficulty in knowing just where and how to draw the line on language stems from the fact that cultural and community definitions of "foul," "disrespectful," and so on, may differ markedly from the teacher's. Thus the teacher must be careful not to let cultural ignorance or bias be the basis for judging language as improper or unacceptable for the classroom. Moreover, it's important to recognize that language must not be considered unacceptable *simply because it's different from the teacher's* (see Dilg, 2003; Powell & Caseau, 2004).

Nevertheless, just because a student uses certain language at home or on the street doesn't make it acceptable in the classroom. In fact, if the teacher doesn't draw clear limits on classroom language, he or she will undoubtedly encounter some very serious behavior management problems. Belligerent language is often a prelude to other aggressive behavior. Flagrantly disrespectful language, if not checked, encourages further disrespectful behavior. Yet, it's important not to let such clearly unacceptable language be the trigger for a teacher's inappropriate or unproductive use of words. Adults are tempted to respond to unacceptable language with outrage, lecturing, shaming, arguing, or even verbal counteraggression. Such responses by a teacher are themselves—or should be—unacceptable. Cool, calm, clear, and respectful responses to unacceptable language are difficult but necessary. They're necessary for two primary reasons: to avoid getting drawn into the student's escalation of misbehavior and to demonstrate to youngsters the behavior we expect of them.

• *How can I make sure I understand and am understood by my students?* Teachers often misunderstand the content of students' language or the intent of their verbal expressions because they don't understand their students' cultures and the language that's part of them. Teachers may not make themselves understood by their students for the same reason. Becoming well acquainted with students' language, including slang expressions within any given culture, is critical to teachers' communicative competence. However, a full discussion of cultural diversity of language is beyond the scope of our task here. Beyond the matter of a teacher's competence in understanding language diversity, there are other issues about listening and talking to students that often make the difference between success and failure in managing behavior.

Listening effectively involves more than hearing the words; it demands attention to context, nonverbal behavior, and affect. The same verbal message may mean different things and require different responses depending on the social circumstances; in one context it's a joke, in another it's a serious matter. Sometimes a student's verbal and nonverbal behaviors are contradictory, as when a student says, "No! I ain't gonna do it, and you can't make me!," followed almost immediately by the first step toward compliance. The teacher who focuses on the tough talk and applies sanctions may miss the real point of the communication and become embroiled in a needless struggle; the one who ignores the verbal challenge and focuses on the student's compliance may artfully sidestep an unnecessary confrontation. The teacher who doesn't understand the emotional meaning of what students say may respond in ways that aren't constructive. Students may not understand the difference between street talk and classroom talk or may not have learned when certain expressions are inappropriate. So, it's important to set clear expectations for classroom talk but to decode students' communicative intentions regardless of the idioms they use.

Making sure that students understand what you say is no simple matter. Some teachers operate under the false assumption that loudness and reiteration will do the trick. Although raising one's voice and repetition are sometimes necessary, more sophisticated communication strategies are required in most cases. The content, timing, posture, and other dimensions of teacher communication are typically the more important keys to being understood. For example, you may want to review our questions and suggestions in Chapter 5 for giving instructions. Sometimes it may be necessary for the teacher to use the idiomatic language of the student's home or the street rather than the typical language of classroom discourse. We discuss other aspects of making oneself clearly understood in subsequent sections of this chapter.

How is talking with students about their behavior related to my teaching goals?

A well-thought-out classroom structure will reduce the amount of time spent on unproductive dialogue about behavior, such as unnecessary repetitions of or arguments about rules, consequences, or classroom routines. A predictable daily routine and smooth transitions between activities allow you to focus dialogue on instruction and expected behavior rather than on misbehavior. Moreover, talking with students about their behavior before their actions escalate to a major disruption is often effective, as we noted in Chapters 4 and 5 in our discussion of the acting-out cycle. (Review Figure 4.2 and accompanying descriptions.) If your overall approach to behavior management is proactive, then your talk will be primarily positive and instructive. This means that the teacher will frequently engage students in conversation when students are in the calm phase, minimize verbal engagement with students during the acceleration phase (avoid getting drawn into arguments), and use talking with students during the trigger and agitation phases to help students resolve their problems.

Many students act irresponsibly. A major reason for talking with students about their behavior is to teach them to assume responsibility for their actions and choices in social interactions and in their work. They may not accept responsibility for their own behavior but, instead, blame their actions on others (usually their parents, teachers, or peers), bad luck, a lack of ability, or the difficulty of the task. One way you can encourage students to assume responsibility for their own behavior is by questioning and commenting. For example, a teacher might say, "Anna, what will happen if you complete your work with 90 percent or more correct by 10:30?" (Pause for correct answer.) "Right, you'll be able to work at the computer until it's time to go to art class." It's usually wise to emphasize the description of the positive events that will follow expected performance rather than the unpleasant consequences of failure or misbehavior. Emphasizing the expected and the positive consequences helps keep the student focused on doing the responsible thing and is part of maintaining a positive, supportive classroom climate.

How can I avoid unproductive talking with students about their behavior?

One of the greatest challenges of working with difficult students is steering clear of nagging, wasted words, and verbal battles. Much of adults' talking with these students is ineffective or actually makes things worse. The students are masters at drawing adults into arguing, yelling, threatening, wheedling, berating, lecturing, and other forms of verbal struggle that they—the students—are very likely to win. They "win" by getting their way, getting the adult upset, diverting the adult from the real issue or problem, making the adult feel out of control or guilty or, in some other way, making the issue the adult's problem. Here are some ways they do this:

- By not responding to your words, ignoring, pretending not to hear
- By doing precisely, deliberately, and obviously the opposite of what you've asked them to do
- By denying any knowledge or perception of something they've been doing
- By repeating a nonsense, inappropriate, or incorrect word or phrase in response to a question
- By repeating a question over and over, never seeming to hear or understand the answer
- By mimicking you or someone else
- By interrupting, not allowing others to express themselves
- By insulting or verbally assaulting you
- By changing the topic

Most teachers have difficulty not responding with corrections, arguments, or other forms of resistance to such verbal challenges. They want the last word. They want to insist on the student's admission of error and on his or her correct verbal representation of reality. And, in so doing, teachers nearly always set themselves up for defeat. It takes experience and a high degree of skill to recognize the bait and to resist taking it. Taking the bait and getting pulled into an unproductive verbal exchange usually involves making one or more of the following mistakes:

- Showing signs of agitation, such as raising your voice, scowling, or making a threatening gesture
- Using verbal counteraggression, such as insults or threats of harm

- Repeating a statement over and over, answering each repetition of the student with your own repetition, which you intend as a correction of the student's statement
- Pleading with the student
- Stating a consequence for the student's behavior that is unrealistic or inappropriate, such as stating that there will be a penalty (one that you can't or won't levy)

Nearly always, teachers lose by these strategies. Usually, it's much more effective to do the following:

- Maintain calmness, showing as little sign of offense or upset as possible.
- Either ignore the student's verbal challenge or respond in a quiet but firm voice.
- Restate clearly and calmly—but only once—your expectation or answer.
- Move away from the student, giving him or her a few moments to calm down or respond appropriately.
- Look for opportunities to respond positively to the student's appropriate behavior, perhaps by changing the topic yourself.
- Give the student a choice of meeting the expectation or experiencing a negative consequence (one on which you know you can follow through).

After an episode of serious misbehavior has occurred and the student has calmed down and is able to engage in a productive conversation, debriefing is important. Debriefing is a private conversation with the student (at least kept as private as possible) in which the teacher tries to structure a dialogue that will help the student understand what happened, why it happened, how to choose a better alternative way of behaving, and how the student and teacher can plan to avoid further episodes of unacceptable behavior. The debriefing should be brief and focused. The teacher should initiate debriefing only after the student has gotten past the emotional arousal that typically goes with a serious acting-out incident and is able to talk about it realistically and without further emotional upset. That is, the debriefing should occur in the recovery phase of the acting-out cycle. Keep in mind that during debriefing, difficult students will not necessarily be completely rational (from your point of view) and may try to derail the conversation or engage you in argumentation. Your task is to stay focused, to avoid invitations to argue, and to move the student—if ever so slightly and grudgingly—toward more adaptive responses to the problems he or she encounters. For example, a useful debriefing might go something like this:

> TEACHER: So, tell me what happened this morning that landed you in detention.
>
> STUDENT: Hell, I dunno. It wasn't my fault. It was Henry who got it going.
>
> TEACHER: Well, let's start with what happened first. What was the first thing that happened?
>
> STUDENT: When I came in, Henry, he started on me. That's what happened first. It was his fault, and you know it, and I don't want to hear about it.
>
> TEACHER: What did Henry do? How did he start on you?
>
> STUDENT: He called me a dope. You heard him, and I'm gonna git that sucker, too. And then he called me other names, like "welfare queen" and other stuff.
>
> TEACHER: So, Henry called you a dope and other names. I understand. That's pretty hard to take, and Henry needs to learn not to do stuff like that. But what happened after he called you names?
>
> STUDENT: I punched him, you saw that! I punched him in his fat mouth, that's what I did.
>
> TEACHER: Yeah, I saw you hit him. And then what?

STUDENT: Well, you know what happened, he hit me back.

TEACHER: Yes, it looked like you guys were gonna take each other down.

STUDENT: We woulda, too, if you hadn't come 'round.

TEACHER: So, what's the rule if you get into a fight in this school?

STUDENT: Detention.

TEACHER: Right, after-school detention, and we call your parents.

STUDENT: And it ain't fair when you didn't start it, and I didn't start it. It was Henry's fault, and you know it.

TEACHER: Well, the rule is, it doesn't make any difference who started it, if you get involved in hitting someone you get detention.

STUDENT: You may think so, but I don't. And somebody calls me those names, I'm gonna hit 'em, and they gonna know it.

TEACHER: I know you'd want to hit 'em, and I probably would too. But what could you do besides hit somebody who calls you names?

STUDENT: I dunno. I'm gonna hit 'em,'cause I can't stand it.

TEACHER: I know it's tough to do, but what are the things we've talked about that you can do besides hit somebody who gets on you?

STUDENT: Ignore them, I guess, but I can't do that.

TEACHER: Right, ignoring them and just going on about your business as if they weren't there—that's a good idea, that's a good alternative. It's hard, but you can learn to do it and not get sent to detention.

STUDENT: But they shouldn't be callin' me names.

TEACHER: You're right. If they're doin' that, then they've got a problem, and they need to learn not to do it. But if they get you to react by hitting them, then what happens?

STUDENT: I get detention. But I don't care. I ain't gonna have it.

TEACHER: Right, if you hit, you get detention, and then it's your problem, too. So, how could we work on your not getting detention?

STUDENT: You stop them calling me names, that's how.

TEACHER: Well, yeah. I'll do what I can to stop that. They shouldn't do it. But if they do, then what can you and I do so that you don't get detention?

STUDENT: You stop them.

TEACHER: How will I know when they're doing it? I couldn't hear Henry this morning when he was calling you names. You guys were over on the other side of the room.

STUDENT: Well, I can tell you.

TEACHER: Right, you can tell me. But how would you do that? Would you yell out, "Hey, Henry's calling me names!" or how would you do it? How about you just walk away and come toward me and give me a signal?

STUDENT: Like what?

TEACHER: Like just walk toward me and pull your ear, like this. That'll mean you are just walking away from somebody who's calling you names.

STUDENT: I dunno, man, I'm gonna just hit 'em.

TEACHER: Well, let's give it a try, OK? Just give it a try next time, and then if you can do it and not hit, you won't end up going to detention. OK? Will you try that?

STUDENT: OK, I can't make you no promises, but I'll try.

TEACHER: Great. We'll give it a shot. Let's just try it.

In this verbal interaction, how did the teacher avoid getting sidetracked into an argument about who was at fault? How did the teacher sidestep invitations to argue about the fairness of the consequence for fighting? How did the teacher avoid lecturing or other forms of unproductive verbalization?

What verbal and nonverbal communication skills must I model and teach?

Teachers must model and teach the self-control skills that are prerequisites for effective communication. Students may need to be taught to:

- Take turns talking, allowing one speaker to speak at a time.
- Not interrupt while someone else is talking.
- Maintain a focus on a topic (especially if it's their own behavior) without wandering.
- Understand how much to say about their behavior without being repetitive or evasive.
- Avoid ambiguity or vagueness while at the same time being polite and considerate.

No adult is likely to teach these critical communication skills unless he or she can demonstrate them in verbal exchanges with students.

The nonverbal prerequisites for effective communication are also important. Students may need to be taught how to:

- Use eye contact during conversations and show understanding that different cultures and individuals have different expectations about looking and talking.
- Listen to what others are saying and use appropriate facial expressions and body language to maintain social connections.

Again, if you want to teach students these skills, you have to use them yourself.

LISTENING   Through the use of **active listening**, teachers can learn to differentiate between the emotional and intellectual content of what students are saying. Active listening requires giving the student your full attention by blocking out other distractions. Pay close attention to the verbal and nonverbal actions of the student and try to decide which parts of what the student is saying are facts and which are emotional messages. It's important to gauge the student's feelings and reactions. Listen long enough to evaluate the student's behavioral status. In addition, because active listening is an intensely individual activity, remember that your personal feelings toward the student will influence the unspoken messages you hear.

Active listening provides the student with an opportunity to deal with inappropriate behavior and frustration. Using good listening skills will also convey a sense of empathy to the student and support the possibility of behavioral improvement. Demonstrating these skills may encourage students to listen appropriately when you talk, but the demonstration alone may not be enough. You may need to describe how people behave when they are listening and ask the student to practice that behavior. However, you must be careful to look for the teachable moment when the student won't interpret your instruction as criticism or nagging.

USING PROXIMITY   Personal proximity is important in communication, especially if the speaker has poorly defined personal boundaries. Being too far from a student while talking may be misinterpreted as disinterest, whereas getting too close may be threatening. A comfortable distance for most students is about an arm's length, although you may find that some students appear to need more personal space than others. Angry and aggressive students probably need more space than calmer or compliant pupils. Proximity during verbal communication is partly a cultural phenomenon; you should be aware of cultural expectations (see Powell & Caseau, 2004). However, even within cultures students may respond very differently to proximity. The key point is to watch for signs that an agitated student is best managed by closer proximity or by keeping more distance.

SPEAKING BODY LANGUAGE   Body language and posture convey a sense of interest or lack thereof. Slouching or leaning back is more likely to communicate disinterest, while leaning slightly forward may indicate an attentive attitude. However, try not to be physically rigid or "posed" either. You want to appear confident, in control, and assured, but not arrogant. Body movement and gestures can be seen as either encouraging or disapproving during a conversation, so be aware of any personal gestures that may interfere with what you are trying to communicate.

Body language varies considerably from culture to culture. It's essential to take the student's culture into account when interpreting the meanings of body language or choosing a posture or gesture. If you're not sure about these meanings, ask an adult who is competent in that culture to help you understand.

ESTABLISHING EYE CONTACT AND VARYING FACIAL EXPRESSIONS   Eye contact conveys a sense of interest and friendliness to most listeners and adds to your credibility. However, staring is usually interpreted as intimidating and should be avoided. Facial expressions can be helpful in conveying what you're thinking during your conversation. It's important to listen carefully to what the student is saying so that you won't be caught off guard and react with outrage. For example, you should not respond with an exaggerated expression to a comment that the student made to try to shock you. In addition, prolonged disapproving expressions can be very distracting. It's more appropriate to match your expression carefully to the conversational content.

Again, you must be aware that eye contact is an aspect of communication that's highly grounded in cultural expectations. In some cultures, students are expected to avoid eye contact most of the time; in others, students are expected to look into the eyes of the adult who is talking to them. Expect and give eye contact that's consistent with the expectations in the student's culture.

PAUSING, REFLECTING, AND PROBING   In talking with students, teachers should make careful use of language to convey very definite and clear messages about their demands. Think through what you intend to say before talking with a student about their behavior. Taking a moment to consider how you'll phrase a question or comment and being aware of your body language can save a great deal of energy and frustration. If possible, put yourself in the student's place and see what it would take to answer your question or respond to your comment appropriately.

Learn to use verbal cues that will enhance conversations about behavior. For example, silence can encourage a student to be reflective or to expand an explanation of his or her behavior.

True, silences that are too long create a disconcerting "dead space." However, most adults tend to rush in, to fill all seconds with words, to be too hurried. This is understandable because schools are busy, even frenetic, places, and many other students besides the one you're talking to at the moment need attention. Still, what you communicate by appropriate pauses is that this conversation is important, that you're thinking carefully about it, and that you want the student to think carefully, too.

You may prompt students by using recognition statements, which simply acknowledge that you've heard what they've said to you (e.g., "I see . . . , yes . . ."). Another way to prompt students is to use reflective statements mirroring what the student has said (e.g., if the student says, "I hate Sally!" you might respond with something like, "So, you hate Sally . . .").

DESCRIBING, NOT JUDGING   Language may be either descriptive or judgmental. *Judgmental language* automatically elevates a situation or behavior to a level at which conflict is more likely. Applying a judgmental label to behavior (e.g., "awful," "bad," "stupid," "wrong") often ruins the chance for further communication. It may be quite true that in the eyes of many people the student's behavior merits a highly negative label. But remember that the objective is to establish and maintain communication with the student, not merely to communicate a judgment. **Descriptive language** is often preferable because it describes what happened without attaching a subjective judgment. Such language doesn't label behavior with an emotional overlay that may truncate communication. The more objective and factual the language, the more precise the feedback to the student about his or her behavior and the easier it is for both teacher and student to remain calm. Furthermore, descriptive language is less likely to provoke an escalation of misbehavior. For example, a judgmental comment might be, "Sean, that was an awful way to treat Jean." A related descriptive comment might be, "Sean, you pushed Jean into the wall."

CHOOSING THE BEST WORDS   The wise teacher selects vocabulary carefully to reflect what has happened or is happening as calmly and objectively as possible. Familiar words are usually better than words the student may not understand. Brief statements are typically better than long ones. Language should be appropriate for the occasion and apply specifically to the student, the behavior, and the social context. This requires careful judgment of the student's language abilities and responses to verbal expression. Sometimes, vivid language in the form of metaphors or similes works well. For example, "Peter, don't take the bait" may either communicate nothing at all or be a clear and effective warning, depending on the student's understanding of and response to figures of speech. Remember, too, that the line between an effective figure of speech and sarcasm is fine and that you should stay clearly out of sarcasm territory.

Specific words may be appropriate and understood in one language but inappropriate or even incendiary in another. The key point is to know your audience. As you are teaching, you must listen carefully for words that are particularly loaded for particular groups or individuals. An expression that has a meaning for your audience that you don't attach to it can lead to a serious social faux pas.

USING THE BEST VOICE   Voice tells us a great deal about the speaker's expectations and emotional state. Students are extremely sensitive to changes in a teacher's voice, including loudness and pitch. In some circumstances, success in talking with students about their behavior may depend as much—or more—on how you sound as the words you say. Your voice should be loud enough so that students can hear you clearly, although talking in too loud a voice is just as detrimental to conversation as speaking too softly. A shouted command may sometimes be necessary, and a strong voice is often appropriate. However, a quieter voice than usual is sometimes highly effective in getting a student's attention. Speaking at one volume level, however, will mean that nothing you say will stand out from your other comments. Varying the volume of your voice will stimulate interest and help the student maintain focus on what you are saying. Varying your voice pitch will convey different messages to students. A shrillness or monotone will decrease your ability to hold a student's attention and is often a good indicator of your emotional state. Some teachers use a tentative or a questioning voice when giving instructions or commands (e.g., "Could you please sit down?"). Typically, it's wiser to use a firmer voice that indicates the expectation that the student will do what you want (e.g., "Rodney, please sit down now"). Practice using a tone and inflections that communicate calmness, firmness, confidence, and assertiveness but not harshness.

SETTING THE RIGHT PACE   The pace at which you converse is also important. There's a good chance that when you're talking with a student about his or her behavior, you may be extremely excited, frustrated, or angry. These emotions may tend to make you speak more quickly. Speak slowly enough so that your words aren't garbled or incompletely formed. Also, don't speak too slowly or hesitantly, as this may communicate that you are unsure of yourself and not in control of the exchange.

Most people have a pace of speaking that's natural for them, and their pace may vary considerably, depending on the culture or geographic home of the speaker. However, some teachers need to slow down and some need to speed up their pace to be most effective.

SUMMARIZING   You may wish to interject brief, intermittent summaries of what the student has been saying. Summarizing student talk will reflect back to the student what he or she has said, and it also provides a point of reference that the student can use for further discussion. Rephrasing what a student is communicating by asking for confirmation may also help (e.g., "Let me see if I understand what you're trying to say. Did you mean that . . . ?"). That is, you may wish to repeat the views of the student without attempting to evaluate the student's feelings or nonverbal impressions. Keep in mind, too, that summarizing or rephrasing can be overdone.

QUESTIONING   Most teachers see questioning as part of teaching academics. It's also a critical part of talking with students about their behavior. The way a teacher asks questions about students' behavior may mean the difference between effective communication and alienation or disruption. Questions may be used to motivate students, help them think about their behavior, or provide them with information about more appropriate behavior.

Questions come in two major varieties: open and closed. Both have advantages and disadvantages. Choosing the right kind is a key factor in a teacher's ability to engage students in productive interactions.

Closed questions are the more restrictive of the two types because they ask for either very specific information or a yes/no response. Their advantage is that they focus on a specific issue or event and typically yield explicit, if limited, information. However, it's wise to avoid excessive use of yes/no questions except as a warm-up for other questions (e.g., "Did you tear the page?" would be a warm-up question for discussing alternatives to tearing pages), as they have several disadvantages. One disadvantage of closed questions is that they allow only a simple choice between two alternatives. This means that the student is forced to choose one answer over another, effectively preventing discussion or reflection on more appropriate behavior. Another disadvantage is that closed questions don't give the teacher much information about what the student is thinking. Also, unless closed questions are used sparingly, teachers often end up asking one yes/no question after another—a practice that's ineffective and frustrating for both teacher and student.

Open questions are less restricting because they allow students to formulate their own answers from an unlimited array of possibilities. That is, students who have to think of their own answers must engage in internal self-talk to select from a variety of responses to your question. For example, instead of saying "Did you tear the book?" (closed question), you may make more progress by asking an open question, such as, "What can you tell me about the torn book?"

Bear in mind that questions should contain natural, everyday language, as opposed to "text-book" or highly formal language, and should be simply worded at a level appropriate to the age and language ability of the child. Many students are easily confused by questions containing unfamiliar words. Make questions brief and ask only one question at a time. Some students find it difficult to remember long or multiple-part questions. Questions should be purposeful and address exactly the behavior you wish to discuss. However, good questions demand that the student think carefully before answering.

WAITING   Wait-time in conversation is especially important when questioning students about their behavior. It's also important when giving commands or choices. Expecting an instantaneous answer or response is a mistake, but so is waiting too long, which indicates either that you aren't monitoring the student's behavior or that you're not following through with an appropriate next step. Waiting patiently communicates that an answer is expected, and it simultaneously allows the student sufficient time to think about a response. Most researchers believe that three to four seconds is appropriate when waiting for a student response. Many teachers don't allow enough time for students to formulate answers before prompting answers or asking another question. Not waiting for a student response may communicate to the student a feeling of being rushed or pressured to answer. However, waiting too long before applying a consequence, repeating the question or command, or taking other appropriate action indicates that you are unaware or unconcerned. There are times, certainly, when you need to disengage from an interaction or avoid a coercive struggle by not responding. Nevertheless, if you intend to continue to interact with the student, then judging just how long to wait for a response is critical.

How can talking with students teach them about personal responsibility?

The ultimate goal of behavior management is to help students become more self-controlled and self-directed. The debriefing session after a major acting-out incident should include a discussion about how to avoid future upsets. During debriefing, you'll want to discuss what led up to the incident, what the student might have done instead of act out, and how future incidents can be avoided. In other words, the object of debriefing is to help the student understand what went wrong and what you and she or he might do to make things go right next time (Colvin, 2004). Furthermore, the idea of precorrection, as we discussed in Chapters 4 and 5, is to work with the student to make a plan and follow it—a plan that will lead to the student's learning strategies of self-management. Externally imposed controls are often necessary, but they're only a first step toward giving the student skills for adaptive independence.

Teaching students to be responsible for their own behavior is a difficult task, so avoid using language that makes someone else responsible for their personal conduct (e.g., "I guess Sally made you very angry"). Instead, describe the situation in language that emphasizes personal decisions and responsibility for one's actions (e.g., "So, you got really angry when Sally . . ."). Try not to become sidetracked by the student's attempts to avoid being held accountable for his or her actions. Many students are provocative or hostile as a means of maintaining their control. For example, if a student can engage you in talking about how others are to blame for his or her behavior, then you will waste valuable time attempting to convince the student otherwise. By this time, the student will be in control of the conversation and an opportunity for teaching will have been lost.

In order to maintain control of the conversation for the purposes of teaching responsibility, you can respond to the student in one of two ways. First, you may use a directive response with students who have limited problem-solving skills. Offer the student one of two choices (e.g., "Either sit down now, or I'll call Mr. Harrison") and allow him or her a few seconds to decide which will occur. Make sure you monitor the student's behavior and follow through with the appropriate consequence after a few seconds.

Achieving a large measure of self-control and autonomous selection of appropriate behaviors is a prime goal in dealing with students with mild disabilities. Talking with students about their behavior is a first step toward getting them to assume control over their actions. Some students consistently show only small gains in transferring what they learn about their behavior in specific situations to more generalized social skills. A major aim of talking with students, therefore, must be to help them monitor, evaluate, and modify their behavior on their own. Your responsibility for student behavior will be lessened over time as the student gains greater self-control.

A student's assessment of his or her own behavior is the initial step toward self-control (Kauffman & Landrum, 2009a). To encourage self-assessment, your first task as a teacher is to help the student decide whether his or her behavior is appropriate or inappropriate. In order to make this discrimination, the student must carefully compare personal actions to the standard set by the classroom rules of conduct, learning, and peer social interaction. If the behavior is inappropriate, encourage the student to modify the misbehavior by considering several possible solutions to the problem. Discuss each option with the student and be supportive of the process of selecting a more appropriate behavior. Reinforce the student for choosing an appropriate behavior to be used in the future.

Self-assessment depends largely on the willingness of the student to change his or her behavior to more acceptable alternatives and the ability to understand why the behavior change is necessary. Negotiation of the new behavior will be shaped by the expectations of both the teacher and the student. Negotiation is effective because there is little point in using teacher-imposed expectations that students are unable or unwilling to attain.

When the replacement behavior has been agreed on, devise a self-recording system so that the student can accurately note how often the new, appropriate behavior occurs and how well it was implemented. The recording system provides a measure of the student's awareness of behavior change. Self-recording of the replacement behavior encourages the student to use self-talk. Further, it helps the student keep a record of the degree of control he or she has over the change in behavior. Self-recording also helps the student internalize control of the new behavior. In turn, the more internal control the student can exercise over his or her new behavior, the greater the likelihood that what is learned in one specific behavioral situation will generalize to other behaviors and situations. Once self-recording has begun, you can talk with the student about his or her progress. Be sure to reinforce increases in appropriate behavior. As the new behavior emerges, the student can evaluate the success of the replacement of the old misbehavior. It's important that you keep a tally of the appearance of the new behavior. When you talk with the student about how well he or she is doing, you can compare your tallies to those of the student. Such a comparison will help refine the accuracy of the self-recording and will be a "reality check" for unrealistic expectations held by you or the student.

As progress is made in a self-assessment program, the student may begin to administer his or her own reinforcement for increased appearance of the new appropriate behavior. At this point, the student can be instructed to rehearse the steps necessary for maintaining an appropriate behavior by internal dialogue. Self-talk (internal dialogue) helps the student improve behavior by talking through the steps necessary to assess and, if necessary, modify behaviors.

How should I talk with students about appropriate behavior?

We hope that you recall our discussion in previous chapters of the crucial role of a teacher's attention to desirable behavior, especially our discussion of positive reinforcement in Chapter 5. Positive recognition of what you want from students is the keystone of behavior management; without it, your other behavior management skills will fail. Positive reinforcement may include special privileges or tangible rewards, but it should be accompanied by your positive comments—social praise in some form.

Experienced teachers know that effective praise is not merely the stereotyped "I like the way you raised your hand and waited for me to call on you," although such statements clearly have their place in good teaching. The trick is, first, to be aware of the student's behavior that is desirable, to catch it in progress, and then to accompany it or follow it immediately with something that communicates approval and encouragement. This isn't as simple as it might first appear. To most teachers, students' misbehavior is more conspicuous than their desirable behavior. If you're dealing with an especially difficult student, you may need to observe carefully to find brief periods of the student's calm, on-task behavior or evaluate the student's behavior carefully to see that it is more appropriate than is typical for him or her. The temptation is to expect too much before you give the praise or recognition. True, expectations for students' conduct can be too low and praise can be too generous. But that's not the failing of most teachers; many teachers are too ready with criticism and too stingy with recognition of the expected behavior. The teachers most students are drawn to, and from whom most students learn best, are those who recognize effort and achievement, even if it's small, who are encouraging and supportive, and who take obvious pleasure in a student's success. The important point to remember is that praise is due for whatever represents improved effort or a worthy achievement *for a particular individual,* not for the typical person or someone of great accomplishment. The beginning student of any age—whether learning the piano, math, writing, or basketball, turning in homework, or behaving appropriately in a group—thrives on recognition and encouragement for what looks like a small achievement to an advanced student.

The language of effective praise is at once simple and complex. Almost everyone knows the typical words and phrases that convey public approval or recognition, and in this sense the language of praise is simple. Certainly, most people also recognize that particular words, phrases, gestures, facial expressions, and other acts can convey a more significant level of approval than others, depending on the person from whom they come and the context in which they are given. Likewise, people understand the expression "to damn with faint praise"—to signify contempt by "praise" that is sarcastic or compares an accomplishment to something worse (e.g., *"That* sentence was not total nonsense!"). It's important that effective praise be a sincere expression, verbal or nonverbal, that recognizes the value of what a student has done in a way that the student understands and appreciates.

Communicating approval and encouragement depends on your understanding the developmental level, individual characteristics, and cultural identification of the student. Some students may react negatively to praise to which others respond positively. Getting a positive reaction may depend on timing, the use of particular words or gestures, or the privacy of the communication. For some adolescents, for example, the typical public praise statement may discredit them with their peer group and be ineffective or worse. For some students, low-key indications of approval are best; for others, an animated display is most effective. The key is understanding how to communicate approval that's meaningful to the individual, and, for that kind of praise, one can make this generalization: Nobody doesn't like it.

The purpose of approval of desirable behavior is twofold. First, it's an invitation to positive social interactions that are adaptive and mutually beneficial. It's the first step toward social bonding.

Second, it's a model that's intended to induce imitative self-evaluation in the student. Our hope is that students will learn to evaluate their own behavior, to see their own accomplishments, to internalize teachers' valuing of them, and to respond with self-approval of desirable conduct. Teachers want students to notice their own improvement and learn to celebrate their own successes. This isn't done by focusing on criticism or correction or by abstaining from any evaluative statements. Rather, teachers do so by showing their approval of students. True, there is a time to ask students for their self-evaluation (e.g., "How well do you think you did just now?" "Do you think you did the right thing?" "I wonder what you think of the fact that you turned in your homework four days in a row"). However, many difficult students have received so little positive feedback and recognition that beginning with self-evaluation leaves them adrift in a sea of uncertainty or starved for a kind and encouraging word. Having so seldom been praised, they don't know how to evaluate their own performance or praise themselves.

We can't overemphasize the importance of noncontingent attention as a preventive behavior management tool, a means of engaging students in positive social interaction before misbehavior has a chance to emerge (Colvin, 2004; Walker, Colvin, & Ramsey, 1995). Noncontingent attention means that you are *not* looking for a *particular* appropriate behavior and making your attention contingent. Rather, you're engaging the student in positive, productive activity *before* he or she has a chance to start misbehaving. Anticipate the student's entry into your classroom. Have a positive comment to make and engage the student immediately in an activity that he or she enjoys—a little chore or a favored activity, for example. Look for opportunities to talk to the student about something pleasant and nonthreatening, if not highly rewarding. Think of it as a preemptive positive strike. "Hi, Chas. Cool shirt! I like those colors. I've got all these books to straighten up on this shelf. Would you help me out by doing this job for me?" Know your student. Short-circuit the tendency to exhibit undesirable behavior by taking the initiative in a positive vein.

How should I talk with students about unacceptable behavior?

Negative teacher talk is often detrimental to appropriate student behavior and achievement. Constant negativity or belittling talk is unlikely to convince a student to improve behavior. It may easily, however, have the opposite effect. There's little point in embarrassing students when talking about their behavior, especially in front of the rest of the class. Resorting to language that causes shame is a personal attack on the student's self-esteem. Your objective should be to address the student's behavior and promote responsible actions. Avoid sarcasm, insults, and offensive language. Courteous language isn't only professional; it also provides a model for students.

If possible, address misbehavior confidentially. When you talk to students about their behavior in the presence of their peers, confine conversation to the behavior itself. If it becomes necessary to confront or reprimand a student, give him or her an opportunity to save face. Keep it as private as possible; position yourself near the student and speak in a soft voice to reduce the chances of other students overhearing what you are saying. Doing this also teaches the rest of the class that they may expect the same dignified treatment.

An increase in positive messages and a reduction of negative messages will extend the chances of favorable behaviors recurring. For example, even critical feedback can be worded without being attacking or personally offensive. Using "I" messages that take responsibility for your feelings are helpful (e.g., "I feel that throwing the book on the floor was a poor choice of behavior"). In this way you express disapproval without attacking the character of the student. It doesn't follow, however, that the more positive the teacher talk, the better the student behavior and achievement. A neutral and businesslike approach in talking with students is at least as effective as an overly positive approach when the topic is misbehavior. More successful teachers maintain a supportive but controlled attitude in their classrooms. Less-successful teachers tend to engage in talk that's either excessively positive or excessively authoritarian and harsh. Also, teachers who are internally controlled take responsibility for what they say. Their students make more progress than those of teachers who blame the way they talk on someone else.

You should have three objectives in communication about misbehavior: (1) indicating clearly that the behavior is unacceptable, (2) indicating clearly what is expected, and (3) finding a way to help the student learn to do what's expected. Your communication shouldn't give the student a reason to flare up. Keep it clear but brief, low keyed, and as private as possible. At the same time, make sure you tell or signal what you want, not just to desist. When you have an opportunity, talk to the student about the misbehavior and how you can help him or her learn acceptable alternatives to it. For example, you may have a brief discussion of specific things the student might do to avoid blowing up in response to not understanding an assignment. You may say something like, "What can we do so that, when you don't understand, you can stay calm and get the help you need?" Look for opportunities to develop precorrection plans, including rehearsal, prompts, and strong reinforcement for the expected behavior.

How should I talk with angry or aggressive students?

Sometimes students who are angry or upset become verbally abusive. They may seem intent on insulting or assaulting the teacher for no apparent reason except to establish their control and dominance in the classroom. For example, students may say to the teacher—or to someone else so that the teacher is certain to hear it—such things as these:

"Man, you a weird lookin' dude."

"Why do you wear such nerdy clothes?"

"She's got the ugliest nose I've ever seen!"

"Your breath stinks like shit."

"You don't know how to teach at all! Why didn't nobody teach you how to be a teacher?"

"Look, you just leave me alone or I'll punch your face in."

"You like your job, then you stay outa my face."

"You don't get off my case, my momma will come get you."

"You're stupid, and you lie!"

"Your class is boring."

"I could teacher better than you."

It's easy to take remarks like these personally and respond in kind, especially because they *are* aimed directly at you. Students know that teachers are vulnerable to personal attacks, and sometimes they seem to have an uncanny sense for knowing what will be especially hurtful and offensive. Refusing to take students' remarks to heart will help you avoid becoming angry or hurt and getting drawn into power struggles. Feeling personally affronted by every negative comment will distract you from the real work of teaching and signal to students that they've found a victim.

Certainly, it's unrealistic to expect teachers or anyone else to have no emotions or no emotional reaction to what students say. Nevertheless, it's critically important for teachers to model restraint in the face of provocation and to show by word and deed that they won't be sidetracked from their professional responsibilities. This isn't to suggest that effective teachers are unfeeling robots who simply grind away at getting through the curriculum. There are times when expressing frustration with a student in a controlled, appropriately responsible way can be extremely effective. Such a strategy, however, should be used sparingly and under extenuating circumstances.

Most prospective teachers haven't carefully prepared and rehearsed responses to angry or aggressive students. Most inexperienced teachers expect their students to be kind and polite to them. Sometimes teachers fail to prepare for hostile, demeaning talk from their students because such incidents are few and far between in idealized classrooms. It's also difficult to prepare for every possible situation because the circumstances of each encounter are unique. You can, however, prepare yourself in a general way. First, define for yourself as carefully as you can the verbalizations that you will tolerate and the types that are unacceptable.

Clearly unacceptable verbal behavior usually involves a situation in which a student says things that are likely to lead to serious classroom disruption or property damage. Such verbalizations may be a clear prelude to fighting, self-injury, or destruction of property. Second, once you have a clear set of limits, think through as many problem situations as possible, envisioning how you will act and what you will say. Work out a "prepackaged" strategy for dealing with the situation and rehearse the physical and verbal steps that will be necessary to regain control of the communication. Third, practice speaking in a calm tone and rehearse giving firm directions and commands. This kind of "imaging" and rehearsal won't prepare you for every eventuality, but it will provide enough preparation so that you'll have time to think of other solutions or, if necessary, get assistance.

When you see a crisis brewing, you may initially try to buy time to allow you to regroup and move into your "prepackaged" verbal strategies or consequence. To buy time, you can direct students to go to different parts of the room, instruct them to engage in a new or different classroom activity, or insist on silence among arguing or fighting students until the situation is calmer. Sometimes an angry student can be deflected by your suggestion of an alternative behavior or activity. This also provides an interim time for the student to regroup and to regain some control. Another useful intervention involves asking the students to comply with a small request rather than insisting on a total move from anger to compliance.

As suggested by our discussion of the acting-out cycle, preventive talking is preferable to reactive talk. More can be gained by nipping a problem in the bud by a simple comment than by trying to deal with a full-blown crisis, where talking with a student tends to become less and less effective as the crisis escalates. As important as it is to try not to let a situation get out of control in the first place, you shouldn't overreact to the buildup to a crisis or a blowup in which the student gets out of control. Overreaction to minor infringements sometimes causes major problems that could have been avoided in the first place. Judging what to ignore and what to attend to will increase with experience, but your decisions will be helped by constant vigilance and a clear understanding of what you are prepared to tolerate in your classroom.

Besides mental or actual rehearsal, you must have an explicit plan for negative consequences that will follow intolerable behavior. Preplanning is absolutely essential. Otherwise, you're likely to find yourself saying that something will happen when you can't be assured that it will. The consequence may involve suspension, calling parents to come to take the student home, calling the police or a probation officer, and so on. Work with your principal and other staff who may be involved and with parents or guardians to make sure that everyone's clear about what will happen as a consequence of the intolerable behavior.

If you're forced to deal reactively with a suddenly out-of-control situation, your first concern should be to prevent harm to anyone in the room and to deescalate the emotionally charged situation as quickly as possible. In this situation, attempting a conversation with the student is rarely effective. For example, if two students are fighting, you are quite unlikely to be successful in asking questions about what started it or how the students feel about it. It's time for clear, short commands related to your preplanned consequence, time to get help, perhaps time for physical intervention.

Assuming that there is no immediate physical danger, talk in a firm yet calm, nonthreatening manner. If an angry student perceives that you are afraid or feeling intimidated, there is a very good chance that he or she will respond with increased aggression. Speak calmly and in a natural voice. Simultaneously lower and relax your hands and arms to appear nonthreatening. Be alert, however, for any physical threat to yourself or other students. Avoid touching the student, as this may escalate her or his anger. Talk only about what is happening at that moment and avoid reciting past problems or transgressions. It's best, too, in spite of any personal feelings that you may have, to avoid having the last word. Do *not*, at all costs, taunt (e.g., "Okay, just try it, go ahead and see where it gets you") or threaten (e.g., "You do that and you'll be sorry!"). Instead, give a clear and simple choice between the expected behavior and a consequence that you know you can deliver (e.g., "Bob, either return to your room now, or I'll call the police"). Don't get in the student's face. Give the student a few seconds to decide what to do. Then follow through, either by resuming the expected activity or applying the consequence.

Once you've given the student a choice, given the student a few seconds to decide, observed that the student is not complying with your expectations, and stated that the consequence will occur, don't let the student talk you out of applying the consequence; you *must* follow through on what you've said will occur. The student may well try to draw you into an argument, protesting that he or she is now complying with your expectation (e.g., "I'm going, I'm going!") or pleading that you're not being fair (e.g., "I didn't know you really meant it," or "You didn't give me enough time"). Decline to be drawn in by ignoring the protestations or pleading. You made your decision; stick with it, or your subsequent statements will be taken as hollow threats.

How should I talk with students who are withdrawn?

Aggressive, acting-out students are an obvious challenge, as you must think on your feet and respond quickly to in-your-face behavior. Withdrawn students are not so obvious a problem in grabbing your attention, but they are no less daunting. The student who shuts you out and won't respond to your questions can be very frustrating indeed, leaving you feeling defeated in your attempts to build a meaningful teacher-pupil relationship.

The rules of engagement with withdrawn students aren't so clearly developed as those with aggressive, acting-out students. However, we can suggest that you avoid several strategies because they are highly likely to fail. You would be unwise to bore in, to insist on a response, or to wheedle and cajole. Often, withdrawn students are highly reinforced by attention from adults who are obviously frustrated by their unresponsiveness and seem determined to hound them into talking. Punishing the student for not talking is foolish. Expecting a sudden or dramatic breakthrough is unrealistic. Other approaches may give you a considerably greater chance of success, although careful observation, sensitivity, patience, and satisfaction with small gains are required.

Spending time in proximity to the student, perhaps engaging in parallel activities and certainly watching carefully for signs of attention, may pay off. Your behavior and speech should indicate awareness of and interest in the student, not criticism. Look for what attracts the greatest interest of the student. Offer opportunities to engage in appropriate activities related to those interests and, if possible, arrange the activities to require some minimal verbal response from or interaction with someone else. Try communicating through written messages or use nonverbal communication (e.g., gestures, signals) if the student is persistently unresponsive to your speech. Be gently persistent, even relentless, in your attempts to communicate, but do so without conveying a sense of frustration or anger. That is, don't give up, but don't try to drag responses out of the student; the student will win this battle easily. Invite at every opportunity, entice if you can, but do so in a way that conveys calmness and confidence that you know what you're doing, not that you are at your wit's end.

A major factor in achieving success with withdrawn students is looking for successive approximations of normal social interaction. That is, you must be able to see and reinforce small steps in the direction of normal interaction. For example, if you have a student who simply won't respond in a large group of peers, then try to include the student in a smaller group, perhaps in a group with just one other student. If you have a student who will respond to your questions with only one-word answers, set your sights first on this student's responding with only a very few words. You may never make—and shouldn't intend to make—a social butterfly of a student who is severely withdrawn. You should, however, attempt to draw the student into successively closer approximations of normal social interaction.

Some students are persistently, consistently withdrawn. Others withdraw periodically, often after an emotional blowup or acting-out incident. In either case, it's critically important to be sensitive to signals that a student wants to be left alone. Nothing is gained by invading a student's "space" when he or she is clearly indicating that you're not welcome to be close by and that he or she doesn't want to talk to you. However, it's also important to monitor the student's behavior carefully, looking for opportunities to draw the student into appropriate interaction.

Summary

Talking with students about their behavior is one of the most complex aspects of teaching. The teacher must understand how classroom language is different from the language that students use at home or in the community. Particular care is required to develop communication skills that are sensitive to cultural differences.

Talking about behavior should be consistent with other instructional goals; the objective is to talk with students in ways that teach self-control. Teachers must learn how to avoid getting drawn into unproductive verbal interactions with students, such as arguments. They must also teach, through modeling and direct instruction, a variety of verbal and nonverbal communication skills such as listening, using proximity and body language, making eye contact, varying facial expressions, pausing, reflecting, probing, describing, choosing words and voice, pacing, summarizing, questioning, and waiting.

Talking with students about their appropriate behavior is critically important. The key is finding ways of expressing approval of the student's behavior that are meaningful to him or her. In talking with students about unacceptable behavior, it is important to keep the communication as private as possible and to highlight what is expected instead. Talking with angry and aggressive students requires preplanning, emotional detachment, and calmness in setting expectations and applying consequences. Students who are withdrawn present a different and daunting challenge. The best approach involves persistent but gentle, calm, and careful attempts to establish communication and induce social interaction.

Case Connection

Talking with students is an issue in every case. However, you might especially consider what teachers could say to students and how they would do so in the following cases:

The Truth About Alice   Janet Lane
They Failed Derrick   Melinda Smith

What You Don't Know Can Hurt You   John McCullum
Where to Now   Connie Ballard

CHAPTER SEVEN

Using Peer Influence

Questions for Reflection

How might I use observational learning and vicarious consequences to affect the behavior of my students' peers?

Models Who Are Likely to Be Imitated

Rewarding the Model and Target Student

Limits of Vicarious Effects

What type of group contingency might I use to create desirable peer pressure?

Independent Group Contingencies

Dependent Group Contingencies

Interdependent Group Contingencies

Cooperative Learning

Schoolwide Plans

Cautions About Group Contingencies

How might I engage peers as confederates?

How might I use peer tutors as a classroom resource?

Choosing and Training Tutors

Limitations of Peer Tutoring

What options should I consider in teaching social skills?

Summary

Case Connection

People usually assume that the most important things students learn in school are the things they learn from their teachers. This assumption may or may not be correct. It's well known that students learn a great deal from each other. Our hope is that what they learn from each other improves their conduct and achievement, but we know that this often isn't the case. Students learn much by observing each other, and their observations sometimes lead to conflicts or withdrawal. Frequent serious conflicts with peers, minimal interactions with peers, and association with deviant peers are indications that a student is likely to have long-term personal problems, as we noted in Chapter 3.

Teaching requires the management of groups to foster positive and satisfying peer relations. Teachers must recognize the pervasive influence of peer groups in nearly every person's life. Even teachers are concerned about what other teachers think. Moreover, the behavior of our colleagues influences our perceptions of important events, many of our decisions, and significant aspects of our professional relationships. But perhaps the peer group exerts its greatest influence during the middle school and high school years. It's not that peers exert no influence at all in other grades, just that middle schoolers and high schoolers seem particularly swayed by peer influence.

Many adults are highly aware of peer influences. We may consciously choose certain friends and imitate our peers to enhance our professional skills, ethical conduct, and personal satisfaction. Many students aren't so keenly aware of peer influence and aren't so astute in choosing their associations.

Teachers have an obligation to do what they can to make positive peer influence an important aspect of their students' lives in the classroom and to help students learn to make wise choices about peer relationships. The vignettes of a teacher, Sally (and pupils Kevin and Derrick) and a student we call Marcus illustrate some of the issues teachers face in helping students get along with and learn appropriate behavior from their peers.

Sally

Kevin, as I said, was a real problem because he didn't comply with my requests or commands. That's the reason I made up little compliance lessons in which I had him practice doing what I told him. My first thought was to teach him individually, but then two things occurred to me. First of all, he didn't interact much with any of the other kids in my class. He was a very, very strange little boy in many ways and didn't seem to pay much attention to his classmates. Most of the time he seemed "spaced out" and not in touch with what was going on around him. Second, I had another child in my class, Derrick, who was a lot more compliant than Kevin but still needed a little improvement. I thought it'd be a good idea to teach Kevin and Derrick together in my compliance lessons. Derrick could serve as a model for Kevin because he would usually do what I asked. My strategy early in the lessons was to get an appropriate response from Derrick to one of my instructions, reinforce him, then ask Kevin to do the same thing. I also alternated instructions so that Derrick wasn't always the first to respond. This approach worked really well because Derrick was, at first, a good model for Kevin. But I also found that Kevin started interacting with Derrick at other times during the day.

Marcus

When he was 17 years of age and a sophomore in high school, Marcus read on a fourth-grade level, and his spelling level was third grade. One of his teachers described him as "hell on wheels." When asked to read silently, he would provoke another student or simply walk out of the classroom. He seldom completed his homework or brought school supplies to class. He had such high anxiety about tests that when he was given his first unit test he stood up, overturned his desk, and left the classroom. He threw erasers or chairs at anyone who disagreed with him. He bullied the boys in his classroom with overt physical threats and bullied the girls with covert, sexually derogatory insults. He made frequent accusations against the teacher and seemed always to want to argue with her. He was a 6-foot-two-inch out-of-control adolescent. His teacher was uncertain just how to talk to him about his inappropriate behavior because he seemed unapproachable in any reasonable way. She found that refusing his invitations to argue and merely stating her expectations as calmly as possible was the best way to avoid Marcus's blowups.

Source: Based on a case described in Stichter, Conroy, & Kauffman, 2008.

Peer pressure will be at work in the classroom whether the teacher harnesses it or not. Social pressure from peers is more obvious in some classrooms than in others. In some classrooms it obviously affects every student; in others it is seen most clearly in an "in-group." In some classrooms the pressure of the in-group is for academic achievement, but in many classrooms there is pressure to resist academic learning and to be disruptive. Some classrooms are characterized by feelings of belonging or togetherness of all the students, whereas others are characterized by tension, divisiveness, scapegoating, exclusive cliques, and destructive competition.

Experienced teachers know that every group, like every individual student, is different from every other. Some groups are easy and some are difficult to manage. The group's character seems to depend on the mix of individuals comprising it and the circumstances that bring it together. The dissimilarities in peer relations that we observe in various classrooms aren't due only to differences in teachers' skills in managing groups. Still, there are enough common or predictable features of groups and peer interactions that we can offer suggestions about strategies that are likely to be useful in accomplishing specific goals. Important questions teachers need to ask themselves about managing peer influence include these:

- How can I harness peer pressure as an effective force for improving my students' behavior and achievement?
- How can I encourage cooperation and caring for each other among my students?
- How can I help students on the social fringes of the class become better accepted among their well-behaved peers?

QUESTIONS FOR REFLECTION

As you contemplate what you might do to foster good peer relations among your students and how you might use group pressure effectively and humanely, you will need to keep in mind the basic psychological processes involved in social groups. For example, people in groups learn much by observing each other, especially by noticing the positive and negative consequences of other students' experiences. Watching what happens to others not only reveals how to obtain consequences but it also allows the observer to experience those consequences *vicariously*—as a substitute for one's own experience. Finally, individuals in groups are loosely or tightly bound together by structures that are imposed by group leaders or by an outside authority. The way individuals relate to each other as group members depends partly on the rules for sharing in each others' success and failure. We suggest that you ask yourself at least the following questions about specific strategies:

- How might I use observational learning and vicarious consequences to affect the behavior of my students' peers?
- What type of group contingency might I use to create desirable peer pressure?
- How might I engage classroom peers as confederates?
- How might I use peer tutors as a classroom resource?
- What options should I consider in teaching social skills?

How might I use observational learning and vicarious consequences to affect the behavior of my students' peers?

Teachers must always be aware that they are serving as models for their students. Youngsters learn a lot about teaching, parenting, relating to peers, and other aspects of socialization by watching adults. You need to be particularly concerned about practicing what you preach because your students probably will learn at least as much from what they see as they do from what they hear. One question that should be in your mind is whether your students would be behaving appropriately if they imitated you. We recognize that adults have prerogatives that children and adolescents don't have. Yet, you don't want to lose sight of the importance of adults providing good models for younger generations.

Children and adolescents are also keen observers of each other. Perceptive teachers use students' tendency to watch and imitate their peers as a means of improving the conduct of those who exhibit inappropriate behavior. They do this by having students whose conduct is desirable serve as models for others who are misbehaving or having difficulty learning. The inappropriate conduct that may be improved through peer modeling includes a wide range of problems, such as being inattentive, aggressive, or socially withdrawn; it may also include lack of study skills or specific academic difficulties.

Using observational learning successfully requires careful selection of the model (student) whom you hope will be imitated. You also must reward the model and the student(s) you want to imitate the model and do this in a way that does not discourage the student who is observing. When you use procedures that are intended to enhance observational learning, it's likely that most or all students in the classroom will experience vicarious effects. That is, when any student receives reinforcing or punishing consequences, those who are watching probably will be affected indirectly through their vicarious experience of the reward or punishment.

MODELS WHO ARE LIKELY TO BE IMITATED   Some individuals are much more likely than others to be imitated by their peers. This means that when you use an observational learning strategy, you must attempt to choose a model whose behavior probably will be most influential with the target student. Research doesn't indicate precisely the type of model who's most likely to be imitated in every circumstance, but we can offer some general guidelines. Usually, you'd be wise to choose a model whom the target student sees as attractive, competent, and similar to himself or herself in important ways (e.g., someone of the same sex and close to the same general ability level). If the behavior you hope the target student will imitate is one that he or she has had considerable difficulty learning, then a coping model is best—a model whom the target student can see overcoming difficulties on the way to mastery, not one who has already mastered the behavior and performs it effortlessly and flawlessly. For example, if you're looking for a model to help a target student overcome a serious fear of talking in class, the best classmate to serve as a model won't be one who enjoys public speaking. Rather, it'll be one who has some hesitation about speaking up but manages to overcome his or her anxiety about it. Watching someone who shares your anxiety or difficulty overcome it and perform successfully tends to make you feel that you can do the same; observing someone who apparently never shared your struggle isn't nearly as encouraging.

Keep two principles in mind: First, the model must be personally attractive to the observer or imitation isn't likely. People tend to imitate those they admire, as well as those they perceive as sharing similar characteristics but as somewhat "better" than themselves along certain dimensions. Second, the model must exhibit behavior that the observer believes he or she can imitate successfully. People often imitate those they admire, even if they're very different from themselves in most respects. In fact, what they imitate may have little or nothing to do with the primary reason they find others attractive. For example, an individual might imitate the dress or mannerisms of popular musicians but have no intention of imitating—and no ability to imitate—their musicianship. If someone is just learning to play a musical instrument, or learning another skill, the best model is someone who can demonstrate a level of skill just above his or hers. Virtuosic performances may provide inspiration to continue learning, but beginners who are expected to imitate a master are likely to get discouraged and give up. Teachers sometimes make the mistake of choosing models who are too "good" or too competent to be encouraging of imitation by the target student.

REWARDING THE MODEL AND TARGET STUDENT   Sometimes models are imitated even though the imitators aren't directly rewarded. However, the target student is much more likely to imitate the model you've chosen if he or she sees the model receiving reinforcement for appropriate behavior.

Thus it's important to provide the reinforcement for the model when the target student is watching. In some cases, if the target student is unaware that the model is to be imitated, you may need to prompt the target student by telling him or her to watch the way the model behaves (or solves a problem). Then you must be sure to reinforce the target student immediately when his or her behavior approximates that of the model. If the target student observes that others receive rewards for a given behavior, but that he or she isn't rewarded for the same behavior, the result may be demoralization or inappropriate behavior. The model's behavior should demonstrate the kind of behavior or performance you expect; your response to the model should demonstrate that such behavior will be rewarded, and the target student's attempts to imitate the model should be rewarded.

In the typical classroom, a lot of things are going on simultaneously. Individual students' behavior is sometimes good, sometimes not so good. You will be more likely to encourage good behavior in the group if you call attention to the specific conduct of well-behaved students. Make your social reinforcement of desirable conduct as specific as possible, so that the behavior you want to encourage in observing students isn't only demonstrated by the model but described. "John, I like the way you waited to be called on" is better than "Thank you, John, for being polite" because it's a more specific description of the behavior you want observers to imitate.

LIMITS OF VICARIOUS EFFECTS   Teachers who are excellent behavior managers often make good use of vicarious effects to encourage good conduct. For example, when they observe minor misbehavior, they ignore it and show obvious approval for appropriate behavior of another student, usually someone in close proximity to the one who's misbehaving. In this way they offer a vicarious prompt to the misbehaving student; they are saying, in effect, "Behave in this way (like the appropriately behaved student), because then you'll get my attention and approval." They focus on desirable conduct, knowing that the observing students may not only be prompted to behave appropriately but also experience vicarious gratification when they behave in the same way as those who are being rewarded.

Rewarding models in the hope that observers will imitate desirable behavior can backfire if you're not prepared for at least two possible complications. First, you must be careful not to rely on a single model or a small group. If only one student or a small group of students is constantly featured as fulfilling your expectations, then the rest of the class is likely to see you as playing favorites or having "pets." This will quickly destroy the effectiveness of the models and undermine your use of rewarding consequences. Make sure that you catch the good behavior of as many different students as possible and call attention to it. Second, in some groups—and this tends to be a particular problem among adolescents—"teacher-pleasing" behavior is anathema, a taboo, something that carries a stigma. You must be prepared for groups in which typical statements of praise or approval aren't rewarding and may, in fact, be punishing. This doesn't mean that you can't use vicarious consequences or that you must become punitive. It means that you must be very shrewd in rewarding the behavior you want to encourage. You may need to keep your praise and approval minimal and emphasize—matter-of-factly—rewarding consequences that are meaningful to the group. These consequences may be activities or privileges that members of the group see as desirable.

We caution further that few people, if any, can live by vicarious effects alone. A person may be able to share to some extent in the joy and pain others are experiencing directly, but others' lives can't become a substitute for his or her own direct experience. Compared to direct experience of consequences, vicarious effects are weak. Furthermore, vicarious approaches typically work well with groups that are generally well behaved; they aren't likely to work with groups that are highly disruptive or out of control. For very poorly behaved groups, frequent direct rewards for individuals who are behaving appropriately are typically necessary.

We offer an additional caution about the limitations of vicarious effects. If an individual observes others receiving consequences for certain behavior but receives no consequences for the same behavior, the effect is likely to be the opposite vicarious consequence. For example, if a student in your class sees others receiving rewarding consequences for certain behavior, yet he or she seldom or never is rewarded for behaving similarly, then the effect will in all likelihood be vicarious punishment—he or she will feel, by comparison to others who are being rewarded or punished. Alternatively, if a student sees others being punished for certain behavior, yet he or she isn't punished for similar behavior, then the effect will be vicarious reinforcement—he or she will feel rewarded. This principle suggests that favoritism or bias in a teacher's consequences will compound behavior problems. Students who observe their classmates receiving rewarding or punishing consequences for a specific kind of behavior should receive the same treatment. If they don't receive at least similar treatment, then the effect on their behavior is likely to be the opposite of that for those who are receiving direct consequences.

What type of group contingency might I use to create desirable peer pressure?

The contingencies of reinforcement that teachers use often apply to individuals without any reference to the peer group. However, contingencies can also be arranged for groups in a variety of ways, some of which produce considerable peer pressure on individuals to behave in ways that earn rewards or avoid punishment.

The phenomenon of group pressure is well known, and it is a pervasive feature of social groups. Consider the group pressure that is part of political parties, unions, professional organizations, fraternities and sororities, and religious groups. All of these rely on peer pressure as one means of controlling the behavior of members and furthering their collective aims. One cannot conclude that group pressure is undesirable, although there are examples in which groups have destructive aims or use excessive and cruel peer pressure. As a teacher, your task is to encourage peer pressure for appropriate behavior and keep it from becoming excessive or inhumane.

Any contingency that's oriented toward a group will create some level of peer pressure. Group-oriented contingencies include those in which the same rules apply to all individuals independently, those in which consequences for the entire group depend on the behavior of one member, and those in which the consequences for the entire group are interdependent (all members of the group obtain the same consequences based on the combined behavior of the members). Each type of contingency has certain advantages and disadvantages in the classroom. Combinations of group and individual contingencies are possible, and you may want to consider how you could combine contingencies to structure the most effective learning environment, for specific individuals and groups.

INDEPENDENT GROUP CONTINGENCIES   Independent group contingencies are those that apply uniformly to each student, regardless of the performance of the group. For example, you might establish the following contingency for students in your classroom: "If you turn in acceptably completed homework, you are allowed to participate in a five-minute period of free time for talking with friends." This is a group contingency, in that it applies to the entire class; it's independent, in that one student's behavior doesn't affect any other student's consequences.

Independent group contingencies have the advantage of focusing on individual responsibility. Their disadvantage in managing a group is that they don't generate much peer pressure. About the only pressure from peers will be that which is already present in the form of friendship ties and the relatively weak and indirect influences of modeling and vicarious consequences.

DEPENDENT GROUP CONTINGENCIES   Dependent group contingencies are those under which rewards are available for all group members only when requirements are met by one member or a small subset of the group. An example of a dependent group contingency is the "hero procedure" used by Gerald Patterson, renowned for his research with aggressive children, and his colleagues. They made class "heroes" of hyperactive, disruptive students by setting a contingency under which these students earned rewards for the entire class by paying attention and behaving appropriately.

An advantage of dependent group contingencies can be positive peer pressure—peers may "root for" the target student and do whatever they can to encourage him or her to behave appropriately because they have something to gain by doing so. Another possible advantage is that the social status of the target student may be improved if his or her behavior becomes a source of rewards for peers. A disadvantage is that the misbehaving student can become a target for peer harassment and the other members of the class can feel that they are being denied an "entitlement" when they don't receive a reward. The way the dependent group contingency is presented, as well as the nature of the group to which it's applied, may determine whether the advantages outweigh the disadvantages or vice versa. The reward earned for the entire group by the target student must be an extra—an add-on to the rewarding consequences routinely available to the group—or there's too much risk of negative peer reactions when the reward isn't earned.

INTERDEPENDENT GROUP CONTINGENCIES   Interdependent group contingencies are those in which a specific requirement for a reward applies to all members of the group but the reward depends on the combined or total performance of the group, as well as the behavior of individuals. That is, the group's combined performance is the criterion for anyone to receive reinforcement, and all share equally in the reward. For example, a teacher might allow the class to participate in a special activity after each member of the class completes an assignment successfully. Basically, team sports are interdependent group contingencies—individuals contribute to the team's success, but it's the team, not an individual, that wins.

The "Good Behavior Game" is an interdependent group contingency that has been used in a variety of forms by teachers (Babyak, Luze, & Kamps, 2000). The essential features of the game are these: (1) the teacher states certain rules that apply to all members of the class; (2) all members of the class can earn points for the class (or their "team," a subgroup of the class) by behaving according to the rules; and (3) the class (or team) earns rewards, depending on the total number of points earned by the group's members. In some variations on the game, the class or team has earned a reward for accumulating less than a certain number of points given for specific misbehavior (i.e., the rules of the game were reversed, with low misbehavior points "winning").

Interdependent group contingencies typically create peer pressure; whether it's primarily positive or negative pressure depends a lot on the composition of the "teams." One member can sabotage the team, creating considerable hostility among other team members. Teams that are clearly unequal in ability quickly create problems. Overemphasis on competition can cause scapegoating and other negative peer interactions. Our suggestion is that you consider using interdependent group contingencies, as they are powerful devices for harnessing peer pressure, but that you use them with considerable caution.

COOPERATIVE LEARNING   Nearly every teacher has at least heard the term **cooperative learning**, if not read about or been instructed in cooperative learning procedures. Many variations on the theme of cooperative learning are possible, but they all have in common the combined use of independent and interdependent group contingencies. Pairs or larger teams of students work under contingencies in which their combined performance, as well as their individual improvement, is evaluated and rewarded. Some variants of cooperative learning deemphasize individual achievement and concentrate on group performance and reward. Cooperative learning procedures hold great promise as a means of fostering positive peer interactions. We encourage the use of cooperative learning strategies with the cautions we offer for all group contingencies.

SCHOOLWIDE PLANS   Sometimes behavior management plans are schoolwide. This is extremely desirable if all school personnel can decide to work together on a plan and carry it out (see Darch & Kame'enui, 2004; Kerr & Nelson, 2010; Lewis, Newcomer, Trussell, & Richter, 2006; Martella, Nelson, & Marchand-Martella, 2003; Walker, Ramsey, & Gresham, 2004). In a schoolwide plan of positive behavioral support, the expectations for students are consistent, and the focus is on approval and reward for desirable behavior. If a schoolwide system of positive behavioral support is implemented well, peer encouragement of appropriate behavior works not just in a classroom but in the entire school, including places like hallways, playgrounds, and cafeterias.

CAUTIONS ABOUT GROUP CONTINGENCIES   Group contingencies of the types we have described can encourage positive peer pressure, but they can also backfire and result in negative pressure and coercion if they aren't carefully managed. We offer five suggestions for avoiding the common problems of threats, criticism, and harassment from peers when a student doesn't perform as his or her peers would like. If, in spite of following our cautions, a group you are managing is putting negative pressure on certain of its members, we recommend that you revise or eliminate the contingency.

   1. Be certain that the performance standard you set isn't too high. You must begin with a criterion for reward that the target student or group can meet easily, then gradually increase the requirement for reward. If you set the standard too high in the beginning, everyone may be disappointed; if you expect gradual improvement over time, however, the target student or group is more likely to win approval from the rest of the class. Early success in achieving the reward should be virtually guaranteed in the beginning by setting a requirement that represents slight improvement over current behavior.

   2. Emphasize reward for appropriate performance rather than punishment for undesirable behavior. Whenever possible, state the contingency positively and reward the group for good behavior (e.g., "We'll all take a 10-minute break when everyone has finished this math assignment" is preferable to "Nobody can take a break until everyone has finished this work"). The alternative—stating rules not to be broken and giving points for misbehavior—means that one or a few students can easily sabotage their peers' efforts by deliberate misbehavior. These "spoilers" may encounter a lot of hostility and threats from their classmates, and this may set the stage for escalating coercive interactions.

   3. Keep the competition fair. If you divide the class or school into teams, make certain that the teams have about equal chances to "win." Whenever possible, allow everyone to earn a reward for good performance and the "winners" to earn a little extra.

   4. When using interdependent group contingencies, encourage everyone to participate, but don't require it. Forced participation will almost certainly set up the group for failure. Group contingencies will not work for all students in all circumstances. Use the group only for students who are willing "players." Let those who don't want to be team members "sit out."

   5. Make allowances for those who don't work well as part of any group you can construct. In spite of your best efforts, some students may repeatedly or purposely torpedo their group's efforts. Don't merely exclude these students from participation in groups. Set up individual contingencies for them, and keep open the possibility of their rejoining a group when they are willing to work cooperatively with their peers. Even in schoolwide plans, individual behavior management plans may be necessary for some individuals (see Darch & Kame'enui, 2004; Lewis; Newcomer, Trussell, & Richter, 2006). Removing one or a few individuals from the group contingency is often better than abandoning it for the majority. For those who are removed, however, you must have individual expectations and provide rewarding consequences for appropriate behavior.

How might I engage peers as confederates?

Students are a potential classroom resource as teachers' confederates—accomplices, allies, or assistants of the teacher in specific interventions. Sometimes a peer confederate is able to extend the teacher's reach by carrying out specific intervention procedures that the teacher can't implement because of a lack of time or because the object of the intervention is to enhance peer relations that only another student can initiate directly. When a peer is serving as the teacher's confederate, the confederate's role may be explained to the target student, but this isn't always the case. Depending on the specific role of the confederate and the nature of the target student's behavior, you may need to obtain parental permission and administrative approval before implementing the intervention procedures. You must exercise careful professional judgment in deciding whether the interactions between confederate and target will be such that parents or school administrators might question their appropriateness. If in doubt, discuss the role you propose for the confederate with your supervisor or principal before proceeding.

Peers are particularly useful as models and tutors for specific skills, as we discuss elsewhere in this chapter. Students may also learn how to give very effective social reinforcers to their peers in naturally occurring interactions. In addition, peers may be very helpful as confederates in initiating social interactions with students who are socially isolated or withdrawn. Confederates must be carefully chosen and trained. The teacher must know precisely the role the student is to play in the intervention, model that role for the confederate, and provide feedback as the confederate rehearses precisely what to do. Moreover, the teacher must monitor the confederate's performance to make sure he or she is implementing the procedures as intended.

Not all students are capable of serving as confederates, and any student who does so will require careful training and supervision. Peer confederates must be reliable in several respects. They should have good school attendance so that you are able to depend on their availability. In addition, confederates should be generally positive in their interactions with peers, able to avoid negative interactions with peers under nearly any circumstance, and able to follow your instructions. You shouldn't select as a peer confederate a student who isn't liked by the target child; the confederate should be socially attractive to the target student or at least socially neutral.

Some interventions may be appropriate if implemented by the teacher but not if they are implemented by a peer confederate. Using a peer confederate to assist in punishment isn't, in our opinion, justifiable (with the possible exception of some peer-implemented conflict resolution procedures). Peer confederates are best used to provide good models, tutor or coach fellow students in specific skills, initiate positive social interactions with target classmates, and deliver positive reinforcement for specific desirable behavior as determined by the teacher.

Conflict resolution by trained peers is a strategy that has been implemented in some schools and classrooms. Students serve as counselors or mediators who try to help their peers resolve disputes in nonviolent ways. They are trained in specific negotiation procedures to resolve minor problems, the goal being to catch conflicts before they escalate into major struggles. Some conflicts clearly are too much for peers to manage, and proper training will help students recognize problems that need to be dealt with by an adult. However, many students at all grade levels can learn to help their peers step back from minor confrontations, to ask questions that clarify each party's goals and point of contention, and to negotiate a nonviolent solution that is satisfactory to both parties. In some schools, mediation or conflict resolution has been made a part of the social studies curriculum. We note that not every attempt to train and use peer mediators has been successful. Training takes time and special expertise on the part of teachers, and peer mediators need time and a private place in which to resolve disputes. The resources required for successful peer mediation are not always available.

How might I use peer tutors as a classroom resource?

Peer tutoring became an extremely popular idea in the 1990s. No teacher should plunge into peer tutoring, however, without a clear idea of what the tutoring is to accomplish (see Kerr & Nelson, 2010). The skills to be acquired by the tutees must be stated explicitly. Also important are the objectives for the tutors. Using a classroom peer as a tutor solely to save the teacher's time and effort is highly questionable. Tutors should be learning valuable skills themselves during the process of tutoring, and the teacher should be able to state exactly what those skills are. Some studies have shown that tutors' academic performance or social behavior improves, but such improvement can't be taken for granted. Before launching a peer tutoring intervention, you should be able to answer these questions:

- What specific skills do I expect the tutee to acquire from this tutoring?
- What specific benefits do I expect for the tutor?
- Is peer tutoring the most effective and efficient way I can attain my goals for the tutee and tutor?

CHOOSING AND TRAINING TUTORS   Ordinarily, teachers assume that when they enlist peers as tutors they're making better use of their time and operating a more efficient and effective instructional program. Before assuming that peer tutoring makes better use of your resources, however, you must consider how much time and effort will be required to train and supervise the tutor(s). Some teachers have implemented relatively unstructured and unsupervised tutoring. The teacher has merely told students to work in small groups and help each other learn academic tasks, such as spelling words. Other teachers have given tutors very explicit and relatively extensive training in how to teach specific skills. This kind of training has sometimes involved modeling by the teacher, rehearsal by the tutor under the guidance of the teacher, and frequent feedback on performance. Obviously, the specific objectives for the tutor and the tutee as well as their abilities will determine how much training and supervision are required and therefore how much of the teacher's time, if any, is saved.

Classwide peer tutoring has been implemented by some teachers, whereas others have involved only a few of their students. Sometimes same-age peers have been used; sometimes tutors have been substantially different from their tutees in age. In spite of the popularity of peer tutoring as an academic intervention, research doesn't yet indicate clearly the characteristics of the optimum tutor-tutee match. In any case, you should consider how a variety of characteristics of the students involved as tutors or tutees might contribute to the success or failure of peer tutoring: relative ages, gender, social class, ethnicity, and skill development, for example. Also critically important are behavioral characteristics, especially the tendency to be punitive toward others, the ability to give contingent praise and other rewards, and susceptibility to peer influence. The specific tutoring arrangements you choose must be based on your knowledge of the individual students involved and your estimate of how they'll interact, given the specific tasks you have set for them.

LIMITATIONS OF PEER TUTORING   Effective teachers and aides aren't easily recruited, trained, and evaluated. We doubt that untrained and unmonitored peer tutors will provide instruction equal in effectiveness to that of most classroom teachers and aides. Although we recognize its potential benefits, the simplicity and cost effectiveness of peer tutoring are exaggerated in some reports of its use. Peers can and often do help each other, but they don't always do so, and they aren't likely to do so without careful planning, monitoring, and training.

Peer tutoring might create more behavior problems than it resolves if it's not carefully implemented. Depending on the match of tutor and tutee, the specific skills being tutored, and the training, supervision, and reinforcement for the students involved, peer tutoring can have remarkably positive or negative outcomes. Some disruptive, unmotivated students will learn a great deal and become more tractable when they serve as a tutor for a peer or when they are tutored by another student. Students who are socially withdrawn and unresponsive in a larger group may develop close relationships and learn critical social skills when involved in a peer tutoring arrangement. Others, however, will carry their behavioral difficulties into the tutoring interactions. Some students may engage their tutees or tutors in coercive interactions or fail to use their assigned time together in the manner intended by their teachers. You must be aware that peer tutoring has the potential for negative outcomes and be ready to modify or terminate tutoring arrangements in which coercion or inappropriate use of time allocated for tutoring is a problem.

What options should I consider in teaching social skills?

Within the past decade, teachers and researchers have begun to recognize the fact that social skills are perhaps as important as academic skills in determining students' futures (see Darch & Kame'enui, 2004). Without good social skills, students' academic progress is likely to be less than optimal, their future educational opportunities are likely to be restricted, and they are less likely to make a successful transition to adulthood and employment. Consequently, most educators now place more emphasis on the social learning that occurs in the classroom (Kerr & Nelson, 2010; Walker, Ramsey, & Gresham, 2004).

Social skills are taught by parents, families, peer groups, and teachers. To a large extent, the social skills training children receive is informal and incidental—we might even say haphazard. Educators are now beginning to realize that many students fail to learn social skills under these conditions, just as they fail to learn academic skills when instruction is haphazard. As is true in the case of academic instruction, most teachers have neither the time nor the expertise to develop their own curriculum and instructional materials for teaching social skills. Fortunately, social skills training programs, including specific materials and lessons, have been developed for students at both the elementary and secondary levels. Regardless of what program you adopt or what social skills training activities you plan for your students, you'll need to ask yourself the following questions:

• *What are the particular social skills that my students need to learn?* Careful observation and reflection may help you understand exactly what it is about the social behavior of particular students that is problematic. For example, the problem might be one or more of the following:

inappropriate eye contact during interactions
lack of response to social initiations from others
maladaptive responses to instructions from authority
giving or responding to criticism inappropriately
impulsive or aggressive responses that provoke social conflict
inability to demonstrate appropriate affect.

Understanding the demands of positive social interactions and relationships is critically important in describing the social skills one needs. Try to describe precisely what your students need to learn to do, as well as what they need to learn not to do, if they're to become more successful in their relationships with others.

• ***Do my teaching strategies promote social competence?*** Some teachers employ instructional approaches that minimize social interaction, providing almost no opportunity to learn social skills. These teaching strategies, which focus almost exclusively on independent work and individual responses, demand so little interpersonal competence that social skills become relatively trivial.

• ***Do I teach social skills explicitly?*** Most teaching activities should encourage social interaction. However, providing opportunities for social interaction isn't enough for many students. Explicit instruction is often necessary. A social skills curriculum must focus on helping students acquire and use an acceptable level of specific social skills. Talking about social skills isn't enough. Rehearsing and practicing them with feedback on performance are necessary.

• ***Am I able to generalize training in social skills from simulated to actual social situations?*** It's one thing to be able to exhibit social skills in a familiar and friendly environment; it's quite another to exhibit the same skills in the presence of unfamiliar and unresponsive or antagonistic individuals. Your curriculum and instructional strategies for social skills must take into account the importance of helping students extend their skills beyond the training sessions in which you teach them.

• ***Is my approach to social skills training consistent with the needs of students with mild disabilities and students at risk?*** Students with disabilities—especially mild mental retardation, learning disabilities, and emotional or behavioral disorders—may need social skills training that most students don't. Likewise, students at risk (i.e., seemingly headed for academic or social failure but not yet identified as having a disability) may not respond like most students to particular social situations. Students with disabilities and students who are at risk may need more explicit and directive instruction in social skills than the more typical student.

Summary

Teaching requires managing the behavior of groups. Peer pressure is always present in groups, whether harnessed by the teacher or not. You must attempt to foster positive and humane peer pressure that encourages a sense of togetherness or belonging among members of the class, cooperation and caring of students for each other, and better acceptance of those who are at the social fringes of the group. Students are keen observers of each other, as well as of adults. Teachers often use observational learning and the tendency to imitate certain peers and adults as a means of improving behavior. Effective observational learning procedures highlight the appropriate behavior of attractive models and that includes rewarding consequences for both the model and those who imitate the model. The vicarious experience of consequences by those who witness models being reinforced for desirable conduct may influence the observers' behavior. Vicarious effects are relatively weak, however, and direct consequences are necessary for managing serious behavior problems.

Group contingencies create peer pressure and can be used in a variety of forms, including independent, dependent, and interdependent contingencies. Cooperative learning procedures involve a combination of individual and group contingencies. Care is needed to avoid possible negative peer pressure when group contingencies are used. With proper selection and training, many students can serve as effective confederates of the teacher in implementing positive behavior management procedures. Also with proper selection and training, most students can also serve as effective tutors for their peers. Teaching social skills necessarily involves group learning and a curriculum designed to teach appropriate interpersonal responses.

Case Connection

Many of the cases in Part II describe situations in which you could think about behavior management strategies involving peers. However, you might find the following cases particularly helpful for thinking about how peers can be involved in managing behavior:

Avoiding the Issue   Johnny's Teachers
The Truth About Alice   Janet Lane
What's Inclusion Got to Do with It?   Anita Atkinson
Winnie   Patty Gray

CHAPTER EIGHT

Working with Other Teachers and Other Professionals

Questions for Reflection

What do I need to know about working with someone whose views are much like mine?

How do I work with someone who doesn't share my views?

Finding Out About Other People's Views

Making Your Views Clear

Finding Mutual Objectives

How and what can I learn from other teachers?

Listening and Reading

Watching

Learning

How do I share my ideas with others most effectively?

Sensitivity and Tactfulness

Clarity and Terseness

Acceptance

What does it take to make collaboration benefit me and my students?

What are the limits of collaboration?

When am I better off "doing my own thing"?

Summary

Case Connection

W orking with other teachers and other professionals (usually called **collaboration**), especially the collaboration of special education and general education teachers, is considered essential in schools of the early 21st century. In fact, there's now a substantial literature on collaboration of general and special educators (see Eber & Keenan, 2004; Friend & Shamberger, 2008; Kerr & Nelson, 2010; Sawyer, 2004; Soodak & McCarthy, 2006; Trent, Artiles, Fitchett-Bazemore, McDaniel, & Coleman-Sorrell, 2002; Trent, Driver, Wood, Parrott, Martin, & Smith, 2003). But collaboration can involve the joint work of any teacher, including only general educators or only special educators. And regardless of whether they teach general or special education, teachers must work with principals, supervisors, psychologists, and other support personnel. So collaboration doesn't involve just the special-general educator distinction.

Teachers must do their best to work well with each other and other professionals to provide the best instruction and behavior management. And although the goal of collaboration is often the inclusion of students with disabilities in general education, that's only part of the story. Teachers need to work with each other as best they can for the benefit of *all* of their students. Probably this is most obvious when the goal is a schoolwide plan for behavior management. In reality, though, successful collaboration isn't easy, isn't simple, and usually is a far longer, more involved story than the instances in which it doesn't work. Consider the vignettes describing the experiences of Jennifer and Penny:

Jennifer

When I first entered Washington School as special education teacher, the school year had already begun, and my caseload had already been determined—IEPs written, homerooms assigned, schedules established. I was responsible for 10 students, most of whom had mental retardation, from three grade levels (K, 1, and 2). Every student had a different schedule, a different homeroom teacher, and obviously, different instructional and behavioral needs. All of my previous teaching experience had been in a self-contained classroom, so I really wasn't sure how to approach this new situation and be sure I was meeting the needs of all of my students. In addition, as the "new kid on the block," I didn't feel comfortable jumping in and changing everything right from the start. That first year, I made a few minor adjustments: I made sure students in the same grade level were assigned to the same homerooms, and I used my instructional assistants to provide instruction and supervision for students when I needed to be somewhere else. However, I never felt good about this arrangement—I knew my students were not receiving the intensive, targeted, coordinated instruction they needed, and I knew they were having to deal with far too many teachers and transitions throughout the day. On the positive side, that first year provided me with the opportunity to work with and observe several general-education teachers and get a feel for their instructional capabilities, behavior management styles, and organizational skills. Then I started planning for the next year.

First, I approached a teacher, Julie, who I knew was very strong instructionally, gentle but firm in her behavior management approach, and highly organized and efficient. I shared with her my idea of selecting a first-grade classroom to be our "partner class." Despite the fact that my students would be from multiple grade levels, academically they were all quite similar, working on pre-K and kindergarten skills and demonstrating serious receptive and expressive language delays and disorders. First grade seemed like an appropriate grade where my students could "fit in" developmentally. I explained to Julie that if her class became our partner class we would follow the same schedule, which would mean going to P.E., art, music, and library at the same time. We would have lunch, recess, and holiday celebrations together to allow for social interactions among the students. We would co-plan field trips and even have class pictures and semiannual award ceremonies together—times when my students traditionally felt left out, not quite knowing where they belonged.

Julie and I usually taught literacy and math separately because my students' needs were not similar to those of her students in these areas, but we co-taught science and social studies, doing our best to integrate the curricula from the various grade levels whenever appropriate and possible. If my students' needs changed and one or more of my students became ready to be integrated successfully into a general education classroom for literacy or math, she and I would work together to adjust that student's schedule.

I could tell Julie was excited about the idea. She had been watching me over the year, too, and she sensed that we had similar instructional styles and behavior management approaches. She had had several special education students "included" in her classroom in the past, and she was frustrated with the way their schedules were always "chopped up," and support from the special education teacher depended upon how many children she was serving and what times worked out well for her. Moreover, despite her efforts to make the special education students feel welcome and important in her class, Julie never thought these students had a "home" in either classroom—general or special education. She agreed to try the new inclusion model if we could obtain administrative support.

The next step was to meet with our principal, Mrs. Graham. Julie and I went together. We started by explaining the rationale for doing things a little differently. I talked about my frustration over not being able to provide intensive, uninterrupted, coordinated, and targeted instruction for my students and the inefficiency of having them make so many transitions throughout the day. Julie spoke about her past experiences with the "revolving door" model of inclusion—how it seemed to leave the students feeling ungrounded and herself feeling unsupported in trying to meet the needs of students with such intense needs. Mrs. Graham listened attentively, clearly impressed with the extent to which Julie and I had thought through the details of this new plan. She had a few questions, mostly logistical, but agreed to support us in any way she could.

The plan worked beautifully. During the first week of school, I spent time in Julie's class talking about the kids in my class (my students were not present). I began by asking students what they knew about me and my class. As expected, students had noticed that I didn't have as many students in my room, but we had more teachers. Some had observed that the kids in my class weren't all in the same grade. And one rather precocious first grader shared that the students in my class had "disabilities." We continued to discuss what it means to have a disability (inability to do something that most can) and how we all have inabilities in some areas. I asked, "Who here knows how to fly an airplane?" Of course, no hands went up. Then I said, "Well, then, I could say that we all have an inability to fly a plane." What makes my kids different, I explained, is that they are unable to do some things that most kids their age can do. Next I pulled out a photo of each of my students, and we talked about him or her. "This is Dylan," I explained. "His disability has to do with talking. It's really hard to understand what Dylan is saying when he talks. Most kids his age can talk well, like you do. If you're being a friend to Dylan, what do you think you should do if he says something and you don't understand?" We brainstormed ideas like asking him to repeat what he said, asking him questions, or even smiling and nodding and talking about something else! We had a similar discussion about every one of my students, and Julie's kids seemed eager to meet them and work with them. This set the stage for our class partnership.

The next week, we began combining our classes for science and social studies. We usually began with a whole-group lesson, during which we introduced and explained a concept. We often split into two smaller groups for additional instruction or guided practice. Grouping students by what they need to work on allowed them to participate more and teachers to monitor attention and behavior more closely. Julie and I adapted written work or projects to make them accessible for my students (e.g., larger print/paper, pre-cut pieces, lower level reading materials, reduced writing demands), and some of her lower students benefited from these accommodations as well. We learned to speak the same language when it came to behavioral expectations, and although we did not use the exact same management system, we communicated frequently and openly about individual student behavior. Students quickly realized that the rules would be enforced, no matter which teacher led their particular group. Sometimes the two classes met in Julie's classroom; sometimes everyone came to mine. This was a nice way to take away the stigma often attached to the special education room.

One of the best elements of our new program was our shared lunchtime. Because many of my students had complex feeding issues and/or became over-stimulated in the noisy, crowded cafeteria, we chose to eat lunch in our own quiet classroom. This also allowed us to work on conversation and social skills, areas of great need for all my students. Julie and I worked out a rotation schedule, so that five of her students were assigned to be our "Lunch Buddies" for a week at a time. Therefore, we had student models of appropriate language and social skills, a quiet, structured environment, and a great opportunity for students to build real relationships and friendships with non-disabled peers. The same was true for field trips. My class takes numerous community-based field trips, whereas the general education classes take only one or two curriculum-centered trips a year. We decided to include five of Julie's students at a time on some of our trips, so that each student had at least one opportunity to go on a trip with us. As we attended a play, rode the Amtrak train, visited a planetarium, and groomed horses at a farm, Julie's students were able to see that my students were a lot more like them than they'd thought. This is "inclusion" at its best, I believe—when students can have their academic needs met in an appropriate (and separate, if necessary) environment and when they have genuine opportunities to interact and connect with similar-age peers who understand their disabilities and can see beyond them.

Penny

The school's speech pathologist, Judy, and I had worked together for years. One year, 11 of the 12 students in my special education class had language difficulties and qualified for speech services. At the beginning of the school year, Judy and I reviewed my students' IEPs and scheduled their speech lessons. Also, we had to plan a special schedule for Eleanor, my student with Down syndrome. When Eleanor's parents signed her IEP in the spring, they demanded two things. First, Eleanor was to participate in the regular classroom science and social studies classes. Second, we were not to remove Eleanor from any classroom for speech therapy. Instead they ordered that Judy sit with Eleanor in the regular classroom during science and social studies classes, help her when she was asked to respond, and write down the speech problems she experienced. Then Judy would discuss these problems with me. I had an undergraduate degree in speech pathology, so Judy and I thought this could work. She could determine Eleanor's problems and then briefly instruct me on how to tutor Eleanor. We also decided to meet with the science and social studies teachers to discuss their lesson plans so that I could help Eleanor understand some of the concepts before the instruction began.

I was encouraged about this plan, but it never worked. While Judy and I were making our schedules, the principal was writing his schedule for the teachers. Because neither of us had homerooms—my students were mainstreamed for homeroom—the principal demanded that we "serve the school." Judy and I were stunned. We didn't have homerooms, nor did we have what the principal termed, "regular size classes." However, both of us taught every day without a break. It's just the way special education works much of the time, so we weren't upset about that. But our principal took every spare minute from us with extra duties: bus duty in the morning, lunch duty when we didn't have the child study committee meetings, and Judy left immediately after lunch everyday to serve other schools. Judy did sit with Eleanor during regular classroom sessions, but neither of us had a half hour a week to meet and plan with each other or with the regular classroom teachers in spite of our begging the principal. I threatened to inform Eleanor's parents that the principal wasn't implementing the IEP, but the IEP didn't state that Judy and I would meet, that we would conference with Eleanor's regular classroom teachers, or that Judy would instruct me; just that Eleanor wouldn't be removed from any class for speech and that Judy would sit with her during Eleanor's regular classroom sessions. So there was no written statement in the IEP demanding that Judy and I collaborate about Eleanor, and that entitled the principal to dispose of collaboration between a special education teacher and a speech therapist, as well as collaboration with the regular education teachers.

Sometimes Judy said, "Our principal just doesn't understand what special education is, let alone what it requires."

He didn't.

As the vignette about Jennifer indicates, collaboration can work out very well, much to the advantage of the teachers involved and their students. In these cases, communication between the teachers is good, and they have compatible views of problems and what to do about them as well as how to teach. The major problems they face are finding time to work together and getting administrative clearance and support for scheduling. The work involved is arduous; the story is usually comparatively long and involved. As illustrated by the vignette about Penny, collaboration failed to materialize because of a lack of administrative support for time for personnel to work together. That's the more usual and much shorter story.

But, besides the administrative support for scheduling time for collaboration, misunderstandings and personal or professional conflicts often get in the way of teachers' working well together. It's one thing to understand collaboration at a theoretical level and quite another to make it work day-in-day-out. Sometimes teachers have extreme differences in their views of students and teaching—opposite or conflicting views of behavior management that just can't be reconciled. Other times, although they agree about most things, they have personal quirks that make working well together very difficult or impossible. They just don't get along personally or don't like each other. Inevitably, time to plan joint work and the very feasibility of doing the kind of collaboration that's expected by administrators or professors become difficult issues, even if teachers see eye-to-eye about what needs to be done or is likely to work, and they like each other.

The same kinds of opportunities and problems go for working with other professionals who may not be classroom teachers. This includes school administrators, psychologists, social workers, consultants, or other human services professionals who get involved with the student or group in question. All of us understand that working together is desirable. Most of us also understand that this is easier said than done. You can't just assume that problems aren't going to arise and that everything will go smoothly when working with other people.

QUESTIONS FOR REFLECTION

Suppose that you're a teacher and want to work with others. What questions should you ask yourself when you see problems? We suggest that you begin with these:

- What do I need to know about working with someone whose views are much like mine?
- How do I work with someone who doesn't share my views?
- How and what can I learn from other teachers?
- How do I share my ideas with others most effectively?
- What does it take to make collaboration benefit me and my students?
- What are the limits of collaboration?
- When am I best off "doing my own thing"?

What do I need to know about working with someone whose views about education are much like mine?

In working with someone who shares most of your views, the problem of collaboration is mainly one of finding the time to schedule teaching together or sharing information about the curriculum or particular students. If your views of teaching are compatible, then negotiating who is to do what and planning how things will be handled is relatively easy. You just need to make sure that you both communicate well.

In working with another teacher who shares your views, you should also get administrative clearance if you want to combine your classes or do other activities together that require administrative knowledge and support. What you *don't* want is a principal or supervisor who's surprised or displeased by where you are or what you're doing or thinks there's something conspiratorial about your working together. Usually, if you make a good case for working together, administrators will encourage you and support you in any way they can. But, remember Penny's experiences. Sometimes, for whatever reasons, administrators don't facilitate collaboration, and their failure is not always the fault of the teachers involved.

Keep in mind the fact that you're probably not going to find someone to work with who agrees with you about *everything*. Keep the focus on a particular student or group. Your collaborations mustn't get sidetracked by other issues, even if they involve your passionate personal beliefs about politics or religion or some other hot-button issue. Students' welfare and learning have to be your primary concern. And, remember that if you present your plan to administrators with the kids' benefit clearly explained, you're more likely to get administrative support.

How do I work with someone who doesn't share my views about how to solve an educational problem?

There isn't any simple answer to the question of how to work with someone who sees things very differently from you. But a lot of the same ideas that we've already discussed in other chapters of this book apply here, too. Working with other adults isn't, in many ways, very different from working with youngsters. Just because you're working with adults with training in education or other human service doesn't mean that you won't run into situations or behaviors calling on your most careful reflection and your most savvy behavior management. And part of your reflection and management must, of course, include self-examination so that you become aware of any way(s) in which you might be contributing to the problem rather than resolving it. If you're wondering about how to work with another professional, you might start with questions like these:

- Do I know what the other person's views really are?
- Have I made my views clear?
- Can I find objectives for which we can work together?

FINDING OUT ABOUT OTHER PEOPLE'S VIEWS   Sometimes people misunderstand each other or get the wrong idea about what someone else really thinks. This might be because they've never really talked about issues or one person just made assumptions about how the other person will see things. Or it could be because one of the people was being sarcastic, just joking around, or hadn't really thought through the issue. In any case, the minds of people may not meet up simply because one person doesn't really know the other person's views about managing behavior problems in general or managing a particular problem.

So, you might begin by asking some questions to get a better handle on the other person's views. But be careful how you do this. You could be perceived as the "grand inquisitor" and put the other person off by appearing to be adversarial. If you want to find out what another person really thinks, you have to have enough rapport with him or her not to be perceived as judgmental and haughty if the way they see things is not the way you see them. Finding out what someone else really thinks requires the same kind of personal sensitivity to others that we've tried to encourage in working with students. Remember that you're trying to get the other person to talk freely, not clam up. And sometimes this can be very difficult because a particular view (for example, of politics, religion, ethnicity, disability, or discipline) might be anathema to you or be considered unacceptable in the school in which you're working or in the group in which you're discussing things. It's relatively easy to work with someone who shares your views; it's not so easy to work well with someone whose views you find disconcerting. And don't forget that the central purpose is trying to find a way to do this for the benefit of students.

MAKING YOUR VIEWS CLEAR   At the same time that you're trying to find out how another person sees things, you've got to be as open about your own views as you want them to be with you. Self-disclosure is sometimes difficult, and you've got to be careful how you do it. You can set yourself up as someone with a "holier than thou" attitude, as judgmental and rejecting, or as overly sensitive and fragile. The trick is finding a way of ferreting out what the other person believes without being nosy and saying what you think without being haughty. This isn't a simple matter, and doing it requires what most adults consider good "people skills."

FINDING MUTUAL OBJECTIVES   Part of the problem of working with someone who doesn't share your views is not personalizing their criticisms of your views, accepting theirs, and trying to find common ground. You have to ask yourself: Are there things on which we *do* agree, and can we find and focus on those? Can we find a mutually acceptable way of dealing with this problem? The assumption here is that you can find a mutually acceptable way of *defining* the problem.

Because you're working with a colleague, not a student, you must keep in mind that negotiation or compromise plays a larger role than when you're working with a student. Surely, there is a place for a student's choice (which implies a degree of negotiated control), but give-and-take is likely to be more important in working with colleagues. On some matters, there may be no compromise, but be very careful what these are. You might well be justified in taking the position that you simply won't use corporal punishment or that you won't compromise by terminating your use of approval and praise as a reward for appropriate behavior. However, you might not be so well justified in refusing to budge on something like your rejection of punishment of *any* kind for undesirable behavior or your insistence that a student not pay for something he broke. Knowing just when to "stick to your guns" and when to be persuaded by others is part of the art of being part of a team. Remember that the idea is to do what's best for your students, not win a battle of wits or principles with other adults.

How and what can I learn from other teachers?

You might learn a lot from other teachers by listening carefully to what they say. You might learn even more by watching what they do. Sometimes, there's a very close correspondence between saying and doing; sometimes there isn't. This is roughly as true for adults as it is for children. You might start with these questions:

- What do I hear and read?
- What do I see?
- What can I learn?

LISTENING AND READING   Teachers often describe their experiences, trials, amusing incidents, and failures or successes. They might do this in a teacher's lounge or in other social situations. And their descriptions can give you important insights into what teachers believe about behavior management and about what's likely to work or not to work with a particular student. Remember, too, that teachers' insights are often included in students' cumulative folders or other permanent records. We're not suggesting that you accept at face value whatever other teachers say, but we are saying you should consider seriously the possibility that they're right. As we've mentioned elsewhere in this book, you shouldn't just assume that in every case and for every problem you'll have to find out for yourself because the teacher you've listened to or the teacher whose comments you've read is wrong. This is especially difficult if the teacher who's letting you know what he or she experienced doesn't share your views on important issues.

WATCHING   Observation is important, too. If these observations can be systematic and extended, that's great. Often, schedules and teacher responsibilities simply don't allow this, and so you have to catch snippets of other teachers' interactions with students. Our advice: Schedule observations if you can, but keep your eyes open for what you can learn even if you can't do a scheduled observation.

LEARNING   What you can learn might help you in your interactions with individuals or groups of students. You might be able to learn something about what's likely to be successful and what's not. As is true in student teaching, we'd like prospective teachers to see and learn about what they *should* do, not just what they shouldn't. But, as is true in all aspects of life—including the lives of our students—we want ourselves and our students to learn important things from both positive and negative examples. That is, we want to help our students learn both what to do and what to avoid. So, your listening and watching may result in your saying to yourself, "Now, there's a good idea, and I wonder whether I can do that?" or "Wow, there's a mistake I really don't want to make!" As is true of students, what we learn as teachers depends on the knowledge and experiences we bring to the situation.

How do I share my ideas with others most effectively?

You may be able to maintain your job as a teacher simply by minding your own business. But we hope you'll share good ideas with others—and warn them away from things that are inappropriate or don't work very well. But there are ways to do this well and ways to do it ineffectively. Ask yourself these questions:

- Have I been sensitive and tactful in suggesting how things might be handled?
- Have I been clear and crisp about what I suggest?
- Have I been accepting of responses to my suggestion?

SENSITIVITY AND TACTFULNESS   We're all understandably resentful of the know-it-all who tries to tell us how to do whatever we put our hand to or seems to have an immediate answer for every problem. At the same time, we're really thankful for the help of someone who sees us struggling with something and helps us see how to do it in an easier or better way. The sensitive helper, the one whose tact and sympathy and knowledge we admire, intervenes at what we see as the right time and in what we see as the right way. That person knows just when to help and when not to and how to do it. This is true whether the job we're doing is construction or playing a musical instrument or teaching.

If you wait until you're asked for a suggestion or if you wait until a colleague's problem is obvious to him or her, then you're likely to get a better response when you do make a suggestion. But be careful how you phrase your advice or help. If you say that you've found something helpful when *you've* had the same (or very similar) problem, then the other person is more likely to take your advice. "You know, when I've had that problem here's what I've found usually works . . ." is a better beginning than something like, "Here's what you should do . . ." or "Well, here's the way to handle that . . ." Pretending to be a paragon who's not had a problem isn't very likely to go over well. Setting yourself up as the expert who knows everything isn't as likely to get a favorable response to your idea, good as it might be, as letting the other person know that you've had that problem, too, and that you think your suggestion *might* work. In other words, being reasonably empathic and humble will go a long way toward getting a favorable response to your suggestion.

CLARITY AND TERSENESS   Sometimes, teachers bury their suggestion in a sea of blather, just as they do with students. Or they don't make themselves clear by using common language. You certainly don't want to be perceived as "talking down" to a colleague, but that person does have to understand exactly what you mean. You might have to give one or more examples or even ask whether the other person understands just what you mean.

ACCEPTANCE   When you provide advice or suggestions for another professional, you have to be prepared for several possible outcomes, just as you do with kids. First, you might get an outright rejection (e.g., "No, that's not going to work."). Second, you might get an agreement from another teacher to try to do what you've suggested, but that teacher never tries it. Your suggestion is just ignored. Third, you might find out that the colleague tried your suggestion but didn't stay with it (i.e., didn't try it long enough for it to be successful) or botched it so badly that you think you might as well not have given it. The implementation of your suggestion was so half-hearted or so poorly done that your idea was ruined. So what do you do now?

In the first case, you have to remember the old saw: "You can lead a horse to water, but you can't make him drink." Sometimes, for whatever reason, your advice or suggestion just "falls on deaf ears." In this case, your best bet is to wait for another request, not to point out that the person didn't do what you suggested.

In the second case, our thoughts about it are much the same; don't push your luck. If the colleague says that he or she tried your suggestion but it didn't work, you have an opening to say that it's not going to work immediately and recommend hanging in there with it. Sometimes, it's helpful to ask for an interim report, to check periodically to see how it's going. You might even see an opportunity to suggest a little refinement that makes a big difference in the outcome.

Our thoughts about the third possibility are much like those for the second. You're probably not going to have a lot of luck if you say anything that could be perceived as demeaning or haughty or frustrated. If asked, you can clarify how what you suggest should be done better or offer corrective feedback; if not asked, save your breath.

Take a deep breath and realize that you're responsible for what you do but not for what others do, that you can't change the world, and that just because this person didn't take your advice or suggestion doesn't necessarily mean that they're totally incompetent or inept in everything they do. It takes a bit of wisdom and grace to realize that not everyone's going to agree with you about everything and that everyone has faults—including you.

What does it take to make collaboration benefit me and my students?

Collaboration with others takes time and energy, and it's not something you'll want to do without benefit to yourself and your students. Useful collaboration offers two-way benefits—it benefits both of the collaborating parties, not just one. Even if the suggestions seem to flow primarily one way, there are benefits both to the one making the suggestions and the one taking them. The first (suggestion giver) derives the benefit of having stronger colleague after the collaboration; the second (suggestion taker) derives the benefit of becoming a better professional and helps more kids. Usually, when professionals collaborate they learn from each other—the suggestions and benefits go both ways.

Successful collaboration requires finding agreement—at least certain points of agreement about how to respond to certain problems. Success doesn't mean that the people who are collaborating have to agree on everything, but it does mean that they have to agree on at least one thing—and more than one thing, we hope. And success also means that the people involved and their students benefit from agreements made by teachers.

Collaboration that benefits you and your students results in more consistent responses to desirable and undesirable behavior. It means, first of all, that the adults involved in collaboration agree on what is and what isn't acceptable conduct. It means that you'll be able to rely on your colleagues and they'll be able to rely on you to respond as you agreed to the student's appropriate and inappropriate behavior. You both end up knowing more about what to do in response to problems. And the benefit to your students will be that they will encounter more consistent responses from adults to their behavior, whether it is desirable or undesirable.

Collaboration offers no magic. It's not an end in itself, and no one should think congratulations are in order just because people have tried to do it. Ultimately, what counts is that professional competence is enhanced and students learn more.

What are the limits of collaboration?

To hear some people talk or read what they write, you'd think that collaboration is to teaching what penicillin is to antibiotics. It's not a new idea, something teachers have never done until someone called it to their attention. It's received a lot of attention in the late 20th and early 21st centuries, but it's not a discovery that's going to revolutionize the way teachers work. Although collaboration can be very beneficial, it also has some distinct limitations that should be recognized.

1. Collaboration isn't the fix for incompetence. It's not the magic elixir that will make schools effective. It can result in a pooling of ignorance or incompetence that could give participants the illusion that they're making progress.

2. Collaboration can't overcome irreconcilable differences. People who can't find common ground can't do it.

3. Collaboration isn't the ultimate "leveler," so that nobody's more knowledgeable or more competent than anyone else, and everyone's dead equal in expertise. Someone who supposes that nobody approaches a problem with more competence in managing it is a charlatan.

4. Collaboration isn't doable as a teacher's add-on responsibility or expectation without time to do it. Administrators have to see that you have time to engage in it to make it work.

5. Collaboration isn't a categorical variable—something that's only categorized as on or off, yes or no, zero or one, and so on. It's a continuous variable. That is, it's something that can be done a little or a lot, ranging from fleeting moments to substantial blocks of time.

6. Collaboration won't be successful if it's forced on people who don't want to do it. It's not something that can be imposed from on high, although it's something that can be encouraged and facilitated by administrative decisions.

7. Collaboration is a tool that can be used well or abused. If it's used well, teachers like it, and they and their students are better off because of it. Used poorly, it upsets teachers and leaves both them and their students having wasted time.

So, don't be fooled by the hype of collaboration into thinking that somehow it's going to bring a new day to teaching. Like any of the other tools that we recommend, it can be used with finesse for what it is or be sold as snake oil—as a can't-fail solution to nearly every problem.

When am I better off "doing my own thing"?

Remember that collaboration isn't an all-or-nothing matter. So, you can do it when and where it works and sidestep it when it's not productive. Knowing just when you're better off working by yourself is just as important as collaborating when you can.

You might recall that in Chapter 6 we discussed knowing when your talking with a student isn't going to go anywhere—when it's useless, and you might as well just wait until a later time when it might be more productive. We suggest that you think similarly about collaboration. If you encounter responses like the following from a colleague or colleagues, then you're probably better off letting attempts to collaborate with them wait for another day:

• The other professional proposes something that's unethical or contrary to the principles you hold nonnegotiable (e.g., proposes using dire threats that can't be carried out or recommends corporal punishment)
• Your suggestion is rejected outright as unworkable, wrong, or unrealistic

- You and the other professional can't seem to agree what the problem is, much less what should be done about it
- You just can't do what the other professional suggests (not because you think it's wrong but because of realistic personal limitations); you've explained this but you're obviously not believed

Sometimes you're going to encounter situations in which collaboration might help but you just can't make it work—it's just not in the cards. It's good to recognize these and set your own course. Don't give up doing what you can for your students on your own, even if you think you could do more if you just had a colleague who would work with you.

Summary

Working with other professionals, usually called *collaboration*, is often expected. When collaboration is successful, it can bring important benefits to teachers and students. However, the requirements and difficulties of collaboration are often misunderstood. It's important to make sure that you understand the views of the person with whom you wish to collaborate and equally important to make your views clear. You can learn either what is likely to work or what isn't by listening, reading, and watching other professionals carefully. In sharing your views, it's important to use good communication skills, just as it is with students. Successful collaboration results in benefits to you as a teacher because you learn new skills and benefits your students because they receive better instruction and behavior management. However, collaboration has its limitations, and sometimes you may be better off working on your own.

Case Connection

Working with other educators is often an issue, but you might find the following cases to have elements of working with other educators that are particularly important:

Caught in the Middle   Leann Grossley
Charley   Ms. Russell

The One That Got Away   Charles Allen
What's Inclusion Got to Do with It?   Anita Atkinson

CHAPTER NINE

Working with Parents and Families

Questions for Reflection

Why should I involve parents and families?

Who are the parents of my students?

Understanding Economic Stresses on Families

Understanding Parents from Different Cultural or Ethnic Backgrounds

What are my prejudices?

What is the reciprocity of parent-child interaction?

What are the school guidelines for communicating with parents?

When and how should I involve parents, especially parents of tough kids?

The Sooner, the Better

Letters

Parent Conferences

Abusive Parents

In what ways can I involve parents and families?

Home-Note Programs

Why is it so hard to involve parents?

Summary

Case Connection

Parents and families play a critical role in the education of all students, including those with disabilities. Some make it their business to remain actively involved in their child's education; others appear to relinquish control to educators. In any case, as a teacher, it's your responsibility to make every effort to involve parents in the education of their children. "The involvement of parents in the education of their children is of unquestionable significance. Scores of studies indicate that student achievement increases as parents become more involved in their children's education" (Whitaker & Fiore, 2001, p. 15). You *can* help students improve their behavior in school, but without parent support and collaboration in the intervention, the behavior changes will be school-specific and won't generalize to other settings (Walker, Ramsey, & Gresham, 2004). Consider the experiences of parent Miss Adams and teacher Marie in the following vignettes.

Miss Adams

Edgar couldn't sit still for more than a few minutes, and according to an analysis of the assistant principal, couldn't focus on a lesson for more than *10 seconds*. When he stood in line to go to any activity outside of the classroom—physical education, music, art, or the library—he didn't stand. He jumped, hopped out of line, sometimes pinched the student in front of him, and never just walked quietly anywhere. He turned over desks, threw things around the room, and sometimes clawed material off the bulletin board. A few days after his transfer to our school, the regular education teachers asked me to please remove him from their classes. The art teacher said, "He's a tornado!" He was. I met with his single and hardworking mother, Miss Adams, and discussed placing Edgar in my self-contained class all day until he could control himself more. "That's fine with me. But he ain't gonna stop jitterin' around. He just ain't."

My aide, my student teacher, and I spent a lot of time talking to Edgar about what he would like to earn in the classroom, and we let him choose his reinforcements. The overwhelming reinforcement and the mild punishment reduced a lot of his tornadoes, and, after three weeks of strong behavior management in my class, Edgar could focus for ten minutes on a lesson. My student teacher, Angie, said, "He's not a tornado anymore, but he's still a bad storm." He was.

Miss Adams couldn't afford a telephone, so I contacted her at work and arranged another meeting at her convenience. She was pleased that her son had improved a lot, but wondered why he hadn't improved *more* considering all the attention he had received. And she also said, "I can't do what you people have done. Don't got the time or the energy."

I was very concerned. The school psychologist and I thought that Edgar was a very hyperactive child and needed medicine, something I rarely approved. I was about to ask Miss Adams about Edgar taking meds, when she said, "Mrs. Hamilton, I been trying for a long time to get some doctor to give him some pills to get Edgar to calm down, but they tell me that he's just a little boy, and that's the way little boys are. They won't give me nothin'. Will you help me?"

I did, and it was interesting. On the way to the doctor, Miss Adams said, "I usually hold onto Edgar when we go to the doctor, and he's pretty good. I'm wonderin'. Maybe we should just turn him loose while we're there."

"I think so, Miss Adams," I agreed. "I think so."

We did. We sat in the examination room, holding onto Edgar, until the doctor walked in. Then we turned him loose and sat there with our hands in our laps. Edgar became the tornado. He opened all the drawers, tore out sheets and gowns, hopped onto the table, and pulled down the blood pressure cuff and the implements to examine eyes and ears. Even in this tiny room, the doctor couldn't control him. After a few minutes, the doctor looked at us, his face taut with fear, and asked us, "Ladies, help me, please!"

The doctor prescribed the highest dose of Ritalin he could, and it worked like magic. Edgar could focus for 20 minutes, and there were no more storms of turning over desks, or rummaging into student's backpacks. We included him in some regular classroom activities, and even though we heard a few complaints, his behavior had improved dramatically. He was learning, interacting appropriately with classmates in special and regular classes, and behaving better at home.

Miss Adams was grateful for Edgar's improvement. I taught her a few behavior management skills, one of which was rewarding Edgar when he had a good day at school. Her acknowledgment of Edgar's success at school was very encouraging for him, and he often said, "Gotta do right here at school for Mamma." He did.

Marie

Rusty Farmer was one of the most violent young students I'd seen in my 15 years of teaching. At age 8, he exhibited very serious aggression in my classroom. He hit other children, he hit me, he threw things—I was concerned about other children in the class being hurt seriously by him. Since the beginning of the school year, I had dealt with his taunting of classmates until they hit him, and then he would hit them back; his attacking me with his fists and feet; his sweeping everything off other children's desks and throwing such items as books and pencil boxes at students and teachers; his overturning desks and throwing chairs. I had not been able to engage Rusty's mother in a serious conversation about his behavior, partly because she cared for several neighbors' young children and didn't seem to have time to talk. But I felt that I had to get her involved and hoped that I'd have a good chance of getting her help in dealing with Rusty's aggression. When I finally reached her and explained my concern about Rusty's violence toward adults and other children, her exact words to me were "He don't give me no problems like that at home. I don't know why you folks let him do that to you at school. He don't try none of that kind of stuff with me no more. Don't you let him rear up like that on you, no ma'am! I don't put up with none of that at home, and I don't want you to put up with it at school neither. You just knock him on his ass. That's what I do with him. I just haul off and knock him right on his ass if I see him doublin' up his fist or somethin'. He deserves it when he acts like that!" What could I say? I was dumbfounded. And what was I to do now? We finally reduced Rusty's aggression in the classroom but anywhere else, including at home, he was violent.

There is general agreement about the importance of involving families of students, including those with disabilities, but there are few guidelines for accomplishing this goal. This transitional, multicultural nation often demands that teachers and parents from different ethnic backgrounds, different races, different socioeconomic backgrounds, or those with vastly different values collaborate for the improvement of students. "We either don't know how or don't consider it important to admit to and examine our prejudices about these many differences. Without this self-realization, we may inadvertently make a mess of our attempts to collaborate with parents" (Pullen, 2004, p. 31).

No wonder some teachers would rather perform odious chores than meet with parents. One colleague who was to meet with a difficult parent commented that she would rather clean the toilets in the boys' bathroom than meet with this parent! When asked why, she remarked that even though cleaning toilets was nasty, she knew that she could do it competently. She said she wasn't sure whether she could have "the collaborative, supportive parent/teacher conference the school system expects with the reincarnation of the Wicked Witch of the West." Depicting a parent as a witch during lunchtime conversation is something we don't recommend, but we also know that this parent had a reputation in the school system for antagonizing school personnel and that the administration had not offered any guidelines and precious little support for dealing with this parent. (Even the *principal* was afraid of the parent, called the WWW!) This parent had fought hard and long to get some of the needed special education services for her child. She came to school ready to rumble, and we're not sure that we blame her.

QUESTIONS FOR REFLECTION

Clearly, you might consider a wide variety of questions about the most appropriate roles of parents and teachers and various strategies for working productively with parents. We've organized our discussion around these essential questions:

- Why should I involve parents and families?
- Who are the parents of my students?
- What are my prejudices?
- What is the reciprocity of parent-child interaction?
- What are the school guidelines for communicating with parents?

- When should I involve parents, especially parents of tough kids?
- In what ways can I involve parents and families?
- Why is it so hard to involve parents?

Why should I involve parents and families?

The Individuals with Disabilities Education Act (IDEA), even its reauthorization in 2004, requires the involvement of parents. In what might be considered the Dark Ages of special education, there were no federal or state guidelines for determining how children qualified for services as a special education student. Special education class roles expanded as general education teachers decided they couldn't cope with particular students and made decisions—pretty much on their own—that a student should be in special education. All that was needed to transfer a student from a regular classroom to a special classroom was verbal permission from the principal and the act of removing a student's cumulative folder in the central office file from one teacher's class to another. You can't imagine the fury and shock of parents who accidentally discovered that their child suddenly was in a class for students with disabilities when they hadn't been consulted or advised. We know that at least one angry parent of that era yelled at the teacher, "Who decided this? *You?*" Then, with even greater anger, the parent said to the teacher, *"No, I guess not. You're too young and too stupid!"* Can't say that we blame her.

Beyond the legal requirements, however, expert teachers realize that efforts to work most effectively with students include help from parents, as the emotional ties between parents and children are immeasurably more binding than those between teachers and students—even students whose parents are abusive. Neighbors of 5-year-old Abigail called child protective services because Abigail and her 3-year-old sister were eating out of garbage cans and sometimes sleeping in the alley behind their apartment. Their hygiene was so terrible that they were infested with lice and had large oozing sores all over their bodies. Both girls were placed in foster care. At age 8, even though Abigail hadn't lived with her mother for three years, she still remembered some of the horrors of her former life. But these memories didn't dim her desire to once again live with her mother. When one of us asked her why, she said, "She's my mom." One of us witnessed this extraordinary parent-child emotional bond as a volunteer for the court-appointed special advocate (CASA) program. We've observed these bonds between parents and their children repeatedly across different ethnicities, religions, and socioeconomic levels.

Also, a child's teacher holds only a limited number and variety of reinforcers for the student. Parents have a large number and variety of reinforcers they can employ with their children. Most important, parents usually know what will provide reinforcement for their children and what won't.

Another reason for involving parents is to minimize the chances that the child will be able to manipulate parents against you—or you against them. To be most effective in managing behavior, teacher and parent need to be united in their expectations and discipline, just as both parents in a family need to present a consistent united front. The only way to avoid the problem of children manipulating differences between adults is to maintain close communication between home and school. Close communication doesn't guarantee that the child won't be unable to play adults against each other, but it does make such manipulation more difficult.

There are no hard and fast rules for determining how to engage parents in a collaborative and supportive relationship, but we can avoid some of the pitfalls. First of all, who are the parents of your students? The 21st century presents different family configurations than in years past.

Who are the parents of my students?

UNDERSTANDING ECONOMIC STRESSES ON FAMILIES   According to the Bureau of Labor Statistics, in 1940 less than 9% of all women with children worked outside the home. The 21st century is different. "Nearly three-quarters of all mothers are in the labor force." (U.S. Department of Labor Statistics, 2009). Also, according to the Labor Department, unmarried mothers are more likely to work than married mothers. There are many reasons why mothers work, but one is that it's an economic necessity. It's more and more difficult to support a family on one income.

Childcare often consumes a large share of the resources of families who live in poverty. The U.S. Bureau of Census reports that in 2005 *poor* families with an employed mother paid more than four times the percent of their budget on childcare as families who weren't poor—about 29% versus about 6%, respectively (U.S. Census Bureau, 2009).

When the economy declines, the number of homeless families increases. And homelessness is highly stressful for the family, particularly the children. According to the National Alliance to End Homelessness, there are other reasons for homelessness. "Domestic violence is the immediate cause of homelessness for many women and children. In November 2006, over 22,000 victims of domestic violence—12,000 children and 10,000 adults—received services" (National Alliance to End Homelessness, 2009a).

Students who are homeless are uncomfortable in new environments, and this can be a gigantic stress on children. They're often ill at ease trying to make new friends or responding in class to teachers whom they don't know. The McKinney-Vento Homeless Education Assistance Act of 2001 helps homeless children stay in the school system they attended when they became homeless. According to this act, if a child lives in a shelter, motel, vehicle, or at a campground, he or she qualifies as homeless. If the student lives on the street, in an abandoned building, trailer, or other inadequate accommodations, he or she qualifies as homeless. If the family is bundled into the home of relatives or friends, they are homeless. This law demands that homeless children also qualify for other rights and protections, such as school systems providing transportation to students who have moved and wish to continue in their school of origin. Also, if the parents or guardians prefer to register children at the school in the area in which they now reside, they may do so without presenting documents normally required for enrollment. For example, homeless parents or guardians don't need to present a birth certificate, proof of residence in the area to which they moved, or immunization records. Also, both school systems—the original or the new—must provide free lunch. During economic downturns, this law can cause financial stress on school systems, but it also provides stability for children and youth who can continue in their school of origin.

But parents' loss of jobs and domestic violence aren't the only causes for children to be removed from their homes. As of 2006, over 2.3 million people were incarcerated in federal or state prisons in the United States (Bureau of Justice Statistics Bulletin, 2007). The female incarceration rate has increased, leaving children of incarcerated single mothers living in foster care (See also National Alliance to End Homelessness, 2009b). Often this incarceration is not for a violent crime. Prisons have become warehouses for the mentally ill and drug offenders, many of whom have no history of violence or high-level drug use. Homelessness, for whatever reason, is very hard on the children and should be considered very carefully by school personnel.

Due to the steadily increasing divorce rate and the rise in teenage pregnancies, single parent families have become the most widely spread phenomenon. According to the Annie E. Casey Foundation (2009a), "Too many children live in communities where a large number of families are absent of fathers" (see also Annie E. Casey Foundation, 2009b). This requires single mothers to do the job of both parents and places children at a greater risk. "An estimate of 32 percent of all children are born into single-parent families" (de Melendez & Beck, 2007, p. 111). This leads to another economic stressor on single-parent families—uncollected child support. For example, in 2009 in the state of Virginia, 441,000 parents owed their children more than $2.5 *billion* in child support (Virginia Department of Social Services, 2009).

Parents who live in poverty are often overwhelmed with worry about how to pay the rent, put food on the table, buy clothing, and provide medical care for their children. The issue of providing the daily necessities for their families becomes consuming, which means that many parents may not have the energy or the time to collaborate with schools. Single mothers who work several part-time jobs probably won't volunteer to bake cookies for the class party or to chaperone the next field trip. But this doesn't mean that these parents don't care for their children. They may be working several jobs and do not have the time or the transportation to come to school for a conference. But they still love their children. For example, the visiting teacher at one school insisted that the father of a very aggressive fourth grader come to school every time his son was violent, which was often. This father was a custodian who took the bus to work, had no sick leave, no vacation time, and no health care. The first time this dad came to school, he spoke with affection about his son, even though he also revealed that his son embarrassed him and that he felt helpless to change his son's behavior. He said, "I want my son to get an education. I'll help however I can." After the third time in a week that the visiting teacher yanked this father off his job and dragged him to school, he angrily told teachers to handle his son's problems at school and to stop bothering him. He said, "I don't get no money if I'm not pushin' the broom. They dock my pay for every hour I'm gone. I live too close to the bone as it is." Sometimes the necessities of life—food, clothing, and shelter—override parent collaboration with schools.

Even though teachers often view these parents as not attentive at best, or neglectful at worst, most parents care deeply for their children. Some are overwhelmed, and often their apparent lack of attention to their children covers a more troubling problem.

UNDERSTANDING PARENTS FROM DIFFERENT CULTURAL OR ETHNIC BACKGROUNDS   One of the authors of this book can say this: "With the exception of my fourth-grade teacher, all my teachers, kindergarten through high school, either taught my parents or went to school with them. For better or worse, teachers and students occupied the same economic, racial, and cultural background in my hometown. Not so today, and sometimes these differences become a quagmire to negotiate."

We can't offer a book on multiculturalism, nor do we wish to stereotype any ethnic group. However, it's important to grasp the fact that most of the views we hold about ethnicity and race are based on what we have learned from our families and from the media. And sometimes these views are distorted.

Ask yourself: *Do my students come from ethnic and cultural backgrounds that are different from mine?* A teacher acquaintance of ours remarked on the culture shock she experienced when she moved to a rural school in the South from an affluent suburban school in the Northeast. She said, "It's been hard to adjust. For example, some of my students' families hunt and eat squirrels! Can you imagine?" She was ready to scuttle back across the Mason-Dixon line when one of us told her that we grew up eating squirrels and that our grandmother liked to fry up the heads, crack them open with her knife handle, and pick out the brains! It's interesting to note that this teacher was of the same Irish American heritage as that of the coauthor to whom she was speaking.

But regardless of where one teaches, it's clear that the demographics are changing in the United States. Presently, approximately 35% of the students in the United States are from ethnic/racial minorities—minorities compared to the majority of U.S. citizens who are predominantly of Western European extraction. However, the 100 largest school districts in the country, which teach one in every four public school students in the nation, already serve populations that are 68% "minority."

And it's projected that by 2050, minorities will *collectively* account for 57% of the student population, so "minority" will actually apply to Caucasian children before too long (U.S. Department of Education, 2009).

Although the numerical majority of poor children in the United States in 2009 is white, a larger percentage of nonwhite populations than of white children experience poverty. This trend is particularly alarming. "Because a student's academic achievement is highly correlated with his or her socioeconomic status, the recent growth in poverty among children is of serious concern to educators" (Villegas & Lucas, 2002, p. 8).

And who is teaching most of the students from diverse backgrounds? Most of our nation's teachers continue to come from a rather homogeneous group; approximately 86.5% of teachers are white and 75% are female. And most are from suburban or rural middle-class communities (Gollnick & Chinn, 2002, p. 4). Indeed, the profile of the teacher education student that emerged from a study in 1987 has not changed appreciably: "the typical teacher education student is a monolingual white female from a low-middle or middle-class suburban or rural home who wants to teach children who are like herself" (Cushner, McClelland, & Stafford, 2000, p. 12).

You might think about the ethnic or cultural identity of your students. For example, you might ask: *Are any of my students Asian?* According to the report from the U.S. Census Bureau, the Asian population rose by 3.2 percent, or 460,000, between 2005 and 2006. Also, the Asian population in 2006 was younger with a median age of 33.5, compared with the population as a whole of 36.4 (U.S. Census Bureau, 2009). Asians come from nearly 50 different countries and ethnic groups, each with distinct cultures, languages, and traditions, and they occupy almost every socioeconomic level from the very rich to the very poor.

Although these groups have wide diversity in religion, culture, and language, there are some similarities to consider. "The concern for maintaining the interdependence of the family and individuals' loyalty to the family is seen in child-rearing practices. Behaviors of the individual are seen as reflecting on one's ancestors and one's race" (Springate & Stegelin, 1999, p. 108). Because teachers in Asian cultures are accorded a higher status than teachers in the United States, Asian American students may be confused by the informality between American teachers and students. This higher status granted to teachers in the United States by many Asian Americans may also contribute to an area of potential cultural confusion for teachers who expect parents to be actively involved in making suggestions for their children's education. Because many Asians view the teachers as experts and authorities on education, they believe that teachers will have all the resources to guide them properly (see Mathews, 2000). Finally, some think that Asian American students function better in a quiet, ordered environment (Springate & Stegelin, 1999).

You might ask: *Are any of my students Latino?* Latinos comprise the majority population in some areas of the United States and will probably be the largest minority in the country in a few years. In 2008, 48% of the public school students in California, 46% in Texas, and about 20% in New York State were Latinos (Gandera & Contreras, 2009, p. 2).

Some Latino educators see a challenge in our school system regarding these students. "Latinos are the largest and most rapidly growing ethnic minority in the country, but academically, they are lagging dangerously far behind" (Gandara & Contreras, 2009, p. 1). Many feel that the gap between Latinos and others is the result of circumstances in this country. For example, many of the schools Latinos attend are de facto segregated, inefficient, and substandard and have inadequate books and materials. Also, many of the teachers in these schools are not bilingual and are unprepared to teach Latino students. "Nationally, a survey of services provided to English learners [Latinos] in 2003 found that more than 40 percent of teachers nationwide had English learners [Latinos] in their classroom, yet only about 10 percent reported that they were proficient in reading and writing the language of their students" (Gandara & Contreras, 2009, p. 147). There's insufficient teacher training nationally, which is attributed to the small amount of funding for teacher education in many school systems. This makes it difficult for teachers to interact with Latino parents. However, as stated previously, teacher interaction with parents, regardless of ethnicity, is very important. "Family involvement is highly desired in education because many studies show student achievement increases when parents are actively involved" (Soto, 2008, p. 250).

Another issue in the United States is the different teaching methods for Latino students. Educators often disagree about whether to use ESL, bilingual education practices, or dual-language in school systems with large Latino populations.

Again, a reminder that this chapter is not a course in multiculturalism and that making generalizations can be dangerous. However, we offer a few generalities that *may* guide today's teachers, even if you have no training in teaching Latino students.

"To be Hispanic is to value children" (Rodriguez, 1999, p. 3). A Latino acquaintance told us how much he enjoyed his children and how he hoped to have more. "The house is so happy with children, even when they cry." This is not to say that other cultures don't value children or that all Latino parents love to hear their children cry. But there is a different emphasis on family and children than in the competitive society that is dominanted by Caucasians in the United States. This may be confusing and may cause conflict when collaborating with Latino parents. For example, Latino children may seem babied and overindulged by some teachers' standards. It may not be unusual for a Latina mother to tie her 6-year-old child's shoestrings or for preteens to sit on their mother's lap, or for preschoolers to still drink from a baby bottle (Brice, 2002). This potential conflict has been described as follows:

> In brief, schools tend to reflect the values of the so-called mainstream, which are highly individualistic—teaching students to become independent and take care of their own needs. In contrast, immigrant Latino families tend to be collectivistic—teaching children to be interdependent with others and to attend to the needs of the family. (Rothstein-Fisch, 2003, p. ix)

And, similar to the attitudes of many Asian parents, Latino parents may *not* view their job as teaching their children academics. "Seeing the functions of teacher and parent as clearly distinct, they may believe that academic instruction should be restricted to school. They may believe that their primary responsibility is to socialize the child, not to teach academics" (Educational Research Service, 2003, p. 74). The preceding may mean that a request for Latino parents to drill their child on a list of vocabulary words you send home may not receive the attention that you hoped for.

You might ask: *Are any of my students African American?* In 1995, African American students accounted for 14.7% of school-age children; however, by 2050, it is predicted that African American children will account for 16% of our student bodies (see Villegas & Lucas, 2002). Even though the population of African American students has increased, the academic gap has not declined. "One reason for this in our view, is that since the end of desegregation, the teaching force has become increasingly White, and many of these White teachers (along with some teachers of color), are ill prepared to work effectively with students of color in urban settings" (Teel & Obidah, 2008, p. 4). However, teachers' color is *not* the only reason for this gap. For example, other contributing factors include ineffective instruction, inadequate and unsafe school buildings, inadequate textbooks and other materials, large class size, inequitable distribution of qualified teachers, and high turnover rate for teachers and administrators. Also, African American and Latino communities have less access to good preschool and daycare programs. Other factors contributing to this gap include economic stress and inadequate housing. Also, poor health care is a significant drain on minorities. "Evidence indicates that race and ethnicity correlate with health disparities within the U.S. population" (U.S. Department of Health and Human Services, 2009). As mentioned earlier in this chapter, the economy of parents becomes a major issue and can lead to stress on parents and students, making teacher-parent interaction difficult.

But we can't deny that there is an academic gap; if we do, we definitely won't fill it. "The achievement gap has a face—it is the faces of our African American, Latino, First Nations, and poor students. We cannot confront it, however, unless we are able to see it, describe it, and talk about it accurately and honestly with the blindfolds off" (Lindsey, Graham, Westphal, & Jew, 2008, p. 9).

Although all minorities experience some form of racism, none experiences such profound discrimination in the United States as that encountered by African Americans (Klein & Chen, 2001). Because of the overt and covert racism, many African American parents encourage independence, assertiveness, and individualism in their children so that they will be able to cope and survive in a racist society. We've heard white teachers complain that African Americans view everything through the prism of racism. "They're all paranoid!" one teacher lamented. What mainstream society may view as paranoia, African Americans historically view as necessary for their survival. According to Springate and Stegelin (1999), African Americans have survived under harsh economic and social restraints and have developed:

- Strong kinship bonds among a variety of family households
- Strong work, education, and achievement orientation
- High level of flexibility in family roles
- Strong commitment to religious values and church participation values
- A humanistic orientation for perceiving the world and relationships

African American children are typically encouraged to learn self-help skills—walking, eating, dressing, and bathing—early and are expected to take on household chores earlier than in most mainstream families. This independence, paired with academic achievement, is also a tool for combating racism.

Parallel with teaching children how to survive racism are (a) the value placed by many African Americans on relatives and friends and (b) the high level of flexibility in family roles. "Reliance on this extended kinship system has important survival value for African American families" (Klein & Chen, 2001, p. 82). This reliance on others, the philosophy that it takes a whole village to raise a child, means that friends and relatives may feel responsible for disciplining children. It also means that there may be multiple caregivers for some of your African American students, and this is often a worry to mainstream teachers who are concerned about a lack of predictability in their African American students' environments and the possible lack of consistency regarding discipline.

Discipline is also an area where African American parents may differ from most of society. African American parents tend to be more authoritarian than most parents, and many are not opposed to corporal punishment. "If your background reflects a preference for nonauthoritarian, relatively permissive discipline practices, be aware that this difference is a particularly difficult one with which to deal unemotionally" (Klein & Chen, 2001, p. 83).

You might ask: *Are any of my students Native American?* American Indians constitute approximately 1% of U.S. school-age children, and that statistic will probably remain stable for the future (Villegas & Lucas, 2002). There are over 500 tribes in the United States, half of which live west of the Mississippi River. These tribes speak over 200 different languages, which require teachers to become familiar with the cultural practices of the American Indian children they teach.

But there are some similarities among the tribes. First, as in the Asian and Latino communities, many American Indians are collectivists who not only emphasize the extended family but also the tribe and the community. This means that parents may identify a friend as spokesperson or as a source of information about the child. A typical teacher with little or no knowledge of the culture of her or his American Indian students may be unnerved that someone other than the parents—aunt, uncle, grandparent, or sibling—is responsible for disciplining the children, or providing pertinent health information (Klein & Chen, 2001).

Often, American Indians encourage their children to manage themselves and to operate independently when the children are very young, which most teachers may view as overly permissive or neglectful. However, even though there is an emphasis on self-sufficiency, many American Indian parents do not encourage competitiveness, and this independence must never be at the expense of the family or the community. "Attempts to convince Native Americans to be competitive (such as being the first, best, fastest, or smartest) are incompatible with their cultural values" (Manning & Baruth, 2000).

Finally, you may ask: *Are any of my students biracial or multiracial?* A growing number of students are biracial and multiracial, and their families may have different preferences about how they wish their children to be recognized. Some parents of biracial or multiracial children prefer to think of their children as "just children." Others acknowledge both backgrounds and have definite wishes about how their children should be treated. Still others may fully embrace the cultural identity of one of the parents.

Be careful! With regard to all of the information we have provided about different cultures, we urge you to be careful. It is imperative that teachers conscientiously not only study the *cultures* of their students but also have enough contact with their students to understand that they are *individuals* with crucial differences. They may or may not conform to the generalizations we have made about their culture. Remember: If you're going to be sensitive to individuals, then you've got to be sensitive to their cultural differences (Kauffman, Conroy, Gardner, & Oswald, 2008). And remember this, too: The single best thing you can do to promote multiculturalism is provide effective instruction for children, regardless of who their parents are.

What are my prejudices?

Before you begin communicating with parents, you must be aware of *your own* views regarding the following:

- How do you view different ethnic and racial groups? Are your views stereotypic?
- How do you view families who are poor? Do you blame them for their poverty?
- How do you view same-gender partners as heads of household?
- How do you view religious differences?
- How do you view single parents?

School systems in the United States serve diverse ethnicities and religions—cultures that all educators may not understand. Unfortunately, most of the views people hold about these differing cultures are based on what they learned from their own families and the media, and sometimes these views are distorted. Therefore, it's essential to examine your personal values and beliefs about these differences. This doesn't mean that we scrap our value system and subscribe to those of others, but it does mean that we understand our beliefs, how our beliefs might cause us to judge others, and how these judgments might interfere with collaborating with parents (Kauffman et al., 2008; Pullen, 2004).

For example, when one of us was a court-appointed special advocate (CASA) volunteer, her director requested that she advocate for a little boy named Martin. In Martin's eight years, except for a 2-year stay with a family friend, he had been shifted among over a dozen homes, and most of his caregivers had been either abusive or neglectful. Needless to say, by the time Martin was 8 years old, he was angry, defiant, noncompliant, and generally difficult. Social services had difficulty placing him, and Martin was having a good time controlling a lot of folks. In the CASA volunteer's first conversation with Martin, he said that he liked "scaring adults and keepin' 'em jumpin'." He was good at it too!

But life had not always been one of shifting families for Martin. One of his first caregivers was a single woman, Miriam, who had kept him from birth to age 2. At that time Miriam was diagnosed with a terminal illness that carried the prognosis of a long and painful death. Miriam sadly relinquished

Martin to his relatives, sold her home, and prepared to die. Six years later, the diagnosis was amended. She discovered that she was not going to die, and she wanted Martin back. The Department of Social Services thought that this was a great idea. However, by this time, Martin had run through all his abusive relatives and was successfully getting banished from one foster home after another, as well as routinely suspended from schools. So the idea that someone actually wanted this extremely difficult child was an answer to a prayer. But there was a problem. Miriam was gay and had a partner. The social worker wanted to know if the CASA volunteer would have trouble advocating for a child to be placed with a gay couple. The advocate asked what a person's sexual orientation had to do with parenting skills. The agency then asked if the advocate would write a report that would reject the fallacy that if a gay couple raises a child, the child is bound to be gay. The state was very conservative, and some of the folks involved with the case also thought that to be raised by a gay couple was "unnatural," or "a sin against God," or "unlawful."

Miriam successfully adopted Martin, but the volunteer advocate's interaction with professionals and other volunteers while working on this case was unnerving. Many spoke of being uncomfortable placing Martin with a gay couple, but they couldn't explain their discomfort. They said things like, "I'm just uncomfortable, that's all." And one of the professional witnesses who had written most of the definitive studies about children raised in homes with same-sex partners said that she would not testify as an expert witness if Martin's family contested social service's decision to place Martin with a gay couple. At other hearings at which she had testified, her life and that of her family had been threatened, and she wasn't willing to risk her family's safety.

Recently, an acquaintance of ours from a southwestern state bemoaned the fact that the Indians were a lost cause in her state. "You have no idea how much money they squander on alcohol." In her eyes, they are "lazy drunks." But she had no knowledge of the 19th- and 20th-century boarding schools that were organized in an effort to assimilate American Indians. Indian children were forcibly removed from their parents and shipped long distances on trains so that the children could learn English and a marketable skill and thereby "assimilate" into mainstream society. Perhaps the motives of the authorities at the time were good (sometimes people are simply misinformed, not mean), but the boarding schools were harsh. The Indian children were routinely punished for speaking their language or practicing their traditional customs. Consequently, because some of these children didn't return home for years and because they weren't allowed to speak their native language or practice their customs, they forgot them. Many blame the boarding schools for the increase of alcoholism among Native Americans, who were robbed of their culture but who didn't fit into mainstream society either. Our acquaintance didn't know about boarding schools, nor did she know that one of this country's founding fathers couldn't decide whether the nation should "assimilate or annihilate" its Native Americans. She also didn't know that many health professionals think that Native Americans have a physical predisposition to diabetes and alcoholism.

As a teacher, one of your jobs—perhaps the most important job for collaboration with parents—is to listen to parents so that you can help your students. That's going to be difficult if you think that a single mom who has to commute an hour on a bus to and from work, while childcare sucks up one-third of her salary, could come for parent-teacher conferences if she *really* wanted to. Or if you think that gay parents are objectionable and make you uncomfortable. Or if you think that illegitimate children are a sin against God. Or you're nervous around those whose race or culture or religion is different from yours. Perhaps the hardest part of teacher-parent collaboration is determining how you think and feel about those who are different from you. But it's the first step to forming a collaborative relationship with parents.

What is the reciprocity of parent-child interaction?

Expert teachers also realize that parents of students with behavior problems are not always the cause of their children's problems. Researchers in recent years have confirmed what many parents have contended for a long time: Some children are born with temperaments that make them more diffi-cult to parent and teach (see Kauffman & Brigham, 2009 or Kauffman & Landrum, 2009a for research reviews and comments). Many parents of more than one child will tell you that almost from the moment of birth they noticed distinct differences between their children. For example, one baby was happy and easy to soothe, the other was irritable and hard to please. Research has now shown that different temperaments can have a powerful influence on how parents deal with their babies and children. Difficult babies can place a great deal of stress on parents. For many years, the dominant child development theorists viewed child-parent interaction as a one-way street running from parent to child. Experts now know that the relationship is reciprocal. Parents can and do influence children, but it is also the case that children can and do influence parents.

That parent-child interaction is reciprocal has important implications for how teachers view parents, especially parents of children with behavior problems. Keep two things in mind. First, parents of children with behavior problems are not necessarily to blame for their children's behavior (Kauffman & Landrum, 2009a). Second, even if you witness poor parenting of children with behav-ior problems, it may not be entirely the parents' fault. Some of the most intelligent and well-intentioned parents can easily get caught up in an interactive pattern that results in their exhibiting inappropri-ate parenting behaviors. It's instructive to keep in mind your own interactions with intractable students. Given that on occasion you've found it difficult to maintain your professional composure with particularly nasty and ill-mannered students, think of having to contend with such behavior daily over the course of several years!

Just as you shouldn't be quick to blame parents, neither should you deny that they can at times be culpable. Poor parenting, especially abusive parenting, can directly cause behavior problems in children. And some parents indirectly contribute to the behavior problems of their children by con-sistently responding in a maladaptive manner to their children's misbehavior. We caution here that you should not assume that parents do not care about their children if they are poor parents (see Kauffman & Landrum, 2009a). Nearly all parents are concerned for the welfare of their children, even if they abuse them. Parents who have poor parenting skills may want to be good parents, but they may simply not have the knowledge of alternative ways of rearing children or have not learned the self-control required to discipline their children humanely.

What are the school guidelines for communicating with parents?

After you've examined your values and your prejudices, you need to understand the school guidelines for communicating with parents—particularly if you're a new or transferring teacher.

- Do written contacts with parents need principal approval?
- Should you have someone from the school accompany you on parent visits?
- What are the school's expectations for how many parents you should meet within a year? If you are teaching 150 students in high school, are you expected to conference with all of them sometime during the year?
- If the parents are divorced, do the records indicate who has custody and with whom you should share the student's progress?
- If the records or teacher talk indicate that the child has a guardian, do you share information with the parents also?
- What should you do if a parent's expectations are unrealistic? For example, if they are:
    Visiting or calling everyday?
    Contacting you by email every day?
    Demanding that you move their child to a higher academic group before the child is ready?
    (see Pullen, 2004)

When and how should I involve parents, especially parents of tough kids?

One of us was told by a fellow teacher on our first teaching job: "You'd better trot right on down to Jake's house and introduce yourself, because you're going to need this grandma. Yes, sir!" This teacher had looked at the class roll and pointed to one of the names.

THE SOONER, THE BETTER The sooner you contact parents, the better. We hope you will have done your homework about your class—read the folders, talked to other teachers—and know the names of the students who will in all probability present problems. Call the parent. Begin by apologizing for disturbing him or her (Whitaker & Fiore, 2001). Usually, it's wise to contact parents of tough kids in the following manner:

> "Mrs. Smith, I'm sorry to bother you at work (or at home). My name is Alice Jones, and I'm going to be Tommy's teacher this year. I hope Tommy can have a good year, and I wonder if you have any suggestions about how I can help him have a good year."

Even if you don't glean any important information from the parent, she or he knows that you're interested in Tommy, that you want parental collaboration, and that you're focusing on the future, not past mistakes. Concentrate on the future! Make the conversation brief, but also tell the parent that you'll check back after school starts to make sure that Tommy isn't experiencing problems that you are unaware of. Give the parents your phone number. Availability is important. But even more important is listening to the parents.

If parents don't work or don't have a home phone, make a home visit. Although this is controversial, many have had success by visiting parents of tough kids before they come to school. But follow these guidelines:

- Make sure that you have examined your prejudices and won't judge the parents or home harshly when you go.
- Find out your school system's policy about home visits.
- Don't go alone. Try to find either someone the family knows to go with you or someone who is familiar with the area.
- If you know that the family has a social worker, the social worker is usually happy to make an appointment for you, and she or he might even accompany you. If you don't know the social worker, apologize to the parents for disturbing them and ask if it would be better if you made an appointment to see them at another time.
- If the parents ask you in, don't sit down unless they ask you to.
- Use the same message you would use if you had phoned the parents—you are looking to the future, you want a good year for their child, and you want suggestions from them.
- Also discuss how you will communicate in the future—perhaps a home-note plan.

As a first-year teacher, one of us didn't follow the colleague's advice who directed us to visit Jake's home before his behavior was beyond control. Here's that experience as one of us remembers it:

> After whining to my mother about the perils in the classroom in general and Jake in particular, my mother directed me to visit Jake's guardian, his grandmother, Augusta. Mother said that Augusta had a hand in raising my cousin Jeff. She went on to tell me that Augusta did not tolerate foolishness from anyone, "whether they be black, white, orange, big, or small." Jake's home had no phone, and when I took Jake home, his grandmother

gave me a cool reception, mumbling something about "teachers all time complaining about Jake." She did not ask me in but stared at me through the screen door until in desperation I asked her if she knew my mother. "I reckon I do," she smiled and asked me to come in. I told her that I thought Jake had a lot of potential and could probably learn a whole lot more if I could get him to behave. She agreed. I didn't elaborate any more than that on his behavior. I didn't have to. Augusta told Jake that he better do what I ask him. "Period! Do you understand me?" Jake wasn't a model student after that, but his behavior did improve dramatically. My only regret was that I didn't follow the teacher's advice and visit Augusta *before* Jake set foot in my classroom—*before* any problems arose. When I left Augusta's house, she said, "The only time I ever saw Jake's other teachers was when he acted up in class. Hope that's not the case with you." I listened to Augusta.

LETTERS   Introductory letters home before students start the school year can be valuable in establishing contact with parents. There are some restrictions, one of which is money. Sometimes neither the school systems nor the teachers can afford the postage to send letters home to parents. If that's the case, then an introductory letter should be sent home the first day of school. Introductory letters to parents should be brief, be simply written, and give information about how to contact you at home and at work. You need to be available so that you can listen. For example:

> Dear Parents,
>   My name is Jeffrey Jones, and I'll be your child's teacher this year.
>   Home phone: 555-1111
>   Work phone: 555-2222
> I don't have a phone in my classroom, so I may have to call you back. But I shall return your call as soon as I can. I'm looking forward to meeting you.
> I need you!
>
> Sincerely,

You might delineate some of the behavioral and academic goals with which you'll begin the year. Regardless of how you choose to contact parents, your first contact should be positive. Remember Augusta. *Don't wait until there's a problem before you contact parents.*

PARENT CONFERENCES   Successful conferences take preparation. The following are a few guidelines for a successful parent conference:

- *Have you done your homework?*
  1. Reviewed the student's cumulative records
  2. Consulted with other professionals
  3. Documented the student's academic and behavioral progress
  4. Established rapport with the parents before the conference
  5. Familiarized yourself with the student and family's culture
- *Have you involved the parents before the conference?*
  1. Discussed the goals of the meeting with the parents and solicited their input
  2. Involved the student, as appropriate
  3. Scheduled a mutually convenient day and time for the meeting
  4. Provided written notice prior to the meeting

- *How do you involve the parents during the meeting?*
  1. Welcome the parents and speak informally with them before beginning
  2. Reiterate the goals of the meeting
  3. Begin with a discussion of the student's strengths
  4. Support your points with specific examples and documentation
  5. Encourage parents to share insights
  6. Ask open-ended questions
  7. Avoid jargon
  8. Practice active listening. Remember, one of your big jobs is to listen to parents
  9. Review the main points of the meeting and determine a course of action
  10. Provide additional resources (e.g., support groups, family resource centers, websites)
- What do you do *after* the meeting?
  1. Document the results of the meeting
  2. Share results with colleagues who work with the student
  3. Follow up with the parents as needed to discuss changes

There are other points to consider before a conference. Ask yourself this: *Am I able to avoid blaming parents?* One of the least helpful things a teacher can do is lay the blame on parents for the misbehavior of their children. Parents will already be on the defensive because you've called them to have the meeting. Weigh your words carefully so as not to give the impression that you think they're the culprits. Even if you're convinced that they're the cause of their children's problems, you should avoid accusations. If they're at fault, it's better to let them arrive at that judgment on their own.

An acquaintance of ours, an immigrant from Great Britain, angrily asked if all teachers in America were bossy or just her 8-year-old daughter's second-grade teacher. This mother was very worried about her daughter, who insisted on taking a nap as soon as she got off the school bus and then wanted to go to bed immediately after supper. The pediatrician assured this mother that her daughter was just small and tired easily and that there was nothing wrong with her. The mother was considering changing pediatricians for a second opinion when her daughter's teacher called and brusquely demanded that she put her daughter to bed on time on school nights because she was sleeping during the day. This mom asked us, "Couldn't the teacher have asked if we've seen the same behavior at home? She just decided that we were awful parents who kept our child up late every night."

Here's another question to ask yourself: *Am I willing to admit it when I'm wrong?* Some teachers, especially those who are relatively inexperienced, feel that it's a sign of weakness to acknowledge to parents that they've made mistakes. We don't think you need to see the meeting as an opportunity to reveal all of your shortcomings, but if you have doubts about how you've handled the student, it's a good idea to concede this point.

Another question: *Am I willing to admit it when I don't know the answer to parents' questions?* Again, be careful not to fall into the trap of feeling that you need to answer every question posed by the parents. Confident teachers are more than willing to say that they aren't all-knowing. In fact, teachers should view the parent-teacher conference as an opportunity to learn more about the child from the parents.

Can I accept the family as it is? Some teachers have the idea that parent-teacher conferences should be quasi-therapy sessions, mistakenly thinking that they try to influence family dynamics. Your focus should be on what the student is doing in your classroom. To be sure, you'll want to talk about how the child behaves at home, and you may want to suggest that parents carry out certain procedures in the home to backup what you're doing at school, but you shouldn't see yourself as a family therapist.

Am I attuned to cultural differences between the parents and myself? It's important that you respect the cultural backgrounds of parents and not misinterpret their behavior or offend them because their customs vary from yours.

Can I find something positive to say about the child and something positive about the parent that I can support? It's very important that you try to find something positive and supportive to say about the child and the parent in every parent contact. Sometimes this may be difficult. A first-grade teacher that one of us worked with began a parent conference with the parents of a very violent and noncompliant child by reporting that Johnny eats his lunch every day. Sometimes you have to really dig to find a few positives to share with the parents. Nevertheless, if all the parent receives is negative information, you aren't likely to get very far in resolving the problem. Dishonesty about your feelings and perceptions isn't helpful. Going out of your way to find something—anything, regardless of how small—that you can be positive about or support will make your attempts to work cooperatively with a parent more likely to be successful.

Meeting with parents about a student's misbehavior demands a delicate balance between providing an objective account of the misbehavior and demonstrating that you're an advocate for the child. Even though you need to be sensitive to the possibility that the parents are going to be unreceptive to what you have to say, it's important that they hear what you have to say about their child's problem behavior. At times it's tempting to spare parents the anxiety caused by information that will likely prove disheartening. Conveying only good news skews their perspective, however, just as much as conveying only negative information. If a serious incident arises, then they have no sense of background or warning. Filling them in at this point may lead them to conclude that you're withholding information and provoke a sense of mistrust. When telling parents unpleasant information, it helps not only to be as objective as possible but also to state the case in a way that clearly conveys your advocacy of the student. It's paramount that you focus on the future—how you and the parents can help the child behave appropriately. When it's obvious to the parents that the teacher is angry or upset with their child, parents become apprehensive about the treatment the child may receive. A common response to this sense of dread is a defensiveness that polarizes parent-teacher relationships.

ABUSIVE PARENTS   Some teachers are lucky enough to have long careers without experiencing an angry or verbally abusive parent. When a parent does become abusive, it can be unnerving or frightening. The following are some guidelines for facing an angry parent.

- Remain calm.
- Do not make angry responses.
- Speak softly.
- If you are in error, admit it. (It's best to contact the parents with the error before they find out from their child.)
- Maintain eye contact.

Sometimes teachers feel sandbagged by explosive parents, and it's not always possible to determine why they're so angry. Parents might feel guilty about their child's lack of achievement, feel overwhelmed by poverty, or have had a bad experience with schools in the past. Whatever the reason for the abuse, remember that you *need* them. And you don't want to give them the ammunition to take to your principal or superintendent. *So keep your cool!* Don't hang up the phone, or walk away, or scream, or respond defensively or angrily. Some consultants suggest that you handle abusive parents in the following manner: "Mrs. Smith, please don't talk to me that way. I will never speak to you like that, and I will never speak to your child like that."

Of course, this means that you know yourself and know that you never would speak to a student that way. And remember that delivery is everything. You must be calm, speak softly, maintain eye contact, and not get into the back-and-forth of an argument that you can't win. If you've made a mistake that has infuriated the parents, admit it, and tell them how you'll prevent this from happening again. Try to focus on the future and how you can prevent this problem from erupting again. Restate that the purpose of the meeting is to help the student in the future.

In what ways can I involve parents and families?

HOME-NOTE PROGRAMS   **Home-school plans**, sometimes known as *home-contingency plans,* can be very effective in helping students control their behavior. With a home-note plan, *you* evaluate the student's behavior, but the parents deliver the consequences. The teacher fills out a brief report on the student's behavior, the student takes it home, and the parents deliver the reinforcement. Although home-notes aren't a panacea, research indicates that they can be highly effective. They are palatable to most parents and students and require a minimum of teacher time. They also provide a means by which parents and teachers can work together in a constructive way. But home-notes shouldn't be used in the following situations:

- If you suspect abuse
- If you think that the parents may not consistently implement the program

There are several other things to keep in mind in setting up a home-note program. Most important, of course, is that you meet with the parents to work out the features of the program. In this meeting, you should leave as many choices as possible up to the parents, especially with regard to the types and amount of reinforcers as well as the schedule of reinforcement (i.e., how many "good" notes it takes to receive a reinforcer). The more they feel they are working with you in the development of the home-note program, the more likely parents are to carry it out consistently. You should also consider the possibility of including the student in on the planning at some point. It's usually best to meet with the parents first and then decide whether to include the student in another meeting.

Although you should be as precise as possible in defining the criteria you'll use in judging the occurrence or nonoccurrence of behaviors, the note home to parents need not be detailed. In other words, the feedback to parents need not be lengthy or complicated. Unless they request it, all you need to do is inform them that the child has or has not engaged in the desired behavior. Perhaps you will leave space for teacher or parent comments, but you might use this option only occasionally.

Most researchers suggest that teachers begin by using the home-note system on a daily basis. Once it has been working successfully for a couple of weeks, you can begin to wean the child from the system by going to a once-a-week note. In the early stages, especially, you should check frequently with parents. Even at later stages, you should make periodic checks with parents to see how they think the system is working. Figure 9.1 is a copy of a home-note used for a third-grade student who refused to complete any seatwork.

If the parents are abusive or won't consistently implement the plan, it's often effective to use a mentor in the school to reinforce the student: another teacher, an aide, the principal, a secretary, or anyone who will show an interest in the student and implement the plan consistently. One student in the school where one of us taught was very fond of the physical education teacher who shot baskets with this student on Friday afternoons if the student had successfully met the terms of the plan.

Why is it so hard to involve parents?

The seeming contradiction—that parents hold a great deal of influence over their children but shouldn't be automatically blamed for the behavior problems of their children—is perhaps what

Name _____

Date _____

Completed reading follow-up

    Neatly   Yes   No

    Accurately   Yes   No

Completed math follow-up

    Neatly   Yes   No

    Accurately   Yes   No

Teacher Comments:

Parent Comments:

_____   _____
Teacher's signature   Parent's signature

FIGURE 9.1   Sample Home-Note for Third-Grader

makes it so very difficult for novice teachers to work constructively with parents, especially parents of students who misbehave. You need to maintain a very delicate balance between recognizing that parents are important to the educational process and not immediately pointing the finger at them when their children misbehave.

Summary

The ability to work with parents is often the critical difference that divides good teachers from those who are truly excellent. Skills in instruction and behavior management serve teachers well, but these skills alone are often not enough. In order to achieve excellence, teachers must be able to communicate effectively with parents. By so doing, they can enhance their behavior management techniques by leveraging the influence that some parents have over their children. Although working with parents doesn't come naturally to all teachers, those who take the time and effort to develop such skills will be rewarded handsomely.

Case Connection

Very seldom, if ever, is working with parents and families unimportant. However, you might consider how it was especially important in the following cases:

Lenny   Sara Olson

Richard's Mother   Polly Dudley

Grandma's Boy   Helen Jamison

When Secrets Disable   Cathy Schrock

The First Parent Conference   Christine Walker

PART TWO

Cases for Analysis, Discussion, and Reflection

The cases are listed in alphabetical order by title. Numbers in parentheses after the cases indicate the chapter numbers for which the case was recommended in Case Connection.

Alone in the Dark *Alan Stean* (5) pp. 138–140

Avoiding the Issue *Johnny's Teachers* (1, 7) pp. 141–143

Caught in the Middle *Leann Grossley* (8) pp. 144–148

Charley *Ms. Russell* (1, 8) pp. 149–153

Grandma's Boy *Helen Jamison* (9) pp. 154–159

James's Uncertain Future *Dan Parker* (4) pp. 160–162

Lenny *Sara Olson* (9) pp. 163–166

One Bad Apple *Elaine Brown* (5) pp. 167–170

Richard's Mother *Polly Dudley* (9) pp. 171–174

Stealing Time *Robert Carter* (4) pp. 175–179

The Contract with Parrish and Son *Rebecca Phillips* (3, 5) pp. 180–183

The First Parent Conference *Christine Walker* (9) pp. 184–188

The One That Got Away *Charles Allen* (8) pp. 189–192

The Truth About Alice *Janet Lane* (2, 6, 7) pp. 193–195

They Failed Derrick *Melinda Smith* (5, 6) pp. 196–202

What You Don't Know Can Hurt You! *John McCullum* (2, 6) pp. 203–205

What's Inclusion Got to Do with It? *Anita Atkinson* (7, 8) pp. 206–210

When Secrets Disable *Cathy Schrock* (9) pp. 211–214

Where to Now? *Connie Ballard* (6) pp. 215–218

Winnie *Patty Gray* (3, 7) pp. 219–225

Alone in the Dark

ALAN STEAN

I was sitting in my classroom waiting to see if any of my students' parents would appear for the October parent–teacher conferences. This was my first year at Junction High, and I wasn't sure what to expect from either the parents or the faculty. My classroom phone rang. It was Steve Lopez, the assistant principal.

"Is a Thelma Crabtree one of your students?"

"Yes, I have her for social studies and geography."

"I just got a call that someone saw her biting her mother out by the road. Does that make any sense to you?" he asked.

"I have never met Mrs. Crabtree," I answered. "Thelma is always cooperative but very quiet in my class. Biting her mother seems very out of character."

"I don't know either Thelma or her mother. Would you mind taking care of it?" Steve asked.

I stepped outside to a rather strange sight. Two women, both looking disheveled and agitated, were standing by the road at the corner of the school lot. I recognized one as Thelma, my quiet, conscientious 15-year-old student, and I assumed the other was her mother. As I approached, Thelma was holding tightly to the corner of Mrs. Crabtree's sweater, appearing for all the world like a little girl desperately clutching her mother's apron strings to save herself from a threatening world.

"Hello, Thelma," I said as calmly as I could, approaching the silent pair. I looked at her mother and said, "I'm Alan Stean, one of Thelma's teachers. Would you like to come to my class?"

"I wanted to, but Thelma wouldn't let me," Mrs. Crabtree explained in a bewildered voice. "It took me 30 minutes to get from the car to the corner of the school, one step at a time. When we got here, Thelma refused to move and started biting me."

I turned to the quiet, frightened girl and asked, "Did you bite your mother?"

Thelma explained, "Carrie (one of the school psychologists) told us both that Mother wasn't to come in the school and talk to the teachers. I can't let her in there."

Mrs. Crabtree turned to Thelma and pleaded, "I just want to ask the teachers if there is anything that I need to do for you. I need to know how much material to buy for your home economics project. It's alright."

Without speaking, Thelma bent down and started biting her mother on the upper arm through her sweater. As Mrs. Crabtree tried to turn away, she cried out, "Ow! Ow! Ow! Thelma, stop! Why are you doing this? Okay! Okay! We won't go into school."

Thelma stopped biting her mother and started sobbing, "You know you can't go in there."

It became clear to me that Thelma was holding her mother's sweater for support and also to keep her from getting any closer to the school. I was shocked. I had never seen Thelma do anything remotely aggressive. This seemed more a desperate attempt to satisfy the conflicting instructions she had received from the important adults in her life than aggression toward her mother. I watched Mrs. Crabtree try to reorient herself and regain her composure. I started to realize that this was a bigger problem than it appeared to be.

As Thelma continued to sob, I told her, "Your mother has a right to know how well you are doing in school. Have you told her that you are getting *A*s and *B*s in my classes?"

Thelma's trembling became more noticeable as she answered, "No. You aren't supposed to be talking to her either."

Mrs. Crabtree, trying to be positive, said, "I know that you are good in school. If you won't tell me what is happening in school, the only way I can find out is to come here and talk to the teachers."

Thelma bit her mother again. I moved toward them but I was afraid to intervene for fear that I might make the situation worse. I told Thelma to stop but I don't think either of them heard me as they engaged in a curious dance around each other.

Finally, the dance stopped.

"You can't go on biting your mother. We need to talk and find a way to work this out."

Thelma did not reply.

Mrs. Crabtree thought aloud: "High school can be scary. I guess there are a lot of things that are different here than at the middle school. I don't want to upset Thelma but I need to know if she is doing okay."

"Thelma's teachers say that she is very quiet in class," I told Mrs. Crabtree. "As of last week when I talked to them, she was getting good grades in all of her classes. Do you know what Thelma means when she says you aren't supposed to go in the school?"

Mrs. Crabtree asked her daughter, "If you are doing so well in school, what harm would it do if I went in for a minute to ask your home economics teacher how much material I need to buy?"

Thelma's only answer was to bite and pinch her mother again. Thelma stopped long enough to say, "I have to pee."

Mrs. Crabtree rubbed her arm and explained. "Whenever Thelma gets upset, I worry that she will pee in the car before we get home. It's a half an hour drive back home, and we left home two hours ago."

"Thelma, do you need to go into the school to use the restroom?" I asked.

"She'll go into the school if I leave her," Thelma answered, pointing to Mrs. Crabtree while looking down at the ground. "Even though she knows she shouldn't."

"Well," I said, playing for time, "we can stay out here and talk until you get back."

Thelma turned and wouldn't face me again. She was becoming more distressed and confused by our inability or unwillingness to follow the simple instructions she had received from Carrie. "No! You aren't supposed to talk to him either. Let's go home!" she pleaded.

"I guess we should go," Mrs. Crabtree said.

I knew further efforts were unlikely to be successful, but I asked Thelma, "Can you wait to use the bathroom until you get home?"

Thelma nodded yes.

"Are we still friends?" I asked.

Thelma stared at the ground and shook her head.

"Maybe by the time we get back to class tomorrow we will be able to talk about this," I said hopefully.

Thelma shook her head and started pulling her mother's sweater toward the car.

"I guess we should go. You won't pee, will you? You promised," Mrs. Crabtree pleaded.

Thelma shook her head from side to side.

As they turned to leave I said, "It was nice meeting you, Mrs. Crabtree. I hope we can talk and be friends again tomorrow, Thelma. Being your friend is important to me."

The pair shuffled away.

Returning to the building, I was worried that I had unintentionally violated Thelma's trust. She was a quiet girl who only talked when spoken to and then always in a monotone. She never interacted with other students in my class. At lunchtime each day I could count on seeing her standing alone in the hall five minutes after being dismissed from my class. I had worked hard to develop a friendly, supportive relationship with Thelma.

Steve Lopez stopped me in the hall. "Well, was your student really biting her mother?"

I briefly related what had happened.

"It doesn't make sense," said Steve, "I don't think there's any constraint keeping Mrs. Crabtree out of the school—she has custody of Thelma, so she should have the right to talk with us."

"Carrie's not here right now," said Steve, "but check with Doris Dexter. I think she has had some dealings with Thelma in the past."

Doris was in her office.

"I remember Thelma. She's the big dumpy girl with old dirty clothes that just hang on her. I've seen her shuffling down the hall. The first time I met her was when she came back to school after a year on a psychiatric ward. It seems that she drove a spike through her foot and then wouldn't let anyone touch her foot to treat it."

"Until this morning Thelma has always been really quiet and cooperative," I said. "This morning I felt that she must have been feeling the same way she did when she drove the spike through her foot. I'd hate to think of her doing anything drastic like that again."

"The first time I met with Thelma's father," Doris continued, "was the only time I have ever been afraid for my personal safety in dealing with parents. Mr. Crabtree acted so irrationally that I was sure I was going to be beaten up at any moment. In fact, I remember removing my watch and glasses—at least they would be safe even if something happened! But back to today. I can't imagine what Carrie might have meant or said to Thelma to give her the impression that we weren't allowed to talk to her mother."

I talked with Carrie a few weeks later, and the picture of the day in the parking lot became a little clearer.

"I asked Thelma's mother to wait in the car on Thursdays when she picks Thelma up after school and brings her to counseling. They need to work on separation. In a few years, Thelma will be out on her own, and they need to start working on that. Mrs. Crabtree insists on meeting Thelma at the school door or even at the classroom door. She claims that Thelma won't be able to find the car on her own. Mrs. Crabtree always arrives at our meeting scratched and bruised, so we haven't been very successful yet. The rule wasn't intended to restrict the mother's access to the high school staff."

When Thelma returned to class, she refused to talk to me or do any work. She sat quietly at her desk waiting for the class to end. When I tried to discuss the incident by the road, she would only say, in reference to what Carrie had told her, that I had lied, that I had broken "the rules" and her trust. Nothing seemed to help.

I felt as if I was in a room with the lights off—as if in my dealings with Thelma I would unwittingly destroy something. At the same time, I desperately needed to get to a door and let some light in.

In spite of my best efforts, I never did.

Avoiding the Issue

JOHNNY'S TEACHERS

As a senior in Southeastern High School, Johnny continued to deal with issues of anger management that had been problems for him throughout his educational career. Johnny's parents and teachers met annually to consider his needs at his IEP meeting. Across the years, his mother had been frequently summoned to the offices of the elementary, middle, and high schools he attended to respond to violations of the school's behavioral codes. Usually, she met with the school officials and was informed that he would be suspended for one to three days or would serve a number of hours of after-school detention.

The oldest of three children, Johnny was described by his mother as having a "very short fuse, just like his father." As a child, he was easily angered and often struck out physically with very little provocation. He was a target for teasing and bullying because he became angry and upset so easily, and some of his peers made a game of taunting him until he lashed out and got into trouble. Johnny was identified as a student with an emotional/behavioral disorder in the third grade. The team decided to serve him in an inclusive setting with accommodations, such as frequent reminders to follow the rules, extended time on assignments, and assigned seating near the teacher. At the conclusion of the third grade, Johnny's teacher admitted that she had seen very little change in his behavior and that, while she felt sorry for him, she was glad that he was no longer *her* problem.

In the fourth grade, a more detailed behavioral plan was written for Johnny due to a series of incidents involving fighting—on the playground, on the school bus, and in the lunchroom. Unsupervised time was a particular problem for Johnny. In the classroom, most of his difficulties occurred during activities that required individual and small-group work. He seemed to exhibit fewer problems during teacher-led, whole-class activities involving little or no interaction with his peers. His teachers noted that he needed a lot of structure, a lot of prompting to stay on task during class activities, and frequent reminders to follow classroom rules. He often refused to continue working when things weren't going smoothly for him, and those refusals were generally accompanied by major classroom disruptions if the teacher insisted he continue on the task. His verbal refusals were more frequently followed by physical outbursts. He began throwing books and pencils, tearing up papers, and hitting other students.

The interventions in the fourth-grade IEP included seating near the teacher, access to a "cool down" room, small-group instruction, and small-group testing. In his fifth-grade year, the school counselor had tried to include Johnny in a few group counseling sessions but dismissed him from the sessions because of Johnny's surliness, arguments with other members of the group, and frequent refusals to participate in the group activities. His teachers reported that they arranged the small groups in which he would work with great care but noted that, even with that attention, he often had problems interacting with classmates.

At the end of his eighth-grade year, his guidance counselor advocated that his IEP include a behavioral accommodation because he was unable to control his temper. She stated that such a plan would be better than any other incentive or instructional program because it would allow him to be "in charge of himself." When the team suggested that the plan be accompanied by instruction in how to avoid becoming so angry that he needed to leave, the counselor pointed to the unsuccessful group counseling attempt and the principal suggested that the school should not be doing this for Johnny.

By his senior year, Johnny had been served for several years under a behavioral plan that allowed him to escape any situation that made him upset. However, he received little or no instruction on strategies that would allow him to confront and deal with those situations. His behavioral plan allowed him to leave the room if he became so upset that he felt he might cause himself problems with school authorities or that might lead to suspension from school. His teachers were aware that, should he leave the classroom, they were to allow him to go without confronting him or asking him for any explanation. Johnny was to locate his guidance counselor so that he could talk through whatever was upsetting him, then return to the classroom when he felt calm enough to continue with the lesson.

In quite a few situations, Johnny took advantage of this plan. At first, any class activity that he didn't enjoy would lead him to leave the class. His ninth-grade teachers complained that it was becoming impossible to get a good sense of what skills he had and the ones he needed to work on because he was missing so much instructional time. As time passed, Johnny felt more and more frustration with class work, as his skills were failing to keep up with the instructional demands. That frustration, in turn, led him to leave the instructional setting more frequently.

In addition, seemingly minor comments from any student that Johnny didn't like, even those that weren't specifically directed to him, could also cause him to decide to leave class. He often complained that things that had happened at home, before or after school, or between classes made him so angry that he was unable even to come to class, much less remain in class. He was not able to put aside difficulties with a particular student in a class even if the incident had happened earlier in the day or even earlier in the week. While his guidance counselor was able to "talk him down" or allow him some quiet time to "get himself together," it did not seem that Johnny had developed any more coping skills than he had had when he entered high school. Even students whom he considered to be his friends could set him off with a poorly timed jest, which most other students would brush off or respond to in kind.

Johnny and Jake had been in the same classes since elementary school and had a history of difficulty with each other. Jake was known as a bully in the school and in the community. Jake had no behavioral intervention plan, and the administration avoided confronting him, as his mother was quick to threaten school officials with legal actions and to complain to the superintendent or school board members when Jake was in trouble. Jake enjoyed teasing other students, but, as most bullies, didn't take well to being teased in return. Johnny and Jake lived in the same neighborhood and had problems both in and out of school. They were assigned to many of the same classes in school. The principal explained that they only offered a limited number of co-taught and self-contained sections of any class and that the students would just have to get along. Most teachers arranged their class activities to avoid interactive group activities or open discussions when both boys were present.

In November, Johnny had a confrontation with Jake that led to serious consequences. This particular incident began during an activity in a senior English class that involved an individual writing assignment. The class was under the supervision of a substitute teacher who had worked in the school before and was familiar with both of the boys because she lived in the same community.

After the class had settled down to work on the assignment, Johnny asked a question. Jake found the question to be annoying and began to belittle Johnny. Johnny responded, and the verbal retorts escalated into a shouting match. When Johnny felt he could no longer handle the verbal sparring with Jake without getting into trouble, he left the classroom in search of his guidance counselor.

Johnny arrived in the guidance office and was informed that neither his regular counselor nor any of the other counselors familiar with his case were available. At this point, Johnny made a sensible decision. Rather than return to class angry, he found the assistant principal in charge of special education. Johnny asked if the AP (assistant principal) was available and if he could have a few minutes to speak with him. When Johnny sat down in the office, he told the AP, "I'm so angry I could kill Jake!" Without any further discussion, the AP suspended Johnny for 10 days based on the school's zero tolerance policy that included verbal threats.

Caught in the Middle

LEANN GROSSLEY

Louise Jones's sixth-grade class seemed to take longer than usual to come in and settle down after their morning break. With the warm sunny weather and the playground right outside the classroom window, they were reluctant to resume the joys of math.

This was my second year as a substitute teacher in the Geneva City school system. Being a substitute teacher gave me valuable learning experiences in a wide variety of classes and schools while I attended East State University where I was working on my master's degree in education. I had been in the system long enough that most of the principals knew me by name and often called me when a teacher or aide was absent.

As the children filed in, I recalled the first time that I had worked with this class three weeks earlier. Shaun Haley, the principal of Church Street Elementary, had called to get me to fill in for Julia Bell, Louise's classroom aide. I remembered leaving Louise's class that day with a renewed excitement about my chosen profession. When Shaun called again, this time to substitute for Louise, I looked forward to working with the sixth-graders again. I recalled that the class was not that large—18 students. They were a lively bunch whose enthusiasm knew no bounds. They were curious, funny, and motivated.

On this second visit, I arrived a little early to get the "feel" of the classroom. I had learned long ago that most teachers who knew they would be absent would leave instructions and materials in plain view on their desks. I checked Louise's desk. Sure enough, there were several pages of detailed notes and directions. As I carefully read Louise's messages, I made a mental note of what I needed to do and jotted down several reminders on a pad. Deep in concentration, I became somewhat puzzled by several inserts in the morning activities where Louise had added post-it notes, all saying the same thing: "Check with Julia for details of what to do here." I felt a little uncomfortable with these mysterious directives—11 in all. I liked to know exactly the way the morning would go. I had had enough unpleasant experiences desperately trying to improvise with children to whom I was a relative stranger!

Activity in the hallways increased, and I made a quick trip to the staff lounge for a fresh cup of coffee before the day began. On the way, I pondered my situation: I was acutely aware that the introduction of a substitute teacher was, at best, unsettling for the students, who almost always perceived that I was "not their real teacher." I had always managed to overcome these perceptions by being well prepared by the start of the day. At least I had worked with this class once before. Louise's little notes meant that I couldn't possibly be as prepared as I wanted to be. Another nagging thought arose: Was I to be the aide to Julia or a replacement teacher for Louise, with Julia acting as my aide? By the time I returned to the classroom, Julia was already there.

Louise had told me that Julia was a competent aide. She had had no prior teacher training except an in-service that the city schools required of all aides working in elementary classrooms. She had been an aide since the in-service several months earlier. A rather large, imposing figure, Julia's long, straggly hair framed her pale face. She wore very thick, smudged spectacles that enlarged her dark brown eyes. She seemed to move quite slowly but with great deliberation. My initial impression was that she appeared very cautious and very tentative. Our conversation went like this:

ME: Hi, I'm Leann Grossley. Shaun Haley asked me to substitute for Louise. You must be Julia Bell?

JULIA: Good morning, Leann. Nice to meet you.

ME: I've already looked over Louise's instructions, so . . .

JULIA: Yes, I know. I'll get things started as soon as the bell rings. In the mean-time, would you mind checking over these math sheets? The answer key is right here.

Julia, it appeared, liked to be in charge, and I didn't feel like arguing. I moved to Louise's desk and began grading the sheets.

Class began at 8:00 sharp. The tardy bell rang at 8:05 and was followed by a series of school announcements over the public address system. A bell signaling the beginning of the academic day rang at 8:10. Julia's teaching style became quickly apparent. She delivered instructions in a booming voice, her ample arms flailing the air to emphasize her point. Her directions were constantly punctured by admonitions to various students who were not complying with her wishes:

JULIA: Now, we're going to begin. Phil, get a move on! We're going to begin our math. Mary, what's the matter with you? Can't you sit still even for a few minutes? Let's begin by opening our math books to page . . . Manuel, are you quite finished with your little private conversation now? Thank you so much. Turn to page 231. Quickly now!

After several more minutes, Julia finally succeeded in getting the class focused. Several students looked somewhat anxious. It was clear that Julia was reveling in her role of "teacher for a day." The math lesson swiftly became a macabre game of Julia doing her level best to catch students in wrong answers. When she did, her punishment was a diatribe that left the offending student mortified:

JULIA: Conchita, what's the answer to number seven?

CONCHITA: Thirteen . . . um, no, twelve, . . . wait . . .

JULIA: Can't you make up your mind? If you'd been listening to what we did in class yesterday, you'd know! Are you sure you're supposed to be in this class? Doesn't seem like you should be from what you're saying. That's the easiest math problem in the whole exercise!

Conchita turned bright red and remained silent for the rest of the lesson. Julia was relentless, but not everyone got the same treatment.

JULIA: Jonathan, number eight.

JONATHAN: Thirty-seven.

JULIA: Exactly! Jonathan, it's so nice to have people in this class who have brains and use them. Why don't you try number nine as well?

JONATHAN: Sixteen.

JULIA: Of course! Conchita, are you getting the picture now?

I felt so sorry for Conchita and several others who failed to escape Julia's wrath, and who never had a chance, it seemed, to redeem themselves. As the unswerving barrage continued, I became increasingly angry. What had children like Conchita done to deserve this? It was clear that they didn't understand the work, but Julia's little game did not involve teaching. Julia changed her focus to Chris, a reedy, sandy-haired boy who, it seemed to me, wore a permanently baffled look. I had noticed that look the last time I had worked with the class. I also remembered that Chris appeared to be one of the weakest students in the class. When Julia called his name, I knew things would go from bad to worse.

JULIA: Chris, number fifteen, now!

Chris was visibly startled. His brow deeply furrowed, he stared at his book. The room was absolutely silent. By this point, nobody was looking up from their books. It seemed that the other students were simply glad that Chris had been chosen and not themselves. Their bowed heads betrayed their wish to hide as much as possible while sitting in a desk facing Julia's stony gaze. Chris began to squirm in his seat, his left leg trembling slightly.

CHRIS: Number fifteen?

Chris was playing for time, hoping to delay the inevitable.

JULIA: What's the matter with you? Are you deaf? If you're deaf, you shouldn't be in here! Deaf people don't belong here. We move too fast! Chris, are you *really* deaf, or as *usual*, just not paying attention? You should, you know, your grades are the worst in this class!

CHRIS: I'm sorry, I thought you said . . .

JULIA: Number *fifteen*. What's the answer?

CHRIS: Twenty-three?

JULIA: Twenty-three? How on earth did you get twenty-three? Are you on the planet here with us? Twenty-three? Twenty-three? Puhhhhleeeease!

Chris looked like a stunned animal. As Julia turned her gaze to another victim, I couldn't stand it any more. I got up and went over to Chris's desk. As I crouched down beside him to help him find his place, Julia turned on me.

JULIA: Ms. Grossley, I'd appreciate your waiting to help Chris until I've finished the exercise. He'd do a lot better if he'd listen and get his homework done. It's really not your problem.

Against my better judgment, I retreated to my seat, just as humiliated as some of the students had been. I felt my cheeks getting hot, and my knuckles were white in my clenched fists. Several students, risking Julia's unwanted attention, looked sympathetically in my direction.

By the time the mid-morning break arrived, I was more than ready to escape the oppressive atmosphere.

The children straggled reluctantly in from their break. Julia positioned herself at the classroom door and, as usual, was yelling at the kids.

JULIA: Move it! We don't have all day you know! Josh, sit down NOW! Felicity, what's your problem? Do you need me to come over there and solve it for you? You'll be really sorry! If you people won't settle down, I'll begin writing down names! You know what that means—name down, then the office! I'll bet you don't want that to happen!

Everyone quickly settled down and looked at Julia—everyone, that is, except Chris, who had his head down on his desk.

JULIA: Chris, get your head up this minute! What do you think this is, your bedroom?

Chris didn't respond. But Jonathan did.

JONATHAN: Ms. Bell, I think Chris is sick. I think he threw up on the playground . . .

JULIA: Nonsense—he was fine before the break, he should be fine now. Chris—up, NOW!

Chris didn't respond. Julia was furious.

JULIA: Get your head up NOW, get with the program, or you can get out and go to the office!

Chris had had enough. Looking up for the first time since entering the class, he gave as good as he had gotten.

CHRIS: I will do anything I want to, and YOU can't make me do anything!

JULIA: I CAN send you to the office!

CHRIS: SO?

The entire class was watching, blow by blow. Julia was trembling as she walked over to Chris's desk.

JULIA: How DARE YOU?

Without warning, Julia turned to me. She turned so swiftly that I jumped.

JULIA: It's either Chris leaves or me. YOU take him to the office and write the referral when you get there.

Reluctantly, I walked to the door, opened it, and waited for Chris to join me. Slowly, he pulled himself up out of his seat, tears streaming down his cheeks. Every pair of eyes tracked us through the door on our way to the office.

There was so much I wanted to say to Chris. I wanted to tell him that it wasn't all his fault. Julia had been awful. It had all happened so fast. One minute we were coming in from break, and the next minute there was this ugly confrontation.

There I was caught between Julia and Chris. I very much wanted to side with Chris, and yet, what example would I be setting for Chris or the other students by taking one side against the other? After all, Julia worked with these students every day and Louise had given no hint to what I had just witnessed. As we slowly walked to the office, I agonized over what Chris must have been feeling.

I filled out the referral for Shaun with a heavy heart. Chris, seated in the office, looked so dejected. He was pale, sweaty, and breathing rapidly. I sent him to the nurse.

As I turned to leave, I made a decision. Returning to the office counter, I attached a note to the referral:

Mr. Haley: I really must talk to you about this referral. If you don't get this before I leave at the end of the day, please give me a call at home.

Teaching for me would never be the same.

Charley

MS. RUSSELL

"I don't feel safe in my own classroom," Ms. Russell shared with the other committee members. "And I don't think my students feel safe either." The building-level assistance committee (BAC) was meeting about Charley Alderman, a second-grade student in Ms. Russell's class. This was the fourth time the committee had met this year about Charley, and each time, the decision to go to Child Study was put off again. Ms. Russell knew that holding a Child Study meeting was the first step in getting Charley evaluated for a possible disability. Yet the principal, Mr. Weiner, and a couple others on the committee always seemed to overpower the group and delay the process once again. "That's fine for them," she thought to herself. "They don't have to deal with the kid every day."

Ms. Russell was not a complainer. In fact, she had a reputation as one of the best teachers at Poplar Ridge School. She was well-organized, highly structured, behaviorally consistent, and extremely precise and competent in her delivery of instruction. She had agreed to take on the "intensive" second grade this year, knowing full well that she would be assigned the students with the most challenging academic needs. More often than not, this also meant that she would have to deal with the most serious behavioral problems as well. For most of the school year, she had done this well—her class was difficult by any measure, but they were making progress academically, and behavioral problems were handled swiftly and fairly without having to send kids to the office. But Charley was the exception. His behaviors had escalated in both frequency and intensity to the point where Ms. Russell could no longer handle him herself—not with 20 other needy students in the room! She had resorted to writing office referrals—Charley had accumulated over 20, but still Mr. Weiner claimed he did not have enough evidence to recommend that Charley be evaluated for a possible behavioral disorder. Nothing was working, and Ms. Russell was scared—for herself (she was five months pregnant), for the other students in her room, and even for Charley, who was headed down a path of frustration, failure, and maybe even tragedy.

The problems were apparent from the beginning. In reviewing Charley's file before he entered her class (four weeks into the school year), Ms. Russell noted that Charley had attended five different schools in just the past two years. Academic concerns were noted on report cards and records from as early as kindergarten. Not surprisingly, behavioral problems had begun early as well. On his kindergarten report card, Charley had all "Ns" for "Needs Improvement" in the conduct areas: getting along with others, following classroom rules, respecting rights and property. Difficulties with reading were noted as well: Charley was having difficulty learning letters and sounds, recognizing rhymes, developing the concept of a word—all essential early literacy skills. Ms. Russell also learned that Charley's home life included some additional stressors: an older brother identified as having an emotional/behavioral disorder, a chronically uninvolved mother, and a stepfather in and out of prison. Who knows why the family moved around so much, but it couldn't be good for the two boys. Ms. Russell found paperwork indicating that the process of referring Charley for a special education evaluation had been started at every one of his previous schools, but Charley always moved away before any substantive actions could be taken. That's why she put Charley's name on the BAC docket early in the school year when she, too, began to have concerns about his academic levels and classroom behavior. She wanted to get him extra help if needed, before he had a chance to change schools again.

At the first BAC meeting, Ms. Russell focused mainly on academics. It was a "chicken and egg" question, she knew, as to whether Charley's academic problems led to behavioral problems or vice versa. But she decided to start with academics. Maybe if he can feel successful and competent with his schoolwork, he won't feel the need to act out. Ms. Russell advocated for and the committee agreed to provide two hours per week of one-on-one after-school tutoring for Charley in reading and math for eight weeks. Ms. Russell also shared with the committee the simple behavioral plan she had designed for Charley. She taped a small chart to his desk and looked for opportunities to "catch him doing good," after which he would earn a sticker. When he accumulated 15 stickers, he could select something from her prize box or earn 15 minutes of one-on-one time with a specialist teacher (i.e., P.E., art, music, library). Charley really enjoyed art, so Ms. Russell thought he might really enjoy some extra time with the art teacher, and the other specialists offered their time as well.

About a week after the BAC meeting, Ms. Russell scheduled a conference with Charley's mother. She shared her concerns about how Charley was falling further and further behind his peers in all subject areas, especially reading, and how the school was going to provide tutoring for Charley to help him catch up. She also gave specific examples of some of the troubling behaviors Charley had demonstrated: putting his hands in his pants during class, touching girls on the behind as they walked by, throwing food in the cafeteria, leaving his seat and hitting other students on the bus, refusing to remove his jacket and "hiding" inside it, even getting into a fistfight with another student on the first class field trip. Charley's mother nodded knowingly—these behaviors did not seem to surprise her—but, at the same time, she shrugged her shoulders as if to say, "I don't know what to do with him either!" Ms. Russell emphasized with Ms. Alderman that the most important thing she could do right now would be to check Charley's homework folder every night, sign his behavioral chart, talk about what happened in school each day, and continue to remind Charley how important it was to her that he do well in school. Ms. Alderman was pleasant but noncommittal: her attitude seemed to say, "Yeah, yeah, I've heard all this before, but nothing ever changes."

The next week, tutoring began, and Charley's new behavioral plan was put in place. The first day went well. Charley seemed motivated by the frequent positive feedback he was receiving and by the chance to earn something "special." But the novelty soon wore off. By the third day, Ms. Russell was having a harder and harder time catching Charley at his good moments, and Charley seemed to be seizing every opportunity he could to agitate other students when Ms. Russell wasn't looking. He even became more defiant with adults, as if to say, "I'm in control here. I can do whatever I want, as long as I make up for it later by doing a few good things." Charley would ignore the teacher's direction asking the students to clear off their desks and prepare for a new lesson. If Ms. Russell spoke to him directly, he would often grunt, slouch, or shove the items off his desk, disrupting the entire group. If she chose to ignore him when he was noncompliant, Charley would soon begin to engage others by leaning over and erasing a peer's work or grabbing something off a peer's desk. Separating Charley from the rest of the class sometimes worked, but just as often, Charley either completely disengaged from the lesson (tucking his head into his sweatshirt and slouching down in his seat) or sought louder, more intrusive ways of gaining the attention of others (throwing objects, making threatening gestures). As hard as Ms. Russell tried to handle these behaviors herself in the classroom, she soon found herself writing disciplinary referrals and sending Charley to the office. "At some point," she thought, "I need to consider how Charley's actions are affecting the rest of my class—interfering with instruction and triggering other behavioral problems. I can't let one child disrupt the learning of 20 other children every day!"

In the meantime, Charley attended tutoring sessions twice a week. The tutor, Ms. Jackson, reported that Charley seemed to enjoy the one-on-one time with an adult, but that he spent a good part of their time together talking about things that were upsetting him at home or at school. Ms. Jackson allowed these stories to distract them from their work at first, thinking part of her role was to build a trusting relationship with this boy, knowing that he may not have anyone else with whom to share his feelings. Sometimes the stories were alarming: once Charley told Ms. Jackson he was sick and tired of seeing his stepdad hurt his mom, but that she needn't worry because he was going to shoot him. Then he laughed and added playfully, "It's just a BB gun, you know. Man, I sure got you worried!"

Charley showed some improvement academically, as Ms. Jackson was able to show through her assessments. But the progress rarely transferred to the classroom environment because, it seemed, as soon as Charley was back in a group situation, his behavioral problems again emerged, and he ended up disrupting the class and/or being sent to the office. He continued to miss instructional time so that even his tutoring sessions became inadequate in helping him stay afloat academically.

The BAC continued to hold periodic follow-up meetings, and Ms. Russell continued to alert the group to her growing concerns for Charley and how he was impacting her entire class. A new behavioral plan was established whereby Charley could earn a star for each period throughout the day when he: a) followed directions, and b) cooperated with peers. Every time he earned a star, he got five minutes of "drawing time." Ms. Russell thought that the more frequent reinforcement schedule might help keep Charley motivated. At the same time, Ms. Russell began using time-outs to interrupt Charley's disruptive behavior before it escalated. If Charley complied with a five-minute time-out and was able to return to class successfully, he was still able to earn his star for that period. Knowing how important it was to Charley to feel "in control" of every situation, Ms. Russell tried to incorporate as many choices as possible into Charley's schedule. For example, he was able to choose the order in which to complete his written assignments, the location in which he wanted to work, and whether or not to work with peers. Ms. Russell also arranged for Charley to join a small group of students who received math instruction from the special education teacher, hoping that the small-group setting would be less stressful and intimidating for him. In addition, a special education aide, who was assigned to work with another student in Ms. Russell's class, began to devote much of her time to Charley, hoping that the extra attention and close behavioral monitoring would help keep Charley on track and prevent his misbehavior.

Ms. Russell shared all of these interventions at the BAC meeting. She brought documentation of the numerous episodes of defiant, attention-seeking, aggressive behaviors Charley had displayed over the past weeks. She invited the specialist teachers (P.E., art, music, library) to attend the meeting to share their many concerns about Charley's behavior in their classes. The P.E. teacher talked about how he carefully chose Charley's partners in gym class, placing him with responsible, cooperative peers who were not likely to be provoked by him. But one day, when the P.E. teacher was busy helping another group, he heard a loud shout and turned around to see Charley shoving one of his partners against the wall and then walking over to another partner and spitting on her. Next Charley kicked over a bucket of equipment before the teacher was able to get to him and guide him away from the group. This teacher was worried, understandably, about the safety of everyone in the gym. "I have close to 40 students in there at a time," he said. "I can't possibly watch Charley's every move and not lose the rest of my class!"

Once again, however, the committee decided to wait before taking Charley's case to Child Study, refusing to move one step closer to having him evaluated for a possible behavioral disorder. "There are too many environmental factors at play here," the school psychologist argued. "If Charley's behaviors are a direct result of his dysfunctional home life, then we cannot call him emotionally disturbed; we are dealing instead with a form of conduct disorder." Ms. Russell had never understood the distinction between an emotional/behavioral disorder and a conduct disorder, and no one had ever explained it in a way that made sense to her: it seemed to be a matter of personal opinion alone. "Even if you could distinguish the two groups of kids," she thought to herself, "would the distinction drastically change the types of services these children need or the kinds of programs from which they might benefit?" It was a mystery to her, that's for sure, but who was she to say? She was merely the classroom teacher; she didn't claim to have any particular expertise in the area of emotional/behavioral disorders. Surely the school psychologist and principal knew more than she, right?

Weeks went by. Charley's new behavioral plan fizzled after just a few days. When Charley did earn his drawing time, he acted as though he had just had a stroke of good luck; he didn't seem to connect the reward to any purposeful behavior on his part. The special education teacher was beginning to question whether she could continue to allow Charley to participate in her math group. Truthfully, her primary responsibility had to be for the students on her caseload with identified disabilities. Working with Charley had been a "bonus": he did not qualify for special education services at this time, and he was interfering with her ability to meet the needs of her "legitimate" students. The aide who had begun focusing her attention on Charley was also becoming increasingly frustrated. She enjoyed the times when she could give positive feedback to him, and he seemed to enjoy their interactions. But when Charley became uncooperative or openly defiant, she really didn't know what to do. He seemed to be making a fool of her, as if he sensed her lack of confidence and decided to use it to his own advantage.

The end of the school year was approaching, and another BAC meeting was scheduled for Charley. Ms. Russell was at the end of her rope: she was ready to demand that something be done this time. When the committee started talking about encouraging the family to undergo an evaluation that could lead to in-home support services and/or counseling, Ms. Russell started to shift in her seat. Then the school psychologist said she would talk to Charley's mom about taking him for a psychiatric evaluation, and papers would be sent home to allow the school and the child psychiatrist to exchange information. Again. Ms. Russell felt uncomfortable: both of these actions were voluntary on Ms. Alderman's part, and Ms. Russell did not hold high hopes that Charley's mom would follow through. Ms. Russell could feel her face turning red as her emotions welled inside her. Finally, she spoke up. "But what about TOMORROW? Can someone here please tell me what I'm supposed to do with Charley when he walks through my door TOMORROW? Someone is going to get hurt. I don't feel safe in my own classroom." Nods of approval and support came from most members of the committee, but once again, the principal and school psychologist prevailed, and Child Study was again postponed, pending the results of the "voluntary" evaluations that Charley's mother was supposedly going to pursue. Ms. Russell left the meeting feeling frustrated and powerless. "What is the purpose of having a committee, if the only opinions that seem to matter are those of the principal and psychologist?" she wondered. She went home with a knot in her stomach, knowing that something bad was going to happen, sooner or later.

The next day, Charley came to school in good spirits. The day started out well, and he earned five minutes of drawing time when he completed his entry assignments without incident.

Then Ms. Russell gave the signal for students to clean up in order to begin social studies. She was excited about today's lesson, which involved having students rotate among four stations where they would complete various projects to culminate their study of Egypt. Charley's first station was pyramid building, something he was likely to enjoy. The stations had all been introduced and explained yesterday, so students were instructed to begin working immediately. Ms. Russell focused her attention at Charley's station first, and just as she had expected, he seemed to be off to a good start, enjoying the project and apparently getting along with his classmates. As she moved about the room to check on other students, it wasn't long before she was startled by a piercing scream coming from Charley's area of the room. She turned to find Charley pinning another student against the wall, raising his fist in preparation for a punch. The other student's ruined pyramid lay on the floor in front of them, having been stabbed numerous times by Charley's pencil. Ms. Russell lunged to reach the boys before the first punch flew, but she was too late. She stepped between the boys before Charley could punch again, thinking only later about the risks she might be taking for the baby she was carrying. She calmly instructed another student to phone the office, and she waited in that position until help arrived. Charley was escorted out of the room, sent home, and suspended pending a completed psychiatric evaluation.

Charley never returned to school that year. He missed the last four weeks because his mother, not surprisingly, failed to keep several scheduled appointments with the child psychiatrist. Shortly after summer break began, a copy of the psychiatrist's evaluation arrived at the school. The doctor had diagnosed Charley with bipolar disorder and prescribed medication to begin immediately. However, Charley's mom reported that he would be spending his summer with an uncle out of state, so she would not be able to guarantee that he would get his medication regularly until he returned home.

"It's out of my hands now," Ms. Russell thought to herself. "But next year, he's going to show up on some teacher's doorstep, and who knows how bad things will have to get before the ball gets rolling once again and his case finally makes it to child study? Are we really helping this child by waiting? What are we waiting for anyway?"

Grandma's Boy

HELEN JAMISON

"I was totally unprepared to deal with those people." Helen Jamison took a sip from the apricot tea that Cindy, her roommate, had just brewed. "All I could think of was poor Justin and how awful it must be for him to live with such a dysfunctional family. I just hope we can come up with something at school that will help this kid."

Helen was a second-grade teacher at C. E. Conners Elementary School. Just two months into her first year of teaching, she had encountered the first rift in what had otherwise been a smooth and gratifying beginning. As a novice in the profession, she had hit the ground running, and her innovations had caught the eye of the central office supervisors, building-level administrators, and parents. For the most part, her 27 second-grade students got along well with one another, and she was excited about the cooperative spirit that she had managed to cultivate in this average-ability group.

At the beginning of the year, Helen had encouraged the students to select a name for the class—a name symbolizing strength, honor, and cooperation. The students had decided to call themselves the Spartans, and at Helen's request, the art teacher had drawn a picture of a warrior on horseback to post on the wall just outside the classroom. Helen had then cut the backgrounds from students' photographs and meticulously positioned and glued each picture over the silhouette of the warrior, creating a beautiful collage. Across the body of the horse, in majestic red, was a salutation: **WELCOME TO ROOM 204: HOME OF THE SPARTANS.**

Helen tried to perpetuate a theme of cooperation throughout the course of each day. She took time during each week to teach, model, and have the students role-play social skills that would encourage cooperation and citizenship. She praised students when she "caught them being good," and she routinely coupled this social praise with "Caughtcha!" stickers that they could exchange for prizes from her treasure chest. She presented "Spartan of the Week" awards to students who worked hard to improve their grades in an area of weakness. Of course, there were times when curiosity and mischief spawned misbehavior and minor noncompliance, but for the most part Helen believed herself capable of using basic behavior management techniques to handle such occurrences.

And so it was that after just two months of teaching, Helen was quite pleased with her performance and the performance of almost all of her students. She was greatly concerned about one of her little "munchkins," however. Justin E. Richardson II had transferred from another school in the county, and he was not keeping up with the rest of the students in the class. He daydreamed constantly, and he completed virtually no assignments. Against the advice of a colleague, Helen had scheduled a meeting with Justin's father, hoping to develop a home-school behavior management program that would motivate the child to increase his productivity. The meeting had been a complete disaster, and now Helen sat in her apartment, totally flustered by her first encounter with irate parents. She was glad that Cindy was home, as she really needed to vent her frustrations, anger, and disappointment about what had just happened. She curled up in her recliner, gazed straight ahead, and began recounting her experience.

"After the first month of school, I reread Justin's cumulative folder and discovered that a confidential folder had also been sent from his old school. Justin's first-grade teacher, Judy Cole, had written on the referral form that Justin's behavior had started to deteriorate toward the end of the year. He daydreamed constantly, was inconsistent in his work habits, and refused to comply with her instructions. She also said that Justin was not an acting-out child, but that he was difficult to deal with because of his passive-aggressive personality. No one at Conners knew anything about this kid, so I called Judy, hoping she could tell me about some 'trick' that worked last year. I can still remember her response after hearing who I was: 'Oh, so you're the lucky one this year!' She told me she felt as if she was on a treadmill with Justin, his father, and the grandmother last year. It's really sad. Judy didn't think she could do anything to help Justin. She believed nobody would be able to help the poor kid until they eased up on him at home."

"Exactly what was happening at home?" Cindy asked as she kicked off her shoes, sat Indian style on the sofa, and began munching an apple. Cindy was an elementary school guidance counselor and a masterful listener. She interjected very little, but she frequently nodded her head and gestured to Helen to continue. For this, Helen was extremely grateful. Having a live-in therapist was great!

"Well," responded Helen, "I questioned Judy further about the home situation and discovered that Justin's parents had just divorced last summer. After the divorce, Justin and his father had moved in with Justin's paternal grandmother, Ann Richardson—better known to school personnel as 'Brunhilda.' Judy also warned me that this grandmother was a real 'busybody' and would make herself a part of every interaction that took place between Mr. Richardson and the school.

"She told me that I'd 'really have to watch that lady.' Apparently, Judy's child study team recommended that Justin undergo a full evaluation, but his father refused to grant the school permission to go through with the testing. Judy didn't believe for a minute that the refusal came from Mr. Richardson. His mother has such a dominating influence over him that Judy was convinced that she's the one who blocked the testing. Grandma came to all the meetings with Mr. Richardson, and she was adamant that Justin's problems in school were all caused by his mother—'his no-good, cheating, lying mother.' "

"Boy, it sounds like this Mrs. Richardson's a real charmer," Cindy concluded, rising to refill their mugs. She reclaimed her spot on the sofa and asked, "Is what she said about Justin's mother true, or did Judy give you conflicting information?"

"Actually, Judy wasn't aware of the causes leading to the split-up of Justin's parents, but she did know that the mother had relinquished custody of Justin and had left the state shortly after the divorce. No one at Judy's school knew exactly where the mother had moved to, and this 'mystery woman' had made no attempts to contact any school personnel. Judy finally told me that because the mother was no longer in the picture I should follow her strategy from last year and try to get help from my school psychologist or guidance counselor. She told me to stay away from the father and grandmother because they're the ones mostly responsible for what this child is going through.

"I now realize that Judy couldn't have been more accurate in her assessment of the situation," continued Helen. "As far as I'm concerned, this meeting was a waste of time. Granny Richardson, even though I didn't invite her, came with her son to the conference and immediately started to blame Justin's mother for all of his problems. I couldn't believe it when she bad-mouthed her 'low-life' ex-daughter-in-law. The way she sat straight up in her seat reminded me of a drill sergeant, and the way she barked at me made me feel like I was a recruit!"

Helen sat bolt upright and proceeded to imitate Mrs. Richardson. Her voice took on a different timbre, and for a moment Cindy actually felt that she was being lectured by a sergeant. "'No matter how hard I try to make that boy realize that he has a no-account for a mother, he still wants to see his parents back together again. He wants them to be a threesome again, so he stages these little games and hopes that Jus will contact his mom.' 'Jus' is what grandma calls Mr. Richardson."

Helen stood, pointing her finger at Cindy and continuing her impersonation. "'Well, the last time he showed off like this, I whipped his ass good and took away his bike, and I know he shaped up for a while. I guess I'm just gonna have to do it again.'"

Helen took her seat, folded her arms, and nodded her head matter-of-factly. Cindy applauded this electrifying performance, concluding that this role-playing was just the thing Helen needed to relieve some of the tension that she was feeling. She motioned for her counselee to continue, and they both giggled as Helen resumed her story, now somewhat more relaxed.

"Cindy, I could not believe what I was hearing or seeing! Just as Judy had told me, Mrs. Richardson monopolized every moment of the conversation. Mr. Richardson occasionally nodded and affirmed what his mother reported, but he contributed little else to the conference. I tried to direct questions his way, but every time I tried, 'Brunhilda' jumped right in. More and more I realized that because of his home situation, Justin was in jeopardy of developing some serious emotional problems."

"So, what did you suggest?" asked Cindy as she slid to the floor and rested her back against the base of the sofa.

Helen sat on the edge of her chair and shared her game plan. "At one point, I had decided to suggest that the family seek counseling, but after just a few minutes I realized that that recommendation would go over like a ton of lead. Also, I'd been warned previously by my assistant principal that such suggestions were frowned on by the school system, because if Justin was found eligible for special education, the system could be forced to pay for this as a related service. So when I wasn't able to think of anything else, I decided to push for my idea of a home-school management program. I also tried to make these people understand that finding a solution to Justin's problems would require much more than spankings and scoldings. I described Justin's behavior, hoping that this would provide me with a lead into my management proposal.

"'Justin,' I said to them, 'sits and stares most of the time. He doesn't interact with the other students in the class. In fact, if they initiate a conversation or ask him a question, he usually refuses to even acknowledge their existence. He looks at one of his books or writes in one of his skillbooks, pretending to be hard at work.'

"I also explained that Justin didn't respond to either praise or criticism, rewards or punishment. He hasn't completed any assignments. He's failed every section of every unit test in reading. On one occasion, I watched him complete the comprehension subtest by merely going down the list and selecting answers at random. He hadn't bothered to read any of the passages in the section, and he failed the test miserably. After this, I thought that Justin was preoccupied and unmotivated. Later, I realized that, on the few occasions when he did try, Justin found it extremely difficult to decode unfamiliar words, and his oral reading was choppy and labored.

"Well, for what it was worth, I shared this information with Justin's father and grandmother. I practically begged these people to understand that we all needed to work together to help Justin. Unfortunately, after hearing my concerns, Mrs. Richardson held on to her notions about what was best for her grandson. When I tried to ease into my proposal, I was interrupted abruptly."

Helen resumed Mrs. Richardson's position and voice. "'Justin don't need no kind of home-school program.' That was Mrs. Richardson's response to my plan. 'You deal with him your way here, and we'll deal with him our way at home. Like I already said, if push comes to shove, we'll just have to beat some sense into him. Once we help him get that woman out of his system, he'll be all right anyway. Just you wait and see, he'll be all right.'

"There was no need for any further discussion," sighed Helen. "After this outburst, I thanked the Richardsons for coming and ended the meeting. As they were leaving my room, I think I may have managed a half-hearted smile, but I couldn't help feeling sorry for Justin. This child is constantly being bombarded with negative information about a mother that he apparently loves, and he's being punished severely when his behavior and feelings are in conflict with those of his grandmother and father. I tell you, Cindy, I was exhausted and depressed after that meeting, and even though talking about it has helped, I just don't know what my next move will be."

Cindy broke the silence that followed with the suggestion that they identify the most salient problems and rank them. The two then spent the next half hour trying to identify possible strategies that might improve the situation.

Helen's session with Cindy had helped her sort out what she believed to be true about this entire situation with Justin and his family. She concluded that there were emotional problems and possibly learning disability problems that caused Justin to experience so much difficulty in school. Helen also believed that she was not equipped to handle these problems and that it was now time to seek the expertise of more qualified personnel. Hence, the week following the meeting with the Richardsons, Helen brought Justin's case before the child study committee and asked that they once again pursue the testing that had been recommended the previous year.

Now, a month after the committee meeting, Helen found Cindy seated before her and once again felt the need to share the details of her most recent episode with Justin. It was a Sunday afternoon, and she and Cindy had just dotted the last "i" and crossed the last "t" of their plans for the week. Plan books, schedules, and teachers' manuals were scattered about the floor. "Though we may toil from sun to sun, a teacher's work is never done," quipped Cindy as she began to clean up her part of the mess.

"You're telling me!" groaned Helen. She began to pack the rectangular laundry basket that she used to transport materials to and from school. "I'm really excited about the activities I've planned for this week, but I honestly dread the thought of dealing with Justin Richardson for another day. I feel like Judy—I feel like I'm on a treadmill with this kid."

"So what's happening now?" Cindy asked. "Didn't you tell me that the child study committee made recommendations that you thought might work?"

"So I thought," agreed Helen as she placed the last stack of materials into her makeshift briefcase. "I shared the experiences I've had with the Richardsons and my conversations with Judy. After hearing my concerns, the team concluded that there was a slim-to-none chance that Mr. and Mrs. Richardson would reconsider having Justin evaluated. Instead, they recommended that we try Judy's strategy. They suggested that Ron Saunders—that itinerant school psychologist assigned to our building—work with me as a consultant. I wasn't exactly thrilled about that decision, but I understood, to some degree anyway, why they didn't want to pursue testing or counseling, and I felt that with help from a more experienced professional I might be able to help Justin."

"Well?" Cindy asked.

"Well, I was *dead* wrong!" replied Helen. "This child is determined to have his way, and he lets me and everyone else at the school know that he simply will not be broken. He is so defiant in a nagging, passive sort of way, and he isn't bothered in the least bit by any of the consequences that we built into his contract. I really want to help this kid, but I'm losing patience. I'm beginning to resent having to meet and plan so much for some kid who just doesn't respond positively to anything."

"Okay, okay!" Cindy interjected, motioning Helen to calm down. "What exactly did the two of you come up with?"

"We worked like gangbusters! After the child study team made its recommendations, Ron and I met several times to discuss Justin's case and brainstorm about possible behavior management strategies. Finally, we decided that self-recording of completed assignments might motivate him to finish more of his work. We developed daily recording sheets and set up a plan to monitor his performance. We had a little meeting with Justin and developed a menu of rewards that would encourage him to complete at least 50 percent of his math assignments per week. We also wrote up a weekly contract that outlined expectations and consequences."

"Well, are you ready for this? The self-recording thing didn't even last a week. Justin rushed through all of his math assignments without reading or copying the problems from his textbook. He simply headed his paper, filled in the blank spaces with numbers that he apparently pulled from the sky, and placed his papers in the 'assignments completed' box. His work completion rate skyrocketed, but his accuracy rate plummeted."

Cindy could understand Helen's frustration, but she could not help chuckling when she realized that Justin had manipulated the situation one more time. "So the infamous Justin prevails again," she noted.

"You guessed it. And at that point I was seeing red. My teeth ached, I was so tensed up. I just felt like grabbing Justin by his shoulders and shaking some sense into him."

"Helen, I know exactly how you feel. It's really difficult to deal with a kid that you just can't seem to reach, even though you've given it your best shot. Try not to take this thing so personally, and remember that Justin's learned to play his games well. It may take a long time to eliminate his inappropriate behaviors."

"I know, I know," continued Helen. "We didn't give up so easily. Ron and I both agreed that we were pretty stupid not to include anything about accuracy in Justin's contract, so we added in a statement that he would also have to complete his math assignments with at least 50 percent accuracy."

"Sounds good," Cindy stated, "but I take it from the look on your face that this didn't work either."

"Right again," replied Helen. "To get around this added contingency, our little friend proceeded to cheat from his neighbors' papers. This time, both work completion and accuracy increased, and of course Justin claimed that he was meeting the terms of the contract. Friday, after carefully observing and documenting Justin's behavior for three days, I decided that I had to confront him. That's when things really got out of hand."

"While everyone else completed their independent practice assignments for math, I called Justin to my desk, reviewed the terms of the contract, and questioned him about the cheating.

"'I didn't cheat off of nobody's paper, you liar!' This is exactly what he screamed at me! The other kids stopped working and looked up to see what was going on. Then Justin really went into his act. He grabbed the contract off my desk, ripped it up, ran into the bathroom in the back of the classroom, and slammed the door behind him. I was totally caught off-guard because I'd never seen him act this way before."

"Yeah, sometimes that happens when you implement a management program," said Cindy. "As you tighten the reigns, the kid resists. So how in the world did you pull things together after that outburst?"

"Believe me, it wasn't easy. I walked to the bathroom door and asked Justin to come out. No response. I opened the door, and I immediately dismissed any thought of trying to force him out.

I mean, he looked crazed! He had his fists clinched, his eyes were bulging, and his whole body was shaking. Hey, I politely closed the door. 'No way,' I thought, 'not today.' I turned around and looked at the other kids. Some of them asked, 'What's wrong with Justin, Miss Jamison?' Others started laughing, and within seconds they were all chattering about what had just happened. I stood in the middle of the classroom, not knowing what to say or do."

"Finally, I remembered Ron's crisis intervention plan, so I sent a student to his office with an SOS card. Ron got there in a few minutes, and while he attended to Justin, I took the rest of the class outside for an unplanned recess period. That seemed to take their minds off of what had just happened."

"Well, young lady, I think you did a super job of handling things," replied Cindy.

"Yeah, I was really glad that I was able to get the other kids out of the room without creating another major scene. After about 30 minutes, Ron convinced Justin to come out of the bathroom, and he took him to his office for the rest of the day. "And what's the plan for tomorrow?" asked Cindy.

"Well, Ron and I talked to our principal after school, and he has put us on the agenda to meet with the child study committee first thing tomorrow morning. I don't know what the final outcome will be, but I do know that something has to change. Justin has some serious emotional problems, and I think it's pretty obvious that, right now, he needs more than I'm able to give."

James's Uncertain Future

DAN PARKER

James Judson was enrolled in my third-grade special education class from the beginning of the school year. James lived with his mother and an older brother, Kenny. Kenny was a tenth-grade straight-A student and an athlete—an all out, good kid. I was not surprised that James idolized Kenny. As was so often the case with my students, Kenny took the place of James's father. James knew where his father lived, but he hadn't had any contact with his father for about a year.

James's mother, Anna, did her best to support the family but had a history of frequently changing jobs. She was very big and tall, an intimidating figure complimented by a generally belligerent attitude. She had a very deep, raspy voice, and when she talked, her comments were so pointed and harsh that they often left me breathless. In our many interactions over the year, she often appeared angry and usually claimed that everyone was picking on James or criticizing her parenting skills. However, Anna was highly verbal and always seemed very interested in James's academic progress. If he took work home, she usually tried to help him.

The family lived in a rundown part of town comprised of mostly Mexican American and African American families of low socioeconomic status. The area had a reputation for gang activity, and children commonly witnessed violence in the neighborhood. The school reflected the neighborhood. West Side Elementary housed 1,200 students with multiple classes for each grade. Official school statistics reported the ethnic mix as 50 percent Hispanic, 45 percent African American, and 5 percent Caucasian and Asian American students.

When I first met James, he seemed nice enough. However, I didn't see James every day—he would only come to me for extra help or reteaching as needed. At first, James would come to my class only once in a while. Even in those early days he was very distractible and talked out of turn all the time. If the class were answering questions from the textbook, for example, he would burst out with "Oh! Oh! Oh! Mr. Parker! Mr. Parker! I know that! Oh! Oh! Oh!" and then, nine times out of ten, he'd give the wrong answer.

What I was seeing in my classroom was soon mirrored by what Jill was experiencing in hers. James had begun picking on other kids. He'd been hitting, pinching, scratching, kicking, and tripping. Students would walk by to go to the pencil sharpener and James would whack them on the back of the head. Soon, Jill started sending James to me much more often—as much for his inappropriate behavior as his schoolwork, I thought.

Although James was labeled learning disabled (LD), he was academically up to par. If his inappropriate behaviors hadn't been so obvious, he never would have been in my room. Everyone knew

James's behavior was the problem. Even his mother acknowledged that: "Well, he's active, that's all there is to it." His activity, however, wore people out. Jill would go home crying almost every day. He just overwhelmed her.

By midyear, James was acting out all the time. We tried a wide variety of behavioral approaches, but none of them worked. The school psychologist tried, the general education teachers tried, the LD teachers tried, and the principal had ideas that she tried, all to no avail. By the middle of the year, we had had four conferences with Anna. In spite of our strenuous urging, Anna would only help with the homework and not much else.

In the fifth conference, we repeated the now growing litany to Anna. She refused to believe that James was misbehaving in class.

"He's not really doing that," she said.

By this point we had all had enough, so we invited Anna to see for herself. We put up some dark paper on my windows with small viewing slits into the classroom so that Anna could observe James in my class without being seen. After witnessing James's behavior for a two-week period, Anna seemed completely overwhelmed.

At our next meeting we saw a different Anna. She broke down, saying she couldn't believe this was her James. We were all touched by her outpouring of frustration as she told us how hard it was for her to hold the family together, her helplessness at not being better able to provide for her children, and her bewilderment that James was "not more like Kenny." I was concerned, though, that she seemed to leave the meeting with a fiercely determined look on her face. Her parting comment that she'd "take care of things" didn't help, either.

Whatever Anna had meant by "taking care of things" appeared to work. James was quiet and compliant for about a week and actually attended to academic tasks. We soon realized, though, that this was not necessarily progress when, one day, he came to school but couldn't sit down at his desk in Jill's class. Jill insisted he explain what the problem was. James reluctantly showed her switch marks from the middle of his back to the middle of his thigh where Anna had "whipped" him. Besides being unable to sit down at all, he was scared to go home without having done his work.

Even beatings didn't help for long, though. Anna was soon "whipping" him at night quite regularly, but the effects of this harsh punishment wore off swiftly, and the misbehavior reappeared as troublesome as it had been before.

County child protective services intervened quickly. When they spoke with Anna, she was defensive. All she said was, "This is *my* child, and he gets a spanking." That's all that ever came out of it. Inexplicably, child protective services never followed up on the incident. I think James slipped through the cracks or the report was simply put under a pile of others somewhere and forgotten. All that came of the report was that our action didn't endear us to Anna. Her growing suspicion that we were all conspiring against her only intensified.

In desperation, I reviewed James's records carefully once more and found that he had been diagnosed as having a severe attention deficit-hyperactivity disorder (ADHD) almost 18 months previously. In spite of the physician's recommendation that James receive medication for his disorder, no further action was noted in the record. I began to wonder. Why hadn't James received the recommended medication? I raised the issue with Jill, and then I learned another piece of the puzzle.

After school and over the weekends, James spent a great deal of time at church. Anna was a devout follower of her faith, part of which frowned on reliance on medical science, including medical treatment for James's hyperactivity. Any mention of medication drew vehement protests from Anna.

With this additional information, I called yet another meeting with Anna and insisted that James be retested for ADHD. Reluctantly, she agreed. The physician's report was the same as it was before. James had severe ADHD, but Anna refused to allow medication. She would not budge.

Her perception that we were all ganging up on her increased to the point that she demanded the appointment of a mediator to serve as a buffer between her and the school. In the last two months of the school year, Anna would communicate only with the mediator, so all of our recommendations had to be relayed through him. We were desperate. Medication was not an option, and nothing had worked with James except, at least for a while, Anna's physical abuse.

Eventually, Anna suggested that she spend a good part of each school day in the building in the hopes that her presence would keep him on track. She began appearing at school for several hours each day. James only knew that she was physically somewhere in the building. Sometimes she would be watching through the peephole. At other times she spent time in the office or walking around the playground.

James's behavior improved, but as with the beatings he received at home, the effect of Anna's presence soon wore off. By the last month of school, Anna's appearances dwindled, although she remained available by phone. Two or three days a week we would call Anna to come and get James by noon. It was the only strategy we had left—to get him out of the way. It stayed that way until the end of school.

The following year, James's home was rezoned for construction of a new school several blocks away. I heard that Anna was very excited that James was going to a new school. She thought he would get a fresh start.

I saw James yesterday. Still energetic, still impulsive, still unmedicated. My thoughts were not positive. He's going to get into trouble not only with authority figures but also with his peers who will understand even less about him than we did. Soon he'll get to high school, where there are more guns, knives, and aggressive behavior. He's going to upset someone so seriously that that'll be the end.

As I tried to look on the sunny side, I couldn't help but remember Anna's parting words to me the year before: "I don't want the teachers spanking him, and I'm tired of having to get James from school when he misbehaves. I'll just have to take care of his sorry attitude at home."

Lenny

SARA OLSON

Sara Olson had been a teacher at Cross Lake Elementary School for 11 years and for the past 5 years had been assigned the kindergarten classroom. Cross Lake was her first teaching job and would probably be the only one she ever had. She loved the Cross Lake community and was active in community clubs and activities. For the past 3 years she had served as chair of the summer water carnival and was an ardent and active member of the Cross Lake Garden Club. She and her husband, Jim, a state game warden, had bought a house on Bad Medicine Lake just west of town. Their two children, Justin and Katy, were well-adjusted and active fourth- and sixth-grade students at Cross Lake Elementary School.

Sara enjoyed her students, and it showed in their affection for her. It showed after school each day when she would say goodbye to them as they got on their buses. Usually, they gave her a big hug. She always hugged them back, though she clearly remembered the warnings she had received during in-service training about the dangers of touching students. Her students' affection for her also showed as they got older and went into secondary school. The only cafeteria in Cross Lake was in the elementary school, and the secondary students walked a block from the high school to eat at the elementary school each day. Sara always saw some of her former students as she brought her students in from recess, and invariably they greeted her with a happy "Hello, Mrs. Olson."

For the most part, Sara really enjoyed her job. There was good comradeship and support among the teachers and with the principal, Jean Ollerud. The school felt comfortable to her, and it certainly didn't have the kind of racial polarity, staff morale, and discipline problems known to be issues at the Cross Lake High School.

Cross Lake was a reservation border town, lying on the western edge of the Forest County Ojibwe Reservation in the northern area of the state. Sara had lived in the community long enough to have seen the transition of the community during the past several years. When she had taken her first teaching job as a fourth-grade long-term substitute, the majority of the students were "town children." Only a third of them were "reservation children." That had changed in the past 10 years; now the majority of her students came from the reservation. Although most of them still came from poor families, there seemed to be a small and growing American Indian middle class, who, unlike the American Indian families Sara had previously known, participated more often in school activities. The middle-class American Indian parents came to parent-teacher conferences, whereas those of lower socioeconomic status rarely came to the school. Several of the middle-class Indian parents served on the school board and the Indian parent committee and were demanding changes in the curriculum to better reflect their Ojibwe heritage. They also were insisting that the school district hire Indian teachers, and, indeed, several Indians had been hired. More recently, Dale Bird, an Ojibwe from Minnesota, had been hired as the high school principal.

For the most part, Sara tried to change with the times by having reservation elders come to her class several times a year to tell legends and stories. Even though some schools had quit decorating during the Thanksgiving holiday, Sara continued to decorate her room and the area outside her classroom. During this time of the year she featured her Indian unit, teaching the children the contributions Indians made to America. Three years ago she had taken a summer school course at Mt. Scenario College called "Teaching the American Indian Pupil." Although none of her close friends was Ojibwe, she felt she harbored no prejudice against Indian people.

With the start of the new school year, Sara was busy getting to know all the children and trying to assess how well prepared they were, both socially and emotionally, for kindergarten. But one of the children, Lenny, was having a difficult time.

Lenny was one of the reservation children from Bull Club, a small community south and east of Cross Lake. From what she had found out by asking one of the Indian teacher aides, Madeline Wind, Lenny had attended Forest County Ojibwe Head Start. Both of his parents worked for the tribal council and had recently built a new home out in the "Mission" area of Bull Club, so-called because an Indian Bible camp was located in the area. According to Madeline, Lenny was "hell on wheels" and had given the Head Start staff fits in trying to deal with him. According to her, Lenny didn't listen to anyone.

"I heard that last year he even bit the Head Start bus driver," Madeline had told Sara. She also indicated that Lenny may be hyperactive.

During the first week of school, Lenny seemed to be adjusting well. Although he was quite active, he seemed to be making an adequate social adjustment.

By the end of September, Sara was sure that Lenny was hyperactive, but she wasn't quite sure that what she was doing to accommodate it was helping. Many times he became over-stimulated. If the other children were very active, Lenny got unusually active. He often ran around the room bellowing. He talked loud most of the time and freely interrupted others. The over-stimulation was also brought on by loud or unusual noises, bright lights, and all the active games played in her classroom. He had other problems as well. He had difficulty with transitions. After playtime, he had difficulty moving to story time. Sometimes she had to lead him by the arm from one activity to the next. He seemed to have unusually high demands for physical contact and emotion, always wanting a hug and wanting to sit on her lap. At other times he was overly aggressive, and more than once she had to deal with his pushing or hitting other students. Although it seemed that he felt remorse for fighting, he would do it again and again. It almost seemed as if he wasn't able to internalize any information or controls.

This wasn't the first time Sara had had hyperactive children in her classroom. Each year she'd had at least one, and some years she'd had as many as two or three of them. Although she had no formal training in working with hyperactive children, she had done some reading on effective educational strategies with attention deficit or hyperactive children. Whenever she explained something to Lenny, she always had him repeat it back to her to check whether he was listening. She set aside a time-out area for him whenever he lost the ability to control his actions or behavior. She tried to put him in group activities with other children who had a high tolerance for this behavior. When he did good work, she was generous with praise. Likewise, she was generous with her praise when his behavior was appropriate. "Good work, Lenny!" "Good job, Lenny!" "You're having a great day, Lenny. Keep it up!"

Lenny often responded to her praise by beaming and giving her a big hug. But it didn't last long; soon he would be disturbing other students or disrupting the classroom.

On one of those cold and drizzly days in mid-October when the children couldn't have outside recess, Sara's frustration with Lenny's behavior reached a point that she knew she needed outside help. The children all had inside recess in the gym; it was full of activity, some of it organized and well supervised, but most of it not. Sara kept her group in one corner of the gym where she had them occupied with "Grey Goose." But Lenny would not stay with the group. There was too much else going on, with at least 100 other children in various organized and unorganized games. Several times she had to physically lead him back into the circle after he ran off to other groups.

"Lenny, you need to stay with our group. Do you understand? Now, can you tell me what we need to do?"

Lenny responded, "We need to stay with our group, Mrs. Olson."

Finally, when it appeared that Lenny was going to be able to control his behavior, she heard a loud scream from Jessica, the girl sitting next to him. She was crying and holding her arm.

Sara immediately went to her aid. "Mrs. Olson, Lenny bit me. Lenny bit me!"

Jessica showed Sara her arm. Sara observed the outline of teeth marks, and the arm was red and swelling. Jessica was sobbing uncontrollably. Sara immediately summoned one of the teacher aides to take over her class, and she took Jessica and Lenny by the hands down to the principal and nurse's office.

Jessica cried softly all the way down the hall to the nurse's office. Sara counted herself lucky to find the nurse's aide in, because the school had only the services of a nurse's aide three days a week. A fully certified school nurse had been trimmed from the staff years ago in budget cuts.

"We can take good care of Jessica, can't we? Now that doesn't look too bad. It looks like we can make you feel better," comforted Lenore Whitehorse, the nurse's aide. She took Jessica's hand and winked at Sara.

"I can take Jessica now. I'll call her mom and tell her what happened."

With a firm, "Come with me, Lenny," Sara led him into the principal's office reception area. No one was in during this time because the secretary was helping Mrs. Ollerud, the principal, supervise the lunchroom.

"I'm going to have to call your parents this time, Lenny. Do you understand what we said about no hitting, pushing, or biting? We know it's wrong, don't we?"

Lenny shook his head in acknowledgment and began to cry, burying his head in his hands and sobbing.

"I'm sorry, Mrs. Olson. Please don't call my mom. Please!"

"We have to this time, Lenny. It's serious this time. It's time she knew about this."

Sara decided to call Lenny's mom. She stepped behind the counter and found the number in the rolodex labeled "Parents' Phone Numbers." The phone rang at the tribal council office, and the receptionist forwarded the call through to Lenny's mother.

"Hello, this is Peggy, can I help you?"

Sara quickly introduced herself and then proceeded to tell Lenny's mother about what had just happened in the gym. There was silence on the other end of the line as Sara told her of the increasing difficulty she was having with Lenny's behavior in her classroom. She informed her that this time she was going to have Mrs. Ollerud deal with Lenny.

"I just hate to introduce myself under these circumstances, but I felt this time it was important that you know about this incident. It's the most serious one we've had to date, and it's so important that we need you to work with us."

There was a painful silence before Lenny's mom answered. Her voice revealed both surprise and anger.

"I just don't know what to tell you, Mrs. Olson. Lenny's a handful, I know, but we've never had this kind of trouble before. Maybe him and you are having some kind of personality conflict or something. I just don't know. I think I'm going to call my husband. You know, we had a hard time deciding where to send Lenny to school—the tribal school or Cross Lake. It's tough for our Indian children because there are so many damn racists there at Cross Lake, and we knew Lenny might have trouble there because he is a full blood. Maybe we should just pull him out and send him to the tribal school."

Sara heard the click of a phone being hung up; the phone went silent.

Lenny was still crying softly.

"Mrs. Olson, I'm sorry I bit Jessica. I won't do it again. I promise."

One Bad Apple

ELAINE BROWN

After 26 years of teaching, Elaine Brown had developed a guiding philosophy that helped keep her goals as an educator in perspective. She believed that, as a teacher, she should get to know each student's distinctive blend of abilities and set her expectations accordingly. As she expressed it, "My expectations are different, not only for different students, but for every subject. If a student has trouble in math, but is extremely gifted in English and reading, I don't expect *As* from him in math, but he'd better give them to me in English and reading because that's his field." As she began her 27th year in the classroom, this year teaching fifth grade, she already had a working knowledge of most of her students' strengths and weaknesses because she had taught this group as fourth-graders last year. She had only two new students, William and Eddie.

William had moved to Pine County from a nearby city because his mother had withdrawn him from the class for children with behavioral disorders and sent him to live with his father. From the little information Elaine could gather, William's parents had divorced when he was a toddler, and his mother was employed sporadically. Often, she and her three children slept in their car or floated from one friend's home to another between jobs. When she enrolled him in Pine County Public Schools, William's mother made one thing clear: She did not want him placed in a class for children with behavioral disorders.

Elaine had serious misgivings about William being so abruptly and completely included, but she felt she had little choice but to make the best of it. So she approached the task with the same philosophy she applied to the other students—determine what is reasonable to expect and then uphold those expectations while always aiming higher. With William, she found that she had to set her expectations far below the average. Although he liked to read, William's reading was approximately two years below grade level. During the first week of school, he absolutely refused to do his work in mathematics. He simply would not pick up his pencil. As the first several weeks of school elapsed, it was also apparent that he was not accustomed to attending school on a regular basis. In fact, he was absent two or three days a week.

Elaine reported this attendance problem to the visiting teacher (school social worker), Jerry West, who went to William's home on several occasions when William did not come to school. When Jerry knocked on the door, no one answered, and everything seemed quiet and still. Jerry spoke with several neighbors who told him that as soon as he left, William—who had been home— opened the doors and windows and resumed watching television. These neighbors also explained that Mr. Payne, William's father, left for work at a pipe-fitting factory at 6:30 A.M. and did not return home until 7:00 P.M. Jerry then went to Mr. Payne's place of employment and spoke with him during a work break. Mr. Payne, a small man who looked to be in his fifties, explained to Jerry in a soft voice that he wanted William to go to school. He told Jerry that he awakened William each morning; but, because he left for work so early, William was able to go back to bed and skip school. "I'll lose my job if I stay home to make sure he gets on the school bus," he explained.

When he did attend school, William was dolorous and withdrawn except when someone did something he did not like, and then he became explosive. Sometimes these temper tantrums came with no detectable provocation. It was through repeated tantrums that William cultivated his teacher's apprehension and his classmates' fear of him. One such incident occurred on a warm September afternoon. The class was subdued from the stuffiness of the classroom and the heaviness of the school lunch. Elaine, perspiring and weary, nevertheless carried on with her lesson on the exploration of the New World. Without warning, William rose from his desk. Wielding the large fifth-grade social studies textbook far over his head, William slammed it forcefully on Chuck's desk, who sat directly behind him. Chuck reflexively jerked his hands from the surface of the desk and pulled his torso as far back as the orange plastic chair would allow before the book struck the desk with an explosive impact.

The class froze. The second hand on the plastic wall clock ticked laboriously before the spell of the moment was broken by William who, glowering at the class with malevolent intensity, shuffled to his seat and faced the front of the classroom defiantly. Elaine realized—and she knew her students also realized—that William had had no intention of altering the direction or velocity of the textbook even if Chuck had not removed his hands with such quickness. Her mind struggled against numbness in an effort to decide what to do. At four feet, eleven inches, she was not prepared for a physical encounter with William, and she was unwilling to risk further violence toward the rest of her students. Besides, she reasoned, although William had disrupted the class, he had not actually caused harm. Her instincts told her that it was best to let the moment pass, deciding that any immediate intervention on her part might send William completely out of control.

Because William was frequently absent from school, Elaine had the opportunity to discuss his behavior with her students, which she did on two occasions. During these exchanges, she acknowledged their fears and apprehensions, and as a class they agreed to treat William carefully so as to avoid provoking his anger. They would not tease him, touch his belongings, or correct him in class if he made a mistake. These were all things for which he seemed to have a very low tolerance. Elaine also asked the class to give William as much encouragement as possible by doing simple things such as nodding affirmatively after he read aloud. She had noticed that he seemed heartened by such approval, and she wanted to take advantage of this to make him feel a part of the class and feel better about himself.

Elaine took comfort in the trust she was able to achieve with this group of students. The bond she had established with them last year now stood them in good stead. This is not to say that the students became less frightened of William; they did not. What they did become, however, was much more astute in reading him and knowing when and how to hide their fear. Elaine quietly observed these developments with a mixture of pride and sorrow. However, she felt that they were all doing the best they knew how under the circumstances.

The only exception to this cooperative effort was Eddie, a small, spare boy who seemed unable to resist attracting William's attention. Elaine believed that, in his own way, Eddie was at least as troubled as William. In fact, his records showed that he had been referred repeatedly to his previous school's child study committee because of behavior problems. His parents had refused to allow a formal evaluation by which the school could establish eligibility for special education services.

Because he was small, his behavior, although erratic, was more of an annoyance than a real problem, except when it came to William. Elaine's students were growing accustomed to Eddie's unexpected bids for attention. At almost any given time or place, Eddie would poke, slap, or punch classmates much larger than himself, apparently without heed of possible consequences. Any opportunity to get out of Elaine's eyesight provided him an occasion to provoke other students. Elaine remembered the day that, returning from lunch, she found Eddie crawling around on the floor, biting his classmates on their ankles. Reprimanding him for such behavior usually brought a blank smile to his face. Although she had attempted to provide meaningful consequences for his behavior, she had yet to find either a positive consequence or a negative one that really seemed to mean anything to him.

As with William, the class demonstrated more patience with Eddie than Elaine felt she could rightfully expect from a group of fifth-graders. To be sure, some students had more patience than others. On occasion, a less tolerant student would reciprocate Eddie's most recent annoyance with a sound slap or a decisive shove against the nearest wall. Because these retaliatory acts appeared neither to faze nor to hurt him and because they rendered at least momentary results, Elaine usually ignored this vigilante form of justice.

It was when Eddie picked on William that Elaine could not ignore the repercussions. Unlike her other students, Eddie simply did not seem to understand that he should not provoke William, nor did he seem to realize that his teacher could not guarantee his safety when he chose to incite William's ire.

That she could not ensure Eddie's safety was clearly illustrated on a crisp November day as she led her class in from their midmorning recess period. She had established the routine of having her class line up for water before returning to the classroom. After each student had gotten a drink, he or she was to proceed to the classroom to prepare for the upcoming lesson. On this particular day, Eddie, who appeared to be bursting with energy from the preceding kickball game, left his place in line. Escaping Elaine's notice, he whizzed past William, giving him a playful push on his way to the end of the line.

Eddie's piercing scream caused Elaine's stomach to lurch and brought her rushing past the line of wide-eyed faces. There she found William on top of Eddie with his right knee planted squarely on Eddie's spine. His powerful arms were pulling Eddie's frail shoulders toward him, and his contorted features conveyed the full force of his anger and rage. Within that crystallized split second, Elaine could almost hear Eddie's spine snap. Forcing a sense of quiet confidence, Elaine reached out, gently placed her hand on his taut shoulder, and whispered, "William." Almost instantly, William's muscles relaxed. He released Eddie's shoulders and slowly rose to his feet. His glaring eyes refused to meet Elaine's as he stated matter-of-factly, "I'm going to hurt him." Eddie rose to a sitting position and sat sobbing on the floor as the rest of the class stood in silent observation.

Turning her attention to Eddie, she asked him if he could stand. He nodded affirmatively, quickly got up, and wiped his tears on the ragged cuff of his blue flannel shirt. Watching William out of the corner of her eye, she reformed the line and directed the students to the classroom. No one spoke.

Arriving at the classroom, Elaine went to Katherine Ellis, the teacher next door, and asked her to watch the class while she made arrangements to have William taken home. She was hesitant to do this because she did not want to compound his truancy problem, but he seemed unable to compose himself. He continued to mumble threats, and his rigid bearing led Elaine to believe that he might explode again at any moment. She did not want to risk a second outburst in one day.

Upon returning to the classroom, Elaine noticed that Eddie's tears had long since dried, and his memory of the incident seemed to have faded almost as quickly. She, on the other hand, would relive those moments frequently in the days to come as she grew increasingly aware of her tenuous control over the situation. She did discover, however, that she could protect Eddie from William's assaults by making sure that she was the first to intervene when Eddie misbehaved.

Although she did not believe in paddling, Elaine found that if she took Eddie out into the hall, borrowed a paddle from Katherine Ellis, and at least created the appearance that she was paddling Eddie for his misbehavior, William would leave him alone. "It was really easy," she explained. "I would take Eddie out in the hall, take the paddle and come somewhere near him [hit him very lightly], and he would scream like someone was killing him. And William thought I was doing my duty. I'd go back in the classroom, and William would be nodding, and he'd leave Eddie alone." Although she felt that this was less than an ideal solution to the problem, her main objective was to protect Eddie from actual physical harm. This tactic seemed to work better than anything else. Therefore, Elaine resigned herself to getting along the best way she could, but she yearned for the school year to end without a tragic incident.

Richard's Mother

POLLY DUDLEY

Richard qualified for special education services the second semester of his first grade. My aide, Martha, had worked in Robert's classroom before she transferred to my class, and she thought that he was a disturbed but precious child.

"Polly, the problem with Richard is his mother, not him," she said to me.

After a few days, Martha and I were on the same page. Richard's mother alarmed me. Richard came to school dressed in raggedy pants and shirts, wearing shredded sneakers without socks. There were days when he would wear the same outfit over and over and over even though the clothes were filthy. I made an unscheduled home visit to discuss this issue. I asked his mother, Lizzie, if she had contacted social services to obtain help. She shrugged and said, "They won't help me no more."

I was puzzled. She wore clean, almost elegant clothes, had polished fingernails, makeup, jewelry, and a fashionable hairstyle. Nothing about her resembled her son's trashy wardrobe. And she seemed not to care that Richard was embarrassed and needed help.

"It's just the way things are. Can't do no better. Just forget about it."

I didn't. I called social services and asked if they would help Richard get some decent clothes. "We've done that, but she spent the money on things other than clothing. So we can't give her anymore money for her children's clothes."

When I asked what she bought with social service funds, the worker said, "I'm sorry. That's private."

So Martha and I bought clothes, shoes, and socks for Richard and asked the principal to give them to him. He did. The next day, Richard came to school, all smiles, dressed in new shoes, new jeans, and a new shirt.

A few days later, he came to school in rags and scraps again. Martha took him in the hall and asked what had happened to his new clothes. He said, "Mamma sold them."

Martha bought him new shoes and socks, and I went after the clothes again. This time, they were second-hand clothes. Only so much a teacher can afford. We never allowed Richard to wear his new clothes and shoes home. He would come to school in his rags, change into his new clothes, and at the end of the school day, he took off the new clothes, and wore the trash home. I'll never forget his squirming his feet on the floor in his good shoes at the end of the day, saying, "These feel so good. So good."

But even though Richard was in the middle of what Martha and I called "the clothing conflict," he loved learning. If there was an assembly that interfered with his reading lesson, he always asked if I would teach him reading later in the day. Sometimes he would ask, "Do we have to go downstairs for the show? Can't we just stay up here and work?"

The following year, we didn't have to buy him clothes. I'm not sure why. The social worker said it was because social services had "interfered." Martha and I had no idea what that meant, but perhaps they threatened to withhold all services to Lizzie if she continued to sell objects they had provided.

The school counselor and I kept trying to connect with Lizzie, but that didn't seem possible. Richard would take a note home, requesting a conference day and time we could meet her at home. Lizzie would return the note, writing when it was convenient for us to visit her. The counselor and I would go, and Lizzie would not be there. Lizzie's mother was usually there, but not Lizzie. One afternoon, Lizzie was outside her apartment when the counselor, Haddy, and I drove Richard home. When Richard spoke to his mother, she just shrugged. But the amazing incident for Haddy and me was when the school buses arrived with his two brothers and his sister. They ran to Richard who hugged them, stroked their heads, and asked them how their day had been. Then they demanded Richard give them a snack. Not one of his three siblings spoke to Lizzie, nor did she greet them. Richard was the parent.

Richard began asking Martha and me about "cookin' stuff." He wanted to know which Campbell soup cans needed water and which ones didn't. And he asked, "How do you make a samwich?"

After Martha and I gave him some cooking instructions, I asked, "Why do you want to know about these things, Richard?"

"Well, you know, my brothers and my baby sister get hungry, and I'm tryin' to figger out how to feed 'em."

The third year Richard was with my class, he said, "Mrs. Dudley, I want to be a preacher when I grow up. Do you know any preachers?"

"Why do you want to be a preacher, Richard."

"'Cause, preachers, you know, they help other people."

I found an African American preacher, Mrs. Jordan, who had a church close to Richard's apartment, and she volunteered to pick up Robert and his family every Sunday. She did.

Mrs. Jordan and I had several conferences. She related that Lizzie never went to church, and sometimes, Richard was the only member of his family to come with her. She also thought that the children seemed hungry, so she had her church contribute to a nearby grocery store in Lizzie's name so that she could feed her children. After a month, her church stopped contributing.

"Polly, we've discovered that even though Lizzie picks up groceries several times a week, she doesn't feed her children."

"Do you know what she does with the groceries?"

"Yes, she sells them."

"And what does she do with the money?"

She looked at me as if she thought I'd had a stroke. "Polly, she's buying drugs. Don't you know that?"

I shook my head. "I guess I suspected that, but I just couldn't stand to think about it. Denial doesn't work, does it?" Not long after the conference with Mrs. Jordan, Martha came into the classroom before the busses arrived. She was shaking.

"Are you okay, Martha?"

"No. Richard *walked* to school this morning and was waiting outside for me. He told me something that you have to hear. He's in the hall, and he's agreed to tell you, but he won't face you.

He's not supposed to reveal his family's private life, but he's scared and wants you to know about this."

I ran to the hall, stood behind Richard, and said, "I'll listen to you now, Richard."

He was trembling, and his voice was a bit shaky, but he told me what happened. Richard said that the previous evening some men from Jamaica knocked down their apartment door, chased the kids outside, and beat his mother. "They broke her arm. They broke my mamma's arm."

He also related how hard it was to gather up his two brothers and his sister who hid under a car in the parking lot and were too scared to come from under the car. After the men left, he managed to guide his siblings inside. He never told me where his mother went for treatment, or how she got there, just that he had to sleep with her when she came home because she was frightened. I leaned over, put my arms around Richard and told him how glad I was that he was safe, and how proud I was that he took care of his family.

"But Richard, it's the law that I must report this to the principal and to social services. I have to tell them."

He put his hands on my arms and said, "Good."

I called the social worker, who said that she would call me as soon as she went to Lizzie's house. She did. And I wanted to kick her to the dark side of the moon. She said that the administrator at the apartment house hadn't heard anyone knock down the door, nor had any of the neighbors.

"And the door was fine when I got there this morning, so I don't think anyone broke down the door. The hinges looked a little damaged, but it's fine."

Then I asked whether Lizzie had a broken arm; she laughed and said that Lizzie had consumed a bit of liquor and had fallen.

"Are you going to investigate this more?"

"No, I don't need to. There's nothing to worry about. Just relax."

After I hung up, I called the three teachers who instructed Richard's siblings, all of whom were in special education classes in different schools. I told each of the school secretaries that this was an emergency, and I asked if I could speak with the teacher. These teachers were on the phone in a minute. They all said that Richard's siblings were a mess that day and that they had no idea why. Richard's baby sister was in a preschool program, and her teacher said that this was the worst she had ever seen this little girl. We agreed that we had to meet with the social worker as soon as possible, and we did. We begged her to find foster care for these children. She sighed and said, "Well, do any of you want to be a foster parent? We've run out of foster parents in this area."

"So you can't do anything to guarantee the safety of these children?" one of the teachers asked.

"No, but I think that they'll be fine."

This was one of the few times that I've been speechless. As soon as the teachers and the social worker left, I went home and called the police. I told them what Richard had told me. The policeman immediately warned me not to go to Richard's apartment.

"Oh, I never go alone. I go with either the speech therapist, my aide, or the school counselor. And sometimes the principal comes with me."

He sighs. "Please do NOT go down there. Period! We're already working on this case, and if they decide to shoot that mother, they won't ask you to leave."

"What will they do with the children?"

More silence. Clearing his throat. Sighing.

"Please, I'm begging you to get those children out of there so they won't get shot."

"I'll do my best," he said. "But promise me you won't go there. Promise me. And please remember that this case is confidential."

Richard couldn't work after this. He was shaky and despondent and could no longer read or even write his name. The counselor saw him every spare minute she had, and Martha and I sat with him as often as we could. We read to him, colored pictures with him, and sometimes just sat beside him while he slept. And then he was gone.

His mother was arrested for drug possession and prostitution, and all the children were placed in different homes in the surrounding county. After a short while, a new case worker called and asked me how Richard had behaved in my class. She related that parents of the children in the new class had requested that he be removed from the class because of his behavior problems. "He's looking up little girls' dresses."

"Well, that's probably one of the few things that he knows how to do in that classroom. That school system has NO special education services, and his skills have probably tanked due to stress. He needs counseling and stability. Could you please, please find a foster parent in *this* district so he can come back to this school?"

"I've already tried. No success."

"Would it be possible to find a foster parent in a school district that has self-contained special ed. classes. I think that he would do better there."

She found a parent and a class and called me to tell me that she was moving Richard "up a couple of counties."

"Will he be close to any of his siblings? He really loves his brothers and his baby sister, and I'm guessing that he's very worried about them."

"No. I'm sorry, but there'll be several counties between him and his family."

That was fifteen years ago. I never heard anything more about him until recently when a friend related that there's a rumor floating around that Richard's in jail. I'm trying to find Richard, but that's easier said than done. I keep hoping that he stayed with one foster parent and was successful in school, academically and socially; that he's not in jail; that he's found his brothers and his sister. And that he's a preacher.

Stealing Time

ROBERT CARTER

Robert's seventh year of teaching began like most of the others. As a fourth-grade teacher, he had learned the value of setting his standards early in the year, letting students know in no uncertain terms the range and limits of acceptable behavior in his classroom. He felt strongly about strict but fair enforcement of rules, and he found that his students soon conformed to the standards he administered. He believed that if he was fair with students, they would be fair with him. As a result, his classroom became like a small community where everyone knew what to expect and how to behave at all times. Robert found that even his most unusual or troubled students soon fell in line with his expectations, and he believed that his classroom management benefited these difficult students as much, perhaps even more, than the other students. In his classroom there was a comfortable predictability based on the mutual understanding of, and adherence to, the ground rules.

Fall semester progressed just as he had assumed it would. He had worked hard to set his "precedents" and, before the conclusion of the first six-week grading period, his students had settled in. He was pleased that Andy and Martin, both children from very deprived, troubled backgrounds who also had behavior and academic problems, had shown much improvement in their ability to fit in. Kara, a student with behavioral disorders who was included in the class, also appeared to be progressing nicely with the help of her special education teacher, as did David, a student from the self-contained learning disabilities classroom who was included for short nonacademic periods of the school day. David came to Robert's class for morning homeroom period, which included roll call, lunch money collection, the pledge of allegiance, and the like. David also went to art, music, and physical education with Robert's class. With the exception of minor and infrequent student transgressions, all was well.

Shortly after Christmas vacation, David's special education placement in the self-contained learning disabilities classroom was submitted for the reevaluation required every three years. The eligibility committee decided, based on his recent assessment results, that David should now be placed in the regular education classroom for at least 51 percent of the day. In other words, he was to receive special education services in a learning disabilities resource room, but more than half of his instruction was to take place in the regular classroom. Robert now had David for mathematics, a subject in which David possessed relative strengths, as well as for science and health. In addition, David ate lunch with Robert's class and attended the regular fourth-grade social studies class with Ms. Gleason across the hall. Because David's participation in his class had not presented a problem before, Robert had no apparent reason to anticipate what was to come.

Within a few days Robert sensed the beginning of the end of what he had considered a pleasant school year. In mathematics, David did not turn in assignments and was soon far behind in his work. While Robert instructed the class, David alternately made strange noises and interrupted Robert and other students by blurting out declarations such as, "I know that," or "Let me do that." He dropped books loudly and deliberately on the floor, banged his pencil rhythmically on his desk, and probed noisily in his desk for lost objects. When Robert requested that he stop these disruptive and highly annoying behaviors, David ignored him. Robert considered David's behavior a relentless onslaught of interruption and rudeness aimed at him and the other students. He reasoned that David was attempting to regain the attention he had been accustomed to in the special education classroom. After all, in there he had been one of only five or so students with one teacher and a teacher's aide; he had been spoiled by receiving so much individual attention. Robert was certain that he was capable of successfully completing his assignments and that he was simply choosing not to do so, just as he was choosing his outrageous misbehavior. Whether David had taken his Ritalin, or had taken it at the proper time, did not seem to make much difference as far as Robert could see. Robert felt that David did what he wanted to do; and, most of the time, he wanted to show off and interrupt the class.

As both David's work and his behavior continued to worsen, Robert's loathing and resentment of him grew. This one student was ruining everything he had worked so hard to accomplish. To add insult to injury, David often stated loudly that he wanted to go back to his "real" class and to his "real" teacher. He was not even giving Robert a chance to be his teacher. He did not like Robert, and he did not like the other students. Robert felt that somehow he had failed to gain David's respect, but he was at a loss to explain why. In the meantime, David's relationships with the other students were deteriorating.

Because Robert's mathematics class was set up in a cooperative learning format, the students were compelled to work together in small groups, the success of which depended on each member's productive contributions and hard work. David's refusal to complete assignments naturally lowered the average of his group. When some of the other students tried to help him, he rebuffed their efforts. Soon, his classmates began to complain. Robert began keeping David in from recess when he refused to complete his assignments, but he continued to neglect his work.

The day David took an assignment that Robert had just distributed and "chucked" it immediately into his desk, deliberately signifying that he had no intention of completing it, Robert went to his desk to declare sharply, "That's not what we do in here, that's not what's expected of you in here, and I've had just about enough of it." David retorted that he wanted to go back to his old class and that he did not like the way the other students looked at him. Robert replied that the other students looked at him because of the way he was acting. He went on to explain that these kids had never seen anybody act like this before and that if he didn't want them to look at him, he would just have to change his attitude and change what he did in the classroom. At this point, Robert dismissed his class for lunch.

After lunch, David's behavior reached extreme proportions. When he reentered the classroom, he was "bouncing off the walls." He began making noises, pulling on the window blinds, and telling his classmates to "shut up." Robert had planned to have the class prepare some answer sheets for the upcoming standardized testing. Because David was not to be tested with the rest of the class, Robert told him to go to the back of the room (to the time-out seat) so that neither he nor the class would disturb each other. David picked up his materials and went to the designated seat; however, when he reached his destination, he slammed his things onto the desk with such force that his pencil bounced off the wall. Robert seized him briskly by the arm, informing him, "You are not going to throw things in this classroom." David replied, "It didn't hit anyone." He was anxiously repeating this assertion for the third time when Robert jerked him up by his arm, pulled him down the hall, and placed him forcefully into a student desk in the principal's office.

After instructing David not to return until he had completed his work, Robert returned to his classroom. David remained in the office until late afternoon. Because school rules dictated that students were not to be kept in from P.E. during formal instruction from the physical education teacher, David was to attend. Before leaving the classroom for P.E., David commissioned a classmate to tell Robert that he wished to talk with him. When Robert received the message, he told his class that David would just have to wait until the rest of the students went out for P.E.

When the others had left, Robert went to the back of the room where David waited. David said, "I hear you wanted to talk to me." Robert replied that he had understood that David had wanted to speak with him and that he was willing to listen to what David had to say. David's response to this was to tell Robert, "Forget it." After sitting quietly in the back of the empty classroom for a while, David approached Robert's desk and explained that he was sorry for his behavior but he didn't like the other kids in the class staring at him. Robert reiterated the previously offered reasons for their staring. He went on to ask David if he might work better if the other students were told not to stare at him. David allowed that this would help him work better, and Robert followed by inquiring whether he or the class could do anything else to help him. David said that it would help if Kevin did not fuss at him in math groups. Robert explained that Kevin wanted his group to do well and that he fussed at him because David was bringing the group's average down. Finally, David agreed that it might be all right if Kevin fussed, but that it would be much better if he did it quietly. During these negotiations, David agreed to bring his materials to class, to treat Robert and the other students with respect, and to complete his assignments. After this discussion, David's behavior and schoolwork improved for the next several days. The following week, however, the situation regressed to its previous state.

Once again, David behaved as if he were angry with everyone. Robert kept him in from recess for not completing assignments, and he spent more time sitting in the principal's office. As Robert explained it, "He was just angry at everything, and the other kids in the class are just so angry at David, and I'm angry at David, too, because of what he's doing with us. He's just pushing my buttons, and it's just like a power struggle between the two of us. He wants his way, and I want my way. As long as I'm the adult in the classroom, it's going to be my way, because it benefits the rest of the class. I can't have David disrupting everybody else in their work just because David's special. Well, as far as I'm concerned, I have 25 other kids who are special, who want to learn, and David has shown me so far that he just wants to learn when he feels like it; when he doesn't, he wants to disrupt everybody else."

While David was out of the classroom one day, one of Robert's students broached the subject of David's behavior. Several of the others joined in, asking such questions as: "Why is he disrupting our classroom? Why isn't he doing his work? Doesn't he know he's going to fail if he doesn't do his work?" They told Robert that the day he had jerked David out of the classroom, they had laughed. Robert responded by admitting to the students that it must have looked "pretty comical." When they inquired "Why did you have to do that?" Robert replied, "I don't think it's fair to you for David to sit in here and disrupt you." He followed this statement by asking, "Do you think it's fair?" The class concurred with his conviction. He went on to explain that he did not understand what made David "tick." By holding this discussion with the other students,

Robert felt that he was being honest and "up-front" with them. Robert could see that the class was beginning to see David as a renegade and a social outcast, as many of them made statements such as, "We don't like David to come in here." David was to provide further fuel for this opinion in a few weeks.

One afternoon, Robert did not allow David to attend recess because he had not completed his assignments. As David was working on one assignment in the empty classroom, Robert stepped out for three or four minutes to copy a worksheet David had not completed. When the class returned from recess, Bob, whose desk was near David's, reported that his watch, which he had left on his desk, was missing. Robert instructed Bob to check his locker and his desk. He had the other students look for the missing watch, too, but no one found it.

The following morning, David immediately rushed up to Robert's desk and announced, "Look at this watch that my daddy gave me!" Robert asked David to take the watch off so he could see it. As Robert examined the watch, he felt his anger, hurt, and suspicion growing. He was virtually certain it was Bob's watch.

As Robert examined the watch, he confronted David indirectly by asking him in a disbelieving tone of voice if he realized what a strange coincidence it was that Bob's lost watch and the one David claimed his father gave him were the same watch. David immediately refuted him, saying, "No, it's not. My dad gave me this one. No, it's not! No, it's not!"

At this point, Robert decided to take David to the principal's office, where he presented the situation to her and David's special education teacher. David's learning disabilities resource teacher, Lisa Griffith, added that she had noticed David was wearing the watch when he came back to her classroom before getting ready to go home the previous day. Still, David insisted that his father had given it to him. Incredulous and frustrated, Robert at last told David that they would just have to telephone his father to verify his story. Surely, he thought, he'll break down and tell the truth now. Offering him one final opportunity to come clean, Robert asked, "Now, are you *sure* your father gave you the watch?" To his utter amazement, David replied, "Yes, you call him up and that's what he's going to say."

Aware that he now had no choice but to phone his father, Robert proceeded to do so. The task was complicated by the fact that David's father worked out of town and had a hearing impairment, making it necessary for someone to serve as an interpreter on the father's end. For these reasons, Robert decided to call David's mother first. After Robert explained the situation carefully, his mother said that David had come home with the watch and claimed that a friend, a classmate, had let him wear it. Robert thanked his mother and promised to keep her informed.

When Robert presented this new and contradictory information to David, he persisted with his original account. This time, Mrs. Griffith appealed to David. "We're getting pretty thick in all of this, David. Are you *sure* you don't want to go ahead and tell us what happened now, before we have to call your father and get him off of his job and also have someone interpret over the telephone?" To everyone's relief, David confessed that he had taken Bob's watch.

Leaving the situation in the principal's hands, Robert and Lisa returned to their classes. When David returned several minutes later, Robert took him out into the hallway and asked him why he had not admitted in the first place that he had taken the watch. David only shrugged his shoulders and evaded eye contact. Robert pursued his questioning, "Well, don't you think there's something you need to say to Bob?" "Yeah," David replied in a weary voice.

When Robert leaned into the classroom and asked Bob to come out into the hallway, several of the students exchanged knowing glances. Bob approached them slowly and eyed David suspiciously. "I'm sorry," David blurted. Turning to Bob, Robert queried, "Bob, is there anything you want to say to David?" Turning to leave, Bob retorted, "I don't even want to talk to him."

As it turned out, the principal did not punish David in any way for his theft of the watch. Robert was surprised that the matter was simply dropped. Following the incident with the watch, however, other students' belongings disappeared. Each time a student reported a missing item, the others whispered among themselves and looked at David. Robert knew that they suspected him. "Well," Robert thought to himself," I don't know what it's going to take for David to redeem himself before me and the other students." At this point, he felt hurt and angry with David. It troubled him that he was never happy to see David enter the classroom in the morning, and he felt guilty that David was probably aware of his displeasure. He could not seem to dispel his disappointment that David had never really given him a chance to be his real teacher.

The Contract with Parrish and Son

REBECCA PHILLIPS

Frustrated and helpless isn't a good way to feel, Rebecca thought. It seemed like such a long time since she had first met Bob Parrish, and she wasn't really sure that the strain was worth the investment of emotional energy she had put into trying to get through to him during the past three weeks. But there he was in her class, in her face, tearing at her heart, and the end of the school year seemed years away.

Rebecca Phillips had been teaching students with learning disabilities for six years. She felt confident now with her teaching techniques and with the progress of most of her students. She had learned the hard way, through trial and error, about discipline. She now understood the importance of setting up a consistent structure for behavior management from the very beginning of the school year.

This year, Rebecca had switched to a new behavior management program to enforce the rules that she and the students had decided on together. It entailed positive reinforcement in the form of free time or time to engage in preferred activities. She had set up a group contingency with which she was quite satisfied. The class or workgroup began every period with 10 minutes of free time "in the bank." She kept a chart on the board reflecting the current allotted time. If students followed the rules, the group had a chance to earn additional time at Rebecca's discretion. She was careful to award additional time intermittently so that her students could not anticipate when their good behavior might pay off. If a student was not following the rules, however, Rebecca simply pulled out her stopwatch and timed the student until he or she complied. She did not say anything to the student nor did she stop her instruction. When the student complied, Rebecca stopped the watch and wrote the amount of time it had taken the student to get back on task in a "time lost" column on her chart. The total minutes and seconds lost would then be subtracted from the group's accumulated minutes of free time.

Rebecca felt her group contingency worked very well because she didn't have to interrupt her instruction with reprimands or reminders. Her students began urging each other to stay on task, a kind of peer pressure Rebecca judged to be effective and appropriate. When she started her stopwatch, one or two students always seemed to notice and either let the offender know that he or she was not behaving as expected or helped the misbehaving student comply. For instance, another student might give the offender paper if he or she came to class unprepared. Even chronic offenders began coming to class with needed materials, participating in class, and helping others behave as expected. Only one of Rebecca's students did not appear to be affected by the fact that he was losing free time for the group by misbehaving. As a matter of fact, Bob seemed to thrive on the negative attention he drew from his peers.

Bob was an uncoordinated, slightly overweight seventh-grader, what some might call "husky." He dragged a large book bag around from classroom to classroom, usually tripping over it at least once in each class. Rebecca wondered whether this was an attention-getting device or simply adolescent clumsiness.

Bob had moved into Monroeville in early January, bringing with him a confidential file indicating that he had previously received instruction in reading, math, and English in a self-contained class for students with learning disabilities. While reading through his file, Rebecca noticed that Bob had a history of frequent moves—five in his eight years of schooling. Almost every teacher had remarked on Bob's attention-getting antics—inappropriate comments, yelling at the teacher, and refusing to remain on task, for example. Rebecca had made a conscious effort not to prejudge Bob because of his history, hoping against hope that he might have learned some coping skills in his last placement. Her hopes were dashed the day she met him. From the beginning, during group situations he volunteered a running commentary on anything she said that could be twisted into a double entendre. In a class of eight adolescent boys, his comments inevitably created a commotion.

"No matter what the topic during my language arts class," Rebecca recalled, "Bob managed to twist the words around in order to get his classmates' attention. One time when we were discussing Prohibition, I asked for a definition of 'speakeasy,' and he said, 'Isn't that where people used to get sex in the 1920s?' The rest of the class responded with laughter to Bob's comments at first, but then began to ridicule him as 'dumb' and 'stupid.' The more the class got upset with Bob for each 'stopwatch' episode, the more Bob seemed to continue and intensify his efforts to get everyone's attention."

Rebecca quickly realized that Bob should not be included in the group contingency, as he was both thriving on the negative attention and reducing the effectiveness of the program for the other seven boys in the class. After only one week, she pulled Bob out of the free-time program and set up an alternative individual contingency for him. She also felt that his parents needed to be made aware of his problems in the classroom. Two weeks after he joined her class, she found herself calling Bob's home.

What she learned from her call led Rebecca to believe that Bob's home life played a significant role in his behavior at school. As far as Rebecca could ascertain, Mr. Parrish had obtained custody of his two sons, Bob and his younger brother, after a lengthy search to locate the mother and the two boys who moved frequently. Bob's father had finally won custody a short time before their move to Monroeville. Mr. Parrish and the boys lived with Mr. Parrish's parents in an upper-middle-class neighborhood. Bob's grandmother had a history of mental illness and was frequently in and out of "rest homes." When she was home, she apparently did not get along well with her husband. It was in this setting that the boys had begun to build a relationship with the father they had never known.

Mr. Parrish had definite ideas about how Bob should be raised. He intended, as he put it to Rebecca, to "make him into a man." When Rebecca had called to suggest that they discuss Bob's misbehavior, Mr. Parrish had not hesitated to agree to a parent–teacher conference.

At their first meeting, Rebecca was struck with how much Mr. Parrish looked like Bob—an older Bob with a clear edge of toughness, she thought. Mr. Parrish was tall, tanned, and obviously lifted weights. It immediately occurred to Rebecca that this totally masculine father figure might present some problems for Bob. Mr. Parrish was cordial and appeared concerned about Bob. He told his story of recently obtaining custody of his sons, stressing how hard he had worked to get his children back from their mother. He informed Rebecca that he punished Bob's misbehavior with a belt—one with a buckle, of course. In addition, he gave the impression that he did not have much patience with either Bob or his younger son. Mr. Parrish felt that Bob's problems stemmed from being babied by his mother for 12 years. His parenting responsibilities, he explained again, included "making a man outta him." One step toward this goal, he believed, was to put Bob on the football team, adding that he attended a "few football practices to help the coach out and kick Bob's ass when he messed up."

Soon after her first conference with Mr. Parrish, Rebecca met with Bob and his father to set up a home-school contract involving Bob's homework and behavior. Bob seemed to want to please his father as much as his father wanted Bob to "act more like a man." Although she had some doubts about what would happen, Rebecca had hopes that the contract would work. She had no idea what the consequences would be. The day after setting up the home-school contract, Bob confronted Rebecca when he came through the door.

"How come you told my dad I was bad in class? He beat me when he got home, and it's all your fault." He stomped to his seat and flopped down, slamming his book bag down on the desk. Rebecca was stunned. Her heart went out to Bob. She was incensed with Mr. Parrish and his "macho" attitude. At that point, she decided that contacting Mr. Parrish about any of Bob's misbehavior would only result in a beating.

During class that day, Bob participated reluctantly for a short time. But he soon began tapping his pencil loudly on his desk. Rebecca reminded him of their contract. "It don't matter," Bob responded. "My dad don't think I can do it. He said so."

Rebecca felt her anger at Mr. Parrish growing by the second. How could he sit there in the conference and agree that the contract was a good idea and say he would encourage Bob and then go home and tell Bob he thinks he can't do it! Sighing, Rebecca tried to focus her attention on her work with the other students, hoping Bob would return to his work. He didn't. A few minutes later, she tried another tack, suggesting that he follow along with a student who was reading aloud from the literature book. His retort was swift and firm.

"I don't care where we are."

Rebecca chose to ignore this comment and went to stand near Bob's desk, cuing him to the sentence the student was reading. Bob continued to play with his pencil. Gently, Rebecca removed the pencil from Bob's grasp. He yielded and turned his efforts to getting another student's attention. Rebecca did not say a word, but she felt that Bob was trying to upset her because he held her accountable for the previous night's beating. Although she felt guilty about this, she refused to let Bob get the best of her. She had worked hard to get the other students to work as a cooperative group, and she didn't want them thinking she was playing favorites by giving Bob more than his share of attention. As the other students finished their oral reading, Bob informed them of his evaluation.

"Man, you guys are the lousiest readers I ever heard."

Always priding herself on accepting each student at his or her individual level of ability, whatever it was, Rebecca responded immediately in a slow, even voice.

"Bob, I would like to talk to you out in the hallway. Please follow me." She began walking slowly toward the door.

"What? Me? What'd I do? It's the truth!" Bob complained.

Rebecca paused at the door, waiting for Bob to comply. A few seconds later, Bob ambled to the doorway. Rebecca struggled to contain her anger, her voice trembling.

"As long as you are in my class, you will not make comments about the abilities of other students. We are all in this class because we all have different strengths and weaknesses, and we are trying to find the best way for us to learn. If you continue to make these comments, I will have to call your father."

Bob stood against the wall, avoiding her stare. He said nothing, nor did he acknowledge her warning.

"Bob, did you hear me?"

Still no answer. Rebecca stuck her head in the classroom and asked her instructional assistant to come out into the hallway.

"Bob needs a little time to think about what I just told him," she explained. "Would you please stay out here with him for a few minutes until he feels he is ready to rejoin the class?"

Bob followed Rebecca back into the room almost immediately, but she waved for him to go back. When he returned several minutes later, he was compliant. He completed all his classwork and showed it to her. Perhaps, Rebecca thought, my troubles with Bob are over. She had been surprised to see that the other boys were simply sitting there, waiting. She thanked them for being so quiet and calm and rewarded them with two extra minutes of free activity time.

When Bob arrived the next day, he immediately searched for his writing journal. Rebecca's students wrote in their journals each day. Rebecca agreed with her students that their journals were confidential, so she read them only if they were intentionally left on her desk. At the end of first period, Bob's journal was on her desk. What she saw when she opened it sent chills down her spine. Bob had drawn an effigy of himself hanging from a tree. On another page, a knife was thrust deep into the head of his likeness. Another page contained a headstone with Bob's name and birth date. Under these scenes, in Bob's characteristic scribble, she read, "I hat life. I wish I wer ded." Rebecca caught her breath. Was this one of Bob's attention-getting ploys, or was he serious?

Realizing that in Bob's best interests she was compelled to break the confidence of his journal, Rebecca consulted the school psychologist, Mr. Moore, at her first opportunity. Mr. Moore suggested that she question Bob carefully to see whether she could determine the reason for his drawings and statements. He also encouraged her to keep anecdotal records of Bob's behavior. He suggested that after a few weeks of observation, they could decide whether there was reason for referral.

Uncertain of how she should react, Rebecca did not write a response to Bob's entry as she usually did; she waited to see what would come next. The following day, Bob again immediately went to his journal. Rebecca watched him open it and quickly close it again. Later that morning, he chose not to write in his journal while the rest of the students did so. From across the room where she was working with another student, Rebecca prompted Bob to get started.

"I don't have nothing to say," he grumbled.

Rebecca repeated her request and began to move toward Bob. He reacted immediately.

"Why do you always hafta come over here? I ain't doin' nothing!"

Irritated at the disruption of her work with a willing student, Rebecca responded, "That's why I'm coming over, because you're not doing anything."

As Bob's face reddened with rage, she regretted her words. Fearing an all-out scene, Rebecca quickly asked her aide to take over while she talked to Bob. The situation was escalating rapidly to a crisis.

"Why are you always picking on me? Hector doesn't always write in his journal, but you don't yell at him!"

Refusing to get caught up in a power struggle, she continued to move toward Bob. She heard him mumbling.

"I don't care, you can't scare me. I can't stand you anyway. I hate this f---ing class!"

At the last comment, Rebecca became indignant.

"In my class, there is no profanity. You know the rule. I'll have to call your father."

"Go ahead," Bob retorted loudly. "Maybe he'll kill me this time and I won't have to worry about you and this f---ing class."

The other students stopped their work, staring at Bob and Rebecca. Rebecca was desperately trying to figure a way to get Bob out of the room, but she was afraid he was too angry to attempt any kind of move.

"Don't think the f---ing principal can help me!" Bob yelled. "Nobody can. Everybody hates me, especially my dad. And I hate you, you f---ing bitch!" With that, Bob pushed Rebecca's aide aside and ran out of the room.

The First Parent Conference

CHRISTINE WALKER

My student teacher, Christine Walker, was noticeably nervous about attending her first parent–teacher conference. She was quiet, very shy, and an easily intimidated young woman who made me wonder how she would manage parent conferences after she landed a job. So this conference with Mrs. Taylor was not only a meeting with a parent, but also, a learning opportunity for Christine.

"Should I say anything? What should I ask Mrs. Taylor about Paul?" she asked.

"Well, Christine, I always start a parent conference with positive statements about the student, and you're teaching him spelling, so let's discuss what you might want to tell his mother about his spelling lessons."

After a few minutes, Christine said, "Paul seems like a phenomenon, Mrs. Adams. He's not only doing great in your special ed. class, but also in Mr. Jordan's class."

Malcolm Jordan taught a class of twelve at-risk children in the room next to mine, and Paul spent most of the day in Malcolm's class. I told Christine that Malcolm and I scheduled a conference with Mrs. Taylor to discuss three topics. First, we thought Paul needed glasses. Second, Paul's repeated absences. Third, Paul was to be reevaluated soon, and Malcolm and I thought that his academic performance was too high—and his behavior too good—for him to qualify for special education again. Malcolm and I had repeatedly discussed Paul's vision problems with his mother, and she always responded that she didn't know about "that problem." So that was the main concern at the moment.

"Christine, Mrs. Taylor calls me every evening, and last night she said that every night she gets down on her hands and knees and thanks God for Malcolm and me. It'll be a pleasant conference tomorrow. She hasn't always parented correctly, but she's always been very pleasant with Malcolm and me."

I also reviewed Mrs. Taylor's overprotection of Paul for Christine. His parents moved to this area in the summer after Paul's first grade because he'd qualified for services as a special education student. They didn't want any labels on their son, so they moved from a nearby county to the city. But they were also fearful that the county would send his records to the city school system, and he would then be placed in a class for the mentally challenged. So they kept him at home for a long time until a neighbor reported them to child protective services who brought him to school in December. He was eight years old and the principal enrolled him in the first grade. When Paul first came to school, he had no self-help skills. His mother bathed him, dressed him, and refused to allow him to ride the school bus. His parents drove him to school, parked, walked him into the classroom, took off his coat, and hung it up. Then they escorted him to his desk. After a year, I persuaded Mrs. Taylor to park, let Paul out of the car, and *watch* him walk into school. It took me a long time to persuade her to do this. "He might get hurt going into the building. Or kids might pick on him in the hallway."

"What child in primary school would pick on a student who weighs 180 pounds?" Christine asked.

"Can't imagine who that might be. And that's been a big challenge for us, also. She refuses to acknowledge that he's obese."

She was also surprised when I told her how helpless Paul was when he first came to school. He didn't know how to pull up his pants or to fasten them after sitting on the toilet. He would shuffle out of the bathroom with his pants around his ankles, walk to where I stood, stand in front of me, and wait for me to pull up his pants. He couldn't tie his shoes. He didn't know how to wash his hands, and he would walk to the sink after going to the bathroom and hold his hands over the sink, waiting for someone to wash his hands. And according to social services, he wasn't allowed to play outside when at home even though a chain-link fence surrounded his yard. Soon after his enrollment, Mrs. Taylor scheduled a conference with me to complain about our "pushing Paul." She didn't want him to learn how to wash his hands, pull up his pants, tie his shoes, or hang up his coat. Paul's independence was horrifying for her. But I asked her to visit my classroom and observe how all of my students, even those younger than Paul, had learned all these skills at home and needed no help at school. After her visit, she was a bit shocked and finally agreed to allow us to teach him how to tie his shoes, wash his hands, pull up his pants and fasten them. She also commented that learning those skills at school didn't mean that she had to allow him to perform them at home. I also tried to persuade her to take Paul to a doctor and make a plan for Paul to lose weight. She refused.

"I was fifty when he was born, and I'm overweight, too. But my life is just fine."

I told Christine that Mrs. Taylor was very controlling, but after three years, she was beginning to allow Paul more independence at home. He was now allowed to undress and dress himself. But she still bathed him.

"As you know," I said to Christine, "we have some major behavioral problems with Paul, but Malcolm and I spend hours discussing these issues on the phone with Mrs. Taylor. I think that all of us will eventually resolve these problems."

Christine was calm the day of the conference. She said, "I'm looking forward to this. Mrs. Taylor sounds a bit goofy, but she also sounds pleasant—just like Paul."

"She is," I said. "Sometimes she hugs me when we meet, and she's always polite."

That afternoon, I was escorting one of my students to the special bus, when Mrs. Taylor stomped into the school. I was startled. The appointment was scheduled for an hour later, and she was obviously very angry; no smile, no greeting, just a nod of the head.

When we walked into Malcolm's room, some of his students were still waiting for their bus. He was very cordial, pointed to a chair, and said, "Sorry, but we can't meet with you until all of the students are gone. Have a seat, please." She flopped onto the chair and never glanced at him. When he looked at me with his eyebrows raised and his mouth open, I just shrugged. This did NOT look good, but I was just as shocked and confused as he was. And then Christine walked into the room.

"Mrs. Taylor, this is my student teacher, Christine Wells, and she teaches Paul spelling. Christine, this is Mrs. Taylor."

"I'm happy to meet you, Mrs. Taylor. Paul is such a sweetheart. I enjoy him a lot."

Mrs. Taylor never looked at her. She just sat there grinding her teeth. Christine looked frightened. This was supposed to be a pleasant and cordial meeting, but Mrs. Taylor was anything but cordial. Malcolm and I were confused—dumbfounded, in fact.

After the students boarded the buses, I expressed concern to Mrs. Taylor that we were not there to greet her, but that we were not expecting her until later. She grimly paced the floor, never smiled, and after sending Paul to the library, she turned slowly, looked at us and said, "I've come to get something straight."

She sat down for an instant and then jumped up to pace again. As she paced she talked loudly and angrily about the "neglect and abuse" of Paul at school. She also untied and tied the belt of her coat over and over again. In order to accomplish this, she had to heave her monstrous breasts out of the way with her forearms and then tie the ends of her belt.

She did this quickly and rather violently. Rather than listening to her, I found myself concentrating on whether or not she was going to perform an accidental self-mastectomy while raging around the room.

At one point, the whole scene was so ridiculous that I almost burst out laughing. But Christine got paler by the minute and resembled a mannequin with fixed eye sockets. Malcolm's mouth became a thin straight line in his very red face. And Mrs. Taylor was flinging her breasts around the room as if she were juggling them. It was no longer funny.

Malcolm and I tried to calm and reassure Mrs. Taylor. She was convinced that we were allowing the other children to abuse Paul. It became increasingly clear that anything I said was worthless. She was really angry with me. I was the cause of *all* of Paul's woes. She paced the floor, screamed and cried, and slung her breasts around.

After an hour, Malcolm repeated what both of us had said several times—a statement that earned nothing more than a grunt and a scowl from Mrs. Taylor. "Mrs. Taylor, I am genuinely sorry that Paul is so unhappy, but I have not seen any of the mistreatment you speak of. All I can tell you is that I've asked Paul to come and tell me when someone picks on him."

She suddenly stopped pacing, leveled a big grin at Malcolm and said, "Now we're getting somewhere. If you work with me, I'll work with you."

Malcolm's complexion had faded to an ashy hue, but he recognized an opportunity to discuss our agenda, and he plowed ahead. He smiled at Mrs. Taylor and said, "I believe that Paul has a vision problem. Has anyone ever mentioned this to you before?"

"No," she said. "But we've had his eyes checked, and the doctor says that they're fine."

Then Malcolm calmly and quietly asked if it would be possible for Paul to bring pencil and paper to school. "He is always borrowing from me or the other children, and they resent it. He says that his parents can't afford to buy him paper and pencils."

She bounced off the chair. "What! Paul is a property owner. He owns property in his name right now. Why would he tell you such a lie?"

Malcolm's voice became very low, soft, and soothing. "That's fine, Mrs. Taylor. Let's talk about how we can help Paul in the classroom. Why don't we both tell him to report to me any time someone picks on him?"

She slowed her pacing and began to cry. "I'm so relieved. You don't know what I've been through. My poor little boy."

She collapsed onto the chair, crying, "You just don't know. I've had headaches, awful headaches. Yesterday, I decided—I have a gun, you know—I had decided that if Paul came home with one more sad story, that I was going to load that gun and come over here and shoot every child and everyone in this classroom."

I became frozen in the reality that this woman was so unbalanced that she could and maybe would empty a loaded revolver into a classroom full of children. I didn't utter a sound. Malcolm had a white-knuckled grip on several pencils that he stared at. Christine sat so erect that I wondered if she had ever had military training. She stared at her hands clasped in her lap, and her face was completely white. All of us wondered if Mrs. Taylor had the gun with her.

After a few seconds, Mrs. Taylor dried her eyes, bounced up, and said, "Well, I'm so glad we worked that out. I feel so much better."

She headed toward Malcolm with outstretched arms and bouncing boobs. She hugged him, and then me, then Christine. She smiled lovingly at us and left.

Malcolm, Christine, and I stood stone still, listening to Mrs. Taylor's oxfords thump out of the building. When we heard the outside door slam, we fell on each other, laughing hysterically. We laughed until we cried. We hugged each other, then howled with laughter, dried our eyes and said, "This is not funny." Then we collapsed in laughter again. Finally, we managed to run to the principal and tell him what had happened.

Adrian, the principal, had not worked at our school when Paul first arrived, and he had limited knowledge of Paul's history. When we explained our ordeal, he was horrified. We were, too. But we couldn't stop laughing.

He carefully wrote down Mrs. Taylor's threat "to kill every child and everyone in this classroom," and he warned us *not* to have any more conferences with Mrs. Taylor without an administrator present.

The next day, he called Mrs. Taylor and questioned her about the conference. "I said to her, 'Mrs. Taylor, my teachers, Mr. Jordan, Mrs. Gray, and Miss Wells, told me something disturbing about your recent conference. They said that you threatened to shoot them and the children in the class. Could you explain this to me?'"

Mrs. Taylor admitted that Adrian had quoted her correctly and said that at the time she meant it. "She told me that she had gotten so upset about Paul's mistreatment in the classroom that she would have done anything for him."

And Adrian warned Malcolm and me again not to have any conferences with Mrs. Taylor without an administrator. Then he quickly related all this information to the superintendent. What is the procedure for dealing with an unbalanced, frightened, desperate woman who had threatened innocent children? We didn't know.

Adrian also alerted the special education supervisor. She called me, very alarmed for my safety. "Don't call child protective services. I don't want you to call them, even if you do so anonymously." She had several more paragraphs of warning before she hung up. I knew her fears were not without basis, but her warning about having the blood of innocent children on my hands was horrifying. But how else could I protect my class, my babies, I called them, unless I informed child protection services (CPS)?

The superintendent's office sent Mrs. Taylor a letter telling her she was not to come to the school without calling first. And after she made an appointment, she was to stop by the office and the principal would escort her to the conference.

I suddenly became ill and went home early. I called child protective services the day my supervisor called me. Mrs. Taylor wasn't rational and could, and maybe would, come gunning for Malcolm, the children, and me. An anonymous caller had put protective services on Mrs. Taylor's trail originally. Why not again? So I lied. I called and said that I was a friend of Mrs. Taylor and that I thought she acted strange sometimes. I wondered if she needed counseling and had heard that there was a rumor that she had threatened the lives of her son's classmates and his teachers. CPS responded immediately.

The next day, the CPS social worker met with Malcolm and related information she had recently obtained from several of the Taylors' neighbors. They had witnessed Mrs. Taylor chasing Paul outside and beating him with a broomstick. After the beatings, she would bake a cake, call Paul inside, and give him the whole cake.

"Mr. Jordan and Mrs. Gray, please watch carefully for symptoms of this abuse. If he has any bruises, broken skin, difficulty walking or sitting, or any lumps on his head, please call us immediately."

Malcolm and I promised to follow the CPS workers' requests. We also discussed the other issues we had with Mrs. Taylor: Paul's repeated absences, Mrs. Taylor's refusal to have Paul's eyes checked, and his obesity—all of which we attributed to Mrs. Taylor's mental health issues.

Christine sat silently throughout the meeting with the CPS worker. But later, she said to me, "I love children, and I love to teach, but I'm not sure that I can do this. Parents have become a primary issue for me. I'm more than a little nervous about interacting with parents."

So was I. I still am.

The One That Got Away

CHARLES ALLEN

Yesterday, I had lunch with Polly, a retired teacher I used to work with. During our gabfest about family and friends, what Polly calls our "catch-up" session, she asked, "Did you know that Calvin is in the penitentiary?"

I had not heard this, but I was not surprised. In my 29 years of teaching physical education to elementary students, Calvin stands out as the most frightening child I have ever taught. He was the only child who could make my blood feel icy when he walked into the gym, and I've taught some pretty tough cases. Over the years, I've had every kind of special education child that administrators can think up labels for, but none of them can hold a candle to Calvin.

Calvin had always been a problem, even in kindergarten, but when he entered third grade a combination of things sent him spiraling into serious behavior problems. Before Calvin started school, his mother and father were incarcerated for selling drugs, so his aunt took care of him. Around third grade, his mother and father were released from jail and resumed caring for him. I never did hear the whole story, but it seemed that his mother and father did not live together, and both lived with other partners. Neither parent seemed real excited to have Calvin, but the dad did try to deal with this little boy. Calvin lived with his dad and his girlfriend.

Polly said, "Well, yes, the dad did seem to care more for Calvin than the mother, from what I heard. Then one night, he and Calvin came back home from somewhere and found that dad's girlfriend had thrown the dad's and Calvin's belongings in the yard. She wouldn't let them back in, even to get Calvin's schoolbooks."

"I never heard that story," I said. "That's really sad."

Polly continued, "This child's whole life was so sad. When Calvin was in the third grade, right after the dad's girlfriend threw them out, Calvin's father lost his job. Social services provided the necessities, but the dad didn't have any money for Christmas. The special education supervisor told me that when she was observing another child in Mary Anderson's class, she became interested in Calvin and his situation and begged some money from her church to give to the dad to buy presents for Calvin. She also thought that Calvin should have some money to buy his dad a gift. She even helped Calvin pick out a gift for his dad."

I said, "Poor fella. He did have a tough life for a young boy."

"He had a tough life for anybody."

Around this time, Calvin experienced a growth spurt and was as large as some of our fourth-graders, our BIG fourth-graders. He was angry, probably frightened, and he had the size and strength to make his anger a real threat.

Polly said, "I don't know how Mary Anderson dealt with that child for a whole year. She had to instruct her class what to do if Calvin 'went off.' I mean, one afternoon when he was absent, Mary told the children where to evacuate the room if he exploded by the side door. Or by her desk. Or by the hall door. I can't believe that parents in that class didn't scream bloody murder, but they didn't."

I said, "The kids might have been too frightened of Calvin to tell anybody anything. You know he extorted money from other children, but no one would tell on him. You had to catch him in the act, which was not always possible."

"Well, yes, I know about that because I caught him in the act, but he promptly told me to mind my own business if I didn't want to get hurt. I left him in the hall with his victims and got the principal to deal with him. Unfortunately, I didn't know the names of the smaller children he was victimizing, and by the time his teacher arrived, the kids were gone. I'm not sure what happened with that situation."

I talked to Polly for about an hour and reconstructed some of the major episodes in our relationship with Calvin. Calvin had always been noncompliant, but my issuing a bottom-line consequence was usually sufficient to keep him from pummeling other students. My calm statement, "Either sit by the wall for a few minutes or go to the office," had worked before his third-grade year. Sometimes he went to the office, and sometimes he sat out for a few minutes. But he usually complied.

The first time I was aware of his defiance was one afternoon when all the students had left. Mary Anderson, Calvin's teacher, had gotten permission from Calvin's dad and school administrators to keep Calvin after school. Apparently he decided that he was not going to stay. I had the misfortune to be in the office, to look out the window, and to see Calvin dragging Mary Anderson down the sidewalk. Actually, she was holding on to one of his arms with both her hands while he walked steadily down the sidewalk. Her feet were planted firmly, but he was so strong that he was able to drag her along as if she were a wagon he was casually pulling. I asked if she needed some help, and she replied that she did. When I approached Calvin and asked that he return to the classroom, he became a tornado, a whirling machine of flailing body parts. I restrained him and took him to the office where the principal, Mrs. Robertson, Mary, and I tried to deal with him. I don't know exactly how it happened, but Calvin and I ended up in the principal's swiveling chair, my legs around his body, my arms holding his arms in the straitjacket hold while he rammed his head backward into my head.

I remember angrily saying to Mrs. Robertson, the principal, "I'm not getting paid enough to do this."

She said, "Let him go."

I did, and he began to destroy the office. He cleared the shelves, the desk, and turned over furniture. He had a wild look on his face, and frankly, he scared me, but when he had pretty much trashed the room, he began to calm down. Then he picked up a pair of scissors, opened the blades, put one blade on his wrist, and threatened to slice his wrist. I was afraid to breathe but the principal talked quietly and calmly, and after what seemed like a lifetime, she got him to put down the scissors. Mrs. Robertson then decided that she would call a cab and send Calvin home.

When the cab came, the three of us escorted him to the cab, put him in the back seat, and watched him leap out the door on the other side and bolt across the schoolyard. Mrs. Robertson said, "Leave him alone. Don't chase him. I'll call the police." Even though I was too exhausted to chase him, I was also worried about him. I wondered how Calvin, who was already frightened and angry, would react to the police.

Before I left school that afternoon, I told Mrs. Robertson, "Calvin needs help. He's gotten worse this year."

Polly said, "You're not the only one who thought that Calvin needed help. His poor teacher must have come to the child study committee every week. She was so good about implementing our strategies, but Calvin needed so much more than any strategy we could offer. And he consumed most of Mary's time and energy."

Polly went on to tell me about the time she had met a parent for an IEP meeting in the office area and had difficulty conducting the meeting because Calvin was destroying one of the offices down the hall. Polly said, "He turned over a heavy bookshelf, one of those that reach from floor to ceiling and was full of books. He then threw the books against the wall one by one and finally punched a large hole in the drywall with his fist. Even though I closed both the door to the conference room and the door to the office, the noise level was distracting. The parents kept asking me, 'What is that racket?' We managed to sign the IEP, but whew!"

I said, "I never could understand why no one saw fit to test Calvin for possible placement in special education."

Polly said, "I have wondered that myself. Some of us on the child study committee pushed for testing, but our concerns always got overruled. Thought you might know why he was never referred."

"Not me. We support folks are out of the loop. We just teach our nine classes a day, do our lunch duty, our bus duty, and try not to complain. Not many folks think to ask us how we see the children. But Mrs. Robertson did try to help me out. Because I don't have an intercom in the gym, Mrs. Robertson put a phone in the gym office so that I could call her when Calvin went off. I did appreciate that. It was frightening to be at the end of the hall, in the basement, not close to any other classrooms, with no intercom, and no way to get help. I certainly couldn't leave the class with him acting out like that. I did carry him a couple of times to the office, but it never looks good for a teacher to subdue a child like that. And besides, I may be an average-sized male, but Calvin was big, and he was becoming more than I could handle. Particularly when he was flailing around."

I told Polly, "I finally learned to 'read' Calvin. I knew when he walked in the gym door if he was on edge, and I would do all I could to keep him from going off. But sometimes he still exploded. I never knew what would provoke him, and, because he was bigger than the other kids, I was nervous the whole time he was in gym. One day, I knew what had set him off. After we had talked a lot about his controlling himself, another student insisted that he have the same gym scooter that Calvin wanted. Can't figure out what the other boy was thinking, most kids were afraid of Calvin. But the other boy did finally back off and let Calvin have the scooter. I was proud of Calvin that he didn't loose it with this other boy, but by the time he finally got possession of the scooter, he didn't want it. And you should have seen him. His eyes got a wild look in them. He walked to the end of the gym away from the rest of us and paced up and down, up and down, real fast. I asked him if he wanted to go back to his classroom, but he refused to answer. When it was time for his class to leave the gym, he refused to go with them. It was one of those rare days when I didn't have a class after his, so I just let him pace the gym until he was ready to go. After about 15 minutes, he calmed down and went back to class."

Polly said, "I'm glad that you had the good sense not to touch him. Do you remember what happened to Mr. Wheeler, the custodian who befriended Calvin? One morning when Calvin had trashed the classroom and was out in the hall threatening to run away, Mr. Wheeler walked up to

Calvin, and said, 'Come on, Calvin. Let's you and me go for a walk.' When Calvin just stood there trembling and clenching his fists, Mr. Wheeler placed his hands on Calvin's shoulders. Before Mr. Wheeler could utter a word, Calvin clawed both of Mr. Wheeler's arms with his fingernails. Calvin left deep wounds on Mr. Wheeler's arms. Poor man had to go to the doctor, and he missed a couple days of work. He said that Calvin looked like a wild animal when he scratched him."

"I know the look. I thought he looked more like a frightened animal. I guess he was frightened. But you know, when he was calm and when you had him one on one, he was a friendly, funny kid. And smart too."

I told Polly about my plan for Calvin in the fourth grade that was partially successful. That particular year, I was blessed as never before and had the last class free on Fridays. So I talked with his teacher and told her that if Calvin had a good week, he could come shoot baskets with me at that time. His teacher, Betty, devised some kind of behavior management plan. I don't remember what it was, but this seemed to help control him. All during the week, I'd remind him to hold it together so we could shoot some baskets. His teacher would remind him also. She would say, 'Calvin, don't spoil it. You're doing great. Try to hold it together so you can shoot some baskets.' He usually did. I don't know. I reckon that helped some. His teacher seemed to think that it did. And you know what, I really enjoyed our time together his last year at our school."

Polly said, "I had hoped that when Calvin went to middle school that he would get a fresh start. You know, sometimes other children at a new school don't know about a child's checkered past, and the kid can sorta' start over. But this didn't happen to Calvin. He started right away trying to be king of the hill."

I had not known that when Calvin went to middle school, the older boys wouldn't put up with his abuse and beat the stuffing out of him. It was rumored that some of the teachers saw him getting beat up and took their time breaking up the fight. I'm not sure about that, but Calvin landed in the hospital as a result of this fight. When he returned to school, Polly told me that he hot-wired a teacher's car, wrecked the car, and went to juvenile detention. It was all down hill from there. He just about stayed in the juvenile justice system until he dropped out of school. As soon as he turned 18, he was picked up for something, Polly doesn't know what, and is now in prison.

I said, "That child needed help so bad. He was smart and could be charming, but he just was an emotional mess. I must have said about a hundred times or more that we had to get him some help. But we didn't."

Polly said, "This is one the school system failed. We let this one get away."

We did.

The Truth About Alice

JANET LANE

Janet Lane often found her Algebra 1A and 1B courses a challenge. These courses were designed for ninth- and tenth-graders who were comparatively slow to grasp the fundamental concepts of the subject. Janet noticed that this course sequence—Algebra 1A (pre-algebra) first semester in preparation for Algebra 1B (regular algebra) second semester—was generally selected by lower-performing students and that she often had particular difficulty managing students' behavior in these classes.

Janet had dealt with her share, or more, of low motivation, inattention, and overt attempts to disrupt the class. In her 16 years of teaching, she felt that she had handled these problems more or less successfully. She had never encountered a problem that, over time, she was unable to resolve—until recently.

During the first semester in Algebra 1A, Janet's class consisted of the usual mix of students. One student, however, distinguished herself from the others on the basis of appearance alone. When Janet looked at Alice, she could not help thinking that she was the most unattractive child she had ever seen. Although she was not from a poor home, Alice wore a pair of baggy dungarees (rolled up at the ankles) and a polo shirt to school every single day. She apparently had three sets of this "out-fit," but she always looked the same. To magnify the frumpy style of her apparel, Alice's physical shape was, well, unusual. From the waist down, she was proportionally much larger than she was above the waist, giving her a peculiar pear-shaped appearance. The way she turned her feet in when she walked made her look almost as if she had an orthopedic deformity. Very thick glasses; dental braces; stringy, oily hair; and a general unkempt appearance all added to her misfit look.

If only Alice performed well academically, Janet thought, her odd appearance could be somewhat compensated for; but, in fact, Alice was also a weak student. Her parents had recently decided to remove her from the learning disabilities program because they did not want her to be in special education in high school. No one had brought this fact to Janet's attention. But she did not customarily seek such information, choosing instead to "let the kids tell me what they are." As it turned out, there was a lot Janet didn't know about Alice.

Alice had been in Janet's class for only a few days when she approached her and stated, "I'm going to have to be late for class." This soon became a frequent occurrence. Because the class met directly after lunch, the first several times Alice was late, Janet didn't see it as a problem. After all, she reasoned, Alice had been nice enough to tell her each time she was going to be late.

When Alice's lateness became consistent, however, Janet became concerned and decided to have a talk with her. When she told Alice that her tardiness to class was becoming a problem, Alice became quite agitated and repeatedly insisted in a squealing voice, "I have to be late for class." Deciding that she must be firm, Janet replied, "I don't care if you're late occasionally, but you can't be late every single day. We have a class to run, you know."

Perhaps she should have expected the earnest flow of tears that ensued, but, in fact, Alice's weeping caught her off guard. At the moment, all she could think to do was to tell Alice not to worry, that they would discuss it later.

That afternoon Janet decided to seek some information and advice concerning this situation. Noticing Martha Keys, the sophomore guidance counselor, in the main office, she greeted her and began an account of the problem she was having with Alice. Almost immediately, Martha began to laugh so heartily that Janet felt a mild surge of confused annoyance. Noting the bewildered look on her face, Martha managed to ask mirthfully, "You don't know?" Janet shook her head "no" while Martha proceeded to direct her toward the guidance office. After closing the door, Martha explained the situation. Alice, she recounted, had attracted a great deal of attention last year as a result of an incident in the girls' restroom that had become, in a short time, almost legendary.

It seems that Alice's mother had insisted that she brush her teeth after lunch daily and had sent her to school with a neat little kit with which to accomplish this task. Too embarrassed to brush in front of other students and too compliant to disobey her mother's orders, Alice solved her dilemma by brushing in the toilet stall. By all accounts, Alice was observed by another student using the water in the toilet to carry out her dental hygiene.

Word of this "incredibly grody act" spread quickly among the students, and when Martha got wind of it, she called Alice into her office to discuss the matter. They resolved the problem by allowing Alice permission to be late for class after lunch so that she could brush her teeth at the sink after the other students had gone to class. Unfortunately, the incident had resulted in tremendous social damage and now presented Janet with some unusual behavioral problems in her Algebra 1A class.

Janet had been aware that Alice's late arrival to her class caused some disturbance among the other students, yet she was unable to fully grasp the situation until she had discovered the reason for Alice's tardiness. It seemed that everyone had been in on the joke except Janet. When Alice entered class late, she was met with greetings such as, "Hello, Alice!" or "Watcha been doing, Alice?" These remarks were conveyed in ironic tones that held, for the informed listener, a thinly veiled reference to Alice's past bathroom misadventures.

Now that she understood what lay behind these "greetings," Janet became increasingly aware of the disruption instigated by Alice's late arrival. The problem had grown to the point that three of the boys were so consistently ugly to her that Janet was compelled to go to the assistant principal and say, "I want those three boys, myself, and you to sit down and have a little talk." The "little talk," however, didn't amount to much. Just the usual "I can't believe you are picking on this girl! Leave her alone! Act your age! Pretend she's not there . . ." During the meeting, Janet decided that she would definitely have to separate these three and Alice in class, surrounding her with a shield of nice kids. This worked well—for about a week.

Having decided that the boys were the instigators, it came as quite a shock to Janet when she discovered that notes were being passed between these boys and Alice. The particular "love note" that came to her attention was written to Alice by Mitch, the ringleader of the boys who were entertaining themselves at Alice's (and Janet's) expense. The note consisted of a simple message: "I like you, Alice. Would you like to go out sometime?" Alice had replied affirmatively and enthusiastically, and the note was on its way back when Janet intercepted it. Several students exchanged meaningful looks as Janet returned to her lesson.

Disgusted and frustrated, Janet took both Mitch and Alice to the office after class and had them assigned to in-school suspension. She tried to reason with Alice that she was guilty for having participated in the note-passing. How could she get Alice to understand that the boys were making a joke of her without hurting her feelings? Alice just didn't seem to "get it," and this made Janet worry even more. Alice, believing that the boys really liked her, could be played for the fool by them. In the back of her mind, Janet also worried about the possibility that the boys might easily take sexual advantage of Alice. There seemed to be no way out of this situation that would avoid Alice's eventual humiliation or further loss of social status.

They Failed Derrick

MELINDA SMITH

I watched through my classroom window as Derrick and his mother got into their car and drove away. I tried not to cry as I gathered up Derrick's textbooks and returned them to the book room. I walked back to my classroom, sat down at my desk, and tried futilely to work on my reading lesson for the next day. I couldn't concentrate. Each time I tried to read something from my teacher's manual I couldn't help but think about Derrick and what I feared was going to happen to him.

And as for that placement team—that wonderful group of concerned educators—well, I was furious with those guys! The decision to transfer this child to a middle school and place him in a class for children with behavioral disorders was the worst possible thing that we could do to him! Even though he had taken me through some real challenges since the beginning of the year, Derrick had made a lot of progress, and I really didn't feel that placing him in a special education class would improve his behavior. You would think that my previous experiences with children with disabilities would have counted for something, but it didn't. We simply didn't give this kid enough time. I will always believe that we moved too early on this one.

I came to know Derrick my first year back in a regular classroom after teaching children with mental retardation for over 15 years. Now that my own two kids were grown up and off in college, I felt that I was losing touch with how normal kids think and operate. I also believed that I was doing a disservice to my little kids who have disabilities. You see, because many of the classes for students with mental retardation were being phased out, my class had become a regional program. Students from all over the county were bused to my school to receive services. I was teaching some of the same pupils for up to five years, and it finally dawned on me that this was not in their best interest—nor in mine. I considered myself a good teacher, and I really cared about these students, but at the same time I felt myself becoming too routinized. I needed a change, and so did the kids. So, I decided to take the plunge. It was time for me to return to the regular classroom.

There were regular classroom vacancies at my school, Essig Elementary, but after considering my options I decided that I needed to make a clean break. Even though I got along very well with the faculty and staff at Essig, I just couldn't imagine watching my kids walking down the hallway with another teacher. So I talked with an old partner in crime, Greg Rodgers, who was the principal of Helmsley Elementary School. Greg and I worked together during my first five years as a teacher, and over the years it seems our paths always managed to cross. After he became an administrator, we were assigned to assist with the development of several countywide in-service projects. I also served as his assistant principal during a few summer school sessions. Greg was a professional in every sense of the word, and I thought that it would be very rewarding to work under his leadership on a full-time basis. After taking care of all of the formalities, Greg offered me a position as the teacher of high-average and gifted fifth-grade students. I looked forward to this change and challenge, and though it was difficult for me to walk away from what had been a major part of my life for 15 years, I packed up boxes of books, teacher-made games, presents collected over the years, and, yes, even my drawer full of confiscated toys.

I started out on my new venture with a feeling of interest and optimism. During the summer, I enrolled in a course on teaching gifted children, and I read related books and journal articles whenever time permitted. I also spent a lot of time just thinking about my experiences and skills as a special educator and wondering how I could transfer these skills to my new situation. I was so excited! I wanted to be ready in September when those kids stepped off the bus and entered my classroom.

Well, even though I would be teaching higher-functioning kids and even though I was in a new school, I found that I had been typecast. I don't know of any other way to put it. Other special education teachers who had returned to regular classroom positions often told me about their experiences. "Once a special educator, always a special educator," they'd say. It didn't take me very long to understand what they really meant. During the first day of teacher work week, Greg called me into his office and asked if I would consider taking a child who had some real emotional problems.

"This kid has shot holes through almost every teacher in this school," I remember him saying. "If there's anyone in the world who can make a change in him, it's you. Will you please consider taking him until we can get the paperwork done to have him placed in special education?"

"Flattery will get you nowhere," I replied. But in the end, I agreed to take on this kid. When I thought of having a student with emotional problems and academic deficits in a class with gifted learners, I felt a tingle in my spine. This would be a real challenge indeed, I thought.

The student was none other than the infamous Derrick Yates. He was 12 years old and functioning at about a third-grade level in all subjects. He had developed a notorious reputation around school. None of the teachers could handle him during the one year he had been at Helmsley. In fact, I found out that last year he hadn't even been able to stay at school all day. Greg had made arrangements with Derrick's mother to have him picked up after lunch until such time that his behavior improved. Greg had also written a contract with Derrick that outlined student, teacher, and administrator responsibilities. The contract also specified the conditions that would allow Derrick's time at school to be extended. Unfortunately, Derrick never made it past lunchtime. He defied and frightened faculty and staff members on several occasions. He never lasted longer than five minutes in physical education, art, or music because he would disrupt the class, curse or threaten a teacher, and be sent to the office.

Honestly, I hardly had time to hang my bulletin boards during in-service week because my room was buzzing with teachers who wanted to give me the low-down on Derrick. The other fifth-grade teachers talked about how their nerves had been frazzled all summer long because they feared that their worst possible nightmare might come true—that Derrick would be assigned to their classroom. Needless to say, they were quite relieved to know that *moi*—Melinda Smith, the new kid on the block—was also certified in behavioral disorders and fit all the qualifications to be the "chosen one."

"He's terrorized everyone," Karen, one of the fifth-grade teachers, told me. "His mother has absolutely no control over him at home, and so he thinks that he can also be the man in charge here. The weird thing about it is that . . . I think he's right."

At this point, I began to wonder what I had gotten myself into. The stories I heard about Derrick's home life were totally unbelievable. Derrick's father and mother were divorced, and Derrick was living with his mother and a younger brother and sister. He was angered by his parents' separation and divorce, and he blamed his mother for the failed marriage. Apparently, he idolized his father, but these feelings weren't mutual. Unable to deal with this rejection, Derrick took his frustrations out on anyone and everyone with whom he came in contact. This included his mother, brother, and sister. Barbara Cole, the school social worker, told me stories that gave me goose bumps.

"This child actually butchered and killed the family dog with a knife. He cut off the poor dog's head and extremities and lined them up in a neat row in the backyard. His mother had locks installed on the kitchen drawers because she was afraid that he would use the utensils as weapons against her and the other children. She's also installed a double-bolt lock on her bedroom door, and she lets the two younger children sleep in the room with her at night. Some people would consider this absurd, but she was wise to take this action."

To say the least, Barbara had aroused my curiosity. "What do you mean?" I asked.

"Well, on one occasion, Mrs. Yates reported that Derrick was angry with her because he was convinced that she had not allowed him to speak to his dad on the phone. Actually, Mr. Yates had called about child support payments and had expressed no interest in speaking to any of the children. That night, Mrs. Yates awakened to the sound of Derrick jabbing a large butcher knife against her bedroom door. After she threatened to call the police, he finally stopped his terrorizing and returned to his room."

I tried to say something, but Barbara didn't give me a chance. Barbara continued to share her experiences with Derrick.

"Shortly after that, I was sent to the Yates's home to conduct an interview with the mother. I found Derrick home alone that day. For no apparent reason, he was absent from school. Now, Derrick is a large kid for his age and coupled with those bucked and crooked teeth and that uncontrollable sick kind of laugh, he really looks like something scary. To see this kid in action is like watching a scene from an Alfred Hitchcock movie. Anyway, Derrick opened the door, stared at me, and asked in a threatening voice, 'What you want, bitch?' Honey, I just politely turned, walked to my car, and got out of there."

As I listened to these horrendous stories, I realized that this would be the case of all cases. But still, I wanted to give this one a whirl. I had a few tricks up my sleeve that I hadn't even tried yet, and from the way everybody described Derrick, I figured that I would finally have the chance to use them. And so my special education training and my natural inclination and desire to work with troubled children prompted me to accept Derrick Winslow Yates into my fifth-grade classroom.

On the day the students arrived in September, it didn't take me two minutes to realize which one was Derrick. Aside from the descriptions that my colleagues had given, one could not help but feel this child's presence. There was a certain "looseness" about him. From the way he moved about the room, I could tell that he knew he could frighten people, and as I told the class to sit down and get settled, I could feel his eyes on me. He took his time getting to his seat, and I had the feeling that he was trying to let me know that he expected me to fear him, too. Just as the other teachers told me, I could see that "look" in his eyes. So, I realized the very instant I met Derrick that I would have to handle him with kid gloves. Even though I had a little fear, I was determined that I would not let him see or even sense this fear. As usual, I tried to think positively, but I also made plans to expect the worst.

Well, to my surprise, the first three weeks of school went by without any major hassles. In fact, Derrick was not really a problem at all. He was talkative, restless, and obviously frustrated because the work was way over his head. I modified his assignments, however and kept a careful watch on him when I assigned independent work or work in cooperative learning groups. I also used proximity control, and sometimes, if he was getting restless or starting to harass one of the other children verbally, I would simply walk over to him and calmly put my hand on his shoulder, and he'd straighten up. Still, he maintained the "look," and I resigned myself to the fact that I could not let down my guard—that I had to watch him every minute he was in the room.

I don't think Derrick knew how to take it that I was not yelling at him, isolating him, or sending him to the office. He really tickled me one day when he walked up to me and asked, "You don't know about me, do you?" When I asked what he meant, he stated that he had a bad reputation and that he had stayed in the office more time last year than he had stayed in the classroom. He told me that the principals, the teachers, and the kids were all afraid of him and that he liked to do mean things. Boy, did he lay it on the line! I had to think quickly before I responded.

"Why, thank you, Derrick," I replied. "Thank you. I appreciate that you told me special things about yourself that will help me plan for you." I also told him that I was pleased with his behavior so far and that I looked forward to having a good year with him in my class. With that, he looked at me as if to say, "No such luck, Lady!" and returned to his seat with one of his eerie chuckles.

A few days later, his mother called me very upset because she said that things were getting worse at home and she didn't know how long she could keep dealing with Derrick. He was driving her crazy, and she was still very much concerned about the safety of her other children. Well, I felt that Derrick, by coming to me and exposing the negative side of himself, was letting me know that our little hiatus was about to come to an end. It was as if he was saying, "Now you know, I've talked to you and my mother has talked to you, and now I'm going to let it all hang out." This is precisely what he did.

I'll never forget the very first major incident. The kids knew about Derrick's reputation, and they came in really upset and a little nervous to tell me that he had a pocketknife on the bus. Joey mustered up enough nerve to make the report. He was shaking like a leaf when he came up to me. He looked over his shoulder constantly to make sure that Derrick wasn't in the room.

"Mrs. Smith, Derrick had a knife on the bus, and he was waving it in all of our faces, and he dared us to tell the bus driver!"

Poor thing, he was gasping for breath by the time he finished, so I used an old tried-and-true trick—"antiseptic bouncing"—to help him get himself under control. This little technique had been a real lifesaver during my years as a special educator. I sent Joey to the office with a note to the secretary requesting that she send him back with some bond paper after letting him sit and calm down for a few minutes. Just as he left the room, Derrick entered as if nothing out of the ordinary had occurred. He walked over to the browsing table and started thumbing through a motorcycle magazine. As usual, I told everyone to sharpen pencils and prepare for work. Then, I breathed a deep sigh and walked over to Derrick.

When I reached Derrick's seat at the table, I kneeled so that our eyes met at the same level. I spoke in a calm voice. "Derrick, I understand that you had a knife on the bus. Is this true?"

"Yeah, I have a knife. So, what of it?" he replied mockingly.

I asked him to give me the knife, and that's when he really lost it for the first time in my classroom. His shout was so loud that I know people at the other end of the hall heard him.

"Who told you, anyway? I'm going to get the bastard who told on me. This is my knife, I bought it with my own money and you ain't getting it—I don't care what you say, you ain't getting it!"

Oh, Lord have mercy! I thought. Here we go. He walked to his seat and started laughing uncontrollably. He had the knife in his hand, but he hadn't opened it. I was more than a little nervous at this point, and I feared that things might really get out of hand. I knew that I had to react in a way that would not reveal my fears, and at the same time I didn't want to do anything that would cause Derrick to react physically. He continued to look at me. The smile on his face showed all of his bucked, crooked teeth, just as Barbara had told me at the beginning of the year. And yes, he *did* look like something very, very scary.

I continued to talk with him and told him calmly that carrying weapons on school property, including the school bus, was not permissible, that I could not let him keep it, and that he would need to calm down. I used a crisis intervention strategy that I learned as a special educator. As I talked with him, whenever I saw anything that resembled calmness, I offered social reinforcement.

"Good, Derrick. You're not screaming now. You're talking in a calm voice, and you're very still. Good job, now let me have the knife."

Finally, to my relief, he extended his hand with the knife and said, "Here, you want the knife, take it. Give it to the principal if you want to."

So we both took the knife to the office, and I explained that we were not coming with just bad news. I told Greg about the knife, but I also explained that Derrick had suggested that we bring the knife to the office. Good idea, but not enough to avoid automatic suspension.

When Derrick returned from suspension, he began testing me. He knew that I had a policy of allowing my very responsible students to go to the restroom without asking permission. All they had to do was get up from their seats quietly, take one of the wooden bathroom passes, and leave with the understanding that they were not to abuse the privilege. Even though the rule wasn't etched in stone, they were to be back within five minutes and were not to leave the room more than once within any given hour. I explained to them all the time that this was an honor, that they were the oldest students in the building, and that I expected them to handle this privilege. I said to them all the time, "If you abuse, you lose." So Derrick took it upon himself to challenge me on this rule. He left the room three or four times one day and didn't use the bathroom pass. He simply got up and left the room and stayed out 15 to 20 minutes each time. I suddenly realized that I had only been through the calm before the storm.

The last time he got up and left the room, he stayed for about 20 minutes. He reentered and walked over to my desk. We had just finished math, and the other students were preparing for their reading lesson. I was gathering the materials that were needed for the lesson, and I tried my best not to show that I was upset with him. He looked at me and smiled.

"I've been out a long time," he mumbled.

I picked up my materials and faced him with a look of concern and answered, "Yes, I noticed you were out. Is everything okay?"

"Yeah, I thought we couldn't stay that long."

I had to use every ounce of restraint that I possessed as I thought about my next response. I knew that any expression of outrage on my part would send him into hysterics and he'd probably wreck the classroom. No, that wouldn't work. It had never worked before. I had to second-guess this child. I had to hit him from an unexpected angle and catch him off guard. So, once again, I decided to downplay the entire episode.

"Well you're right. You were out for quite a while—but you know what, I trust you. I thought you needed to be out."

"Naw, sometimes I had to use the bathroom, but sometimes I was just walking around in the halls. One time, I even went outside and walked around."

"Keep your cool," I thought. "Remember, you have to figure out a way to make the whole thing—Derrick's game plan—backfire." I decided to use the old 'honesty is the best policy' routine once more.

"Well, Derrick, I must thank you again for being up-front with me. I really appreciate that you have been honest about what you did. You know, some students would not be truthful in the way that you have been. Now, I want you to understand that if this happens again, you are going to lose the privilege of going out of the class to use the bathroom or get a drink of water without permission. I hope you understand this."

Not giving him the opportunity to respond, I made a shushing gesture with my hand and told him to prepare for the next lesson.

After I spoke, Derrick stared at me with a puzzled look on his face. "Ah-hah! My little strategy is working," I thought. He didn't know what to think of me. He anticipated that I would start yelling and screaming at him and send him to the office—just as all his other teachers had done. When I chose something positive about the situation, he did not know what to think or say. He just stared at me for an instant without the air of confidence and control that I had observed earlier. Once more, I was hopeful. Maybe this approach would work.

For the next month, things did go rather smoothly. Oh, there were several times when Derrick decided to show off or create a disturbance, but I continued to remain calm throughout. I was trying hard to let him know that I was not going to give in to his desire to make me "lose it" in the classroom. For a month, though he had his little outbursts, he never won. Occasionally, he beat on his desk with a pencil, rattled papers, made animal noises, and burped loudly, but these episodes started to occur less and less frequently. Once again, proximity control and signaling were all that it took to get him back on track.

The fact that my other students were just the best kids that any teacher could ever hope to have also helped the situation. Whenever Derrick was absent or out of the room, I would talk to them about ignoring inappropriate behaviors. We would even practice how to respond when he left the room and reentered after a long period of time or reentered after I had had to take him outside of the classroom for what I called a teacher–student interaction.

Things were going great, and just when I thought we were out of the woods, Derrick decided to try a new tactic. I came to the conclusion that he could not be satisfied if we were functioning in a state of equilibrium. The child liked excitement and adventure in his life. So, since he couldn't coerce me into a standoff in the classroom, he started to terrorize the other students.

Once, he decided to get his kicks by ripping up his classmates' spelling papers. Literally, before I could get to him, he got up and proceeded to rip the papers of all the students in his row. The poor kids didn't say a word. They were angry and frightened. As quickly as I could, I got over to Derrick and told him to stop—that his behavior was inappropriate. He looked directly at me and laughed, but he stopped tearing the papers. Then I asked him to step outside so that we could have our little interaction. By now the others knew that when I had to do this, they were to continue working quietly. Anyway, I had to do this because I didn't want to embarrass this kid or set him off in front of the other students. So, we stepped outside the door of my classroom and talked. As usual, I talked to him about his inappropriate behavior and described to him what he should have been doing. Then I described his punishment. He would have to apologize to the students and stay after school to tape the ripped papers back together. It worked pretty well.

When we reentered the classroom, the other students didn't say a word. They didn't even look up, but continued to concentrate on their work until I announced that Derrick had something to say. They accepted his apology and went right back to their assignments, just the way we had practiced. What a wonderful class! They were with me all the way on this one. In times to come, I realized that I couldn't have handled Derrick without them. They were truly a great bunch!

Sometimes during our discussions when Derrick was out of the room, they would ask me what they were supposed to do when he took one of their pencils and broke it or what to do if he ever hit one of them. I told them that I watched Derrick as closely as possible and that I would continue to intervene when I saw him do something inappropriate. If he did something that I was unaware of, I told them to get to me and let me know. We continued to practice ignoring skills when he decided to have his uncontrollable hiccups or burping spells. I explained that Derrick had gotten the attention of everyone else by doing things that were not acceptable to others. If we could ignore those behaviors and try to look at the good things that he did and tell him about it, then maybe he would change.

Because Derrick never hit one of the students, their fear of him began to wane and eventually, if he worked well in a cooperative learning group or if I made a big deal out of some good work that he'd completed, they praised him just as they praised anyone else in the class.

Finally, Derrick started to take to this special treatment. By Christmas, the frequency of his outbursts in the classroom had decreased drastically. The students were more comfortable with him, and they really wanted to see him make it in our class. Things were much better within the confines of our classroom, but . . . well, . . . outside the classroom Derrick continued to seek ways to satisfy his insatiable need for calamity. Still, I felt that his improved behavior in the classroom was a giant step in the right direction.

It was just about time for Christmas break, and I was really feeling good about Derrick. I thought we might end the first half of the year on a pleasant note, but Derrick decided otherwise. One day I saw him get up quietly, get the bathroom pass, and leave the room to go to the bathroom. From the corner of my eye, I could see that he had been working nicely, and he appeared to be working at a steady pace. I was simply thrilled! Even his academic work had improved a great deal. It just so happened that on this day there was an overflow in the first floor boys' bathroom, and the custodian blocked the doorway so that he could clean up the mess. Apparently, Derrick decided to proceed to the second floor bathroom. The rest of the story is a nightmare. I looked at the clock and realized that Derrick had been out of the room for about 15 minutes.

"That's strange," I thought. "He hasn't done this in weeks." I started to get a little worried, so I sent another student, Andre, to the restroom to find him. In a few minutes, Andre rushed in to tell me that Derrick was upstairs and was holding up Mr. Douglas, the assistant principal, in the bathroom. Later, Mr. Douglas related that he had seen Derrick wandering around upstairs, so he had asked him what he was doing there. He reported that Derrick walked up to him with a crazed look in his eyes and shouted at him repeatedly, "You must want to die today, huh?" Mr. Douglas was frightened at this point, and he ran into the bathroom and closed the door. After hearing calls for help, one of the fourth-grade teachers sent for Greg, and he arrived upstairs with the custodian within minutes. The three men physically took Derrick to the office. This was two days before Christmas break. Derrick was suspended from school until after the holidays.

When we returned to school in January, the placement team went into high gear to get Derrick evaluated for special education. Near the end of January, Derrick was identified as having a behavioral disorder, and the team recommended—because of his size and because we did not have such a class in our school—that Derrick be sent to the nearby middle school. This really bothered me. All things considered, I thought we were doing pretty well. In spite of acting out, leaving the room, and the incident with the assistant principal, we'd had no major catastrophes. Nothing happened that I hadn't been able to handle within the classroom single-handedly. I thought that Derrick was on the road to existing in a classroom without feeling he had to be in total control of the teacher and the other students. I tried to convince Greg and the team to give us more time, but there was no way that I could change their minds.

And so Derrick's mother brought him to get his things, and I gave him a pad and pencil set as a going away present. I told him that the kids and I would miss him and that the class wouldn't be the same without him. He began to sob uncontrollably, and he just kept telling me over and over again that he didn't want to leave. All I could do was hold him until his mother pulled him away and led him out of the classroom. I couldn't move. I was drained. I was devastated. We had worked so hard, and we were making progress. Now, it seemed that all of our efforts had been in vain.

We failed Derrick Yates. He went to the middle school program and within two weeks was expelled for cursing his teacher. Shortly after that, he was admitted to the local mental hospital, where he's been for the last month.

What You Don't Know Can Hurt You!

JOHN MCCULLUM

When John, a student teacher, thought about his seventh-period class, his breathing became shallow and a radiating knot of anxiety formed in his stomach. This class, the only one that proved to be troublesome for him, consisted of 15 eighth-grade students—seven very high-achieving students and eight who performed considerably lower academically. Of these eight, five talked, laughed, and attempted to dominate the class and him throughout the period. Although John had managed to cope with these problems on a more or less passable basis, doing so had taken a great deal of energy. John had a difficult time concentrating on his lesson delivery as he was constantly distracted by the students who seemed to want to set up a situation in which either he or they won control of the class. He braced himself daily to confront this group. He thought he was familiar with the problems and potential pitfalls in this class. But John was soon to learn that it is easier to fall prey to the dangers of the unexpected and that they often hold the most dire consequences. He was to learn this lesson from a usually quiet student in this seventh-period class.

One afternoon, John planned to conduct a test review in the form of a quiz-show game. On this particular day, his supervising teacher was absent and a substitute teacher was in his place. The supervising teacher seldom if ever attended class, so this day was much like any other for John. He was accustomed to having complete freedom to plan for and instruct this class as he deemed best. Because he was given this autonomy, he chose to take a different approach with the class than that of the supervising teacher. The supervising teacher had usually given the students individual written assignments to complete, and he used very little direct instruction or group work approaches with them. John felt that it was important to use a variety of instructional techniques for these students.

After directing the students to form groups of their choice, he began the game with the expectation that although the class would be rowdy, the game would prove to be an enjoyable and effective review technique. Very little time had elapsed before John realized that the students had selected themselves into groups along racial and academic achievement lines. Six high-achieving white students formed two groups of three each. Only one black female was a high achiever. Of the low-achieving students, seven were black and one was a white male. These remaining nine students formed three groups of three each. John knew that the white students also came from upper-middle-class neighborhoods, whereas the other students came from relatively poor homes. Although he was aware of these factors, he was yet to appreciate the potential volatility of the situation.

When an argument erupted between one of the students from a high-achieving group (Chris) and one of the low-achieving students (Richard), John immediately rose and stepped between them. Ignoring the obscenities being exchanged, John moved quickly to separate them because they had already begun pushing and shoving each other. After separating the students, he was able to recommence the game, which continued more or less successfully until the end of the class period. As the class was dismissed, however, the two students resumed their hostile exchange at the door.

Again, John moved to intervene, calling both students back to the classroom. Only Chris complied. Richard ran down the corridor and turned the corner. Because Chris did not start the argument and because John thought that it would have been fruitless to discuss the issue with only one of the students involved, he released Chris to go home.

In the empty classroom, John reflected on the incident. Despite Richard's academic difficulties, he had not been, up to this point, a behavioral problem in class. In fact, John knew very little about him beyond the fact that he was an academically weak student and had been retained several times. Consequently, Richard was much older and larger than his classmates. John felt that he should not allow Richard's flagrant disobedience to go unaddressed. He decided to go looking for Richard. Finding Richard at the bike rack just outside the building, he approached him and said that he wanted to talk. Richard responded by jumping on his bike and stating, "I don't got time for this," as he rode away. John, stinging with indignation, immediately went to the office and submitted a disciplinary referral.

Upon Richard's arrival at school the following morning, John presented him with the referral notice and walked with him to the office for a conference with the vice principal. On the way, John explained that the referral meant an automatically assigned afternoon detention period in his classroom for refusing to stop when he called. Less than half an hour later, John went to the office to complete some copying and noticed Richard still waiting outside the office for his conference with the vice principal. As he went about his chore, Richard began to make comments in a somewhat staged whisper to the student next to him. These comments amounted to threats directed toward John, such as, "I'm going to break his jaw." At this point, John decided to ignore the remarks.

As he was leaving, he once again encountered Richard, who had gone to the hallway water fountain. John glanced at him as he walked by, and Richard retorted sharply, "Don't be looking at me, boy." John was becoming increasingly angered by Richard's exhibition in front of another student. Although he thought it best to ignore the remarks, he wheeled around and faced Richard. Taking a deep breath to catch himself, he slowly hissed through clenched teeth, "Go in, sit down, and don't make anything worse for yourself. Just sit down and shut up and wait for Mr. Roberts to see you." After mumbling a few unintelligible remarks, Richard complied.

Although Mr. Roberts had agreed to keep Richard in in-school suspension (ISS) rather than sending him to John's class that afternoon, Richard showed up in class. Obviously, Mr. Roberts had bungled the ISS schedule somehow, and now John had to deal with Richard in spite of the tensions created by the situation. Fortunately, Richard remained quiet and low-key throughout class.

When John reminded him of the detention that afternoon, Richard declared that he had to catch his bus or he would have no way home. Doubting that this was the case, John told Richard that he could go home as long as he made arrangements to stay the following day. He also warned him that failure to do so would result in a re-referral and possible suspension.

John's difficulty with Richard escalated the next day during the suspension period. Ironically, John had not seen Richard in class because he had been kept in ISS. He couldn't help feeling a little resentful that Mr. Roberts had failed to keep Richard the day before and then kept him when it no longer mattered. At least, he thought, they could give me a little support downstairs. How hard could it be, after all, to keep a simple ISS schedule straight?

Upon arrival for his afternoon detention, Richard announced, "The only reason I'm staying this detention is because Mr. Roberts said I had to." When John attempted to explain to him exactly why he was given detention, Richard's behavior became erratic. A sickening knot formed in John's stomach as he realized that he was losing control of the situation.

Because Richard refused to be seated and walked around the room striking the computer, walls, desks, and other objects with a yardstick, John was forced to ask the students who had remained after school to complete a project to go to the library. John told him several times to be seated and tried to explain to him why he had gotten the referral. Each time, Richard retorted, "How come Chris didn't get a referral?" John attempted to explain several more times that the referral was not given for fighting, but for running away and refusing to return. Several times during John's explanations, Richard covered his ears and began singing a rap tune. With each explanation, he repeated the same refrain, "How come Chris didn't get a referral?"

Soon, Richard began performing a rap song with graphic lyrics that detailed his plan to beat up Chris. Several times he told John that he was going downstairs to tell the vice principal that "you were trying to beat me up, that you were trying to hit me with the yardstick, and that you were trying to slit my throat." He called John "stupid" and "peanut-head," declared that he hated him, and asked him why he didn't go back to the university. John began to sense that the differences in race and backgrounds had something to do with the animosity he was receiving from Richard.

At intervals, Richard pulled a small bottle from his jacket pocket and drank from it. The contents looked like water, but he called it his "beer" and "wine." Twice during this period, Richard wandered outside of the classroom. Both times, John followed him, reminding him that during detention he must stay in the room. When Richard decided to return to the classroom, he preceded John inside, pulled the door closed, and held it so that John could not get in.

Once inside the classroom, John attempted to get some work done, but Richard's singing was too loud for him to concentrate. When John delivered a stern look in his direction, Richard leaped from his chair and confronted him. "You staring at me? Don't be looking at me. Have you got a problem?" Implicit in this confrontation was a physical threat. John sensed that Richard was soliciting a fight. His pulse quickened and, much to his chagrin, John found himself sizing up Richard's physical bearing, comparing it to his own, inch by inch, pound by pound.

At that moment, John saw a student walking down the hall. Slipping out of the room, he asked the student to get the teacher next door. The teacher, who happened to be Richard's English teacher, was quick to grasp the situation. Stepping inside the classroom, she ordered him in a stern tone of voice to sit down. Richard retaliated with several sharp remarks. It was clear that he was ready to take her on as well. Realizing this, she went downstairs to the vice principal, who told her to release Richard from detention.

Before he released Richard, John told him that he intended to report his behavior and to re-refer him. Initially, Richard refused to leave until he had completed his detention because he thought that John would not be able to re-refer him if he stayed for the duration of the period. Finally, John told him that he could stay if he wanted, but he would still get re-referred. Richard insisted on remaining for the entire period.

John left school that afternoon with an abysmal sense of failure. He mentally reviewed the events leading up to this afternoon like a bad song that he could not get off his mind.

Two days later, during a discussion with the English teacher and a special education teacher, he discovered that Richard had been attending classes for students with behavioral disorders for the past two years. Still, Richard had not been a problem before during this class, and John blamed his own ineptness for creating the situation. If only he hadn't . . .

What's Inclusion Got to Do with It?

ANITA ATKINSON

Anita Atkinson walked from her third-period U.S. history class in a daze. "I've been teaching for 27 years," she thought, "twenty-seven years and I've never had a class of students who are so needy. I don't know, maybe I'm just getting too old for this. Maybe it's just time for me to retire."

There were so many changes at McGinnis High School this year, all in the name of educational reform and improved outcomes for students. Anita's classroom was no longer in the main building, but in a mobile unit. She and her students had been displaced to make room for a computer lab. Most of her students returned to McGinnis from early morning classes at the county's vocational and technical center, and they were finding it difficult to get from the building to her class on time. She frequently found herself interrupting lessons to check in tardy students and redo her attendance sheets.

For the first time in 20 years, the school administrators had abolished ability grouping. The district superintendent's cry for higher standards was now trickling down to the school and classroom level. "We have to become more competitive with other developed nations," Anita had heard her principal say time and time again at faculty meetings. "All students need to be exposed to a more rigorous and comprehensive curriculum." So now all students were placed without consideration of their achievement levels. Well, almost all students. The classes for average to above-average and advanced placement students were now combined; however, X-level classes were maintained for students who were functioning below grade level. Anita's class, for example, was supposed to be an inclusion classroom where students with disabilities were main-streamed with nonlabeled students. For the past three years, special education teachers had been assigned to co-teach with general education teachers who had large numbers of students with disabilities enrolled in their classes. This year, Anita was assigned to work with Jennifer, a second-year teacher of students with behavioral disorders.

Anita made her way to a study room in the library for her planning period. She had every intention of planning for next week's lessons, but she couldn't get her mind off her motley crew. She made it to the study room, closed the door, and just sat, reflecting about her students and what had just transpired in her class. In her mind's eye, she pictured her students sitting in their assigned seats at the beginning of class. Before her sat 20 students—15 males and 5 females, 16 white and 4 black. Most were from low-income families. Of the male students, 10 were labeled as having learning disabilities, and 2 were diagnosed as BD (behaviorally disordered). All 5 female students and 1 male student were labeled as at-risk for dropping out of school. "What a bunch," she said aloud as she opened her NEA tote bag and pulled out her planner, teacher's manual, and supplementary materials for the Revolutionary War. She ran down the list of her most needy students.

Floyd, a 19-year-old white male, was severely learning disabled. Anita couldn't remember when she had worked with another student as low-functioning as Floyd. He was basically a nonreader who required someone to read everything for him. He hated writing anything because of his poor writing skills. The school psychologist told her at the beginning of the year that Floyd had a very low IQ and had come very close to being placed in a class for the mentally retarded.

Greg, an 18-year-old African American student, was bright but unmotivated. He had failed every class for the marking period and was chronically absent from school. He was either sound asleep or on top of things, contributing intelligently to class discussions. Unfortunately, he worked a 3:00 to 11:00 shift at Mr. Joe's Sub Shop down the street and always complained of not getting enough rest. He could've made it in one of the heterogeneous sections, but he'd opted to remain in X-level.

Kendell, another African American student, had a severe learning disability. He read at the second-grade level, was chronically absent from school, and was just barely passing. Kendell had one thing going for him, though. He was a star on the football team, so every marking period he managed to get grades high enough to keep him on the squad. He wasn't concerned about passing the competency exam, earning a high school diploma, or playing football in college. "Um just coasting, Mrs. A.," he told Anita once when she was pushing him to try harder. "I can't read, can't write, ain't nobody gonna accept me into no college. Umma just be satisfied with my certificate of attendance."

Mitch, a 17-year-old white male, was diagnosed with a behavioral disorder. Mitch had a lot of potential, but he was always getting into trouble with the law. At the end of one class, he had come up to Anita and volunteered: "Mrs. A., I might not be here next year. This might be my last day. I haven't told anybody else, but I got in trouble again, and the judge said if I got in trouble again, I was a goner. I was driving without a license and got caught." Prior to this incident, Mitch had gotten busted on school property for selling drugs.

Thinking about these and other students, Anita wondered how she was supposed to get them interested in U.S. history when many of them were just trying to survive from one day to the next. Was she kidding herself, or what?

Anita awoke from her daydream but jumped right back into it as her mind switched to another problem—working with Jennifer, her special education co-teacher. At the beginning of the year, Jennifer had asked if she could co-teach with Anita, as her behaviorally disordered (BD) students and several learning disabled (LD) students had been placed in Anita's so-called inclusion classroom. Anita had been involved in a very successful and mutually satisfying relationship with Carol—another special education teacher—two years before, so she was thrilled when Jennifer requested to work with her. She missed having that extra pair of hands to deal with all the unique needs present in her classroom.

Unfortunately, though, things hadn't gone as smoothly with Jennifer as they had gone with Carol. "It's just not the same," Anita told Carol one night during a telephone conversation. "You and I talked, we shared, we planned together on a regular basis. You were always in my room on time, and you were always willing to modify worksheets, group assignments, tests, and stuff like that. You got all those kids on track when it came to being organized. You did more than just walk around and keep them awake and on task. It was like a 50/50 split, a 50/50 partnership. But this one . . . Well, I don't know, she just doesn't take the lead, and even when I ask her to do something, she doesn't follow through. Now she's missing at least two to three days a week from my class even though I have two of her BD students. It won't surprise me if by the end of the year she's not coming at all."

Anita was startled by the sound of sledgehammers and bulldozers outside the library. A crew of construction workers were building a new addition to the library that would be equipped with state-of-the-art instructional technology. She smiled as she thought about the messiness that accompanies new construction and compared it to the messiness of school reform. "I've seen the pendulum swing from one end of the spectrum to the other so many times over the past 27 years," she thought as she bit into a big, red, juicy apple. "I've always managed to survive the changes and even grow as a result of them. But this time, for some reason, I can't see my way through the messiness. What will be the end result? When it's all said and done, what difference will it all make?"

Anita now turned her attention to what had transpired in class today. If she concentrated, maybe she could come up with some problem-solving strategies that might help her reach the kids and deal more effectively with Jennifer. Her mind raced back to the beginning of class. It was 10:27, and the tardy bell had just sounded. Jennifer was nowhere to be found. She was supposed to have constructed a study guide for the mid-term exam and begin going over it in class. Anticipating a no–show, Anita had developed the study guide herself and was preparing to review with the students.

Jennifer burst through the door at 10:35, apologizing that she was late and hadn't done the guide because she'd had to call several parents to arrange IEPs for newly labeled BD students. Anita couldn't believe her ears. "Carol would never have done this," she thought. "I would never have done this. I would've been here at 5:00 in the morning or called after school or at night." Still, she wasn't one to make waves, so she maintained her composure and acted as if Jennifer's tardiness hadn't fazed her.

"That's okay, hon," Anita replied. She wanted to kick herself for not telling Jennifer what she was really thinking. "I already did the study guide, and now I'm going to put them in cooperative learning groups and have them search for the answers to the questions. You can help me monitor them and make sure they're finding the correct answers." She handed Jennifer a copy of the study guide with the correct answers written in red ink.

"Cool," Jennifer responded, impressed by the organization of the guide. "Wow! This is a really neat study guide with page numbers where they can find the answers!

And I see you divided stuff up so they won't have such a large bank of words to choose from for the fill-in-the-blank questions."

"Oh, I learned that from my other co-teacher a couple of years ago. Yeah, it really helps the kids stay focused and makes them feel like they don't have so much to do at one time. They can break it down into chunks." Anita stopped talking, thinking to herself, "Duh, Jennifer, it would be nice if you would do something like this every once in a while!"

They then quickly got the students into five groups of four students. Unfortunately, the students weren't interested in completing the sheet even though it would help them prepare for their midterm exam. Anita had just attended a workshop on cooperative learning and had spent last week talking to students about how it works. Today, she'd started out by videotaping the cooperative learning groups so students could assess the quality of their teamwork and performance. Around 10:38, Jennifer approached a group that wasn't working and urged them to complete the assignment. As Anita walked around videotaping, she discovered that only one group was following instructions. Disappointed, she turned off the camcorder, put it away, and tried to come up with a way to get the students on task.

"I'll give three points extra on the exam to the group that gets the right answer to the first three questions on the study guide," she called out, thinking that this announcement might spark some enthusiasm. Unfortunately, there were no takers. At this point, spitballs were flying, attackers were being cursed by the attacked, and no one seemed to care that the midterm exam was next Wednesday.

At 10:42, Anita was experiencing serious stress. She decided to refocus, to try another approach. She called "time" and told the students to prepare for a whole-class activity. "Yeah, that's it," she speculated silently. "Maybe I can get more out of them if I pull everyone together in one large group." She called on students from each group and asked for answers to the questions. Jennifer was standing next to her at the front of the room, looking on in silence.

As Anita continued her reflection, she still couldn't believe what had gone down in her class-room. She'd lost all control. All around her, students were engrossed in private conversations. Kendell threw a spitball at Lakeesha from across the room. Lakeesha turned around in her seat, looked Kendell in the eye, spotted a smirk on his face, and shouted, "Go to hell!" as loud as she could. Needless to say, no one responded to Anita's question about the Revolutionary War.

In desperation, Anita had shouted out to the class. "Now wait just a minute! I'm not going to stand here and try to talk when everyone else is talking, so knock it off right now!" She was furious, and the students knew it. Jennifer continued to stand beside her with a blank look on her face.

The students sensed Anita's anger and decided to comply with her demand for their undivided attention, at least for a few minutes. Anita asked her question again, and a few students raised their hands and answered correctly. Some of them even seemed a little interested in the discussion about events that led up to the Revolutionary War. After several students responded correctly to questions on the guide, Anita attempted a discussion about excise taxes, but noticed she was once again losing the students. At this point, Jennifer must have noticed her frustration, for she walked around the room awakening sleeping students, breaking up private conversations, and telling students to raise their hands if they wanted to speak.

Anita called on Kendell to answer a question, trying to get his mind off harassing Lakeesha. "Kendell, can you give us an example of how the colonists protested the excise taxes placed on them by England?"

All eyes were now on Kendell, and he saw this as an opportunity to disrupt the class further. With that infamous smirk on his face, he responded, "This is what happened when those colony guys threw a bunch of whiskey in the ocean and everybody got drunk and had a big PARTAY. Even the fish!" The class broke up in laughter. Students were holding their stomachs. "I'm through, I'm finished!" screamed Lakeesha. Floyd reached over and gave Kendell a high five. Anita looked at Jennifer and saw the tiniest of smiles on her face.

Anita was at her wit's end. "You know, Kendell, you're really getting on my nerves. Now, what did you tell me just yesterday when I asked you to stop goofing off and get serious about school?"

No response.

"I want an answer from you now, Kendell!"

In a terse and apathetic tone, Kendell uttered, "Sorry, teach, that's the way I am. When I work, I work. When I don't, I don't."

"Well, you need to work, then; get in your working mood. You need to get it together so you can stay on the football team."

This statement jolted Kendell into reality. He sat up in his seat, thumbing through the pages in the book to find the answer. "Okay, okay," he responded. He found a picture depicting the Boston Tea Party and tried to read the caption underneath it. "This is a . . . um . . . this is a um. Damn! Mrs. A., you know I can't read this crap!" Several students giggled and teased Kendell because he couldn't read such a simple sentence. Floyd proceeded to imitate Kendell's attempt to read the caption, being careful to capture the puzzled and frustrated look on his face. Kendell was furious.

"If I was you, I wouldn't be makin' fun of nobody's readin', boy, cause you can't even read 'I see the cat.' You need to shut up before I come over there and bust you in yo mouth!"

"Come on, then. I ain't scared of you just cause you the big man on the football team. Come on over here and try to bust me in my mouth and see what you get."

The bell rang, ending the period just as the two boys were rising from their seats to attack each other. Anita quickly told the rest of the students to go to their fourth-period classes, and she and Jennifer escorted Floyd and Kendell to the office. "Yes, there is a God," Anita thought as she realized that the bell had saved her from having to deal with a fight.

When the bell rang signaling the start of fifth period, Anita still had not thought of solutions, no answers to her questions. She packed her tote bag and headed for her class full of above-average and advanced placement (AP) students. Right now, she had to shift gears and think about the planning for the reenactment of the Yorktown surrender with this talented group. She would grapple with the messiness of inclusion later. She needed help desperately, but she didn't know where to turn.

When Secrets Disable

CATHY SCHROCK

I never thought I would see Kate Morrissey sitting with a group of girls and boys laughing and talking. The change in her had been remarkable. In a little more than a year, she had gone from a sullen, introverted, unpopular fifth-grader to just another good kid.

Looking back, I remember thinking how confident I was starting the school year. I had been teaching for two years, I still loved teaching despite the long hours it demanded, and I had handled several difficult situations successfully since I left college—I was ready for anything, or so I thought. I looked at my roster of new students and wondered what surprises would be in store this year. In the first two years there had been challenges, but so far none that I couldn't handle. Had I known what was ahead, I probably would have taken a leave of absence. This class would require strength and energy I didn't even know I possessed.

It started with a note from the resource teacher telling me the names of the six students with learning disabilities who would be in my room. Our school had been using an inclusive model for resource help for several years now, so I knew I would have these students in my room most of the day. This didn't bother me because I had been successful in the past working with students who had both behavioral and academic problems.

I decided to read the green files before meeting the students, so I could make preparations for their arrival. I made a list that included students' names and disabilities. Most of them were having difficulties with reading and math. A couple had behavioral problems as well as academic problems, but still I thought I could handle these issues with help from the special education teacher. I must admit I did become concerned when I discovered that one of the students had severe emotional disturbances and had been violent in the past—punching a hole in the wall, breaking a window with his fist, and dislocating the principal's shoulder. It was definitely going to be an interesting year!

After school began, I noticed there were many student issues I had not expected—two students were identified for the gifted program, one student had been diagnosed with ADHD but was not on medication, one student had behavioral problems stemming from sexual abuse, another student's mother was terminally ill, and then there was Kate. With everything else I had to do, how would I ever find the patience to deal with the tantrums, screaming, stubbornness, and neediness of Kate? I knew teachers were supposed to be able to do it all, but this seemed overwhelming.

I had never run across a child like Kate. I knew from the moment I met her that she was incredibly bright. Unfortunately, her appearance and behavior put people off so quickly that most never took the time to get to know the "real" Kate. There may be more diplomatic ways to say it, but she was dirty, "smelled like a dog" (as a fellow student described her), and was totally unsociable. She always had her nose in a book—at lunch, at recess, and any time there was a break from structured activities in the classroom. I had to hand it to the other kids in class—they didn't tease; not much, anyway. Some of the children I had known through the years would have been unmerciful. Most of the students in the room ignored her. There was little interaction between Kate and the rest of the class.

It was obvious that Kate loved to read, but still I was somewhat surprised by her score on the reading assessment—her instructional level was seventh grade. Her spelling inventory, however, showed she was a level-one speller. The disparity was stunning. Any kind of writing, even the unstructured variety in her journal, was extremely frustrating for her. Every Monday morning I had a battle with Kate when it was time for word study. The task was to use each word from the word list in a sentence. She hated to write. She would whine and mope, and often when I insisted she do the work, she became belligerent—she simply refused to write. The other children observed these episodes, of course, and sometimes they were frightened by Kate's actions. On more than one occasion Kate screamed at me and pushed her book off the desk.

"Okay, Kate, take your word study journal out of your desk and begin your sentences for this week," I said one morning. Kate just sat there staring defiantly at the floor. "Kate, it is time to start." Kate blurted, "I'm not going to do it, and you can't make me."

The mornings I could not cajole Kate into participating, I would give her a choice of going to time-out in the room to do her work or going to the office. Once, when Kate chose not to work or go to time-out, I called the office and asked the assistant principal to come to my room, which was actually a trailer outside the building. The assistant principal arrived and told Kate that she must go to the office to finish her work. Kate held on to her desk and would not move. I sensed that Kate was on the verge of an emotional explosion, so I had all of the other students line up to go to the library. Kate lined up too. As we walked to the library, the assistant principal followed the group. When we passed by the office, the assistant principal told Kate to go into the office, and Kate complied. I felt lucky that the strategy to get Kate to the office had worked without having a violent confrontation in our classroom.

Kate was puzzling. She could be so difficult. It was almost impossible to get her to do anything she didn't want to do. She would dig in her heels psychologically and simply refuse to cooperate. You could see her resistance in her posture. She folded her arms tight against her chest and looked off into space. What seemed totally incongruent and very surprising to me was Kate's sophisticated sense of humor. Early in the year she had begun to bring in cartoons from *The New Yorker* and show them to me. The two of us would howl as we read them. The other fifth-graders looked on in confusion, trying to understand what was so funny.

When I met Kate's mother and her mother's boyfriend at Back-to-School night, I didn't form much of an impression for good or ill. Her mother looked fairly plain. "Please tell me, Ms. Morrissey, do you work in the home or outside?" I asked. She replied, "I recently completed my master's degree in social work. I am a caseworker for the county social services department." Apparently she put in long hours, because she did not spend much time at home. "I'm glad to be finished with the long, frequent drives to night school. For several years I have been unable to spend much time with Kate in the evenings. I gave her so much independence in those days that now she resents it when I tell her what to do." Ms. Morrissey's boyfriend was a little rough around the edges—short, chubby, a couple of days' growth of beard, and remarkably odoriferous. He wore a hunter's cap and his shirt and pants had the kind of gray cast that my family's clothes get when I use cheap detergent. What little he said was virtually inaudible, because he mumbled.

Ms. Morrissey asked some good questions about Kate. She expressed some concerns about her friendships, or lack of them. When I broached the topic of Kate's uncompleted homework assignments, Ms. Morrissey remarked, "That is Kate's responsibility. She knows what she is supposed to do. If I make suggestions she either acts as if I'm not there or refuses to do it." I also summoned up my courage to tell Ms. Morrissey about Kate's body odor. Her response was essentially the same: "That's her job too. She knows she is supposed to bathe every night. When I tell her to shower, she usually responds by throwing a tantrum that may last as long as half an hour."

Time might have passed with only minor rough spots in our classroom had I not decided to visit Kate's home. That visit set us up for what turned out to be a tense, troubling, and fairly long-lasting confrontation. It was in February after I had developed what I believed was a mutually caring relationship with Kate, even though I was beginning to discover that Kate was tight-lipped, even secretive, about her life outside of school.

I was becoming increasingly concerned because Kate had confided reluctantly that frequently nobody came home until 11:00 or 12:00 at night. Many nights, she was in the trailer-home all by herself, except for Sandy, her pet rat, and Rover, her beloved dog. She boasted that she could take care of herself and was not afraid, even though her trailer was in an isolated area. On these nights she fixed macaroni and cheese and treated herself with bags of Oreos—in fact, her reliance on sweets had begun to be apparent. She also told me about how messy things were at her house. She seemed quite pained to tell me these things. Kate would say things like, "You wouldn't believe what a mess my house is. You wouldn't want to come to my house."

When I looked back over my own journal, I realized that I had actually been building a case for making a home visit. Or, more accurately, my letters to myself seemed to compel me to visit Kate and her mother in their home. The opportunity for making a home visit fell into my lap when Kate sneaked her pet rat to school on the bus. Students are not allowed to have animals on the bus, so that evening I offered to give Kate a ride home and to take Sandy the Rat with us. In fear of what I might find, I invited the assistant principal to go with us.

When we arrived at the house, I discovered there was good reason to be concerned. The trailer was down a long, bumpy driveway, nowhere near any other houses. The trailer was old, the front steps sagged, and the storm door, hanging from its hinges, had a broken pane. The yard looked like the local junkyard and included an old refrigerator that had been used for target practice. But the worst was yet to come. Inside, half of the living room was piled from floor to ceiling with trash. A spot had been cleared on the couch just large enough for Kate to sit and watch television. I could see how Kate might be overwhelmed by the enormity of the task of cleaning up the mess.

Kate had been assigned a Big Sister through a program at the university. Ms. Morrissey had told Kate that she couldn't see her Big Sister until the house had been cleaned. With the three of us working together—Kate, the assistant principal, and I—I figured we could at least take care of Kate's room. It didn't take long to discover that it wasn't possible. Her room was covered with trash, books were on the floor, all of her clothes were scattered around the room—not one piece of clothing was in her closet. We started to pick up the trash, but soon stopped when I picked up a book and found dog feces on it. I looked down and realized I was standing in dog poop! Kate was right. The problem was just too big.

All of this happened on a Friday. I did not see her until the following Monday. When Kate arrived at school she was very angry with me. She gave me the cold shoulder. "Hi, Kate!" I said as she walked in the door headed toward her desk. Kate did not respond.

I should have known not to press her, but she had made me angry too—she had been rude all morning. Once again, it was time to collect the sentences for word study. Kate would not hand in her notebook. I gave her an ultimatum and told her she must hand it in now. She looked at me and yelled, "This is my book. You can't have it. This is all your fault!" She threw the book at me, continued screaming, and started tipping over desks.

It took both the assistant principal and me to calm Kate. When she finally settled down, I was so emotionally exhausted that I could have walked out the door and never returned. Following the confrontation, the assistant principal and I agreed that what we needed was an all-out program to bring Kate into the mainstream of life in school, and somehow this effort had to include her mother. We had the will, and we hoped we had the energy, but what we didn't have was a strategy.

Where to Now?

CONNIE BALLARD

Connie had always been a diligent student, and her commitment to academic success was very strong. At the beginning of her college career she had decided she could best serve her future students and teaching career by obtaining both an elementary education teaching degree and a special education license to teach students with emotional and behavioral problems. She wasn't daunted by the extra year's worth of coursework the extra license entailed. Now, close to graduation, Connie knew that she had made the right decision. Not only had she been consistently named to the dean's list, but she had even managed to take a few extra electives in areas she thought might someday be helpful in her own classroom.

With the end of her college preparation now clearly in sight, Connie enjoyed another sense of accomplishment knowing that she would not begin her first teaching job deeply in debt, as was the case with many of her friends. From her first year at McNair State University, she had worked in a busy branch of Smith's Discount World, a large regional store whose merchandise included clothing, sports equipment, household goods, and furniture. She smiled as she remembered her first few hectic days at Smith's—trying to learn her work routine as quickly as possible, making mistakes that sometimes embarrassed her, all the while doing her best to balance her work with her equally weighty responsibility of being a college freshman.

Connie's efforts had all converged in substantial success. Her academic record reflected a 3.98 GPA, and at Smith's she had been promoted from a stocker to being in charge of the store's security detail. By late fall, Connie was looking forward to the end of her final year. She anticipated that she would continue excelling at her college courses and that her work at Smith's would result in a fine letter of recommendation. Connie was well liked by the six security personnel she directed. She was able to apply many of the collaborative techniques she had learned in her teacher preparation program in managing the workers. All in all, things were going very smoothly.

On the Saturday before the start of the spring semester, Connie went to work feeling especially buoyant and optimistic. Over the hectic Christmas season there had been relatively few security problems, and she had been voted one of the two Smith's employees of the year. She was also delighted that she had just received word of her assignment to a plum student teaching placement at Harrison Junior High, a school noted for its excellent services to students with emotional and behavioral problems.

The store was unusually busy, even for a Saturday afternoon. As usual, Connie had two of her security personnel, Steve and Nancy, walking the store floor while she attended to some paperwork. Connie had developed a plan that allowed each security employee to circulate through the entire store in just over an hour. Their task was to monitor the aisles for any signs of illegal activity, usually shoplifting. It was common knowledge that the store lost a substantial amount of money each year to shoplifters, and Connie's patrolling plan had proved remarkably effective. Since implementing her plan, shoplifting had fallen by almost 75 percent.

Connie remembered the time Steve had knocked at her office door and entered quickly.

"Connie, looks like we've nabbed a shoplifter. I passed her twice in the jewelry department after I saw her stuffing some merchandise into her coat pocket. I alerted Nancy when our security routes crossed, and she saw more of the same. I'm sure we've got it on the security videos, too."

Connie had dealt with this situation many times before. Most often, the culprit would confess to stealing the items and show them to her in short order. Jewelry was one of the most popular targets of shoplifters. If the thief was 18 or older, company policy dictated that the police be called and the suspect booked on suspicion of shoplifting. After making statements to the police, the matter was referred to court as a misdemeanor charge of theft. When the suspect was younger than 18, however, it was store policy to interview the culprit, obtain detailed identification information, warn that such behavior was legally prosecutable, and then contact a parent to remove the minor from the store. Second offenses by the same person were referred to the juvenile justice system.

"Okay, so, what do we have this time?" Connie inquired.

"Female, about 13 or 14, I'd say. She's in the waiting room with Nancy. She's denying that she took anything. All we've done so far is to ask her to accompany us to the waiting room."

"Okay, let's take a look," Connie sighed.

They walked into the small "waiting room" adjoining her office. Beside Nancy, a girl slouched in a chair—sullen, disheveled, and sporting bright pink and green hair, rows of earrings up both of her earlobes, and a large silver nose stud. Before Connie had a chance to speak, the girl interjected with a preemptive strike.

"I don't need this shit, man. This is, like, harassment, you assholes! Why don't you, like, get a life? All you do is pick on kids because we choose to look different instead of frigging nerds like you all . . ." Her voice got louder the more she spoke. She was clearly angry.

"Hi, we need to sort some things out . . ." Connie began.

"Screw you, bitch! I'll make sure YOU get sorted out!" came the reply.

"Hold on, no one's accusing you of anything, so just chill out so we can send you on your way, okay?" Connie kept her cool. The girl, still angry, hesitated.

Nancy played a supporting role. "Hey, c'mon, if there's nothing going on you'll be on your way in a minute."

Steve chimed in, "Sure, we're just doing our job, so . . ."

"You call this stinking treatment WORK? How piss-poor pathetic!" The girl turned her face to the wall and began kicking the side of her chair.

Connie tried again. "Let me tell you what happened. Nancy and Steve are security officers for the store. It's their job to walk around and make sure nothing illegal is happening. Most of the time it's pretty boring work. If they see anything happening that looks suspicious, they have to investigate."

"Oh, yeah, like, guilty until proven innocent, right? Are we, like, in a war? What are you gonna do? Take me out behind the store and shoot me before putting me in the dumpster? I don't need this crap."

"Easy, easy now," Steve said sympathetically, "There's no need to get this blown all out of proportion."

"Let's just start with your name," Connie suggested.

"Jenna."

"Jenna who?" Connie thought she'd made a good start.

"None of your goddamn business, that's who!"

Connie dodged that challenge. "Okay, Jenna, how old are you?"

"Two hundred and fifty-seven, slut—in fact it's my birthday today. I'm like, immortal, get it?"

"Well, I'd guess that you're about 13 or 14 . . ." Connie felt she knew how to deal with bluster. "So what if I am?"

"Well, we need to see some identification, or you can tell us who we can call."

"I'm Satan's wife, so go ask him—it's 1-800-GoToHell!" Hmmm, thought Connie, whoever Jenna is, she's getting pretty creative.

Nancy tried again. "Jenna, please . . . let's try to be reasonable about this. We just want to be sure you're not involved in something illegal here in the store. We think you lifted some jewelry and put it in your coat pocket . . ."

"See? I'm friggin' guilty! Here, string me up. I confess, I confess! Oh Lord, take thy wayward servant quietly to the stake! Send me to hell, O Lord!"

Exasperated, Jenna jumped from her chair with such force that it startled Connie. Jenna's sudden movement also ejected several boxes of jewelry out of her pocket and sent them clattering to the floor. The room was deathly quiet. Jenna, resigned to her fate, slumped in the chair, tightly folded her arms, and closed her eyes. Nancy retrieved the items from the floor. Along with the jewelry was Jenna's school ID card.

Nancy was matter-of-fact in summarizing what she found. "Okay . . . So, you're Jenna Morris. You're in the eighth grade, and you live at 324 River Course Drive. Here's your home phone number, too . . ."

"WHATEVER!" shouted Jenna.

Connie continued, "You understand that shoplifting is a crime, Jenna, I'm sure. Here's what's going to happen. Because you're under 18, and this seems to be your first offense, we'll let you off with a warning, but we'll keep your ID on record. That information will be kept private and confidential here in my office to protect you. However, if this ever happens again, we'll refer you to the juvenile authorities."

"SO F---ING WHAT? You think I can't screw them over as well? Geez, like, you don't know who you're dealing with, babe! I have a lot of connections, so watch out when you're driving down the street, like, know what I mean?"

Steve, Nancy, and Connie had heard this kind of thing before and were adept at ignoring such threats.

"I'll call your home right now for your mom or dad to come get you," Connie informed Jenna.

By the end of the shift, Connie had all but forgotten the incident. It was, unfortunately, one of many that blurred together quite quickly. Jenna's mother had come to pick her up, and all three employees were somewhat surprised that, unlike most parents, Jenna's mother seemed neither embarrassed nor angry, simply even more sullen than her daughter.

By the time Connie arrived at Harrison the following week, she was excited and ready to teach. This was her final student teaching experience, and she was elated, knowing that after this practicum the next students she would teach would be in her very own classroom. Gillian Frontera, the school secretary, walked her down the hall.

"I'm sure you'll love it here, Connie," Gillian told her. "These seventh- and eighth-graders are a tough bunch, but your supervising teacher, Martha Seeger, is excellent. She's been teaching emotionally and behaviorally disorders (EBD) kids for years and really does a good job. I'm sure you'll learn a lot from her."

Gillian opened the classroom door. Martha, just returning to her desk after checking students' work, smiled and came right over.

"Hi, you must be Connie. Welcome! Thanks, Gillian. I'll take Connie off your hands."

"Thanks, Martha. It's nice to meet you after only having spoken with you on the phone. I'm really looking forward to this."

"I'm sure it'll be fine, too!"

Connie admired Martha's energy and positive attitude. She looked around the room. Eight students were seated, two to a table.

"These are the seventh-graders. The eighth-graders will arrive after lunch," Martha informed Connie.

Connie spent the morning familiarizing herself with the classroom. She discovered where many teaching materials were stored, and, in snatches of time between lessons, Martha filled her in on the classroom routine, rules, and a host of other details that Connie tried to remember. Lunch was pleasant enough. Returning to the classroom with Martha, Connie was looking forward to meeting the eighth-graders.

As the eighth-graders arrived, Connie was preoccupied with some paperwork. She heard Martha giving rapid, clear instructions as the students got settled, but she was not prepared for what she saw when she looked up from her work. Seated in the front row, close to the door, was Jenna Morris. Connie caught her breath as a surge of adrenaline made her heart thump and her head throb. What would this mean? She quickly tried to determine whether Jenna recognized her. Connie hoped she looked quite different dressed for school than she did in her Smith's uniform.

"Class, this is our new student teacher, Connie Ballard," said Martha by way of introduction.

Connie smiled as best she could. Jenna's face grew increasingly cloudy. Ah, Connie thought, she remembers me.

The lesson passed quickly, and the eighth-graders were soon gone.

"Well, what did you think?" inquired Martha.

Connie knew she sounded much better than she felt, but she needed time to regroup and decide what, if anything, she should do about the fact that she knew something about Jenna and had interacted with her in another context.

"I think they'll be fine. I like teaching this age group, so I'm ready to jump in whenever you want me to."

"Okay, why don't you plan on teaching the eighth-graders tomorrow? They'll all be bringing work from their regular math class. Here's the teacher's manual. They're reviewing Chapter 9, so be sure to look over it tonight and be ready for them tomorrow."

That night, Connie didn't get much sleep. The next day, she caught herself trembling slightly as she waited for the eighth-graders to appear. Martha had already left the classroom to make some phone calls to parents. As the students approached the classroom, Connie could tell that Jenna was being very noisy and disruptive. Taking a deep breath, Connie began to assert her authority.

"All right, everyone, time to settle down before we get to work. Quietly, now, come on in and get out your math books. We have a lot of ground to cover."

The students filed in, Jenna last. As Jenna walked past Connie, she whispered, "Hey, it's Ms. Connie *Smith*, ain't it? Still working that loser's job?"

Connie did her best to ignore the remark and began giving instructions to the class. Everyone complied reasonably well—except Jenna. Flopping into her seat, she stretched apathetically and yawned. Looking directly at Connie, Jenna didn't wait a moment longer.

"Ooooohh, it's our loser student teacher! Hey, Ms. SMITH, whaddya gonna do to us?"

"I'm Ms. Ballard. Please address me by my last name," Connie said calmly but firmly.

"No it ain't, it's SMITH, get it guys? As in SMITH's Discount World over on 12th Avenue. This loser works over there. Whassa matter, you can't get no friggin' teaching job? Know what she does, guys? She's the store GESTAPO! I swear, goes around hasslin' little kids and being really nasty. It's a wonder anyone shops there! She tried to mess with me one time, but me and my mom took care of her sorry ass. Ain't that right, SMITHIE? Checked your car tires lately? How about your apartment? That dog of yours still alive and kicking?"

Connie hesitated. She knew that venting her rising fury was not going to be effective, but this was the first lesson of 15 weeks of student teaching . . .

Winnie

PATTY GRAY

8/27

Well, journal, it's my first day back at school. I'm beginning my second year of teaching, and I think that this time I'm in for a real treat. This year, I'll be teaching a group of "at-risk" first-graders. When my principal first asked me about this class, I wondered, "What in the world do you mean by 'at risk'?" I'd heard so many different definitions while I was in college. Well, as he explained the situation, it didn't take long for me to understand. The students I would have had been in our prekindergarten program, our kindergarten program, and most of them had been retained in first grade. My goodness! I had taught a class of average students last year. This year, most of my kids would be 8 years old in first grade. Mr. Brown (my principal), the reading specialist, and the Chapter 1 teacher decided that instead of using the standard phonetic reading program, I'd use a basal series that combined phonetic and whole-word approaches. I was also told that I should contact the consulting teacher at our school to find out about supplementary materials and behavior management techniques that I'd probably need.

9/1

Wow, it's Friday already. I haven't had time to do much writing. We've been running from one in-service program to the next all week long. Boy, these workweeks are real killers! I'll get my bulletin boards up before Monday if I work all day on Saturday and Sunday. Fortunately, Mr. Brown will be here to let us in. Oh well, such is life in the fast lane.

Betsy, the kindergarten teacher who had many of my kids last year, gave me the low-down on many of the students during lunch today. Man, I'm going to have a class full of boys—11 of them and only 3 girls. Half these guys are on Ritalin. With such an active bunch, at least I don't have to worry about being bored this year!

Betsy also schooled me about one kid in particular. He's called Winnie. His real name is Winslow. He is 7 years old and the only student in the class who was not retained in first grade. He's really tiny for his age, but he's also a real pistol. Betsy shared that Winnie could be so obnoxious that last year he was passed around from one kindergarten teacher to the next. She could only tolerate him for so long, and then she'd have to send him to another teacher for about 30 minutes just to catch her breath. Winnie followed her everywhere—even into the bathroom. Many times she would use the class bathroom so that she wouldn't have to leave the room. The door wouldn't lock, so Winnie would just walk right in. Betsy would be sitting on the commode, and he'd just walk right in.

I kid you not, Bets had me in stitches when she told me about this. She would look at Winnie with an I-can't-believe-you're-doing-this stare on her face and say, "Winnie, I'm using the bathroom." This didn't faze him in the least bit. He'd just simply respond, "But Mrs. Thompson, I have to tell you something." And then he would just say what was on his mind, turn, leave, and shut the door behind him. That's just one of the things he did all year that almost drove poor Bets crazy. I hope that knowing all this will help me cope with these problems. I'm also hoping that Winnie has matured some over the summer. Well, must get back to making the nametags for the kids. I'll try to write again soon.

11/3

My, how time flies when you're having fun! Sorry, I know it's been a while. I must be more consistent with my writing. Someday, when I'm old and gray, I'll be able to look back at these entries and have a laugh or two. For now, though, let me fill you in on how things are going.

It's now been about two months since school started, and although I'm really enjoying my class, I've already had to get some help to deal with both their academic and behavioral problems. Everybody told me at the beginning of the year that I needed to talk with Jackie, the consulting teacher at our school, for help. And so I did. Jackie has a very interesting job. Unlike us regular classroom teachers, she is not assigned to teach a group of students each day. Instead, she's available to provide consultation to those of us who have students with academic and behavioral problems. We meet with Jackie on a one-to-one basis or with a group of teachers referred to as a teacher assistance team. Frankly, I've preferred working with her on an individual basis and you know what—she's really been great! We've been meeting, planning, and implementing for only a couple of weeks, and already I can see a difference in my group.

First of all, Jackie really helped me with the reading program. It didn't take me long to realize that the basal reading program I was given to use was not the answer for my children. I mean, my kids have such limited experiences and vocabularies that they simply can't relate to the material. I needed to make reading more relevant for them. So, I talked to Jackie, and she agreed to help me supplement my reading program with a whole-language component. We're going great guns with this approach.

For Halloween, for example, we made a witches' brew. This was really neat because we were able to build on what the kids already knew to increase their vocabularies. Jackie brought in this huge black pot and a long wooden spoon, and I brought the ingredients for our brew. We had all kinds of nuts, raisins, yogurt raisins, pretzel sticks, malted milk balls, and—you know—the stuff you use to make granola. Both Jackie and I were dressed in witches' costumes, and we started the lesson by having the kids identify the ingredients and taste them. As they munched, we had them come up with words that described the taste—words such as *salty, sweet, crunchy, chewy*. As they sampled each ingredient, we poured that ingredient into our "caldron." As we stirred, we danced around the "caldron" and sang a tune about witches' brew. This continued until each student had "taste tested" all of the ingredients. Finally, we had them sample the brew to note the difference in taste after all the goodies had been mixed together. The kids thought this was great! They were having fun, and they were building their vocabularies at the same time.

Jackie also helped me with behavioral problems. In other words, she helped me with Winnie. From the very beginning of school, he would never raise his hand. Whenever he had something to tell me, he would just blurt it out. Jackie and I talked about this, and together we came up with a plan. We decided that we would try to modify Winnie's behavior by ignoring him when he did not raise his hand and wait to be recognized. Of course, we sat Winnie down and told him what we were planning to do. To draw attention away from him, we told the class that this was something that we were doing with everyone. We expected everyone to raise their hands when they wanted to speak. Jackie did a few demonstration lessons to show me how to react to different degrees and variations of the target behavior, and then I followed through with the implementation of the procedure. She was—and remains—available to observe and coach me when I'm trying a new teaching strategy, and this really helps me refine my skills. I really do hope this plan will work. I'm already beginning to feel the way Bets did last year.

11/19

Well, it's been two weeks since I last wrote. We've been using our B-MOD plan with Winnie, and it seems that things are getting worse instead of better. You won't believe this, but as I walk around the room, he continues to call out my name constantly. If he calls my name and I don't answer him right away, he forgets what he's planning to tell me. When I finally do acknowledge him he'll say, "Mrs. Gray," and then he'll snap his fingers and go "uhh, uhh, uhh." I guess that's why he feels he has to blurt out whatever he needs or wants to say—if he keeps quiet, the poor thing knows that he is going to lose whatever's floating around in his little head. The kids have started to pick on him when he does this. I really can't afford to let things get any worse, so I'll plan to meet with Jackie and develop a modified strategy. Will try to see her tomorrow if I have the time.

11/21

Boy, it's really nice to have someone around who is so readily available. Today, I met with Jackie after school, and we modified Winnie's behavior management plan. In addition to ignoring his call-outs, we also came up with a chart system for Winnie. I made a chart and divided it into sections for reading, language, spelling, social studies, and science. If at the end of one of the blocks he hasn't blurted out an answer or called my name without acknowledgment, he'll get a plus (+). If not, if he does call out, he'll get a minus (–). If he's gotten no more than three minuses in a day's time, I'll let him do something special, like read to the class. He's coming along nicely with his reading and he really enjoys showing off his skills to the rest of the class.

12/30

I know, I know. I've been bad. I said that I would write every day. Things just got so hectic after Thanksgiving that I just could not get to you. I had a wonderful Christmas! Went skiing with some friends and had an absolute blast! Got some really nice presents, too! Jerry gave me a new compact disc player. I really love the sound. Will really enjoy it.

Well, I guess I'm writing because it's getting close to that time again. On Monday, vacation will be over and I'll be back at school with my class. I'm sure Winnie will be in rare form the minute he steps off the school bus. Honestly, you'd think he'd miss a day once in a while. He's the only kid in the class who has perfect attendance!

I mentioned on November 21 that we started using a chart with Winnie. Well, before we got out for Christmas break, it finally started working to where we could get him to raise his hand before he yelled out for help or just blurted out whatever was on his mind. But you know, with all the nervous energy that this kid has, the problem just started to manifest itself in other ways. One day the psychologist came into the room to observe another student. It seems that each and every one of them has some problem or another. Anyway, Winnie raised his hand, but I didn't call on him. Well, as loudly as he could, he just slammed his hands down on his desktop. I kept on ignoring him, and the longer I ignored the louder he got. He was tapping his pencil, kicking his desk, and he continued to slam his hands against his desktop. Finally, I just looked at him and said, "I simply refuse to speak to you while you are acting this way. When you can start to act like a 7-year-old, then I'll look at you." At that point, he was really angry. He put his head on the desk and pouted. He wasn't disturbing anyone else so I just let him sit there until he cooled off.

By our last day before the start of Christmas break, I wanted to SCREAM! I just wanted to change my name because even though he was raising his hand more often, now Winnie was really into the same act that he so artfully performed in Betsy's class last year. He was constantly out of his seat, following me around everywhere I went. He followed me to the office. If I left the room to get something from another teacher I'd look back and there he was behind me. I didn't dare use the class bathroom when he was anywhere in sight. One day, he called my name so much that I just started to count the times. By the end of the day, he had called my name 37 times without raising his hand. Can you believe it? It seems like this was an improvement over his performance before we started using the chart, but he also has regressed to the point where he can never be wrong. If you tell him that he has missed two words on a spelling test—TWO WORDS—he just loses it! He bangs his head against the top of his desk, he crosses his arms and pokes out his lips, or he'll simply sit and sob incessantly. Oh, what a kid! What a kid!

I tell you about all the problems I have with Winnie, but you know, this kid is no dummy. He is the sharpest reader in my class. He can sound and blend like a champ and his comprehension is not at all bad. In math, he's a little slow with word problems, but he's great with computation and he's learning his facts with no problems. I honestly don't think that he has a learning problem. He's the youngest kid in my class, but academically, he's the strongest. Well, I'll see how he's doing in just a few days. Give me strength.

1/2

A nice day! The kids—all of them including Winnie—were well behaved and cooperative. They all shared their Christmas vacations with me, and later during the day I had each of them go to the story-telling station and record what they had done over the holidays. I'm going to do a whole-language thing with their stories for the next few weeks. I really like this approach. I'm still using the basal and doing some phonics, too. The use of many approaches with these kids seems to be the best way to teach them. Winnie was really calm today. He did a great job with his chart, and at the end of the day I let him go down to one of the kindergarten classes and read a story. He really enjoyed that. I hope he stays this way for a while. To say the least, such a change would be extremely therapeutic for me.

1/9

Since the last time I wrote, despite all of my positive reinforcement, Winnie has slipped back into his old ways. He's still raising his hand, but if I don't call on him right away, he continues to get upset and he acts out. He's now getting in trouble with the physical education teacher and the music teacher. He just doesn't click with either of them. Every time I go to pick up the class from music, I find Winnie in time-out because he blows up at the teacher if the instrument he wants to play is given to someone else. The same thing happens in P.E. because he can't seem to follow directions.

Both teachers, though, say that Winnie's biggest problem is his mouth. They say that he just talks out. He just comes up with something out of the blue and will totally disrupt any activity to "share" whatever he's thinking. The little scenario he describes might have occurred three weeks ago, but he just has to get it out—he just has to tell you. Now Journal, I ask you, does this sound familiar, or what? I must admit that I'm somewhat relieved. I was beginning to think it was me.

2/16

The other kids really tickled me today. I'm so glad that they haven't picked up on Winnie's behavior and started to imitate him. In fact, they have started to imitate me when I praise Winnie or try to stop an outburst before it occurs. When I see him about to lose it, I have a habit of going over to him and saying, "Be strong, Winnie, be strong. I know you can do it. Just be strong."

Today, I noticed that the kids around Winnie can also see when he is about to lose it. When I was passing out paper today, Jeremy, who sits right next to Winnie, said to me, "Mrs. Gray, Winnie is doing good today." Later, when he was getting restless and tapping his pencil on the desk, I heard a group of them saying, "Winnie, don't pout, don't pout, you can do it, be strong." How perceptive! They can predict when he's about to start his little episodes, and they try to intervene. Surprisingly, sometimes it works. In this particular instance, I didn't have to say a word to him, and he stopped the tapping.

2/27

Winnie is still doing great academically, but we just can't seem to get his impulsivity under control. Today, I was giving directions to the class, and he just interrupted me to tell me about a television show he had watched last night. I walked over to his desk and gave him a check minus mark and explained to him why. Before I could get back to the front of the class, he was calling my name again. This time, I wrote his name on the board and put a check by it. He continued to talk. Nothing phases him.

3/5

Today, my central office supervisor came to observe me. This was my last observation for the year, and I was really nervous. I told the kids that I'd buy a popsicle for everyone who was good and didn't get their name on the board during what I called "my test." Wouldn't you know it—Winnie was the only student who got his name on the board. He spoke out whenever he felt the urge. I was so embarrassed. I must have turned three shades of red. I tried my usual ignoring trick, and that didn't work. I tried going over to him and talking to him quietly, and that didn't work. I wrote his name on the board, and that didn't work. Finally, I threatened to take a minute from his recess every time I had to write his name on the board. With this threat, he finally settled down, and I was able to continue with my lesson without further interruptions.

Fortunately, my supervisor was aware of Winnie's problems, and because all the other kids were okay and because I had performed satisfactorily during my other observations, I passed the assessment. Still, after this incident I realized that Winnie is really draining me. He makes me feel anxious. He makes me feel like I want to scream! I want to look at him and say, "Don't talk, don't open your mouth, JUST DO NOT TALK."

Anyway, after the observer left, I just lost it with Winnie. I took him out in the hallway and decided that I would just try to reason with him. Yes, maybe if I tried to reason with him he'd realize how inappropriate his behavior really was and try to make a change. So I went up to him and said,

"Winnie, do you realize what you are doing? Do you realize that you are driving me and everybody around you crazy?"

Surprisingly enough, he said, "Yeah."

I continued. "You're tapping your pencil or raising your hand, you're screaming out, you're pouting, you're walking off, you're putting your head down, and people aren't going to like you and accept you for that." Boy, I really let him have it! He said he understood and that he would try to do better. We returned to the classroom and Winnie went straight to his seat looking really sad. I think he's truly sorry when he behaves this way, but I'm convinced that he can't really control his behavior. He wants to be good, but for some reason, he simply has to say what's on his mind whenever it's there. Anyway, he was pretty solemn for the rest of the day, and my other students realized this. They felt sorry for him, and several of them walked by, patted him on the shoulder, and said, "Be strong." This really made me feel like a rat. Out of sheer frustration I had really jumped all over Winnie, and I was really sorry. Still, I think he needed to know that I was upset with him, that his behavior was really getting on my last nerve.

3/6

I met with Jackie again today. She's been so GREAT! My very own private support system. Anyway, I told her what happened during and after my observation. I also told her about how the threat of losing recess time had worked in getting Winnie to settle down. We decided to start from scratch. We drew up a contract stating that we wanted to cut down the amount of call-outs Winnie had during the course of a day. We started with 10 being the maximum number and then we decided that after 10, I'd write his name on the board. For every call-out after 10, I'd place a check mark signifying that he'd lost a minute's worth of recess time. We figured that this would really kill him because all of the other boys would be outside ripping and running, and he'd have to sit and watch. More important, if he was able to limit the number of call-outs to 10 or fewer, he'd earn tokens that could be traded for prizes from Jackie's store.

3/7

We met with Winnie and I explained to him that I was losing a minute from teaching every time I had to stop what I was doing, go over to the board where his name was written, make a check mark, and return to what I was doing. Because I had to do this, he would owe me a minute when he couldn't control himself—when he called out without permission more than 10 times during the day. Winnie understood the terms of the contract. I wrote a long note to his mother explaining what we were going to do, and I indicated that I would place the contract and the chart on his desk on Monday and I would send it home on Friday for her to sign and return.

3/30

We've been implementing our new plan for almost three weeks now with only marginal success. Winnie has not once gotten 10 or fewer call-outs in a day despite the fact that I always prompt him. I'll say, "Winnie, you're doing so good! It's 12:00, and we're going to go out at 1:30 and you haven't lost any minutes yet." Or he can get to the end of the day with only a few check marks on his contract and I'll say, "If you hold on for a few more hours, you'll have a treat to take home." This makes him happy, and he tries really hard, but he hasn't reached his weekly goal for one of the three weeks that we're tried this new approach. He doesn't seem to have the ability to hold out for that long-term goal. Sometimes I think that something comes over him and he just snaps—his mind just snaps, and he's like a different person. He'll try so hard, and then all of a sudden he'll lose it. He'll start with the call-outs or the pouting and lose everything he's worked for. Today, things got so bad with him that I had to send him to another first grade teacher during math just to get a break for myself. For once, I felt I needed to get through an entire lesson without any major interruptions.

4/5

Bless her heart, Jackie is still trying to help me improve Winnie's behavior. We have continued to plan, and today, she showed my class a filmstrip about pouting. The characters in the strip talked about how pouting made everyone miserable and that there were better ways to solve a problem. After the filmstrip, we tried to engage the kids in conversation about what they had learned. Winnie tuned us out totally. He pulled out a piece of paper and started to scribble. I made him put his paper away, but he continued to tune out everything. Wouldn't say a word to anyone.

You know, I think he figured out the filmstrip was directed at him. In fact, so did the other kids. During our discussion, one of my kids said that the boy in the filmstrip reminded him of Winnie. We could tell that the activity was beginning to upset Winnie, so we cut it short. So what do we do next? **WHAT ON EARTH AM I GOING TO DO WITH THIS CHILD?**

5/6

Wow! The gaps between entries just keep getting wider and wider. Well, the school year is about over, and I must admit that I'm glad that the end is near. It's all been so very frustrating. You have so much ground to cover, your students are already behind all the other classes on your grade level, and you don't have time to teach anything because you're always dealing with some sort of behavior or attention problem. Still, I'll miss all of my kids a great deal, but I don't think I want this type of group next year—especially Winnie. If I got my class role for next year and his name showed up on it, I think I'd run out and jump off the nearest bridge. Even so, I feel that we did cover a lot of ground and that some progress was made. I had two students who we were able to get placed in the LD class for next year. Even though all of my students were ineligible for retention, I'm confident that most of them will do well in second grade next year. And yes, Winnie—even Winnie—made *some* progress. When he came to me he was a nonreader, but now he's the best reader in the class. One thing further. I learned so much from these kids and from Jackie this year. I know that my behavior management will be much better next year, and I know I'll be more competent at modifying curriculum to meet the needs of special students. So, I guess, in the long run, this has been a good year for me. Still, if the powers that be decide that I am to have another class next year like the one I had this year, I don't know what I'll do. If I have to deal with another Winnie, how on earth will I cope?

REFERENCES

Alberto, P. A., & Troutman, A. C. (2009). *Applied behavior analysis for teachers* (8th ed.). Upper Saddle River, NJ: Merrill/Pearson Education.

American Civil Liberties Union. (2009, February). *A violent education: Corporal punishment of children in U.S. public schools.* Retrieved March 31, 2009 from www.crin.org/docs/us0808execsummary.pdf

Annie E. Casey Foundation. (2009a). Responsible Fatherhood/Healthy Marriage. Retrieved April 4, 2009 from http://www.aecf.org/Home/OurWork/SpecialInterestAreas/FatherhoodMarriage.aspx

Annie E. Casey Foundation. (2009b). Data on Foster Care from the Census Bureau. Retrieved April 4, 2009 from http://www.aecf.org/~/media/PublicationFiles/FosterChildrenJuly2508.pdf

Babyak, A. E., Luze, G. J., & Kamps, D. M. (2000). The good student game: Behavior management for diverse classrooms. *Intervention in School and Clinic, 35,* 216–223.

Bateman, B. D. (2004). *Elements of successful teaching: General and special education students.* Verona, WI: Attainment.

Brice, A. E. (2002). *The Hispanic child and speech, language, culture, and education.* Boston: Allyn & Bacon.

Bureau of Justice Statistics Bulletin. (2007, December). Prisoners in 2006. Retrieved April 20, 2009 from http://www.ojp.usdoj.gov/bjs/pub/pdf/p06.pdf

Cantrell, R. P., & Cantrell, M. L. (Eds.). (2007). *Helping troubled children and youth.* Westerville, OH: American Re-EDucation Association.

Carnine, D. W., Silbert, J., Kame'enui, E. J., & Tarver, S. G. (2005). *Teaching struggling and at-risk readers: A direct instruction approach.* Upper Saddle River, NJ: Merrill/Pearson Education.

Carnine, D. W., Silbert, J., Kame'enui, E. J., & Tarver, S. G. (2010). *Direct instruction reading* (5th ed.). Upper Saddle River, NJ: Merrill/Pearson Education.

Colvin, G. (2004). *Managing the cycle of acting-out behavior in the classroom.* Eugene, OR: Behavior Associates.

Colvin, G., Sugai, G., & Patching, B. (1993). Pre-correction: An instructional approach for managing predictable problem behaviors. *Intervention in School and Clinic, 28,* 143–150.

Coyne, M. D., Kame'enui, E. J., & Carnine, D. W. (2006). *Effective teaching strategies that accommodate diverse learners* (3rd ed.). Upper Saddle River, NJ: Merrill/Pearson Education.

Cullinan, D. (2007). *Students with emotional and behavioral disorders: An introduction for teachers and other helping professionals* (2nd ed.). Upper Saddle River, NJ: Merrill/Pearson Education.

Cushner, K., McClelland, A., & Safford, P. (2000). *Human diversity in education: an integrative approach* (3rd ed.). New York: McGraw-Hill.

Darch, C. B., & Kame'enui, E. J. (2004). *Instructional classroom management: A proactive approach to behavior management* (2nd ed.). White Plains, NY: Longman.

Dilg, M. (2003). *Thriving in the multicultural classroom: Principles and practices for effective teaching.* New York: Teachers College Press.

de Melendez, W. R, & Beck, V. (2007). *Teaching young children in multicultural classrooms: Issues, concepts, and strategies* (2nd ed.). Clifton Park, NY: Thompson/Delmar Learning.

Eber, L., & Keenan, S. (2004). Collaboration with other agencies: Wraparound and systems of care for children and youths with emotional and behavioral disorders. In R. B. Rutherford, M. M. Quinn, & S. R. Mathur (Eds.), *Handbook of research in emotional and behavioral disorders* (pp. 502–516). New York: Guilford.

Educational Research Service. (2003). *Culture and learning.* Alexandria, VA: Author.

Individuals with Disabilities Education Act Amendments of 1997, Pub. L. No. 105–17 (1997). Available online at: http://www.ed.gov/offices/OSERS/IDEA/the_law.html

Engelmann, S. (1997). Theory of mastery and acceleration. In J. W. Lloyd, E. J. Kame'enui, & D. Chard (Eds.), *Issues in educating students with disabilities* (pp. 177–195). Mahwah, NJ: Lawrence Erlbaum Associates.

Evertson, C. M., & Poole, I. R. (2008). Proactive classroom management. In T. L. Good (Ed.), *21st century education: A reference handbook: Vol. 1* (pp. 131–139). Thousand Oaks, CA: Sage.

Evertson, C. M., & Weinstein, C. S. (Eds.) (2006). *Handbook of classroom management: Research, practice, and contemporary issues.* Mahwah, NJ: Lawrence Erlbaum Associates.

Forness, S. R., Kavale, K. A., & Walker, H. M. (1999). Identifying children at risk for antisocial behavior: The case for comorbidity. In R. Gallimore, L. P. Bernheimer, D. L. Speece, & S. Vaughn (Eds.), *Developmental perspectives on children with high-incidence disabilities* (pp. 135–155). Mahwah, NJ: Lawrence Erlbaum Associates.

Fox, J., & Gable, R. A. (2004). Functional behavioral assessment. In R. B. Rutherford, M. M. Quinn, & S. R. Mathur (Eds.), *Handbook of research in emotional and behavioral disorders* (pp. 143–162). New York: Guilford.

Friend, M., & Shamberger, C. T. (2008). Inclusion. In T. L. Good (Ed.), *21st century education: A reference handbook, Vol. 2* (pp. 124–131). Thousand Oaks, CA: Sage.

Gandara, P., & Contreras, F. (2009). *The Latino education crisis: The consequences of failed social policies.* Cambridge, MA: Harvard University Press.

Goor, M. B., & Santos, K. E. (2002). *To think like a teacher: Cases for special education interns and novice teachers.* Boston: Allyn & Bacon.

Gresham, F. M., Lane, K. L., McIntyre, L. L., MacMillan, D. M., Lambros, K. M., & Bocain, K. (2001). Risk factors associated with the co-occurrence of hyperactivity-impulsivity-inattention and conduct problems. *Behavioral Disorders, 26,* 189–199.

Hallahan, D. P., Kauffman, J. M., & Pullen, P. C. (2009). *Exceptional learners: An introduction to special education* (11th ed.). Upper Saddle River, NJ: Prentice-Hall.

Kauffman, J. M. (1999). How we prevent the prevention of emotional and behavioral disorders. *Exceptional Children, 65,* 448–468.

Kauffman, J. M. (2003). Appearances, stigma, and prevention. *Remedial and Special Education, 24,* 195–198.

Kauffman, J. M. (2010). *The tragicomedy of public education: Laughing, crying, thinking, fixing.* Verona, WI: Attainment.

Kauffman, J. M., & Brigham, F. J. (2009). *Working with troubled children.* Verona, WI: Attainment.

Kauffman, J. M., Conroy, M., Gardner, R., & Oswald, D. (2008). Cultural sensitivity in the application of behavior principles to education. *Education and Treatment of Children, 31,* 239–262.

Kauffman, J. M., & Landrum, T. J. (2009a). *Characteristics of emotional and behavioral disorders of children and youth* (9th ed.). Upper Saddle River, NJ: Merrill/Pearson Education.

Kauffman, J. M., & Landrum, T. J. (2009b). *Cases in emotional and behavioral disorders of children and youth* (2nd ed.). Upper Saddle River, NJ: Merrill/Pearson Education.

Kauffman, J. M., Mock, D. R., & Simpson, R. L. (2007). Problems related to underservice of students with emotional or behavioral disorders. *Behavioral Disorders, 33,* 43–57.

Kauffman, J. M., Simpson, R. L., & Mock, D. R. (2009). Problems related to underservice: A rejoinder. *Behavioral Disorders, 34,* 172–180.

Kazdin, A. E. (2008). *The Kazdin method for parenting the defiant child.* Boston: Houghton Mifflin.

Kerr, M. M., & Nelson, C. M. (2010). *Strategies for addressing behavior problems in the classroom* (6th ed.). Upper Saddle River, NJ: Merrill/Pearson Education.

Klein, M. D., & Chen, D. (2001). *Working with children from culturally diverse backgrounds.* Delmar, CA: Thomson Learning.

Kolodner, J. L. (2003). Case-based reasoning. In J. W. Guthrie (Ed.), *Encyclopedia of education* (2nd ed., pp. 1154–1159). New York: Macmillan Reference.

Landrum, T. J., & Kauffman, J. M. (2006). Behavioral approaches to classroom management. In C. M. Evertson & C. S. Weinstein (Eds.), *Handbook of classroom management: Research, practice, and contemporary issues* (pp. 47–71). Mahwah, NJ: Lawrence Erlbaum Associates.

Landrum, T. J., & McDuffie, K. A. (2008). Behavioral. In T. L. Good (Ed.), *21st century education: A reference handbook: Vol. 1* (pp. 161–167). Thousand Oaks, CA: Sage.

Lane, K. L. (2004). Academic instruction and tutoring interventions for students with emotional/behavioral disorders: 1990 to the present. In R. B. Rutherford, M. M. Quinn, & S. R. Mathur (Eds.), *Handbook of research in emotional and behavioral disorders* (pp. 462–486). New York: Guilford.

Lewis, T. J., Newcomer, L. L., Trussell, R., & Richter, M. (2006). Schoolwide positive behavior support: Building systems to develop and maintain appropriate social behavior. In C. Evertson & C. Weinstein (Eds.), *Handbook of classroom management: Research, practice, and contemporary issues* (pp. 833–854). Mahwah, NJ: Lawrence Erlbaum Associates.

Liaupsin, C. J., & Scott, T. M. (2008). Disruptive behavior. In R. J. Morris & N. Mather (Eds.), *Evidence-based interventions for students with learning and behavioral challenges* (pp. 59–78). Mahwah, NJ: Lawrence Erlbaum Associates.

Lindsey R. T., Graham S. M., Westphal, R. C., & Jew, C. L. (2008). *Culturally proficient inquiry: A lens for identifying and examining educational gaps.* Thousand Oaks, CA: Corwin.

Manning, M. L., & Baruth, L. G. (2000). *Multicultural education of children and adolescents* (3rd ed.). Boston: Allyn & Bacon.

Martella, R. C., Nelson, J. R., & Marchand-Martella, N. E. (2003). *Managing disruptive behaviors in the schools: A schoolwide, classroom, and individualized learning approach.* Boston: Allyn & Bacon.

Mathews, R. (2000). Cultural patterns of South Asia and Southeast Asian Americans. *Intervention in School and Clinic, 36,* 101–104.

Mostert, M. P. (1998). *Interprofessional collaboration in schools.* Boston: Allyn & Bacon.

National Alliance to End Homelessness. (2009a). Domestic Violence. Retrieved April 5, 2009 from http://www.endhomelessness.org/content/article/detail/1647

National Alliance to End Homelessness. (2009b). Mothers' Incarceration: Effects on Children's Education. Retrieved April 5, 2009 from http://www.hearus.us/projects/reach/video.html

Newsom, C., & Kroeger, K. A. (2005). Nonaversive treatment. In J. W. Jacobson, R. M. Foxx, & J. A. Mulick (Eds.), *Controversial therapies for developmental disabilities: Fad, fashion, and science in professional practice* (pp. 405–432). Mahwah, NJ: Lawrence Erlbaum Associates.

Pinker, S. (2002). *The blank slate: The modern denial of human nature.* New York: Viking.

Powell, R. G., & Caseau, D. (2004). *Classroom communication and diversity: Enhancing instructional practice.* Mahwah, NJ: Lawrence Erlbaum Associates.

Pullen, P. L. (2004). *Brighter beginnings for teachers.* Lanham, MD: Roman and Littlefield Education.

Reinemann, D. H. S., & Schnoebelen, S. (2008). Depression and related difficulties. In R. J. Morris & N. Mather (Eds.), *Evidence-based interventions for students with learning and behavioral challenges* (pp. 103–132). Mahwah, NJ: Lawrence Erlbaum Associates.

Rhode, G., Jenson, W. R., & Reavis, H. K. (1998). *The tough kid book: Practical classroom management strategies.* Longmont, CO: Sopris West.

Rodriguez, G. (1999). *Raising nuestros ninos: Bringing up Latino children in a bicultural world*. New York: Fireside.

Rosenshine, B. (1997). Advances in research on instruction. In J. W. Lloyd, E. J. Kame'enui, & D. Chard (Eds.), *Issues in educating students with disabilities* (pp. 197–220). Mahwah, NJ: Lawrence Erlbaum Associates.

Rosenshine, B. (2008). Systematic instruction. In T. L. Good (Ed.), *21st century education: A reference handbook: Vol. 1* (pp. 235–243). Thousand Oaks, CA: Sage.

Rothstein-Fisch. (2003). *Bridging cultures, teacher education module*. Mahwah, NJ: Lawrence Erlbaum Associates.

Sawyer, R. K. (2004). Creative teaching: Collaborative discussion as disciplined improvisation. *Educational Researcher, 33(2),* 12–20.

Silverman, R., Welty, W. M., & Lyon, S. (1992). *Case studies for teacher problem solving*. New York: McGraw-Hill.

Skinner, E., & Greene, T. (2008). Perceived control, coping, and engagement. In T. L. Good (Ed.), *21st century education: A reference handbook: Vol. 1* (pp. 121–130). Thousand Oaks, CA: Sage.

Soodak, L. C., & McCarthy, M. R. (2006). Classroom management in inclusive settings. In C. M. Evertson & C. S. Weinstein (Eds.), *Handbook of classroom management: Research, practice, and contemporary issues* (pp. 461–489). Mahwah, NJ: Lawrence Erlbaum Associates.

Soto, D. L. (Ed.). (2008). *Latino education in the U. S., 2008*. Lanham, NY: Rowman & Littlefield Education.

Springate, K. W., & Stegelin, D. A. (1999). *Building school and community partnerships through parent involvement*. Upper Saddle River, NJ: Merrill/Pearson Education.

Stichter, J. P., Conroy, M. A., & Kauffman, J. M. (2008). *An introduction to students with high-incidence disabilities*. Upper Saddle River, NJ: Merrill/Pearson Education.

Sudzina, M. R. (Ed.). (1998). *Case study applications for teacher education*. Boston: Allyn & Bacon.

Sudzina, M. R. (Ed.). (1999). *Case study applications for teacher education: Cases of teaching and learning in the content areas*. Boston: Allyn & Bacon.

Tankersley, M., & Landrum, T. J. (1997). Comorbidity of emotional and behavioral disorders. In J. W. Lloyd, E. J. Kame'enui, & D. Chard (Eds.), *Issues in educating students with disabilities* (pp. 153–173). Mahwah, NJ: Lawrence Erlbaum Associates.

Teel, K. M., & Obidah, J. E. (2008). Setting the stage. In K. M. Teel & J. E. Obidah (Eds.), *Building racial and cultural competence in the classroom: strategies from urban educators*. (pp. 1–11) New York: Teachers College Press.

Trent, S. C., Artiles, A. J., Fitchett-Bazemore, K., McDaniel, L., & Coleman-Sorrell, A. (2002). Addressing ethics, power, and privilege in inclusive classrooms in urban schools: A cultural-historical approach. *Teacher Education and Special Education, 25*(1), 11–22.

Trent, S. C, Driver, B. L., Wood, M. H., Parrott, P. S., Martin, T. F., & Smith, W. G. (2003). Creating and sustaining a special education/general education partnership: A story of evolution, change, and uncertainty. *Teaching and Teacher Education, 19,* 203–219.

U.S. Census Bureau. (2009a). Child Care 2005. Retrieved April 4, 2009 from http://www.census.gov/population/www/socdemo/childcare.html

U.S. Census Bureau. (2009b). Child care constraints among American families. Retrieved April 4, 2009 from http://www.census.gov/population/www/socdemo/child/child-care-constraints.pdf

U.S. Department of Education. (2009). Status and trends in the education of racial and ethnic minorities. Retrieved April 15, 2009 from http://nces.ed.gov/pubs2007/minoritytrends/figures/figure_7_3.asp?referrer=report

U.S. Department of Health and Human Services. (2009). Women's Health 2007. Retrieved April 8, 2009 from http://mchb.hrsa.gov/whusa_07/popchar/0204wp.htm

U.S. Department of Labor Statistics. (2009). Working in the 21st Century. Retrieved April 4, 2009 from http://www.bls.gov/opub/working/page16b.htm

Villegas, A. M., & Lucas, T. (2002). *Educating culturally responsive teachers: A coherent approach*. Albany: State University of New York.

Virginia Department of Social Services. (2009). Virginia Child Support Enforcement Program, 2008 Fact Sheet. Retrieved April 9, 2009 from http://www.dss.virginia.gov/files/division/dcse/facts_statistics/FACTSHEET2008-Rev.pdf

Walker, B. A., & Fecser, F. A. (2007). Elements of an effective Re-Education program for the 21st century. In R. P. Cantrell & M. L. Cantrell (Eds.), *Helping troubled children and youth* (pp. 141–169). Westerville, OH: American Re-EDucation Association.

Walker, H. M., Colvin, G., & Ramsey, E. (1995). *Antisocial behavior in school: Strategies and best practices*. Pacific Grove, CA: Brooks/Cole.

Walker, H. M., Forness, S. R., Kauffman, J. M., Epstein, M. H., Gresham, F. M., Nelson, C. M., & Strain, P. S. (1998). Macrosocial validation: Referencing outcomes in behavioral disorders to societal issues and problems. *Behavioral Disorders, 24,* 7–18.

Walker, H. M., Ramsey, E., & Gresham, F. M. (2004). *Antisocial behavior in school: Strategies and best practices* (2nd ed.). Pacific Grove, CA: Brooks/Cole.

Whitaker, T., & Fiore, D. J. (2001). *Dealing with difficult parents and with parents in difficult situations*. Larchmont, NY: Eye on Education.

Wong, H. K., & Wong, R. T. (2009). *The first days of school: How to be an effective teacher*. Mountain View, CA: Harry K. Wong Publications.

INDEX

A

ABC analysis of behavior, 42, 43, 51
Academic failure, 29–30
Acting-out cycle, 46–47
  acceleration, 72–73
  agitation, 72
  calm, 72
  de-escalation, 73
  interruption, 71–73
  peak, 73
  recovery, 73
  trigger, 72
Action, in cases, 3, 5–6
Affect, 66–68
Aggression, 30–31 (*see also* Developmentally significant behavior)
Antecedents identification, 41
Aversive consequences (*see* Punishment)

B

Behavior management, 16–19, 22
Behavior problems, 21, 35
  antecedents identification, 41
  behavior pairs, 33
  bothersome, 27–28
  categories, 37–38
  chains of events, 42–43
  coercive interactions, 44–45
  cognitive and affective aspects, of misbehavior, 47–48
  consequences, 42
  control of misbehavior, 39–40
  curriculum/teaching, as management problem, 23–24
  defining, 40–41
  developmentally significant, 29–32
  functional behavioral assessment (FBA), 50–51
  measurement of, 48–50
  misbehavior, causes of, 38–39
  patterns and stages, of misbehavior, 45–47
  positive behavior intervention plan, 51
  prevention, 51–52
  problem, resolving, 33–34
  prohibitions of teachers, 24–25, 26–27
  resolving, 50
  teachers demand, 24–26
Behavioral change, 53
  approaches, 59–60
  attempt to modify behavior, 68–69
  cognitive and affective aspects, 66–68
  corporal punishment, 66
  digital resources, 73
  extinction, 63–64
  instructional approach to, 69–73
  negative reinforcement, 63
  positive reinforcement, 60–63
  punishment by presenting aversives, 65–66
  response cost punishment, 64–65
  strategies, 55–59

C

Case analysis, 2, 3
  in classroom, 3
  consequences, 8–9
  issues, 4–6
  knowledge required in, 6–7
  perspectives of individuals in, 7–8
Chains of events, 42–43
Choice as behavior change strategy, 58–59
Coercive interactions, 44–45
Cognitive and affective aspects:
  of behavior, 66–68
  of misbehavior, 47–48
Collaboration (*see* Other teachers and other professionals, working with)
Colvin, Geoffrey, 45
Communication:
  body language, 83
  choosing words, 84
  describing, 84
  eye contact, 83
  listening, 82–83
  pacing, 85
  with parents, 129
  pausing, 83–84
  physical proximity, 83
  questioning, 85–86
  summarizing, 85
  voice, 84–85
  waiting, 86
Comorbidity, 32
Conceptual modes, 37–39, 59–60
Conduct disorder (CD), 51, 52
Consequences:
  in ABC analyses, 42–43
  anticipated in cases, 8–9
  in behavioral operations, 60–66
  choosing, 67
Corporal punishment, 66
Court-appointed special advocate (CASA), 127
Culture (*see* Multicultural)
Cumulative folders, of students, 14–15
Curriculum/teaching as management problem, 23–24
  precorrection and, 69–70
  social skills, 68–69

D

Debriefing:
  example, 80–82
  importance in recovery, 73

Defining behavior:
  as coercive, 44–45
  as excess or deficiency, 33
  as measurable response, 40
  as sequence, 42–43
Demands of teachers, 24–27
Department of Social Services (DSS), 9
Depression, 31–32 (*see also* Developmentally significant behavior)
Developmentally significant behavior:
  academic failure, 29–30
  aggression, 30–31
  depression, 31–32
  multiple problems, 32
  peer problems, 32
Digital resources, 73

E

Educational problem, solving, 112–113
Examples in teaching, 57–58
Expectations:
  demands, 24–26
  individualization, 24–25
  prohibitions, 26–27
Extinction as behavioral operation, 63–64

F

Functional behavioral assessment (FBA), 50–51

G

Goals of behavior change, 50, 86–87
Group contingencies:
  cautions about, 101–102, 104
  confederates, 102–103
  cooperative learning, 100–101
  dependent, 100
  independent, 99
  interdependent, 100
  schoolwide plans, 101
  tutors, 103–104

H

Home-contingency plans, 134
Home-note for third-grader, 135
Home-note programs, 134, 135
Home-school plans, 134

I

Individualized education programs (IEPs), 6
Individuals with Disabilities Education Act (IDEA), 121
Information, getting, 13
Instruction:
  academic failure, 29–30
  as behavior change strategy, 55–57

Instruction (*continued*)
  behavior problems, 23–24, 25, 69–73
  best practices in, 24, 25
  CLOCS-RAM mnemonic, 24
The Intern Teacher Casebook, 42
Internet resources (*see* Digital resources)
Issues, in cases, 3–4

K

Knowledge, required in cases, 6–7

L

Language:
  acceptable in classroom, 77–78
  body, 83
  classroom *versus* language of home, 77–78
  multicultural aspects, 77–78
Legal issues, 4
Listening to students, 75, 82–83

M

McKinney-Vento Homeless Education
    Assistance Act, 122
Misbehavior:
  causes, 38–39
  cognitive and affective aspects, 47–48
  control, 39–40
  patterns and stages, 45–47
Models:
  communication and, 82–86
  examples as, 58–59
  likely to be imitated, 96–97
  limits of, 98–99
  rewarding, 97–98
Multicultural:
  expectations, 28
  language, 75–78, 82–86
Multiple problems, 32

N

Negative reinforcement (*see* Reinforcement)
No Child Left Behind Act (NCLB), 23

O

"Operant" behavior, 60
Other teachers and other professionals,
    working with, 107
  benefits, 115, 116–117

educational problem, solving, 112–113
learning from, 113–114
limitations 116
sharing information, 111–112, 114–115

P

Parents and families, working with, 118
  abusive parents, 133–134
  blaming parents, 134, 136
  conferences, 131–133
  cultural and ethnic differences, 123–127
  economic stresses on, 122–123
  home-note programs, 134, 135
  introductory letters, 131
  parent-child interaction, 128–129
  prejudices, 127–128
  reasons for involvement, 121
  school guidelines for communication, 129
  the sooner, the better, 130–131
Peer influence, 94
  as confederates, 102–103
  as models, 96–99
  peer pressure, 99–102
  social skills, teaching, 104–105
  tutors as classroom resource, 103–104
Peer pressure, 99–102
Personal responsibility, teaching, 86–87
Perspectives of individuals in cases, 7–8
Positive behavior intervention plan, 51
    (*see also* Reinforcement: Positive)
Positive reinforcement (*see* Reinforcement)
Precorrection, 41, 69
  example of, 71
  interrupting acting-out cycle, 71–73
Prohibitions of teachers, 24–25, 26–27
Punishment:
  aversives and, 65–66
  response cost, 64–65

R

Reinforcement:
  extinction and, 63–64
  negative, 63
  positive, 60–63
Response cost (*see* Punishment)
Responsibility, personal, 67

S

Safety issues, 4
School social worker, 9
School year and physical environment,
    planning and managing for, 11
  academic evaluation, 15–16
  behavior management, 16–19
  cumulative folders, 14–15
  information, getting, 13
Self-control, 67
Sharing information, 111–112, 114–115
Simplicity in intervention, 55–59
Social skills:
  teaching, 104–105
  training, 67
Special education, 121

T

Talking with students, 75 (*see also*
    Communication)
  angry/aggressive, 90–92
  about appropriate behavior, 88–89
  example, 80–82
  language of classroom *versus* language of
    home, 77–78
  personal responsibility, teaching, 86–87
  teaching goals, 78–79
  about unacceptable behavior, 89–90
  unproductive, avoiding, 79–82
  verbal and nonverbal communication,
    82–86
  withdrawn, 92–93
Teachers demand, 24–26
Teaching (*see* Instruction)
Transitions in activities, 70

V

Verbal and nonverbal communication,
    82–86

W

World Wide Web (*see* Digital resources)